# A Cultural Encyclopedia of Lost Cities and Civilizations

# A Cultural Encyclopedia of Lost Cities and Civilizations

Michael Shally-Jensen and Anthony Vivian

ABC-CLIO®

An Imprint of ABC-CLIO, LLC
Santa Barbara, California • Denver, Colorado

Copyright © 2023 by ABC-CLIO, LLC

All rights reserved. No part of this publication may be reproduced, stored in a retrieval system, or transmitted, in any form or by any means, electronic, mechanical, photocopying, recording, or otherwise, except for the inclusion of brief quotations in a review, without prior permission in writing from the publisher.

**Library of Congress Cataloging-in-Publication Data**

Names: Shally-Jensen, Michael, author. | Vivian, Anthony, author.
Title: A cultural encyclopedia of lost cities and civilizations / Michael Shally-Jensen and Anthony Vivian.
Description: Santa Barbara, California : ABC-CLIO, An Imprint of ABC-CLIO, LLC, [2023] | Includes bibliographical references and index.
Identifiers: LCCN 2022022011 | ISBN 9781440873102 (hardcover) | ISBN 9781440873119 (ebook)
Subjects: LCSH: Extinct cities—Encyclopedias. | Cities and towns, Ancient—Encyclopedias. | Civilization, Ancient—Encyclopedias. | Geographical myths—Encyclopedias. | BISAC: HISTORY / Ancient / General | HISTORY / World
Classification: LCC CC176 .S485 2023 | DDC 930.003—dc23/eng/20220801
LC record available at https://lccn.loc.gov/2022022011

ISBN: 978-1-4408-7310-2 (print)
       978-1-4408-7311-9 (ebook)

27 26 25 24 23    1 2 3 4 5

This book is also available as an eBook.

ABC-CLIO
An Imprint of ABC-CLIO, LLC

ABC-CLIO, LLC
147 Castilian Drive
Santa Barbara, California 93117
www.abc-clio.com

This book is printed on acid-free paper ∞

Manufactured in the United States of America

# Contents

List of Entries   vii

Geographic Guide to Entries   ix

Preface   xi

Introduction   xiii

Maps   xvi

A–Z Entries   1

General Bibliography   325

About the Authors and Contributors   327

Index   329

# List of Entries

Abu Simbel
Abydos
Ai-Khanoum
Ajanta Caves
Aksum
Alexandria
Amarna
Ancestral Puebloans
Angkor
Antioch
Anuradhapura
Assyrians
Athens
Ayutthaya
Baalbek
Babylon
Bagan/Pagan
Borobudur
Cahokia
Carthage
Chan Chan
Chang'an
Chavín de Huántar
Constantinople
Ctesiphon
Cyrene

Deir el-Bahri/Djeser-Djeseru
Delphi
Easter Island
Ephesus
Giza
Granada
Great Zimbabwe
Harappa and Mohenjo-Daro
Hittites
Ife
Indigenous Australian Cultures
Iroquois Confederacy
Kilwa
Knossos
Kyoto
La Tène Celtic Culture
Lapita People
Machu Picchu
Madurai
Maya
Memphis and Saqqara
Meroë
Moche Culture
Mongol Empire

Monte Albán
Mughal Empire
Mycenae
Nazca
Old Goa
Olmecs
Olympia
Paestum
Pataliputra
Pecos Pueblo
Pergamon
Persepolis
Petra
Phoenicians
Pompeii
Roanoke Colony
Rome
Scythians

Shaker Villages
Spanish Missions in North America
Stonehenge
Susa
Syracuse
Taxila
Tenochtitlán
Teotihuacán
Thebes
Timbuktu
Tiwanaku
Troy
Tula
Ur
Van
Vijayanagara
Vinland
Xianyang

# Geographic Guide to Entries

*Every entry is listed once, even though many entries fall into multiple categories.*

**Africa**
Aksum
Great Zimbabwe
Ife
Kilwa
Meroë
Timbuktu

**Americas, Meso**
Maya
Monte Albán
Olmecs
Tenochtitlán
Teotihuacán
Tula

**Americas, North**
Ancestral Puebloans
Cahokia
Iroquois Confederacy
Pecos Pueblo
Roanoke Colony
Shaker Villages
Spanish Missions in North America
Vinland

**Americas, South**
Chan Chan
Chavín de Huántar
Machu Picchu
Moche Culture
Nazca
Tiwanaku

**Asia, Central**
Ai-Khanoum
Mongol Empire
Scythians

**Asia, East**
Chang'an
Kyoto
Xianyang

**Asia, South**
Ajanta Caves
Anuradhapura
Harappa and Mohenjo-Daro
Madurai
Mughal Empire
Old Goa
Pataliputra
Vijayanagara

**Asia, Southeast**
Angkor
Ayutthaya
Bagan/Pagan
Borobudur

**Egypt**
Abu Simbel
Abydos
Alexandria
Amarna
Deir el-Bahri/Djeser-Djeseru
Giza
Memphis and Saqqara
Thebes

**Europe**
Granada
La Tène Celtic Culture
Stonehenge

**Mediterranean**
Antioch
Athens
Carthage
Constantinople
Cyrene
Delphi
Ephesus
Knossos
Mycenae
Olympia
Paestum
Pergamon
Phoenicians
Pompeii
Rome
Syracuse
Troy

**Near East**
Assyrians
Baalbek
Babylon
Ctesiphon
Hittites
Persepolis
Petra
Susa
Taxila
Ur
Van

**Pacific**
Easter Island
Indigenous Australian Cultures
Lapita People

# Preface

Our world is changing at a rate faster than ever before, and the specter of climate change haunts our present. Now more than ever, our world's continued survival calls for a deeper understanding of cities and civilizations that once flourished but no longer do. This volume's 10 Investigative Boxes analyze 10 major cities that face extinction today. These come from every inhabitable continent on earth. Coastal cities everywhere are at risk of a rising sea level, but our future includes much more than just flooding. Changing climates mean more fires and droughts and more obstacles to our food and water supplies. Those who are already in the most vulnerable circumstances will be the hardest hit, but everyone is at risk.

Beyond the 10 Investigative Boxes, climate change has been an impetus for this whole project and underlies every aspect of this entire volume. Change is a constant in human affairs; cities and civilizations are continuously rising and falling. First and foremost, this volume proves again and again that cultural influence, economic strength, and military might are guarantees of security only for those willing to lie to themselves.

The book is written for a general audience, for anyone curious about lost cities and civilizations. In addition to the wide spectrum of detailed facts presented in each entry, the reader stands to gain a general appreciation of urban atrophy and the constancy of change. On top of the 10 Investigative Boxes described above, 25 sidebars outline mythical cities created by the human imagination.

The pulp of the volume is the 86 main entries on lost cities and civilizations. The entries, which appear alphabetically, all include the following subsections: Inhabitants, Historical Background, Culture and Society, Demise, Recent Discoveries, Current Status, and Further Reading. The entries—as well as the investigative boxes and sidebars—come from every region of the globe that has been home to humans. The time span is likewise broad, spanning all of human civilization, from several millennia BCE to the present.

The authors and contributors have backgrounds in the fields of anthropology and history. We have been constructing the entries and other components of the volume from 2019 through 2021 using the leading and latest works on the specific locations and cultures.

# Introduction

The accelerating threat of climate change challenges us to analyze our own communities' relationships with the wider world and to contemplate their very existence. This volume explores the span of human history—and plenty of prehistory—searching out prominent and fascinating examples of cities or broader civilizations that shifted from a position of influence to a lack thereof. The results offer a rich mosaic of detailed descriptions from every corner of the globe. These lost cities and civilizations provide much-needed perspective for our present moment.

The flux in size and importance of human settlements has been central to our study of history from the field's inception. Herodotus, the fifth-century BCE historian, sometimes labeled the father of history, centers this theme within his programmatic statement early in Book 1 of his *Histories*:

> I will proceed with my narrative, going through small and great towns of people alike. Because many of those places that were once great have become small, and those that are great in my time were small before. Knowing that human fortune never remains in the same place, I will make mention of both alike. (Herodotus 1.5.3–4, translation mine)

Aware of the constant flux in human affairs, Herodotus promises not to discriminate against small or diminished cities in his writing. In this volume, we focus in on this theme even further, analyzing the flux itself. When we study a lost city, we are not looking at a snapshot of the city at its height, nor are we simply illustrating the archaeological ruins that still exist today. We are instead looking at the fluctuations in the city's fortunes over time: why it grew, how its people thrived, how its culture flourished, and finally why it fell.

In the remainder of this introduction, we will explore the contents of the volume, region by region. This will take us on a very brief tour of human history in which various trends in the world's lost cities will become apparent. From there, we will introduce the contents and functions of this volume's investigative boxes and sidebars. We will conclude with a look at how one theme—colonialism—weaves its way through this volume's contents.

Africa was the birthplace of humankind, and this volume's various entries on Africa feature the continent's diversity of habitats and peoples. The lost cities of Ife, Great Zimbabwe, and Kilwa flourished in vastly different regions of sub-Saharan Africa. Timbuktu and Cyrene show the wide range of identities that cities in North Africa could take on, with the former being a powerful desert trading post and the latter a Greek colony on the Mediterranean. The region of Africa with the most entries is Egypt. As one of the globe's three initial cradles of civilization, the land of the Nile boasts very ancient lost cities as well as more recent ones. The antiquity and richness of Egyptian culture, coupled with a hot, dry climate ideal for preserving certain materials, render Egypt rife with lost cities.

Eurasia, the largest continent on earth, hosts the most entries in this volume, spanning a vast spectrum of dates and settlement types. Besides the Nile, humankind's two other oldest cradles of civilization are found on Eurasia: the Indus valley and Mesopotamia. We explore the Indus valley civilization in the entry on Harappa and Mohenjo Daro. Later periods from this extended region are covered in entries on cities and empires on the Indian subcontinent and in the eastern Near East. These include Anuradhapura, Madurai, the Mughal Empire, Pataliputra, Vijayanagara, and Taxila. Mesopotamia, the other original—and oldest—cradle of civilization, is featured in entries on the Assyrians, Babylon, and Ur. We also embrace the broader Near East in entries for Antioch, Persepolis, Petra, Susa, and Van.

Eurasia came to host an eclectic mix of settlements over multifarious regions outside of India and the Near East, some as far apart from one another as 8,000 miles. We delve into the Mediterranean world through cities such as Knossos, Troy, Delphi, Syracuse, Pompeii, and Rome, among others. Moving farther north into Europe, we encounter the La Tène Celtic culture as well as sites such as Stonehenge. To the east, China, the fourth cradle of civilization, appears in entries on Chang'an and Xianyang. Southeast Asia is home to lost cities that include Angkor, Ayutthaya, and Bagan/Pagan. Borobudur and Kyoto stand among the lost cities on Asia's Pacific Rim. The vast Pacific was first settled from peoples coming from the ocean's west. More precisely, the Polynesian people, who settled huge swaths of the Pacific, can be traced back to the island of Taiwan, off the coast of mainland China. We analyze the vast Pacific through entries on Indigenous Australian cultures, the Lapita people, and Easter Island.

The Americas showcase a diverse range of peoples as witnessed through the continents' lost cities. South America exhibits a wide range of pre-Columbian sites; these include Chavín de Huántar, Chan Chan, Machu Picchu, and Tiwanaku. Like South America, Mesoamerica contained pre-Columbian settlements that ranged from powerful empires to smaller regional settlements. We explore the Mesoamerican sites of Monte Albán, Tenochtitlán, and Teotihuacán as well as the broader civilizations of the Maya and the Olmecs. North America housed the Pecos Pueblo and Ancestral Puebloans in the deserts of the American Southwest as well as the Iroquois Confederacy in what is today the American Midwest and Northeast. Later settler communities also appear as lost cities, such as the Roanoke colony and the Viking settlement of Vinland.

This volume's 10 Investigative Boxes study 10 current cities and locations that face extinction today. These bring the breadth of the challenge of climate change to the fore. Every continent has urban areas both small and large currently at risk of destruction from our world's changing climate. The rising sea level will put coastal cities everywhere at risk. Beyond flooding, an increase of fires, droughts, and disruptions in food and water supply also threaten various regions. Among

# Introduction

xv

this volume's list of places at risk are thriving megacities such as Manila and Jakarta as well as wealthy strongholds such as Venice and the Maldives. While the threat of climate change acted as an impetus for this volume and underlies the entire work, it is in these investigative boxes where it is treated most directly.

The 25 sidebars survey 25 mythic cities and places. Constructed by the human imagination, these legendary locales take on multiple different forms. There are mythic cities that appear in literature, such as Camelot, the castle and court of Arthurian fame, and sometimes the creation of a mythic city can be narrowed down to a specific author, such as Plato's construction of the original Atlantis myth. Other mythic lands are religious in nature, conceptualized by a religion or group of religions, such as the Abrahamic Garden of Eden and the Buddhist Shambhala. Some sidebars examine entire fictional continents, such as Kumari Kandam, Lemuria, Mu, and Terra Australis. Other sidebars feature historical cities that have been mythologized, like the Seven Pagodas and Xanadu/Shangdu. Taken together or individually, these sidebars complement the volume's main entries. The mythic cities and lands provide a set of cities constructed—and often destroyed—by the human imagination. How they compare and contrast to real lost cities can tell us much about their authors and those who have promulgated their stories.

Before concluding, it would be helpful to look at how the theme of colonialism weaves its way through this volume. Many readers will approach the entries herein one at a time, seeking out a specific city that they are researching. Yet, for those inclined, the breadth of the volume may also allow one to see patterns and themes that appear across numerous entries and regions. By briefly analyzing how the theme of colonialism appears in this volume, we see how the volume can illuminate broad themes and historical phenomena. The theme of colonialism within this volume proves interesting for several reasons—not least among them the fact that we as authors did not set out to write about colonialism. Unlike the flux of human fortune that we purposefully thematized in writing this volume, the theme of colonialism has arrived here inadvertently. Nevertheless, given its importance to world history, it crops up all over the place and in many different forms.

By the mid-second millennium CE, European powers began colonizing and exploiting the remainder of the globe. This trend can be seen in the demise of some Indigenous lost cities and civilizations, done in by the arrival of Western imperialists. Among others, these include the Pecos Pueblo, which was abandoned after the Spanish took control of the region, as well as the Indigenous Australian cultures, who faced a genocide from British settlers. Sometimes the colonizers' settlements become lost cities of their own, such as Shaker villages and the Spanish missions in North America. Some of the mythic cities featured in the sidebars are imperial fantasies of colonized land, like Ciudad Blanca and El Dorado.

Finally, many lost cities were looted by Western powers, and their artifacts are still displayed to this day not in situ but in museums back in London, Berlin, or other European metropoles. Just as the theme of colonialism has seeped its way into this volume, so too have other themes and historical phenomena ready for analysis.

# AFRICA

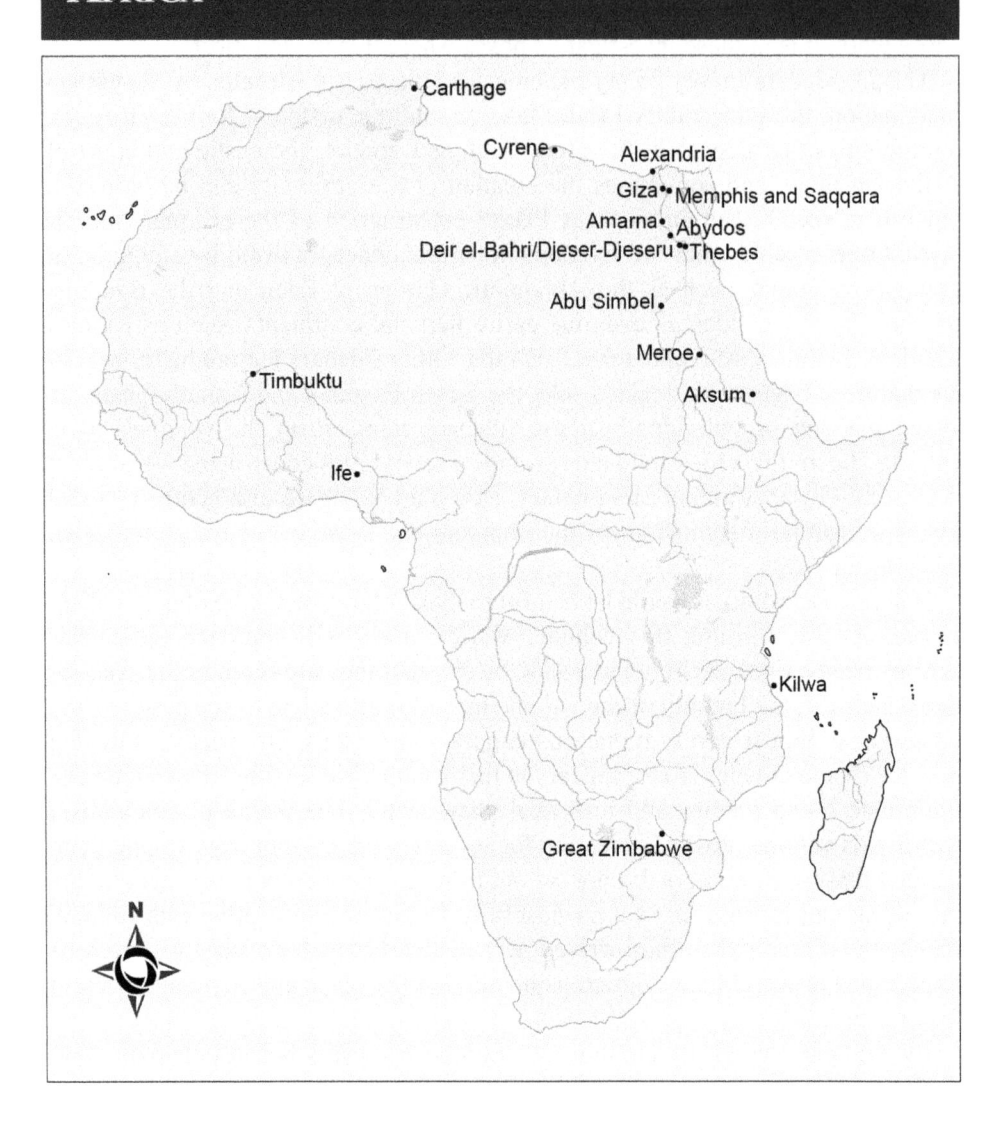

# North America and Mesoamerica

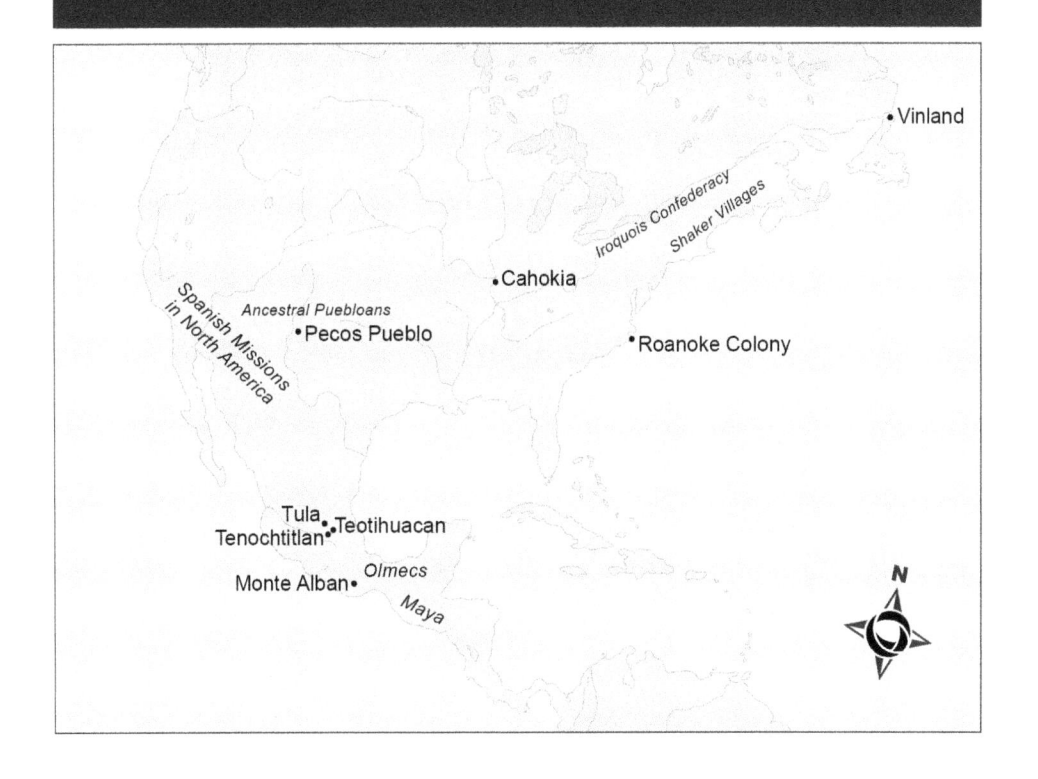

# South America

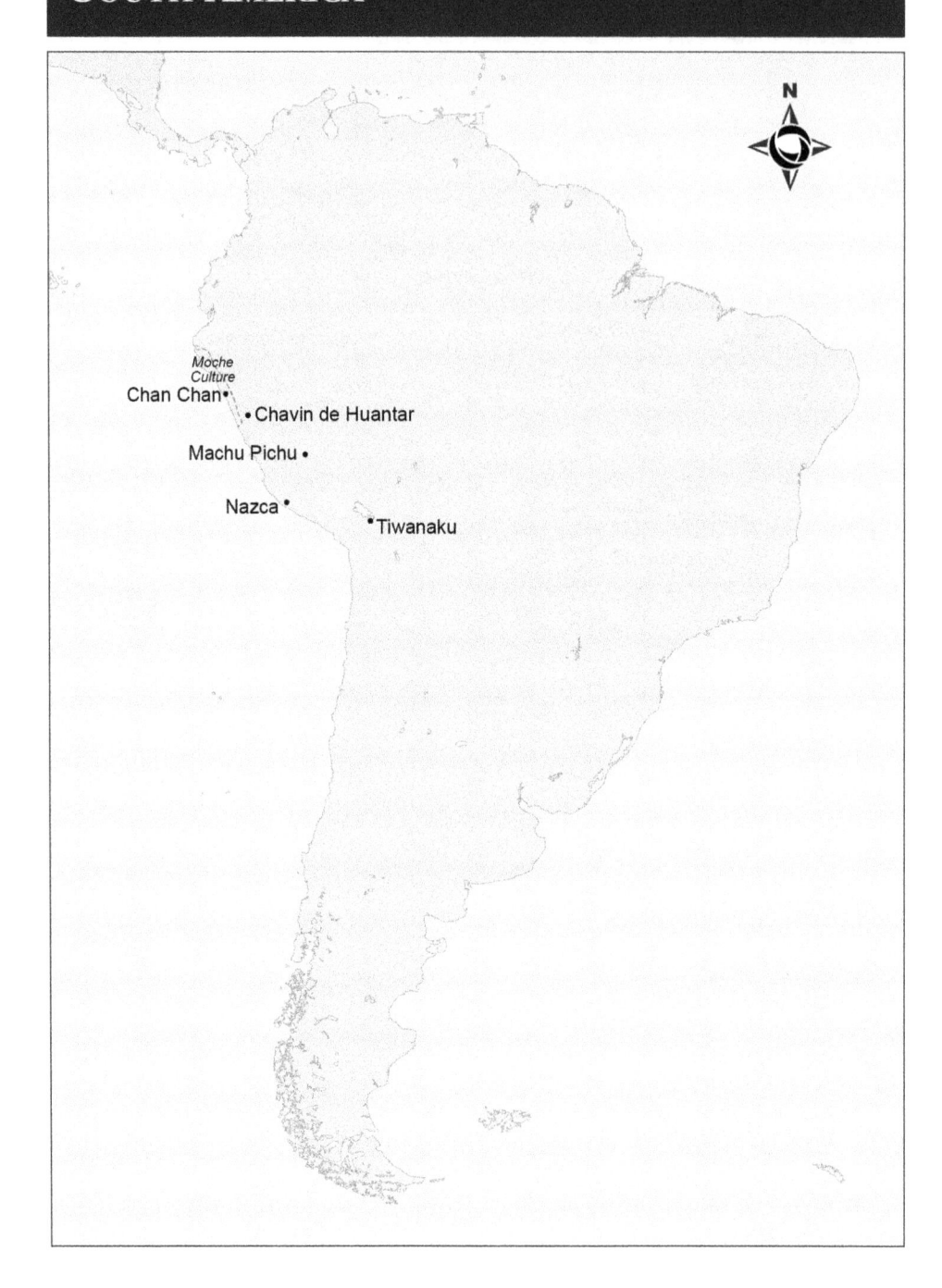

- Moche Culture
- Chan Chan
- Chavin de Huantar
- Machu Pichu
- Nazca
- Tiwanaku

# EURASIA

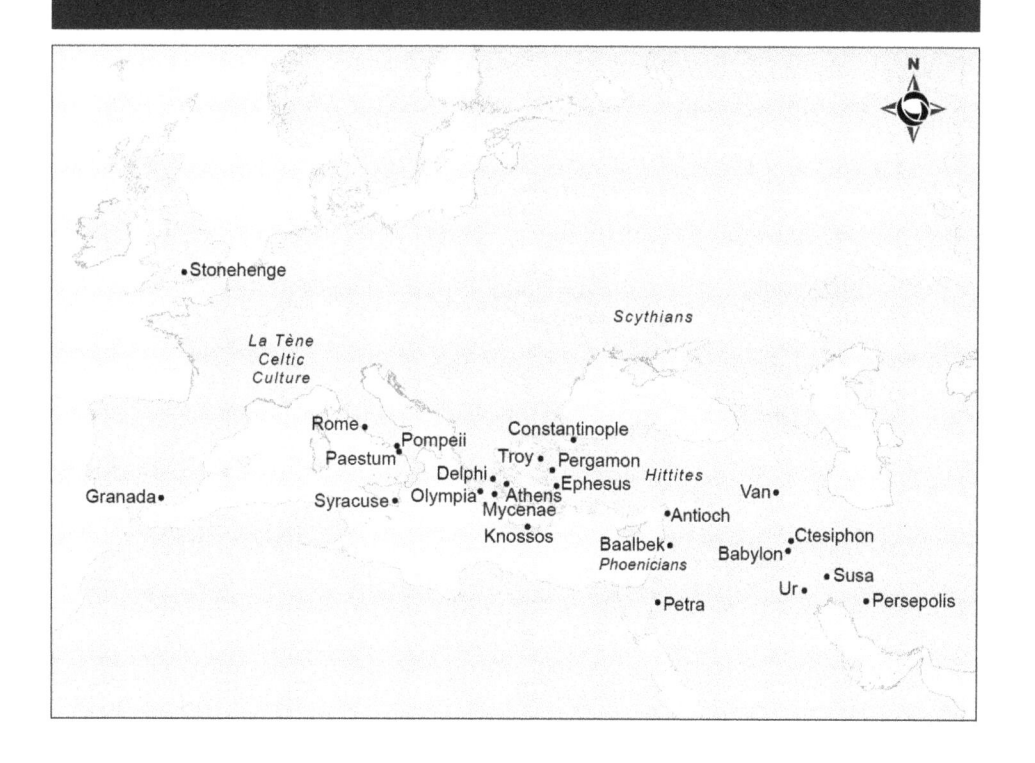

# Asia and the Pacific

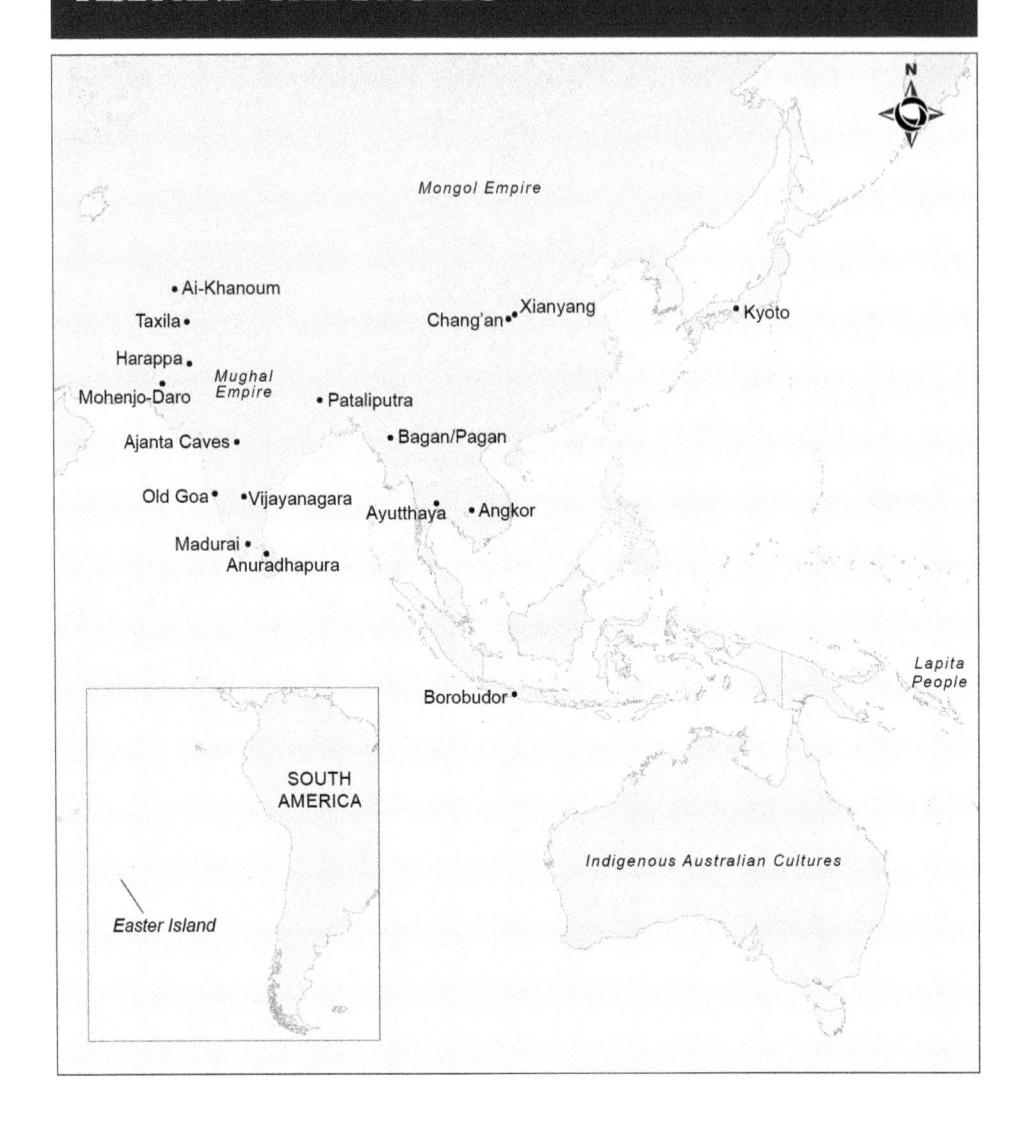

# A

## Abu Simbel

Around 1260 BCE, Ramesses II was the pharaoh in Egypt. At his direction, the massive monument now called Abu Simbel was created in Upper Egypt (southern Egypt), near the second cataract of the Nile River. While there are multiple theories about exactly why the temple was built, there is no doubt that it celebrated Ramesses II in some way. The temple was discovered near the town of Aswan by Europeans in the mid-1800s, and it was carefully excavated and studied. However, in 1960, the Egyptian government's decision to build a dam on the Nile River caused a situation in which the area where the temple stood would be flooded. The United Nations Educational, Scientific and Cultural Organization (UNESCO) thus undertook a massive project to relocate the temple to an area where it would be protected from the rising waters, going so far as to build a man-made mountain to preserve the original feel of the temple and carefully maintaining its orientation toward the sun.

### INHABITANTS

In ancient times, Aswan was known as Swenett and served primarily as a modest trading center or market town. Although the old capital of Thebes was nearby, Ramesses established a new capital far down the Nile, on the eastern delta.

Much of what direct knowledge we have of the ancient Egyptians comes from scribes, who were understandably most interested in recording the lives of their superiors (much like modern writers tend to be more focused on celebrities than on average people). We do know that professions were commonly passed from parent to child. While women did spend much of their life having and caring for children, they were also able to hold other roles in society, such as priestesses, stone workers, or brewers. And despite the common belief that the great stone creations of the Egyptians were built by slaves, slaves held a much lower position in Egyptian society. Craftspeople created the pyramids and other works, such as the Abu Simbel temple; extraordinary skill was required to carve the stone and place it properly. Even the unskilled laborers who moved the stone from one place to another were properly compensated; the work was considered too important to be entrusted to slaves. (Slaves were those who had accumulated too much debt, conquered peoples, and criminals.)

Ramesses II became pharaoh around 1279 BCE, and his reign lasted until roughly 1213 BCE. His most celebrated military campaign was the Battle of Kadesh, fought against the Hittites. The battle was not a great victory, however.

These four colossal figures sit outside the entrance to the Great Temple at Abu Simbel. All four seated figures are over sixty feet tall and were made in the likeness of Ramesses II, who oversaw the temple's construction. (Christophe Amerijckx | Dreamstime.com)

Neither side won decisively, and this ultimately resulted in the first known peace treaty (1258 BCE). Although historians disagree about the precise details of his life, Ramesses is said to have been ninety years old when he died (a very advanced age, considering that the average Egyptian's life expectancy was somewhere around thirty-five years). At the time, he had more than 200 wives and concubines and had outlived most of his children (96 sons, 60 daughters). He lived for so long that many of his subjects had been born while he was the pharaoh and feared that the world would end when he died.

## HISTORICAL BACKGROUND

During the last half of the New Kingdom (1540–1075 BCE), Egyptian pharaohs engaged in virtually continuous foreign wars in an attempt to hang on to their imperial possessions. Ramesses II was one of those pharaohs. Although he failed to defeat the Hittites, he did build monuments such as Abu Simbel and the temple at Karnak that projected images of Egyptian power and preserved his legacy.

Abu Simbel is made of two temples: the Great Temple and the Small Temple. The Great Temple is nearly 100 feet high and more than 100 feet long. On either side of its entrance, there are four huge stone figures of Ramesses II, each over 60 feet tall. Smaller statues (though still bigger than they would be in life) are also around the entrance, representing the people conquered by the pharaoh, including the Hittites, the Libyans, and the Nubians. Moving into the temple, the interior is decorated with images of both Ramesses and his queen, Nefertari, worshipping the gods. His great victory at Kadesh is shown. Some scholars use this to date the temple's construction to approximately 1264 BCE, when the victory of Kadesh would have been part of the people's recent memories. Others believe that the temple was constructed later, around 1244 BCE, after Ramesses and his sons began a war with Nubia, the region south of Upper Egypt and home to the Kingdom of Kush. In that case, the Abu Simbel temple complex would have been created to project Egyptian power.

In the early 1800s, the temple was discovered by Europeans; at that point, sand had covered the stone figures so that only their heads were visible. The ancient name of the temple, if it had one, was lost; the name Abu Simbel is said to have come from a boy who led the Italian explorer Giovanni Belzoni to the location.

The Small Temple is approximately forty feet high and ninety-two feet long. Colossi also adorn the front of the temple, surrounding the entrance. These include four statues of Ramesses and two of Nefertari (not to be confused with Nefertiti), who is said to have been his first and favorite wife. Her status is shown in the proportion between the two figures on the temple; Ramesses and Nefertari are roughly the same size. In most temples, wives are depicted as much smaller than their husbands, and they are rarely dedicated to the pharaoh's wife. Along with the images of the pair making offering to the gods, the interior of the temple shows images of Hathor, the goddess of love, fertility, women, and the sky.

## CULTURE AND SOCIETY

Much of the indirect knowledge we have regarding the ancient Egyptians comes not from their own writings but from those of the Greeks who regularly visited the area. Based on the latter's writings, it is generally believed that the Egyptians had a complex religious system, were an agricultural society, and were focused on living the best lives they possibly could. Their understanding of the afterlife was that it was simply a continuation of this life; Egypt was the best place a person could possibly live, so the afterlife would simply be a continuation of that. In fact, although marriage alliances with other foreign powers were common, girls would almost never be sent to other kingdoms to live; it would have been considered disrespectful to the girl to force her to live somewhere inferior to her homeland. Foreign queens, however, were welcome in Egypt and were treated like natives once they were there.

The ruling elite in Egypt—above all the pharaoh but also high priests and the hereditary nobility—served as guardians of the religious tradition. The pharaoh's commands were absolute, even while surrounding himself or herself with advisers, generals, governing officials (viziers), wives, and bureaucrats of all sorts. The pharaoh's family made up the royal court, which was participated in by nobles, priests, scribes, and others. All aspects of life, from religious rites to wars to food production and building construction, emanated from the royal court.

The Egyptians were an agricultural society that used complicated irrigation systems to water their crops. Unfortunately, while their palaces and temples were constructed from stone, the homes of those who were not royalty were generally constructed of mud bricks and had roofs made from plant stems. These have not survived, giving archaeologists a somewhat limited picture of what the average person's life might have been like. In recent decades, nonetheless, excavations at a variety of different workers' villages have begun to shed light on this aspect of Egyptian society.

Egyptian society is sometimes thought of as dour and death obsessed; however, contemporary records from Greek and Roman writings say that it was quite the opposite. Egyptians of all classes believed that they should enjoy their lives as much as possible. Even criminals were generally treated well, as long as they were not guilty of capital crimes, such as looting temples, rape, or robbery. At the opposite end, the life of the pharaohs, and of all high-born royal and priestly figures, was extravagant to the extreme. Pharaohs were considered deities, and all of society bent to their wishes.

## DEMISE

By the time of Ramesses II's rule, Egyptian power was on the wane. It has long been thought that shortly after 1200 BCE, a large wave of migrants known as the Sea Peoples came to threaten Egypt and other nations in the region. Ramesses III (r. 1187–1156 BCE) managed to stem the tide, but only at great cost to Egyptian military might. This, along with unfavorable environmental changes, contributed to the continued decline and ultimate demise of classical Egyptian society.

As for Abu Simbel, in the 1960s, the Egyptian government drew up plans to build the Aswan High Dam on the Nile River. This would have diverted enough water to cause the sacred site to be flooded, destroying the ancient temple and all of the surrounding structures. Between 1964 and 1968, a team headed by UNESCO worked to relocate the temple almost 700 feet from its original location. The temple had originally been built into a cliff; now the massive stone monument had to be relocated onto the plateau above the cliff. The stones making up the temple were carefully cut into sections in locations where they would be least visible once reassembled and then secured in place at their new location using cement and desert sand. The interior of the temple was supported by reinforced concrete. An entire man-made mountain was created to maintain the appearance of the temple carved into a cliffside. The smaller statues and items from the original temple complex were also moved and preserved. Abu Simbel in its new location was declared a UNESCO World Heritage Site in 1979.

## RECENT DISCOVERIES AND CURRENT STATUS

As has happened with many Egyptian finds, early explorers looted the temples in the years after their discoveries. Some items made it to museums in European countries, but many have disappeared, either into private collections or simply destroyed through a lack of proper preservation. In 2016, however, it was confirmed that a pair of mummified legs in an Italian museum that were taken from the queen's tomb in the Valley of the Queens were almost certainly those of Queen Nefertari. She is believed to have died around 1250 BCE; depending on when the temples at Abu Simbel were constructed, they may have truly been a memorial to the queen that Ramesses II loved the most.

*Michael Shally-Jensen*

*See also:* Deir el-Bahri/Djeser-Djeseru; Meroë; Thebes.

## FURTHER READING

Hawass, Z., and H. E. Farouk Hosni. 2001. *The Mysteries of Abu Simbel: Ramesses II and the Temples of the Rising Sun.* Cairo: American University in Cairo Press.
Pruitt, S. 2018. "Archaeologists Identify Mummified Legs as Queen Nefertari's." History, August 30, 2016. https://www.history.com/news/archaeologists-identify-mummified-legs-as-queen-nefertaris
Shaw, I. 2003. *The Oxford History of Ancient Egypt.* New York: Oxford University Press.

## Abydos

The city of Abydos is one of the oldest in Egypt. Rather than being an urban center, the city primarily served as a religious site, home to the tombs of many pharaohs as well as the supposed resting place of the god Osiris. The most famous temple is that of Seti I (r. ca. 1294–1279 BCE), the father of the more well-known Ramesses II. Much of the work on the temple was completed after Seti's death, and although Ramesses continued the work, his craftsmen appear to have been inferior to those hired by Seti. Ramesses II also had a temple constructed in Abydos, but it has not been as well preserved. The sacred city hosted the yearly festival of Osiris, the god of both fertility and death, who had his own impressive temple at the site.

### INHABITANTS

While Abydos does not appear to have been an urban center, the city did have a residential community to the north during the Predynastic period (from the earliest records of human settlement to around 3100 BCE). Although the cemetery was in continuous use and the temple and town were rebuilt over time, the buildings may have been destroyed during the construction of the great tombs. As such, archaeologists know comparatively little about those who originally lived in the area. That said, the area was continuously occupied from the Predynastic through the Roman periods.

The Egyptians of the New Kingdom period (ca. 1540–1075 BCE), which occurred in the latter part of ancient Egypt's long history, were fundamentally the same as those of earlier eras. They adhered to the ancient polytheistic religion and treated the pharaoh as a divine personage. They maintained an agricultural economy centered on the floodplain of the Nile River, and their society was strictly hierarchical, divided into royals, priests, merchants, commoners, and slaves.

### HISTORICAL BACKGROUND

Seti I, son of Ramesses I, who founded Egypt's Nineteenth Dynasty (1290–1189 BCE), made his mark by launching a series of campaigns in which he punished disloyal people and cities for not properly acknowledging his power. Seeking to restore the New Kingdom's strength, he undertook military campaigns in

Syria-Palestine. His capture of Kadesh in Syria along with the Kingdom of Amurru—both Hittite possessions—was his most notable achievement. Other campaigns were made against the Libyans.

At Abydos, Seti built two elaborate temples with extensive historical and religious decoration. The Hall of Records depicts Seti and his young son Ramesses II honoring a list of pharaohs inscribed on a wall. Seti also constructed a royal residence near his ancestral home around Avaris in the northeastern Nile delta. His son and successor, Ramesses II, expanded this palace into his new capital, Pi-Ramesses.

## CULTURE AND SOCIETY

By the time of the New Kingdom, Egyptian priests, whose office was hereditary, were virtually a separate caste. Each temple had its own priestly hierarchy responsible for maintaining it and conducting religious rites. Religion was woven into the very fabric of Egyptian social and political life.

The first temple at Abydos seems to have been dedicated to the deity Khentiamentiu, whose name roughly translates to "Foremost of the Westerners"—the term *Westerners* here referring to the world of the dead. Over time, the temple came to honor Osiris, the Egyptian god of the dead and the underworld. Mythology at that time held that Osiris's head was buried at Abydos, making it the appropriate spot to honor the god. The cult of the afterlife entailed the use of elaborate funeral rituals designed to move the dead on to the next life. Osiris judged the deceased and determined whether they deserved eternal bliss or punishment.

The Temple of Seti, often referred to as the Great Temple of Abydos, is the most famous monument within the city. It is an L-shaped building with two front courtyards and seven chapels dedicated to major Egyptian deities. Along with its purpose as a memorial to Seti, the temple was designed to show appropriate reverence to all the pharaohs who had come before. For scholars, the temple contains one of the most important finds for understanding Egyptian history: the Abydos king list. This is a listing of all the pharaohs of Egypt, from Menes through Seti himself—although a few names were conspicuously left off the list. Seti's tomb, looted in antiquity, remains one of the grandest in the Valley of the Kings. His mummy, found in a royal cache in secondary burial, is the finest of the royal mummies.

Directly behind the Temple of Seti is a room referred to as the Osireion. Unlike the more delicate work of contemporary Egyptians, the room was created in a style similar to older work. Excerpts from the Book of the Dead and other ancient texts are included on the walls. Large columns and subterranean vaults are present. Each year, it seems, to celebrate the summer to fall Nile "inundation" season, there was a procession from the Osiris temple to the necropolis itself. This festival may also have included mystery plays that celebrated the cycle of life and death.

The Temple of Ramesses II is located nearby but has been poorly preserved. It also contained a slab carved with the names of the Egyptian pharaohs; while Seti's list has been preserved in its original location, the slab from Ramesses's tomb was moved to the British Museum in London.

Rulers of the earliest Egyptian dynasties are also buried nearby, approximately one mile into the desert. This area is now known as the Umm el-Qa'ab ("Mother of Pots"). Sherds of devotional objects and shattered pottery that were brought to Abydos by pilgrims are frequently found in this area. Early tombs in this area are simple brick-lined chambers of roughly ten feet by twenty feet; the tombs slowly increased in size and complexity. Some of the oldest Egyptian writings discovered by Europeans were found in these tombs. Members of the kings' courts also appear to have been buried in pit tombs in the vicinity.

## DEMISE

Egyptian might was in decline by the time of Ramesses II, despite the ever-larger building projects of the later New Kingdom. In later Egyptian history, a succession of invaders attacked and occupied different parts of the country, from the so-called Sea Peoples in the twelfth century BCE to the Assyrians in the seventh century BCE. The last building added to Abydos was a temple to Nectanebo I (r. ca. 379–361 BCE), built during the Thirtieth Dynasty of Egypt. Shortly after that, the Greeks occupied Egypt, followed by the Romans. The area was no longer used for royal burials and fell into some obscurity.

As European interest in ancient Egyptian artifacts increased in the late 1800s, the archaeologist Émile Amélineau began to excavate the Umm el-Qa'ab section of Abydos between 1894 and 1898. Subsequently, the British researcher Flinders Petrie, considered a pioneer in systematic excavation and preservation, encouraged an associate to excavate farther in the area and was furious when he discovered how much damage Amélineau had done at the site. He demonstrated that Amélineau's records were poorly kept or falsified and found that the previous dig had destroyed some artifacts while uncovering others intended for sell.

## RECENT DISCOVERIES AND CURRENT STATUS

Recent years have seen a return to careful excavation at Abydos. In the tombs of the oldest pharaohs, some of the oldest objects and writings currently known have been found.

In 2017, researches described a striking boat burial at the site. The vessel, likely part of the tomb of Senusret III (r. 1878–1839 BCE), was probably intended to assist its owner in reaching the afterworld. In this case, the walls surrounding the boat featured decorative scenes depicting ancient Egyptian watercraft and other historical details. Earlier research had found as many as twelve boats buried on their own within Abydos, dating back to 3000 BCE.

Meanwhile, in 2019, researchers found a walkway adjoining the Temple of Ramesses II that led them into an ancient Egyptian palace. Inside, they found walls adorned with the name of Ramesses II. The researchers suggest that the new finding shows that Ramesses, like his father Seti, considered Abydos to be the symbol of royal power; after all, it was the resting place of Osiris, the omnipotent controller of human life and death.

*Michael Shally-Jensen*

*See also:* Amarna; Deir el-Bahri/Djeser-Djeseru; Thebes.

**FURTHER READING**

Dodson, Aidan. 2019. *Sethy I, King of Egypt: His Life and Afterlife.* Cairo: American University in Cairo Press.
Hignett, Katherine. 2019. "Ancient Egypt: Archaeologists Discover Hidden Palace Marked with Symbols of Ramesses the Great." *Newsweek,* March 28, 2019. https://www.newsweek.com/ancient-egypt-palace-ramesses-ii-archaeology-1378627
O'Connor, David. 2009. *Abydos: Egypt's First Pharaohs and the Cult of Osiris.* New York: Thames & Hudson.
Urbanus, Jason. 2017. "A Pharaoh's Last Fleet." *Archaeology,* January/February 2017. https://www.archaeology.org/issues/242-1701/trenches/5097-trenches-egypt-middle-kingdom-boat-burial

# Ai-Khanoum

Ai-Khanoum—which means "Lady Moon" in Uzbek—is the name that has been given to a Hellenistic Greek city founded in Bactria, present-day Afghanistan. We do not know what its ancient name was, but it was an active part of the Seleucid Empire and then the Greco-Bactrian Kingdom. Upon its discovery in the twentieth century, some suggested that it was Alexandria on the Oxus—one of the many Alexandrias founded by Alexander the Great in the late fourth century BCE—but this proposal has since been superseded by theories suggesting a slightly later founding.

The town sits on a fertile elbow where the Kokcha River flows into the Panj River. The latter is a large tributary of the Amu Darya, which was known in antiquity as the Oxus. The town's location was chosen for its fertility and accessibility. The access to the Oxus river system allowed the town to stay connected to the wider Hellenistic world despite its relative isolation. Although the site existed thousands of miles from the Aegean Sea, it featured many of the staples of an ancient Greek city, including Greek temples, a gymnasium, and an amphitheater. Audiences that attended the amphitheater had sweeping views of both the town and the meandering Panj.

---

*Kingdom of Prester John*

Prester John was a mythical Christian patriarch king who ruled over a legendary Christian kingdom in the East in stories beginning in the Middle Ages. The first stories of Prester John were written in the twelfth century in the context of the Crusades and depict Prester John as a Nestorian patriarch and descendant of one of the three Magi present at Jesus's birth. The location of the mythical kingdom has shifted over time: at first, it was said to be in India, then more accounts began to portray it in central Asia or Ethiopia. The stories drew heavily on contemporary literature about the exotic East, such as the Alexander Romance and stories of Sinbad the Sailor. For the writers of these stories and their readerships, Prester John and his kingdom represented the strength of Christianity in a distant and mysterious land, and the stories dramatized Christian Europe's imperialistic fantasies.

## INHABITANTS

The surrounding region had already been inhabited for some time when the Greeks and others under Alexander the Great first entered Bactria. The site at Ai-Khanoum seems to have been first established soon after Alexander's life in the late fourth century or early third century BCE. The Macedonians and other Greeks settling from the West mixed with local peoples to form a heterogeneous population. Both Greek and Bactrian—an eastern Iranian language—were spoken. The population here and throughout other sites in Hellenistic Bactria developed a unique culture, fusing East and West.

## HISTORICAL BACKGROUND

The exact date of Ai-Khanoum's founding is uncertain, as is its original name. When it was rediscovered in 1961, many thought it could be Alexandria on the Oxus. While this argument has since been eclipsed, it is possible that an early iteration of the site was settled in the late fourth century BCE, perhaps even as early as Alexander's initial invasion of Bactria.

After conquering the massive Persian Empire in the late 330s BCE, rather than heading back west or consolidating his newly conquered lands, Alexander the Great pressed his army on. In 329 BCE, he headed north and east in an attempt to conquer the regions known to him as Bactria and Sogdiana. These regions were less populated than the urban centers of the Persian Empire, and it proved more difficult for him to force decisive battles. After about two years in the region, he moved on to India, having married Roxana of Bactria and founded many new settlements: Alexandria on the Oxus, Alexandria in the Caucasus, Alexandria in Margiana, and Alexandria Eschate. He or one of his generals may have also settled the site that is today known as Ai-Khanoum; if not, his presence in the region made the later settlement possible.

Whether a late fourth-century iteration of the settlement existed or not, the first major foundation occurred under Antiochus I. His father, Seleucus, was a general under Alexander the Great. When the latter died and his empire fragmented, Seleucus founded the Seleucid Empire, taking the lion's share of Alexander's empire. His new empire ranged from eastern Asia Minor through Mesopotamia and Persia to Bactria and the Indus valley. Antiochus inherited this empire from his father. On an expedition through Bactria ca. 280 BCE, he (re)settled Ai-Khanoum and commenced a major building project there. Bactria was relatively sparse, so this town would have been a regional power player.

The town served as an important settlement and trading post within the Seleucid Empire for a few decades until Diodotus, the Seleucid satrap (governor) of Bactria, declared its independence ca. 250 BCE. Ai-Khanoum then served as an integral part of the smaller Greco-Bactrian Kingdom for the next century—the remainder of its existence. Although the Greco-Bactrian Kingdom was smaller than the sweeping Seleucid Empire, it thrived and expanded during this century, especially to the east. While retaining trade with the Mediterranean world to the

A third-century BCE coin depicting Antiochus I. This Seleucid king is largely responsible for (re)settling and building up Ai-Khanoum. (Yale Gallery of Art)

west, Ai-Khanoum and the Greco-Bactrian Kingdom also had contact with powers on the Indian subcontinent as well as Han China.

Eucratides I was the last ruler of Hellenistic Ai-Khanoum. He overthrew his predecessor and undertook an aggressive foreign policy. He also seems to have conducted a building program at Ai-Khanoum. We know that he was the last Hellenistic king there based on numismatic evidence: plenty of coins from his reign and his predecessors' have survived at the site but none from his successors'.

## CULTURE AND SOCIETY

Ai-Khanoum's status as a trading post connecting East and West defined both its culture and society. On the one hand, Ai-Khanoum featured many of the marks of a quintessential Greek town, not unlike what one might find on an Aegean island. The amphitheater and gymnasium dominated the townscape, Greek inscriptions dotted the ruins, and olive oil jars attest to an active trading relationship with the West. On the other hand, material evidence also shows an active trade network with the powers to the east. Indian coins have been found among the local Bactrian and other Hellenistic-style coins. One narrative plate that has been excavated seems to display the Indian myth of Kuntala. The inhabitants made use of the plains rendered fertile by the adjacent rivers. There were also many mines in the region, both mineral and gold. The inhabitants were heavy traders. Their trade networks connected them with societies from the Mediterranean to the Indus valley and beyond.

## DEMISE

Affairs thousands of miles to the east set off a chain of events that led to the abandonment of Ai-Khanoum. In the second century BCE, the Yuezhi, nomads who roamed the steppes bordering China, were pushed from their ancestral pastures by the Xiongnu and began making their way east. They displaced the Saka, who, in turn, invaded Bactria around the 140s BCE. Although other parts of the Greco-Bactrian Kingdom were still resisting, the Saka took Ai-Khanoum during the reign of Eucratides. According to archaeological evidence, the Saka settled into the site for several years. The advancing Yuezhi eventually finished off the Greco-Bactrian Kingdom and forced the Saka from Ai-Khanoum, where it lay abandoned for centuries.

## RECENT DISCOVERIES AND CURRENT STATUS

On a hunting expedition in 1961, Mohammed Zahir Shah—the king of Afghanistan—and his companions found the ruins of Ai-Khanoum. Excavations by French and then Russian archaeologists commenced within a few years. However, the Soviet-Afghan War in the 1980s and America's "forever war" that began in 2001 halted fieldwork and badly damaged the site through looting and fighting.

*Anthony Vivian*

*See also:* Taxila.

## FURTHER READING

Boardman, John, Jasper Griffin, and Oswyn Murray. 2001. *The Oxford Illustrated History of Greece and the Hellenistic World*. Oxford: Oxford University Press.
Cohen, Getzel M. 2013. *The Hellenistic Settlements in the East from Armenia and Mesopotamia to Bactria and India*. Berkeley: University of California Press.
Mairs, Rachel. 2016. *The Hellenistic Far East: Archaeology, Language, and Identity in Greek Central Asia*. Berkeley: University of California Press.
Tarn, W. W. 1984. *The Greeks in Bactria and India*. Chicago: Ares.

# Ajanta Caves

The Ajanta Caves are a series of about thirty human-built cave temples in Maharashtra, a western state of India. They are located along a cliff face in the Indhyadri hills, on the northern shore of the Waghora River in eastern Maharashtra. Altogether, the caves extend for about 600 yards. Construction of the caves began in the second century BCE and continued intermittently into at least the sixth century CE.

The Ajanta Caves contain great artistic and religious achievements, including monastic residences and wall paintings, that can still be observed today. All the pillars are exquisitely carved, and the doorframes are decorated. The walls, ceilings, and pillars of nearly all the caves were once painted. The life story of the Buddha is one of the most popular themes seen in the murals that adorn the caves.

The project of constructing and expanding the caves was primarily carried out by Mahayana Buddhists during the rule of the Gupta dynasty. The caves were abandoned during the seventh century CE and seemingly remained untouched for over a millennium.

## INHABITANTS

During its peak, the Ajanta Caves were home to over 200 Mahayana Buddhist monks. These monastic residences are called vihāras and were originally conceived for the purpose of providing shelter to Buddhist monks during the rainy season. However, the monasteries were not carved until the first century BCE, probably 200 or so years after the first caves were excavated. It is fairly certain that the first caves were carved with the intention of making them into residences. Much of what we know about the history of the caves has been determined through inscriptional and archaeological evidence.

Another important feature is the caitya (worship) halls that served as spaces for veneration. Many of the walls throughout the thirty or so caves feature illustrations of scenes from the Jatakas, stories of the former lives of the Buddha. Because the original excavators and inhabitants of the Ajanta Caves were Mahayana Buddhists, the carvings and paintings represent religious and spiritual images and ideas.

Out of the thirty caves, twenty-five appear to have served as vihāras, and the remaining five are understood to be caitya halls. It is clear that these structures were incredibly difficult to carve, requiring strategic planning, group effort, and ingenious design to excavate inhabitable structures out of a cliff face. The Ajanta Caves are sometimes referred to as a monastic village, demonstrating that at certain historical moments, the caves were such an active site for Buddhist devotees that together they comprised an entire community.

## HISTORICAL BACKGROUND

There is no adequate evidence to establish the exact chronology of when the caves were built. A handful of caves were probably excavated in the second and first centuries BCE; then there was a period of stagnation for around 400 hundred years until the second phase of excavations started around the fifth century CE. We cannot necessarily date when the murals on the caves were produced; some may have been at the same time as the carving out of the caves, and others could have been after. It is likely that these early inhabitants were influenced by early Buddhist devotees who came to western India during and after the spread of Buddhism under the reign of Ashoka in the second century BCE. Ashoka was India's most famous Buddhist king and a major patron of Buddhist architecture.

The second phase of excavations took place during the supremacy of the Vakatakas, who were related via marriage to the preeminent Gupta dynasty.

Votive inscriptions of ministers who worked for the king of the Vakataka dynasty, Harisena, confirm that this second set of caves took place around the late fifth century CE. The inscriptions describe that Harisena's empire spanned across all of central India, from the Arabian Sea on the western coast to the Bay of Bengal on the eastern side.

Almost all of the remaining caves were built during the Gupta period, which was considered by many to be the golden age of ancient India. This was also the era during which the wall paintings reached peak artistic achievement. The Gupta style represents a celebration of both sacred religiosity and aristocratic elegance. The carving and decorating of the Ajanta Caves during this period were made possible by the relative stability of the territories governed by the Vakataka dynasty and their patronage.

## CULTURE AND SOCIETY

The Ajanta Caves were primarily excavated and inhabited by members of the Mahayana Buddhist tradition. Mahayana, translating to "great vehicle," is one of the two main strands of Buddhism. It developed on the Indian subcontinent starting around the first century BCE. One of its primary distinguishing features is its inclusion of the idea of bodhisattva, or people who are on the path to enlightenment for the benefit of all beings. Much of the artwork seen in the Ajanta Caves attests to this belief in the idea of bodhisattva, thus evidencing that many of its creators and inhabitants were followers of the Mahayana school of Buddhism. However, archaeologists and other scholars have determined that a small handful of the caves were likely populated and utilized by devotees of Hinayana Buddhism, which translates to "small vehicle" and is now more commonly referred to as Theravada Buddhism (Theravada means "teaching of the elders"). This group followed a more literal interpretation of the original, pure teachings of the Buddha.

Archaeologists have determined that much of the excavation, decoration, and veneration at the Ajanta Caves took place during the Gupta period of ancient India. This era, from the third to sixth century CE, is commonly considered the golden age of India. The empire ruled over much of the Indian subcontinent and boasted high periods of cultural and artistic development, the Ajanta Caves being just one testament to those achievements. Due to the coastal location of the Ajanta Caves, the site was in proximity to stops along caravan routes of trade, connecting central and western India. As a result, traveling pilgrims, monks, and merchants would have visited the Ajanta Caves and interacted with its inhabitants.

Eventually, the caves even had international influence. The Gupta style of wall paintings seen in the Ajanta Caves influenced the painting style of the Tang dynasty period in China, many Chinese pilgrims having visited the site. Hiuen Tsang, a Chinese traveler, stayed in India for fifteen years in the first half of the seventh century CE. His writings are the earliest known records making reference to the caves, although historians have not determined whether he ever actually visited them or just wrote based on hearsay, as their artistic achievements were so renowned. He wrote that "the walls of the temple had depicted on them the incidents of the Buddha's career as bodhisattva, including the circumstances of his attaining *bodhi*," meaning enlightenment, and "outside the gate of the monastery on either side north and south was a stone elephant."

## DEMISE

The project of constructing and expanding the caves was primarily carried out by Mahayana Buddhists during the Gupta dynasty. After the heyday of the Indian golden age, especially as Buddhism declined as a prevalent religion in India, it seems that the caves were abandoned during the seventh century CE. They remained seemingly untouched for over a millennium and lost their reputation as a prominent religious and artistic site. Because of this, the sculptural and artistic works there were not maintained and preserved, resulting in decay.

While the caves went dormant, their primary occupants were bats and insects, who unfortunately contributed to the decay. As a result, many of the murals, especially those near the floor or ceiling, have been completely destroyed. Although all of the caves had once been exquisitely painted, now only thirteen contain paintings of some value. Luckily, some of the paintings in the middle of the walls (and a few on the ceilings) remain visible. In fact, murals on two of the cave walls are the oldest Buddhist narrative paintings surviving in India.

## RECENT DISCOVERIES AND CURRENT STATUS

After more than a millennium, the caves of Ajanta were rediscovered by British army officers in 1819 as they were hunting tigers. There is a record of officers of the Madras Army seeing the paintings: one of them left an inscription on a pillar in one of the caves that reads, "John Smith 28th cavalry/28th April 1819."

The Ajanta Caves were designated a UNESCO World Heritage Site in 1983. It was one of the first four World Heritage Sites chosen in India and is one of the largest historical sites on the UNESCO list. Today, the Ajanta Caves are one of the most renowned monuments of Buddhism in India.

*Rebecca Waxman*

*See also:* Mughal Empire; Old Goa.

## FURTHER READING

Singh, Manager, and Babasaheb R. Arbad. 2013. "Architectural History and Painting Art at Ajanta: Some Salient Features." *Arts* 2, no. 3: 134–150.

Somathilake, Mahinda. 2016. "Ajanta Murals and Their Chronology: A Critical Analysis." *Journal of the Royal Asiatic Society of Sri Lanka* 61, no. 1: 1–31.

# Aksum

Aksum (or Axum), located on the fertile plateau of northern Ethiopia near the Eritrean border, was the capital of an Ethiopian empire that existed from the first to the eighth century CE. The city features the remains of a number of ancient monuments, notably a collection of tall, sculpted stone stelae (obelisk-like structures) honoring past leaders. Aksum was a major trading and religious center whose reach extended west from the Red Sea, through Eritrea and northern Ethiopia, and into Sudan. It served markets in India, Arabia, Greece, and Rome. The Christian inhabitants, then as now, hold that the biblical Ark of the Covenant (housing the original Ten Commandments) was brought to the city by Menelik, a descendant of King Solomon and the Queen of Sheba. The ark is said to reside in the cathedral of Maryam Seyon (St. Mary of Zion).

## INHABITANTS

The name *Ethiopia* derives from the Greek *Aithiopes*, or "burnt faces." The ancient lands of northern Ethiopia and Eritrea were also called Abyssinia, from the Arabic *al-Habash*. Aksumite civilization thus represented a mix of Indigenous Ethiopian elements; southern Arabian elements brought by migrants from Saba, the territory of Sheba (present-day Yemen); and influences from Hellenistic (or Greek-influenced) Egypt. The main language was Ge'ez (Amharic), a Semitic language from South Arabia that, along with Egyptian and Meroitic (from Meroë), was among the earliest written languages on the African continent. Christianity was introduced from Egypt by Saint Frumentius in the fourth century, during the reign of Emperor Ezana. Aksum's link to Sheba, across the Red Sea, was lost for a period but then renewed in the sixth century under Emperor Kaleb. After the Muslim conquest of Egypt (640), Aksum was cut off from the outside world and evolved into a Christian island surrounded by Islamic neighbors. The people, then as now, practice Ethiopian Orthodox Christianity, a form of orthodoxy similar to, yet distinct from, the Coptic Christianity found in parts of Egypt.

## HISTORICAL BACKGROUND

The founding of Aksum is linked by legend to the biblical figures of Solomon and the Queen of Sheba. Sheba ruled the area of South Arabia in the 900s BCE. In the Hebrew Bible, Sheba is described as bringing a caravan of valuable gifts to King Solomon of Jerusalem. Her son, Menelik, is believed by the Ethiopian Christians to be the offspring of Solomon and Sheba as well as being the ancestor of later Ethiopian rulers.

Around 500 BCE, the people living in Ethiopia were joined by settlers from Sheba. Later centuries saw the addition of Hellenistic Greek elements arriving from Ptolemaic Egypt—particularly Alexandria, where the Copts eventually arose. The Kingdom of Aksum emerged in the first century CE. In the 200s CE, Aksum gained control of Yemen (Sheba). In the following century, Christianity was introduced from Egypt by Saint Frumentius. (Frumentius is called Abba Salama, "Father of Peace," in Ethiopian literature.) About 340, Frumentius was made the first bishop of Ethiopia, and since that time, Ethiopian Orthodox Christianity has thrived in the region.

Also in the 300s, Ezana rose to power in Aksum, becoming emperor and adopting Christianity. He became an example for his people and sometimes also spread the message of his faith through the sword. In about 350, Aksumite forces conquered the Kingdom of Kush and its capital, Meroë, in what is now northern Sudan. Thus, one nearly thousand-year-old African empire came to an end while another expanded.

## CULTURE AND SOCIETY

Aksum's early success lay in trade. One anonymous first-century CE Greek source titled *Periplus of the Erythraean Sea* portrays Aksum as the center of a thriving state whose economy was based on trade in ivory (transported from the African interior), raw gold, and aromatics. These goods were shipped from the Red Sea port of Adulis (near present-day Zula, Eritrea) to Arabia, India, and the Mediterranean region, particularly Rome. Local farmers grew spices and gum arabic along with domestic food crops. Fine pottery was also produced and may have been exported. Aksumite coins, each bearing a cross symbol, were widely used and admired and have been found as far away as China. The Iranian philosopher and prophet Mani (ca. 216–274 CE) identified Aksum as one of the four great empires of the era, along with Rome, Persia, and Sileos (probably China).

Aksum was a monarchy whose king appointed local ministers to collect taxes and run the empire with the aid of midlevel officials and other bureaucrats. Merchants and skilled craftspeople plied their trades along with priests, professional soldiers, farmers, and laborers. Slavery does not appear to have had a major presence in Aksum, though slaves may have been among the empire's exports. An elaborate irrigation system supplied water and helped maintain herds and crops.

The city had a variety of architectural structures, including stelae (stone pillars), tombs, palaces, and houses. One stele, perhaps broken during it final stages of manufacture and never erected, measures about 100 feet long (30 meters) and weighs an estimated 550 tons. Most of the stelae were carved from single stones taken from a quarry four miles away and used to mark the graves of kings. The carved decorations make the stelae resemble multistory palaces. There were also tombs, or catacombs, associated with the stelae, though most of these were looted at some point in the distant past.

## DEMISE

Aksum's decline was mainly due to a shrinking of its trade as Arabian and Persian traders in the Red Sea began to assert greater power. After Muslims from Arabia conquered Egypt in 640, Aksum was cut off from the outside world. Although Christian, Axum became a place of refuge for early persecuted believers of Islam—including, at one point, one of Muhammad's eventual wives. This helped to protect the Aksumites from subsequent Arabic conquests. Nevertheless, the empire's main trading port at Adulis was captured by Muslims in the 700s.

This both deprived Aksum of access to the Red Sea and facilitated the spread of Beja tribes from the northeast into its territory.

Besides outside pressures, Aksum also experienced internal conflict among its ruling class. Overexploitation of natural resources and changes in rainfall likely also contributed to the city's decline. When the Aksumites finally abandoned the capital in the seventh century and moved southward into the interior of the plateau, they came into conflict with the Falasha. The Falasha were an Agaw people who had been converted to Judaism (and are known as Beta Israel, or Ethiopian Jews). In the 900s the Falasha destroyed the kingdom's new capital city. (This city was also called Aksum.) They did not, however, retain control of the kingdom. Eventually, a new Orthodox Christian Agaw dynasty, the Zagwe, became the major power in the region. It restored order, and for 300 years, it ruled the area once controlled by Aksum. One of the Zagwe's legacies is the holy city of Lalibela, which contains several churches carved entirely out of volcanic rock.

Legends about a powerful and wealthy Christian empire in Africa—including myths about a Black Christian king called Prester John—grew during the European Middle Ages. These myths served as a stimulus to Portuguese exploration of Africa in the fifteenth century.

## RECENT DISCOVERIES AND CURRENT STATUS

The Aksum ruins were designated a UNESCO World Heritage Site in 1980. Political unrest has occasionally impacted research, yet archaeologists have continued to work the site when feasible.

One of the city's ancient stelae had been removed in 1937 by Mussolini's Italian army, which had occupied Ethiopia the previous year; it was erected near the Colosseum in Rome. In 2005, however, it was returned to Aksum, although by then it had been damaged by air pollution and a 2002 lightning strike. Restored and reassembled, it was reerected in its original position in 2008 as part of a joint UNESCO, Italian, and Ethiopian project.

In 2015, eleven ancient graves were uncovered. Some of the graves contained the remains of male warriors wearing iron bangles and buried with Roman artifacts. One grave held a high-status woman whose body had been adorned with beaded jewelry and was positioned next to a Roman bronze mirror along with a cosmetics kit. Pottery vessels in the grave are thought to have held food and drink for use in the afterlife.

*Michael Shally-Jensen*

See also: Alexandria; Meroë.

## FURTHER READING

*Archaeology*. 2015. "2,000-Year-Old Roman Artifacts Unearthed in Ethiopia." June 8, 2015. https://www.archaeology.org/news/3385-150608-ethiopia-aksum-burials

Burstein, Stanley, ed. 1998. *Ancient African Civilizations: Kush and Axum*. Princeton, NJ: Markus Weiner.

Munro-Hay, Stuart. 1991. *Aksum: An African Civilization of Late Antiquity.* Edinburgh, Scotland: Edinburgh University Press.

Phillipson, David W. 2012. *Foundations of an African Kingdom: Aksum and the Northern Horn, 1000 BC–1300 AD.* Woodbridge, UK: James Currey.

## Alexandria

The great city of Alexandria, founded by Alexander the Great in 331 BCE and still present in modern-day Egypt, existed at the center of a series of curious events. When Alexander died, the city was thrown into chaos because the Macedonian conqueror had not designated an heir. After several years of war, Ptolemy I became the city's leader, remaining stalwartly Greek while also being an Egyptian pharaoh. This situation continued through the Ptolemaic dynasty, which lasted for about two centuries; the famed Cleopatra (Cleopatra VII) was the last Ptolemaic pharaoh before the city was burned during civil wars.

In between its founding and demise, Alexandria became home to one of the original Seven Wonders of the Ancient World, the famous Lighthouse of Alexandria, not to mention such wonders as the Library of Alexandria and later marvels such as a Roman colosseum and an extraordinary collection of catacombs that blend Roman, Greek, and Egyptian elements. In its time, Alexandria was at the center of Western culture, even as it was steeped in Egyptian and Eastern traditions.

### INHABITANTS

It was Alexander the Great's unsurpassed effort to establish his Macedonian empire that served to spread Greek culture from the conqueror's own small corner of the globe to most of the Mediterranean, northern Egypt, and much of central Asia. With his death, however, the short-lived empire broke up, leaving the individual states to war among themselves. Even then, Greek culture and customs continued to be cultivated and disseminated, a process called Hellenization (after the Greek name for Greece, *Hellas*). The resulting Hellenistic age, as it is termed, represented a hybrid civilization in which Greek, Egyptian, Roman, and West Asian cultures mixed and created something new.

The Egyptian city of Alexandria established itself as a major center of Greek learning. One of Alexander's former top officers, Ptolemy, set out to create an institute for advanced study there called the Temple of the Muses, or Museum (which contained the great library). Claiming to have personally buried Alexander at a site nearby (although the tomb has never been found), Ptolemy assumed the title of king in 305 BCE, and after he died in 283, he was succeeded by his son. Thus, the dynasty of the Ptolemies arose and continued to rule Egypt, from Alexandria, until the end of the reign of Cleopatra in 31 BCE and Rome's absorption of the city into its empire.

While Alexander had envisioned a kind of multiethnic empire—and Alexandria to some extent embodied it—Egypt under Ptolemaic rule was run by a Greco-Macedonian elite, with Greek being the official language of business and politics. (Cleopatra was the only Ptolemaic ruler who spoke Egyptian as well.) The

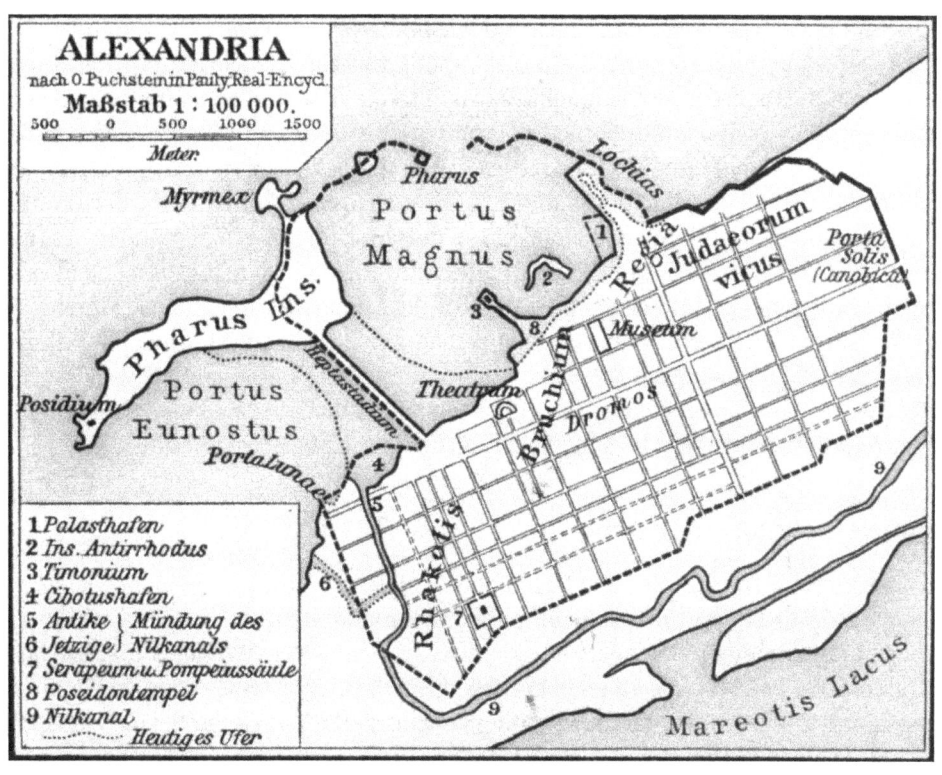

As a planned city, Alexandria was composed of well-ordered streets abutting two large Mediterranean harbors. The island of Pharos (or Pharus) helped form the harbors and boasted the famous lighthouse of the same name. (F.W. Putzgers *Historischer Schul-Atlas*, 1901)

Ptolemies also became renowned for their wealth, which was accrued on the basis of a system of taxation whereby everyone from fishermen to beekeepers had to pay their dues. Moreover, little of what was collected was spent on addressing the needs of the peasants; rather, most of the revenue went to building up the Egyptian navy and army or was directed to members of the royal dynasty. This was more like the Egypt of old than any pluralistic society imagined by Alexander. Yet, the Ptolemies did try to appease the populace by staging horse races and other sporting events as well as occasional public festivals. There was also a modest-sized Jewish population in the city whose members could enjoy synagogue services conducted in Greek.

## HISTORICAL BACKGROUND

Alexander the Great was one of the most prominent conquerors of the ancient world; his empire ranged from Egypt to India and is generally considered to have initiated the era of Hellenistic civilization. The Romans ultimately conquered much of Alexander's former empire in the west, while the Indo-Scythians, a loose group of Iranian and southern steppe peoples, conquered the east and established the Seleucid Kingdom, among other entities.

Alexandria was conquered early in Alexander's campaigns; in roughly 332 BCE, after conquering Syria, he moved south and captured the small Egyptian port town of Rhacotis. He then made a trek into the desert to consult the oracle of Zeus-Ammon at Siwa and learned that he was welcomed in Egypt as the son of god and the true pharaoh. He founded Alexandria at Rhacotis before moving on to additional campaigns; his commander, Cleomenes, was left to expand the city, which would eventually become one of the most famous places of its time.

When Alexander died in 323 BCE, he had not named a successor, and his empire was plunged into chaos (the Wars of the Diadochi). Eventually, Ptolemy I took control of Alexandria, noting that he had made good on Alexander's wish to be buried at Siwa, the site of the conqueror's revelation. Although Alexander is clearly associated with the city, it is the Ptolemaic dynasty, particularly Ptolemy I and his son Ptolemy II, who saw the city grow into its true greatness.

## CULTURE AND SOCIETY

The Greek historian Strabo wrote about Alexandria toward the end of its heyday, saying that it had magnificent public areas and attracted scholars, philosophers, artists, mathematicians, and scientists from all over. We know that Euclid, Archimedes, and Hypatia all lived and taught in the city at some point. Alexandria was home to Pharos, the famous lighthouse considered one of the Seven Wonders of the Ancient World and a symbol of human vision and knowledge. Ptolemy I also founded the Library of Alexandria, regarded as the single greatest archive of knowledge in the ancient world, as well as the Temple of Serapis, in honor of this hybrid Greek-Egyptian god.

The city was designed on a grand scale, with a broad central avenue lined with bazaars. The main building was the royal palace, which was both home to the Ptolemies and the seat of government. It was surrounded by gardens and fountains. In the great Museum of Alexandria, besides the library, there were lecture halls, observatories, a park, and a zoo. The residents of the city came to see themselves as the first cosmopolitans, or citizens of the world.

While Hellenization did lead to some social and economic changes, old patterns remained in place. The well-off citizens of Alexandria continued to own much of the land in and around the city, and they used slaves or immigrant labor to perform tasks. The remainder of the land was owned by the king or pharaoh and was worked by peasants and slaves, as it had been for millennia in Egypt.

A main center of activity was the harbor, one of the largest and busiest of its times. Large permanent docks and warehouses serviced traffic from the Mediterranean, the Nile, and the Red Sea. The Pharos lighthouse, named after the small island on which it stood, guided mariners with its mirrored lantern sitting atop its 440-foot tower.

There are two opposing stories about how the library was destroyed. First, the library may have been burned around 48 BCE; Caesar was then pursuing Pompey but was stopped by an Egyptian fleet outside of Alexandria. He ordered that the ships in the harbor be burned, and the fire spread into the city, destroying the library. Other scholars believe that many volumes were destroyed by the various religious groups that inhabited Alexandria over the years. There is no definitive answer to this lingering mystery. Scholars disagree, too, about how many volumes the library may have contained, perhaps as many as 500,000 (including scrolls, papyri, ledgers, sewn volumes, clay tablets, etc.).

## DEMISE

Other than Ptolemy I and II, the Ptolemaic rulers of Alexandria were generally considered to be fairly incompetent, both in their management of Alexandria and in their roles as pharaohs of Egypt. Members of the dynasty frequently married siblings or cousins in the interest of keeping the bloodline pure; at the time, this was not an uncommon practice, and both Egyptian and Greek religions featured gods following this practice. The interfamily relationships, however, caused constant infighting and questions of divided loyalties. The later Ptolemies did little to expand their power beyond Egypt; when they did so, they were easily turned back. Starting in 200 BCE, other empires with more resources and ambition began to chip away at the edges of the empire created by Alexander the Great.

Rule in Alexandria rapidly changed hands from one pharaoh to another over the next hundred years, and amnesty between the Egyptian citizens and the royal family grew rapidly. After 100 BCE, Ptolemy XI was placed on the throne by Roman powers but was quickly murdered by the Alexandrians. His son took the throne and was expelled within twenty years; he regained the throne with Roman support and managed to maintain it only by bribing Roman officials for their continued protection. This carried on until roughly 48 BCE, when Cleopatra took the throne upon her brother's death. It is commonly believed that she poisoned him.

Cleopatra was highly educated—one of the first of her family who spoke Egyptian (along with several other languages)—and participated in Egyptian festivals and celebrations. She also maintained friendships with Rome; her contact with Julius Caesar has been the subject of literary speculation for 2,000 years. When Mark Antony decided to fight Octavian for power in Rome, Cleopatra sided with him; Antony then lost at the Battle of Actium. Cleopatra committed suicide, and her children were taken to Rome to be raised as citizens there. Egypt did not fight Roman rule, and the Ptolemaic dynasty came to an end after nearly 300 years.

## RECENT DISCOVERIES AND CURRENT STATUS

Alexandria still exists today. But with the destruction of its library, the toppling of its lighthouse by earthquakes, the damage done by different outside powers over the centuries, and, above all, the loss of much of the ancient city to rising sea levels, little of Ptolemaic Alexandria remains.

Today, Alexandria remains a vibrant metropolis with great historical appeal to tourists. The foundations of the ancient lighthouse can still be seen, and one great Roman column survives from the temple attached to the library. A Roman amphitheater was discovered while excavating a nearby site and is an excellent example of classical architecture. The city's striking catacombs are from early medieval times. Modern archaeologists are also beginning to realize that much of the modern city was quite literally built on top of the old city. By carefully digging under roads and sidewalks, additional valuable artifacts have been retrieved. Divers, too, have begun locating remnants of old quays and sections of the royal quarter. Some archaeologists believe that they may have found the palace of Cleopatra herself, but the tomb of Alexander remains elusive.

*Michael Shally-Jensen*

*See also:* Giza; Memphis and Saqqara; Rome.

**FURTHER READING**

Blakemore, Erin. 2019. "New Clues to the Lost Tomb of Alexander the Great Discovered in Egypt." *National Geographic,* February 28. www.nationalgeographic.com/culture/2019/02/lost-tomb-alexander-great/

Casagrande-Kim, Roberta. 2014. *When the Greeks Ruled Egypt: From Alexander the Great to Cleopatra.* New York: Institute for the Study of the Ancient World; Princeton, NJ: Princeton University Press.

Manning, J. G. 2010. *The Last Pharaohs: Egypt under the Ptolemies.* Princeton, NJ: Princeton University Press.

Pollard, Justin, and Howard Reid. 2007. *The Rise and Fall of Alexandria: Birthplace of the Modern World.* New York: Penguin Books.

# Amarna

The Amarna period in ancient Egyptian history retains its fascination for students today. For thirteen years, the "heretic king" Akhenaten (r. ca. 1353–1336 BCE) had outlawed forms of worship that were hundreds (or perhaps thousands) of years old and dramatically changed art and culture in his country. Finally, he was succeeded by a pharaoh, his son, who is probably the most famous Egyptian king to non-Egyptians, Tutankhamun. Furthermore, Akhenaten was married to one of the most preeminent women of the ancient world, Nefertiti. Yet, Akhenaten's rule was so despised among Egyptians that after his death, his name was struck from the list of Egyptian kings, his temples and monuments torn down, and his presence was essentially erased from written history—until, that is, the nineteenth century, when the remains of the city of Amarna were discovered by Europeans.

**INHABITANTS**

The Egyptians of the New Kingdom era (ca. 1540–1075 BCE) were more "internationally" focused than those of the preceding eras. During the Old and Middle Kingdoms (ca. 2575–2130 BCE and 1938–ca. 1600 BCE, respectively), manufacturing and foreign trade had played only a small role in the development of Egyptian civilization. The Egyptians' agricultural self-sufficiency, based on their cultivation of crops in the Nile River valley, lessened their need to look elsewhere for provisions; this was evidenced by the absence of a large commercial class in Egyptian society. However, having obtained new territorial possessions in Nubia and the Levant (Palestine and Syria), the New Kingdom's political elites were now obliged to expand the nation's economic operations. Even while doing so, they continued to make or obtain goods designed to support their extravagant lifestyles, as Egypt remained a most divided society, with elites at the top and a large populace of commoners and slaves at the bottom. The "middle class," such as it was, was fairly small and made up of artisans, builders, agricultural managers, and the like.

## HISTORICAL BACKGROUND

As a pharaoh of the Eighteenth Dynasty in the New Kingdom period, Akhenaten's rule was initially uneventful. He came to power around 1340 BCE, though he may have been a coruler with his father, Amenhotep III. Initially, he was referred to as Amenhotep IV, but he changed his name in the fifth year of his reign, as he had outlawed worship of the deity of Amun, one of many in the Egyptian pantheon, and proclaimed himself to be the living incarnation of Aten, a single, all-powerful deity. By the ninth year of his rule, all the existing temples had been closed, and new roofless ones arose dedicated to Aten, a sun god represented by a golden disk. Akhenaten (meaning "servant of Aten") declared that Aten was the one true god, and the names of other gods were destroyed on monuments and in scrolls.

Once Akhenaten had declared himself the incarnation of Aten, it appears that he had little time for affairs of state. He transferred the Egyptian capital from Thebes to Amarna, about 250 miles north, to mark the break with the past and to reduce the power of the old-line priests. Previous allies of the dynasty often wrote to him, asking for help in one way or another, but he ignored or denied most such requests. Some of these letters have survived and are called the Amarna Letters. While some of them do show Akhenaten responding to matters of state, and demonstrating that he had a keen mind for foreign policy, they also show that he was only primarily interested in that topic when it benefited him. The years of Akhenaten's rule were those of an internally focused regime occupied with a kind of religious fundamentalism.

## CULTURE AND SOCIETY

Throughout recorded history in Egypt, Egyptian religion was polytheistic, meaning that it revolved around the worship of many different gods. Each god had a particular domain that he or she oversaw, and worshippers asked for help from the appropriate god based on what they needed. The pharaoh was supposed to ensure *ma'at*, or harmony of relations between gods and humans. The Egyptians believed that the pharaoh embodied the will of the gods and that their kingdom represented the sacred world; humans therefore had a responsibility to sustain it by behaving appropriately. When Akhenaten closed the old temples and declared Aten the one true god, he upended the traditional Egyptian belief system, not just in terms of religious devotion but in terms of people's general outlook or worldview.

Prior to Akhenaten, many pharaohs associated themselves with a particular god from the Egyptian pantheon and called themselves that god's servant—this was most commonly Horus, the god of kingship and the sky. Akhenaten's transformation, however, was the first time that a pharaoh had identified himself as the living embodiment of a god; this was also the first known instance of monotheism, albeit of a kind still steeped in polytheistic sympathies and not taking deep root in the culture as a whole.

While some scholars believe that Akhenaten experienced a genuine religious conversion, others suggest that he embarked on the religious path that he did to counter the growing power of the cult of Amun, which had defined his father's reign and previous kingships. Virtually every god in the Egyptian pantheon had a cult of some kind, but the cult of Amun had been growing since the time of the Old Kingdom. Amun was eventually associated with Ra, the god of the sun, to the point that he was referred to as Amun-Ra. When Akhenaten became pharaoh, the priests of Amun were as powerful and rich as the pharaoh himself. Thus, claiming devotion to Aten, like moving the capital to Amarna, may have been a way to eliminate the power of the Amun priests at the royal court.

Regardless of the reason, Akhenaten's reforms radically upset the Egyptian way of life. Closing the temples, in the view of Egyptians who did not adhere to the cult of Aten, effectively cast out their gods from the world. There was also a dramatic change to artwork depicting the royal family during this time. Aten was often centered in the images as a disk at the top of the image, its rays pointing down at the images of the pharaoh, his queen (Nefertiti), and their children. Their figures were depicted as almost spindly, with elongated necks, arms, and legs. Some scholars believe that the king suffered from a medical disorder (acromegaly) that could have given him this sort of appearance; others think such figures were simply stylized for effect—and, indeed, Nefertiti and the couple's children were depicted in the same manner, lending support to this idea.

Nefertiti's presence in such images is itself notable. Most images of pharaohs, both before and after, showed the king as a lone figure, hunting or standing in the company of a god. Images from Akhenaten's reign, however, show the couple or the entire royal family. This may have been designed to show the influence of Aten and the god's transformation of the royal family, or it may have been meant to convey the status and influence of Nefertiti and the upcoming generation.

## DEMISE

Akhenaten died around 1336 BCE, and the throne passed to his son, Tutankhaten, who was about eight years old at the time. Tutankhaten inherited a country in chaos. Akhenaten's neglect of state affairs had emboldened the enemies of Egypt, and parts of the Egyptian empire had been claimed, primarily by the Hittites. Tutankhaten renamed himself Tutankhamun, renounced the supremacy of Aten, reopened the temples of Amun and other gods, and moved the capital back to the traditional location at Thebes. Yet, Tutankhamun was but a boy king for most of his reign, dying before he was twenty years old. There is some question, therefore, as to whether the changes he wrought stemmed directly from him or whether they had come from his advisers or other members of the royal court.

The demise of the Eighteenth Dynasty had already begun by then. When Tutankhamun died, his wife, Ankhsenamun, wrote to the Hittite king, asking him to send her one of his sons to marry so that she would not have to marry one of her servants. This was a novel idea, for while Egyptian men often took foreign wives, Egyptian women never married foreign men. In this case, the Hittite king did send one of his sons, but he never arrived. Ankhsenamun disappears from the historical record at that point, and Horemheb, the commander of Tutankhamun's army, eventually took control of the country. The last member of the Eighteenth Dynasty, Horemheb affiliated himself with Horus, saying that he had been chosen to restore the orthodox Egyptian religion. He duly set about destroying any record of both Tutankhamun and his father. His work was so effective that the two pharaohs were virtually unknown until their tombs were accidentally unearthed by archaeologists in the twentieth century.

## RECENT DISCOVERIES AND CURRENT STATUS

Because Amarna had been abandoned by Akhenaten's successors, it has proved more accessible to study than most other ancient Egyptian sites, with their various layers of history complicating the picture. The main districts of Amarna, which Akhenaten called Akhetaton ("realm of the Aton"), were made up of ceremonial, residential, and agricultural structures. In the northern part of the city, the royal palace sat adjacent to the ceremonial center called the Great Aton Temple. To the west was another palace, and to the south was a residential area for priests and government officials. Artisans, including the grave tenders who managed the nearby cemetery, lived in the eastern quarter, which was drier and less desirable. The most southerly area consisted of religious shrines, pavilions, and walkways around artificial ponds and lakes. The different quarters of the town were linked by a broad avenue. The tomb of Akhenaten lies outside the city to the east. When it was discovered in 1893, it was empty, the pharaoh's body having been removed in ancient times and probably either reburied (perhaps in the Valley of the Kings) or abandoned.

Nefertiti was originally intended to be buried in the royal tomb along with her husband, but because he predeceased her, this may not have occurred. Her body was absent from the tomb and likely never placed there. A pair of mummies found in the Valley of the Kings in the early 2000s gave researchers hope that they had located Nefertiti's remains, but subsequent laboratory analysis indicated that neither of the bodies was hers.

Tutankhamun became the most famous of Egyptian rulers when his tomb was discovered in 1922. Unlike most all other such burial sites, Tutankhamun's tomb had never been raided by ancient robbers and emptied of its valuables. It thus contained the richest hoard of Egyptian artifacts ever encountered, including the boy king's striking golden mask. Most of the items from the site are on display in the Egyptian Museum in Cairo, though they also have made several world tours on the museum circuit, to great popular renown. Artifacts from Amarna have also made the rounds, and a solid collection of them is held by the Petrie Museum of Egyptian Archaeology at the University of London.

*Michael Shally-Jensen*

*See also:* Hittites; Thebes.

**FURTHER READING**

Dodson, Aidan. 2016. *Amarna Sunrise: Egypt from Golden Age to Age of Heresy.* Cairo: American University in Cairo Press.
Kemp, Barry. 2012. *The City of Akhenaten and Nefertiti: Amarna and Its People.* London: Thames & Hudson.
Ridley, Ronald T. 2019. *Akhenaten: A Historian's View.* Cairo: American University in Cairo Press.
Stevens, Anna. 2020. *Amarna: A Guide to the Ancient City of Akhetaten.* Cairo: American University in Cairo Press.

## Ancestral Puebloans

The Ancestral Puebloans were a Native American people of what is now the southwestern United States. They are considered the ancestors of the existing Pueblo peoples, such as those inhabiting the villages of Acoma, Isleta, Laguna, San Ildefonso, Taos, Zuni, and the Hopi Reservation of present-day New Mexico and Arizona. Ancestral Puebloan culture flourished from about 300 CE to 1500 in what is today known as the Four Corners region of the Southwest, where the states of Utah, Colorado, Arizona, and New Mexico meet. The people built and lived in large communal structures, which were called pueblos ("towns") by the sixteenth-century Spanish explorers who encountered them.

The Ancestral Puebloans are also sometimes referred to as the Anasazi. However, that name is generally not used by their descendants and is considered slightly offensive by some. *Anasazi* is a Navajo word meaning "ancestors of our enemies." It was first used in the mid-nineteenth century by American military surveyors who came upon mysterious ruins in New Mexico and asked their Navajo guides about the people who had lived there.

Ancestral Puebloan culture is probably best known for the stone and earth dwellings that its people built on cliff walls. Some of the most notable examples of these structures are preserved in the Mesa Verde area in Colorado and in Canyon de Chelly and Navajo National Monument in Arizona. Another dwelling style, that of the so-called great houses erected on flat terrain, can be viewed at sites such as Chaco Canyon, in New Mexico. Farther south and west, the related Mogollon peoples erected the Gila cliff dwellings, and in what is now central Arizona, the (non-Puebloan) Sinagua Indians built what is popularly known as Montezuma Castle.

**INHABITANTS**

Because contemporary Pueblo peoples exhibit a fair degree of linguistic diversity, it is thought by scholars that in prehistoric times, the Puebloans represented different peoples who lived as neighbors in a common region and eventually grew together culturally. Today's Pueblo peoples speak languages of the Tanoan family, including Tiwa, Tewa, and Towa, as well as Hopi, Zuni, and Keres, a language isolate with several dialects. It is not known what languages the Ancestral Puebloans spoke, as they left no written records, but the assumption is that their languages might well have been related to those of modern speakers.

The Puebloan people inhabited about ninety separate villages at the time they were contacted by the Spaniards in 1540. These settlements and their predecessors ranged along the Rio Grande Valley in northern New Mexico and northeastern Arizona. Some sites of the Ancestral Puebloans lie outside this area as well. In general, the Pueblo were village-dwelling cultivators. They built multistory apartment houses and other structures focused around subterranean ceremonial chambers, or *kivas*. The main political authority was in the hands of sacred societies. Each member of a Puebloan village took part in the intense religious cycle that defined the calendar year. Warrior societies also existed, but they were mainly for defensive purposes. As with most Pueblo peoples today, kinship was likely traced through the female line, giving some prominence to women in social affairs.

## HISTORICAL DEVELOPMENT

Maize (corn) cultivation first appeared north of Mexico around 200–100 BCE. Agriculture was developed in the Southwest by the Hohokam, an ancient culture centered in southern Arizona. By the start of the millennium, the Mogollon people were making pottery in a Mexican style, painted red. They became experienced farmers and built stone terraces along hillsides and small dams across arroyos to hold soil and moisture in the arid climate. The Mogollon people lived in shallow "pit houses" dug into the ground and roofed over with logs, branches, and mud.

The Ancestral Puebloans adopted some aspects of their culture from their predecessors. Their own cultural evolution is marked by several different stages, from Pueblo I (750–900 CE) through Pueblo IV (1350–1600). At its peak, between about 1050 and 1150, Ancient Puebloan society was centered on Chaco Canyon in New Mexico, best known today as the site of the great house called Pueblo Bonito. The canyon as a whole included more than a dozen great houses consisting of closely arranged, generally multistoried, dry-masonry structures and accompanying pit spaces or kivas. The dwellings were built with defensive features in mind, such as smooth outer walls that required entry by ladder. Chaco was connected to smaller, more distant great houses by hundreds of miles of paths and roadways; in some places, steps were cut into steep grades of sandstone to facilitate passage. Crop cultivation at Chaco was supported by an elaborate system of water control, including storage of water in reservoirs atop mesas, from where it was led by conduits and ditches into the fields.

## CULTURE AND SOCIETY

Ancestral Puebloan society revolved around the changing seasons—the solstices, equinoxes, and the like—and the routines of agricultural production, especially the cultivation of corn, and they participated in an active network of trade. Communities in warmer areas with a longer growing season traded produce, pottery, and cotton goods to Puebloans at higher altitudes for meat, hides, and wild plants. Some exchanges, however, took place across greater distances. Since early times, shells from the Pacific coast and Mexico have found their way to Arizona and New Mexico, probably by trade from one community to the next over long stretches of time. Eventually, tropical birds, feathers, copper bells, and iron pyrite mirrors were brought to Chaco Canyon by traders from Mexico, who returned south with turquoise and well-designed pottery bowls from New Mexico. Chaco was at the center of this regional trade network, which likely had as religious significance as well as economic and political importance.

Goods were not necessarily evenly distributed among the Ancestral Puebloans. Archaeologists have surmised, based on the study of burial remains, that there were three classes of people in classical Chacoan society. An elite class lived in the largest great houses and wielded the most power. The class below them lived in the outlying great houses of smaller size and prestige. And at the bottom of Puebloan society were the farmers. They produced corn, beans, and squash for their families and the community at large. At different times of year, seasonal ceremonies were held involving the exchange and distribution of food and other necessities brought to the Chaco area from afar. It is believed that elites with political standing and the proper ritual knowledge would oversee these exchanges, thus adding to their prestige through the redistribution of goods.

The classic cliff dwelling consisted of a compact assemblage of connected rooms, numbering from a dozen to over a hundred, often terraced toward the cliff wall. The whole complex was set into an enormous natural cave or contoured geologic "shelf." The individual sleeping rooms were about six-by-eight feet, sometimes larger, with ceilings ranging from four feet to eight feet in height. Toward the front of the complex, ceremonial chambers (kivas) were embedded in the earth, leaving their roofs at "terrace" level. These rooftop terraces, as in the case of contemporary Pueblo peoples, were probably a focus of everyday life. Each cliff site, complete with living spaces, corn-grinding rooms, storage rooms, and ceremonial chambers, constituted a single "town" or pueblo.

The classic great houses were similar to the cliff dwellings in style and function but were laid out more horizontally than vertically. The houses were built in a row or arc with a large pit-house structure—the kiva—in the foreground. The latter was designed for religious ceremonial use. Entry into the kiva was through the roof, and the entryway also served as a ventilator shaft, which was needed to disperse the smoke from the burning substances used in religious rites. Inside, deities represented by doll-like figures (*kachinas*) or drawings were presented to religious adepts as part of the indoctrination process—at least this occurred in the later phases of Pueblo cultural history. Puebloan religion was focused on crop fertility, moisture, and the harmony of life-forms in nature.

The pottery made by the Chacoans varied over the ages, but one distinct style featured geometric designs in black mineral paint over a white slip. Since the potter's wheel was not employed in the New World, pottery was constructed of coils of clay built up from base to top and then pressed and smoothed into elegant shapes. It was then wood-fired in an earthen trench to produce a fine, utile vessel.

## DEMISE

After about 1150 CE, a fifty-year drought came to impact the southern Four Corner region. Trade subsided substantially, and many farming communities were forced to abandon their land. The population declined, new conflicts arose, and Ancestral Puebloan society began to break apart. The surviving Puebloans headed to nearby uplands for safety and to capitalize on the melting winter snows for water and irrigation. Within a couple of generations, new and somewhat larger settlements were established at several locations. These included present-day Mesa Verde and Bandelier National Monument. Once again, natural water sources were tapped and fed into the pueblo. And once again, around 1300, a sustained drought set in and forced the people to leave. This time, they moved to semipermanent creeks and rivers at lower elevations, including the lands of the historic Hopi, Zuni, and Acoma pueblos, where they rebuilt their farming societies. Each was based on an independent, self-sufficient pueblo. These "modern" pueblos witnessed the arrival of the Spanish conquistadors in the sixteenth century; unlike many other Native American communities, they actually survived the encounter and stand today as monuments of endurance.

## RECENT DISCOVERIES AND CURRENT STATUS

Although most archaeologists hold that the Anasazi were the ancestors of today's Pueblo peoples, there is a minority view among some researchers and activists, especially in the Navajo community, that says the ancient Southwest was more of a "melting pot" than has been commonly thought and that the Navajo too likely descended from the Anasazi. The evidence here is thin, but these researchers point to various cultural similarities and to Navajo oral traditions to support their view (see Kloor 2009).

Another recent point of controversy has been the degree to which the Ancient Puebloans may have practiced cannibalism during times of drought and conflict. The image goes against the classic New Age picture of harmony-loving Anasazi people peacefully raising corn and worshipping their gods. Nevertheless, a number of scholarly studies support the idea that during times of extreme famine, the practice took place.

Today, visitors to the Southwest can look into such matters, and much more, at Chaco Canyon and the various other sites mentioned above, most of which function as both tourist centers and active research areas.

*Michael Shally-Jensen*

See also: Pecos Pueblo; Spanish Missions in North America.

## FURTHER READING

Fagan, Brian. 2012. *The First Americans: An Archaeological Journey.* New York: Thames & Hudson.
Kloor, Keith. 2009. "Who Were the Anasazi?" *Archaeology* 62, no. 6. https://archive.archaeology.org/0911/etc/insider.html
Stuart, David E. 2014. *Anasazi America: Seventeen Centuries on the Road from Center Place.* 2nd ed. Albuquerque: University of New Mexico Press.

Thomas, David Hurst. 2000. *Exploring Native North America*. New York: Oxford University Press.

Vivian, Gwinn R. 2012. *The Chaco Handbook: An Encyclopedic Guide*. Salt Lake City: University of Utah Press.

# Angkor

The city of Angkor, in north central Cambodia, was once the seat of power of the Khmer Empire, one of the largest and wealthiest kingdoms in Asian history. Established as the capital by the Khmer king Yasovarman I (r. 889–910 CE), the city quickly grew into one of the largest in the world, housing a million people or more. Angkor served as a religious center. Its Great Temple complexes are larger in scale than the Egyptian pyramids and are rated today as among the masterpieces of world architecture. Angkor Wat, the most famous of the city's temples, had long been dormant and hidden beneath jungle overgrowth when it was rediscovered by European explorers in the 1860s.

## INHABITANTS

The Khmer Empire, which incorporated present-day Cambodia as well as parts of Thailand, Laos, and Vietnam, existed for over six centuries, between the 800s

---

*Manila*

Manila, a cultural and economic powerhouse of Southeast Asia, faces imminent flooding.

Manila surrounds the point where the Pasig River issues into Manila Bay. The city is on the isthmus that separates Laguna Lake from this bay on the western shore of Luzon, the largest and most populous island in the Philippines. The area of Manila has been inhabited for millennia. Early on, two separate polities—Tondo and Maynila—politically and economically dominated the region. Together, they wielded a monopoly over Chinese trade to the rest of the Philippines and entered the written record as early as 900 CE. A fortified Indianized settlement thrived at the location from the thirteenth century, and a Muslim settlement flourished from the turn of the sixteenth.

From the time when the Spanish arrived in 1571, the city played a central role in Spanish trade in the Pacific. Since the late nineteenth century, the city has continued to expand and thrive despite repeated destructions: the Americans took Manila from the Spanish in 1898 and then conducted a brutal multiyear war against the locals to establish their imperial leadership. The Japanese captured the city during World War II, and the Americans recaptured it in one of the bloodiest and most destructive battles in human history in early 1945. Through it all, Manila has retained its cultural and economic prominence. Its varied history has produced a vibrant and layered megacity.

All coastal cities are at risk with sea levels on the rise, but a few details exacerbate Manila's circumstance. These include its vulnerable position on a low-lying isthmus and ongoing land subsidence. The latter refers to the physical sinking of the ground caused by the removal of groundwater. Experts expect worsening cyclones that already cause extensive flooding in the city. Moreover, Manila is among the most densely populated major cities on the planet, which adds both urgency and obstacles to its fight against climate change.

Suryavarman II oversaw the construction of Angkor Wat in the early twelfth century CE. Made of limestone and covering about 400 acres, the temple complex is dedicated to the Hindu god Vishnu. (Littlewormy | Dreamstime.com)

and the 1400s CE. The Khmers are known to have first lived along the lower and middle Mekong River in northern Cambodia and southern Laos. Their original capital was near Kampong Thom, to the southeast of Angkor, but King Yasovarman I moved it to Angkor and built up the city. Besides Angkor Wat, the Bayon and Banteay Srei monuments (all built after Yasovarman's rule) represent outstanding examples of Southeast Asian art and architecture.

The Khmers were often engaged in wars against the surrounding Mon, Cham, Annamese, and Thai peoples. In fact, their dominance in the region was first challenged by the Chams in the twelfth century and finally extinguished by the Thais in the fifteenth.

## HISTORICAL BACKGROUND

The site of Angkor was first settled in 819 CE by Khmer under the rule of King Jayavarman II (r. 802–850), the founder of the empire. It was under Yasovarman I, however, that Angkor—or what was then known as Yasodharapura—was made the capital. The city became the center of religious devotion and featured an elaborate system of agricultural production, including reservoirs, dikes, irrigation channels, and raised roadways. Rebuilt and expanded by King Rajendravarman II (r. 944–968), Angkor came to include the terraced Phnom Bakheng temple, one of the lesser yet still notable monuments.

The splendid Temple of Angkor Wat, originally dedicated to the Hindu god Vishnu, was constructed by the Khmer ruler Suryavarman II (r. 1113–1150).

Constructed of carved limestone, the entire temple compound occupied an area of about 400 acres. It featured a series of concentric gallery corridors surrounding a large central edifice that was crowned by five great lotus-shaped towers, intricately worked and gilded with gold leaf. Angkor Wat impressed visitors with almost 1,300 square feet of bas-reliefs: the entire Vishnu legend was depicted along with pictorial representations of Khmer life.

Ultimately, the city came to hold seventy-two major temples and hundreds of minor temples, spread over a vast area of some 400 square miles. Perhaps the most prolific builder in Angkor's history was King Jayavarman VII (r. 1150–1218 CE), who greatly expanded the city's size and led a transition from Hinduism to Buddhism. In doing so, he directed artisans to alter many of Angkor's sculptures and friezes to reflect the new worldview.

The last great Khmer ruler, Jayavarman VII (r. 1181–1219), built Angkor Thom as a new capital after conquering the Chams; it lies adjacent to the Phnom Bakeng and Angkor Wat monuments. At the city's center was the Bayon, a Buddhist temple with some fifty towers decorated with the monarch's half-smiling face.

## CULTURE AND SOCIETY

For much of its early history, Hindu cults devoted to Shiva and Vishnu and, later, Mahayana Buddhists thrived in Angkor. Besides being a religious center, the city served as the chief political capital of the Khmer Empire. Angkor's planning reflects the importance of religion and politics. Khmer style was strongly influenced by Indian culture but also displays distinct features of its own. The entire city was intended to symbolize Hindu cosmology. It was built around a central pyramid temple, symbolic of Mount Meru, the home of the Hindu gods. The canals that fed the city wells and rice fields were designed as symbolic representations of the life forces at work throughout the cosmos.

The first temples were constructed using brick; in the later ones, from around 1020, dressed stone was used. All these "temple mountains" featured elaborate designs and figures serving as ornaments and sacred images. The central icon represented the monarch in the guise of his patron deity. The two earliest surviving structures, built during the reign of Yasovaram I, are the Bakong (881) and the Bakheng (893), which had 108 tower shrines around its central sanctuary. Angkor Wat was considered the dwelling place of Vishnu, the principal Hindu deity responsible for protecting the world against evil. The compound is surrounded by a 590-foot-wide moat. The causeway leading to the enormous entrance is flanked by balustrades shaped as giant serpents.

Near the end of the twelfth century, the Khmer ruler Jayavarman VII took the radical step of adopting Mahayana Buddhism as his personal faith, turning his back on the Hindu tradition of the region. He went on to make Buddhism the kingdom's official religion when he constructed the Buddhist temple known as the Bayon at the heart of his new capital city of Angkor Thom. In the famous face towers of the Bayon, the king represented himself as a bodhisattva (i.e., a person on the path to Buddhahood) who is motivated by the love of his subjects. Jayavarman was thus able to begin the transition of Angkor and Khmer culture to

Buddhism by resorting to compassion and divinity rather than to war and destruction (in the vein of the cult of Shiva).

## DEMISE

Regardless of Jayavarman's efforts, the Khmer Empire began to fall into decline soon after his death. Part of the reason was conflict over the transition from Hinduism; another part was external pressure from the Chams (of the Champa state). Angkor was sacked by the Chams in 1177 and partly abandoned. It was again captured and sacked in 1431, this time by Thai forces. The Khmer were forced to abandon the city and relocate their capital farther south, near Phnom Penh. Many statues and treasures were looted in medieval times, irrigation and roadway systems fell into disuse, and most of Angkor was eventually covered by jungle. The ruins were only rediscovered by the French in 1861, with some restoration work not beginning until the 1920s.

## RECENT DISCOVERIES AND CURRENT STATUS

Cambodia experienced devastating war and radical government changes between the 1960s and the 1980s. Worldwide, there was concern for the safety of Angkor and other such sites, yet there was no opportunity for inspection let alone conservation. Finally, in 1987, the Archaeological Survey of India, in collaboration with the Cambodian government, launched a restoration effort. King Norodom Sihanouk pressed for reopening the site for archaeological studies and worked to return the site to its former status as a major tourist attraction. Even then, however, the lack of security or control allowed for looting, and sculptures from Angkor continued to appear on the art market. Since then, the picture has greatly improved. Angkor has been a UNESCO World Heritage Site since 1992.

In 2007, using satellite images, researchers discovered that the settlement surrounding Angkor Wat was at least three times larger than previously thought. The irrigation system was found to be larger and more complex, and researchers identified at least seventy-four additional temples at the site.

In 2011, an effort started in the 1960s to reconstruct the eleventh-century Baphuon tower at Angkor Thom was finally completed. By this time, security was reliable, and the complex was attracting some two million tourists annually.

A variety of more recent finds have been made as well. These include several buried or hidden statues and stone heads along with a large bronze workshop at Angkor Thom. Researchers have also uncovered evidence that drought, in addition to conflict, may have played a role in Angkor's demise.

*Michael Shally-Jensen*

*See also:* Ayutthaya; Bagan/Pagan; Borobudur.

## FURTHER READING

Coe, Michael D., and Damian Evans. 2018. *Angkor and the Khmer Civilization.* 2nd ed. New York: Thames & Hudson.

DiBiasio, Jame. 2013. *The Story of Angkor*. Chiang Mai, Thailand: Silkworm Books.
Higham, Charles. 2001. *The Civilization of Angkor*. Berkeley: University of California Press.

## Antioch

Antioch on the Orontes, or Syrian Antioch, was situated about 10.5 miles (17 km) from the Mediterranean Sea on the site of the older villages of Meroë and Bottia. Its ruins lie in the Amuk Valley near the current city of Antakya, Turkey, which is named for the ancient city. It was on the eastern bank of the Orontes River between two of its tributary streams: Parmenius and Phryminus. Mount Silpius was to the southeast, and to the north, where the Orontes and Parmenius met, there was a large island in the middle of the Orontes. The island was incorporated into the ancient city, but the west bank would only ever serve as a buffer zone for the city.

Antioch's mild climate, central location, and ample water supply made it an ideal location for this once great capital city. It was part of the spice trade, Silk Road, and Royal Road. According to legend, in 333 BCE, Alexander the Great drank the water of one of Antioch's local springs and declared it was sweeter than his mother's milk. Located in an active volcanic zone, the fertile soil allowed for abundant orchards and fields. Fish and wild game were also readily available, keeping this large city fed.

### INHABITANTS

Antioch, as part of the Seleucid Empire, had a diverse population that included Greeks, Armenians, Persians, Medes, Assyrians, and Jews. After it was founded in 300 BCE by Seleucus I Nicator, Antioch was filled by Athenian Greeks from a nearby town, Macedonians, and Jews. During the late Hellenistic period and early Roman period, they city's population swelled from a humble 25,000 to over 250,000 inhabitants, and Antioch became the third-largest city in the empire after Rome and Alexandria.

The population of Antioch was a mix of pagans, Jews, and Christians, and they lived in relative peace. The large Jewish population was centered in the Kerateion quarter of the city. St. Paul traveled there on his first missionary trip to convert the first Christians. Greek, Syrian, Armenian, and Latin monasteries surrounded the town. After the fall of the Roman city in the sixth century CE, Antioch was continuously conquered for the next 600 years, incorporating Crusaders and Seljuk Muslims into the population.

### HISTORICAL BACKGROUND

In prehistory, there was a grouping of small villages in the area that would later become Antioch that included Meroë and Bottia. Little is said about these settlements or area, but legend holds that Alexander the Great camped for a time in the area that would become Antioch, drawn in by the beautiful landscape and delicious water. Upon Alexander's death in 323 BCE, his generals (the Diadochi) fought for and divided up the territory he had conquered. Seleucus I Nicator claimed the territory of Syria and founded Antioch (named after his father) in 300 BCE.

Antioch became the capital of the region soon after its founding. The original city was laid out in a grid plan mimicking Alexandria, Egypt. A fortified section of the town was on Mount Silpius with the majority of the city on the low ground to the north along the river. Antioch expanded quickly, and another zone was laid out, most likely to the east and enclosed by a separate set of walls. A third walled city was built to the north on the large island in the Orontes River. A fourth and final town was added later at the beginning of the second century BCE. Since Antioch was made up of these four distinct zones, it was known as Tetrapolis. The whole area was filled in with gardens and covered about four square miles (6 km).

Not much else is known of Antioch during the Seleucid/Hellenistic Period (ca. 300–63 BCE), except that large-scale building in the city continued and the population was large, prosperous, and learned. Its location was in an active and destructive seismic zone, which necessitated constant rebuilding and updating. Politics in the city and the Seleucid Empire overall were just as volatile; a series of rebellions and skirmishes in this period ended with Pompey annexing Syria as a province of Rome in 64 BCE, with Antioch as its capital. The Romans began building monumental structures in Antioch almost immediately, and the province retained independent rule of itself as long as it complied with Rome's wishes. The monumental buildings included a forum, theaters, a circus, an aqueduct, and colonnades. Antioch flourished under the Romans, though it did suffer many earthquakes, including a large one in 115 CE that restructured the landscape.

Antioch was a Christian center in the Roman period that held numerous church meetings. It also had a large Jewish population that lived in a separate quarter called the Kerateion. In 387 CE, there was a large rebellion against a new tax levied by order of Theodosius I, and the city was punished. He divided the Roman Empire, and as a result, Antioch was no longer a capital city but under the rule of Constantinople. Antioch and its port, Seleucia Pieria, were severely damaged in a fire in 525, followed by earthquakes in 526 and 528; the city never fully recovered. The city was temporarily captured by the Persians in 540 and 611 before being thrust into conflict for the next 600 years.

## CULTURE AND SOCIETY

Antioch was a bustling metropolis for several centuries before its gradual decline beginning in the sixth century CE. It was a thriving commercial town connecting the Far East to the Mediterranean world and was considered one of the finest cities in the Greek world, filled with philosophers and scholars. Rome occupied Antioch beginning in 64 BCE, seizing the opportunity to control this strategic and prosperous location as the Seleucid dynasty weakened. It became the capital of the Roman province of Syria and as such was gifted with monumental Roman buildings, such as its famous circus for chariot racing. Meanwhile, it enjoyed Roman military protection. This protection allowed the city to flourish on all social and economic fronts, including religious diversity. Pagans and Jews were already in the region when Rome arrived, and Christianity followed.

Antioch was well connected by both land and sea, and as such, it served as a hub for the exchange of goods and ideas. It was an ideal base for the early missionary efforts of Paul, Peter, and Barnabas, and it served as one of the most important Christian cities outside of Jerusalem. Antioch gave its name to a school of Christian thought that was distinguished by the idea that Jesus had human limitations as well as a literal interpretation of the church writings. In the second half of the third century CE, ten church assemblies were held at Antioch, and later in the sixth century, it became one of the five original seats of power for Christianity, a pentarchy.

## DEMISE

Antioch prospered under Seleucid and Roman rule, but the sixth century CE brought a series of disasters from which the city never fully recovered. A large fire in 525 was followed by earthquakes in 526 and 528. In its state of disrepair, the city was captured temporarily by the Persians in 540 and 611, ending the supremacy of Antioch within the region. Just twenty-six years later, in 637, it was absorbed into the Arab caliphate and dwindled to the status of a small town. In 969, the city fell back into Byzantine hands, where it remained for over a century, before being controlled by the Seljuk Turks and Crusaders in turn. Finally, the Mamluks destroyed the city in 1268.

A small village was rebuilt in its place and taken by the Ottoman Turks in 1517. It was part of the Ottoman Empire through World War I and then briefly became Syrian territory before rejoining Turkey in 1939.

## RECENT DISCOVERIES AND CURRENT STATUS

Few remains of the ancient city are now visible aside from parts of its fortification walls and aqueducts. Most of the Roman city is now buried under the sediments of the Orontes River. Excavations in 1932–1939 in Daphne and Antioch uncovered about 300 mosaic floors from both private houses and public buildings dating to the second through sixth centuries CE. The mosaics depict copies of famous ancient paintings and a variety of original scenes, including animals, plants, and mythological characters, as well as scenes from daily life. The majority of the mosaics are now exhibited in the Hatay Archaeology Museum in Antakya, Turkey, and the Princeton University Art Museum in Princeton, New Jersey. Since the excavations in the 1930s, smaller rescue excavations have uncovered more mosaics, statues, and small finds, but the major buildings of the city are yet to be uncovered.

*Katie Tardio*

See also: Alexandria; Ctesiphon.

## FURTHER READING

Christensen-Ernst, J. 2012. *Antioch on the Orontes: A History and a Guide*. Lanham, MD: Hamilton Books.

Downey, G. 1963. *Ancient Antioch*. Princeton, NJ: Princeton University Press.
Sartre, M. 2005. *The Middle East under Rome*. Cambridge, MA: Belknap Press of Harvard University Press.

# Anuradhapura

Anuradhapura, a city in central Sri Lanka, served as the capital of the Anuradhapura Kingdom for well over a millennium, from 377 BCE to 1017 CE. The city resides on Sri Lanka, a large (25,000 square miles) tropical island off the southern tip of India. The ruins of the erstwhile powerful city sit on the Malvathu River, north of the modern iteration of the city, itself a provincial capital.

Many ancient structures remain from the ancient city. Most famous among these are the Atamasthana, or Eight Sacred Sites. These include the Jaya Sri Maha Bodhi, a sacred fig tree planted by Devanampiya Tissa in the third century BCE as a sapling from the famous Bodhi Tree, where the Buddha achieved enlightenment. The second-century BCE king most responsible for contributing to the construction of the Atamasthana was King Dutugamunu. He built the first iteration of three of the Eight Sacred Sites: Ruwanwelisaya, Lovamahapaya, and Mirisaveti Stupa.

## INHABITANTS

The region around Anuradhapura has been inhabited for thousands of years. According to Pali chronicles, the town of Anuradhapura was settled in the first

### Maldives

As the globe's lowest-lying nation, the Maldives stand on the front lines of the fight against the rising sea.

The archipelago stretches north to south across a swath of the Indian Ocean southwest of Sri Lanka and consists of over a thousand coral islands spread out across about a couple of dozen atolls. The islands were first inhabited before the third century BCE, when they first appear in the historical record. At this time, Buddhism spread across the already settled archipelago with help from Ashoka, the influential Mauryan emperor. Buddhist stupas and other structures constitute the oldest surviving ruins on the islands. Buddhist culture flourished for fourteen centuries, until Dhovemi, the king of the Maldives, converted from Buddhism to Islam in the twelfth century CE. Islamic culture has thrived on the archipelago since. The Maldives were controlled by the Portuguese, Dutch, and British in turn, until they won their independence in 1965.

On average, the Maldives landmass sits less than five feet about sea level, and the highest natural point on any of the islands is less than eight feet. This makes it the lowest and flattest nation on earth. Composed of tiny islands, it also has the smallest landmass of any nation in Asia, yet the islands are spread over a large stretch of ocean. All this leaves the Maldives particularly vulnerable to the elements. It faces monsoons, particularly but not exclusively in the summer and fall, which commonly lead to flooding. However, the biggest threat to the low-lying nation is the rising sea. The United Nation's Intergovernmental Panel on Climate Change has warned that if seas continue to rise unabated, the Maldives may become uninhabitable within the twenty-first century.

wave of the Indo-Aryan migration to Sri Lanka in the sixth century BCE. It was reportedly settled by a minister of Vijaya. The Indo-Aryan immigrants mixed with the Indigenous population in Anuradhapura as well as elsewhere on the island to form the Sinhalese people, who speak an Indo-Aryan language of the same name. The Sinhalese comprised a large portion of the Anuradhapura Kingdom for its entire history, just as they have remained the largest segment of the population of Sri Lanka to this day. Also similar to today, a diverse tapestry of different ethnicities inhabited Anuradhapura and its kingdom alongside the Sinhalese.

## HISTORICAL BACKGROUND

Sri Lanka's historical period begins with Prince Vijaya, and much of its early history is intertwined with legend. According to the Pali chronicles, Prince Vijaya arrived in Sri Lanka with 700 followers after being expelled from Sinhapura for violent deeds. The location of Sinhapura is disputed, but many point to eastern India or even farther east to present-day Thailand. He set up his capital in Thambapanni, thereby founding the Thambapanni Kingdom, a predecessor to the Anuradhapura Kingdom. Vijaya's life is dated to the sixth century BCE, and he is credited with initiating the Indo-Aryan migration to Sri Lanka. The Sinhalese people who populated the Anuradhapura Kingdom and still make up three-quarters of Sri Lanka's present-day population are the result of this Indo-Aryan migration.

After two centuries of the Thambapanni Kingdom, King Pandukabhaya established the Anuradhapura Kingdom in 377 BCE. He moved the capital to Anuradhapura, where it remained for nearly fourteen centuries (except during the reign of Kashyapa I, who ruled from Sigiriya in the fifth century CE). Anuradhapura had existed before Pandukabhaya's reign, possibly founded by one of Vijaya's ministers. Pandukabhaya fostered Anuradhapura into a thriving capital city, just as he reorganized the kingdom as a whole. He developed a more effective court administration and officially demarcated the kingdom's many villages. After defeating many enemies, he consolidated a larger part of the island within Anuradhapura's borders.

Buddhism arrived in Anuradhapura in the third century BCE. The island of Sri Lanka has hosted an assortment of religions for as long as we have a historical record. For its first century and a half of existence, the kings and their courts practiced Brahmanism. Tissa, the king of Anuradhapura, had a favorable relationship with Emperor Ashoka of the Mauryan dynasty on the mainland. The latter sent his eldest son Mahinda as a Buddhist missionary to Anuradhapura. Mahinda first met the king on Mihintale, a mountain near the capital. The king converted to Theravada Buddhism and took the name Devanampiya ("Beloved of the Gods"). He likewise converted his court, and the religion spread quickly.

Reigning in the second century BCE, Dutugamunu gained renown and became one of Anuradhapura's most influential kings. He took the throne from Elara, a Tamil prince from the Chola Kingdom on the mainland. Anuradhapura kings had typically ruled Rajarata, the northern third of Sri Lanka, sometimes more and sometimes less. However, after Dutugamunu took the throne, he went about expanding his territory until he ruled the entire island—the first time that Sri Lanka had been united under one leader. Dutugamunu was also influential in areas beyond military matters. He enacted a large-scale building program, most famously commissioning Ruwanveliseya, a massive stupa to house the Buddha's begging bowl.

In the early fourth century CE, an even more prestigious Buddhist relic made its way to Anuradhapura. Princess Hemamala and her husband, Dantha, brought a tooth of the Buddha himself from the mainland to Sri Lanka. King Guhasiva had ordered them to smuggle the relic from his realm of Kalinga to preserve it from his enemies. Sirimeghavanna, the king of Anuradhapura at the time, received the tooth with great pageantry. He led the relic in a procession to its new resting place, an event Sri Lankans still commemorate every year. The tooth became a symbol of Sri Lankan kingship and remained in Anuradhapura for centuries, that is, for as long as the Anuradhapura Kingdom survived.

## CULTURE AND SOCIETY

The kingdom of Anuradhapura's diverse culture reflected the diversity of its population. Arriving in the third century BCE and soon becoming the primary religion of the kingdom, Buddhism played an influential role in the kingdom's culture. We have multiple influential Pali chronicles from the Anuradhapura period that mix history and religion into epic poems. Brahmi inscriptions have survived from the first half of the kingdom's existence. The Sinhalese script formed from the Brahmi script, and there are plenty of Sinhalese inscriptions as well as a few Sinhalese books that have survived from this period. Frescoes and sculpture were two popular art forms and often revolved around Buddhist motifs. The architecture likewise showcased Sri Lankan twists on established Buddhist themes, particularly with a wide variety of stupas.

The kingdom of Anuradhapura was primarily an agricultural society, with Buddhist prohibitions on meat consumption obviating the demand for most animal husbandry. Rice was the primary agriculture product. The kingdom included wet and dry landscapes, and advances in irrigation became important in cultivating the dry areas. Cotton, sugarcane, and sesame were also grown, and cinnamon is native to the region and became a popular export. Anuradhapura became a trading hub, forging trade networks east and west, including with Mediterranean powers such as the Roman Empire. The Sangha, or Buddhist clergy, had close ties to the court in the capital city of Anuradhapura and held a prominent status within the society.

## DEMISE

The kingdom of Anuradhapura survived multiple invasions from the mainland before the Chola invasions at the turn of the eleventh century CE ended the kingdom for good. The previous invasions were often successful, with mainlanders ruling parts of Sri Lanka for brief periods of time in the third, second, and first centuries BCE as well as the fifth, ninth, and tenth centuries CE. These occupations all proved temporary, however, as Sri Lankans always regained power and reinstated self-governance centered in Anuradhapura.

In some ways, the occupation of Chola forces under Emperor Rajaraja I and his successors was similar to invasions of centuries past. A powerful mainland force invaded the island, overthrew the king at Anuradhapura, and occupied the island for several decades before being driven off the island by local forces. However, there were key escalations: they conquered the entire island as opposed to only the northern region, which was more densely populated and closer to the mainland. Their control of the southern regions, however, proved tenuous. The major difference between this and early invasions was that the Chola emperor Rajendra Chola I, the son of Rajaraja I, razed Anuradhapura. The Chola occupiers ruled from Polonnaruwa, which they called Jananathamangalam, about sixty miles southeast of Anuradhapura. When Vijayabahu I drove off the Chola occupiers and restored local control of Sri Lanka, he retained the new capital of Polonnaruwa as his own.

### RECENT DISCOVERIES AND CURRENT STATUS

Anuradhapura is listed as a UNESCO World Heritage Site as the Sacred City of Anuradhapura. Excavations have been ongoing since the late nineteenth century. Many sites from the Anuradhapura Kingdom are popular among tourists, especially the Atamasthana, the Eight Sacred Places.

*Anthony Vivian*

*See also:* Pataliputra; Vijayanagara.

### FURTHER READING

Herath, Sudhira. 2001. *Anuradhapura, the City of Splendour.* Ann Arbor: University of Michigan Press.
Seneviratna, Anuradha. 1994. *Ancient Anuradhapura: The Monastic City.* Ann Arbor: University of Michigan Press.
Strickland, Keir Magalie. 2017. *Time of Change: Questioning the "Collapse" of Anuradhapura, Sri Lanka.* Oxford: Archaeopress.
Weerakkody, D. P. M. W. 1997. *Taprobane: Ancient Sri Lanka as Known by Greeks and Romans.* Chicago: Brepols.

## Assyrians

The Assyrians created a powerful military state that dominated Mesopotamia and, indeed, the entire ancient Near East for centuries. Although the fortunes of the empire waxed and waned throughout the period of its greatest reach, ca. 911 BCE to 627 BCE, it was the largest imperial state up to that time; later empires, such as Persia, Macedonia, and Rome, strove to achieve what the Assyrians had. In addition, like a number of their Mesopotamian counterparts, the Assyrians worked to preserve their civilization by establishing large libraries (such as those of Ashurbanipal at Nineveh) that housed a variety of texts, some of which had been composed 2,000 years earlier.

## INHABITANTS

The Assyrians were a Semitic people who largely inherited—and cultivated—earlier Sumer-Akkadian traditions. Known for their powerful, aggressive rulers whose armies frequently were engaged in foreign conquest and domestic defense, the Assyrians also represented the last great culture of Mesopotamia. Like the later Romans, the Assyrians built cities, constructed roads, recorded (and translated) information in documents (clay tablets), laid down laws, and had a trade system based largely on silver. Like the Hittites before them, the Assyrians played a significant role in transmitting Mesopotamian civilization down through the ages. They were also known for exhibiting brutality toward their enemies and treating subject peoples harshly.

## HISTORICAL BACKGROUND

A region known as Assyria is attested as early as the third millennium BCE; it then consisted of a collection of autonomous city-states that included Ashur (Assur), Nineveh, and Arbela (Arbil or Erbil). These city-states were likely under the control of the Akkadian Empire and the third Ur dynasty between ca. 2,300 and 2,000 BCE. By the start of the second millennium, however, they had regained their independence. Sometime around 1750 BCE, the Amorites, a seminomadic Semitic people from Syria in the west, imposed themselves on the Assyrian heartland. As a consequence, the Assyrian city-states diminished in importance and eventually fell under the control of the Mitanni Empire (ca. 1600–ca. 1350 BCE).

After the neighboring Hittites destroyed Mitanni (ca. 1360 BCE), Assyria became an independent, unified state. Its ruler, Ashur-uballit I (r. ca. 1363–ca. 1330 BCE), led a military expansion aimed at making Assyria a major power in the Near East. For the next 150 years, Assyria held sway over Babylonia to the south, controlled territory once held by Mitanni to the west, and stood nearly on par with Egypt and the Hittites, the two greatest powers in the region. However, while the Assyrian ruler Tukulti-Ninurta I (r. ca. 1244–ca. 1208 BCE) had conquered Babylonia, his son lost the gains of the father and became a vassal of Babylonia. Only under Tiglath-pileser I (r. ca. 1115–ca. 1077 BCE) did Assyria start to reclaim its former glory. This ambitious king fought campaigns in the north and west, capturing former Hittite areas after the latter's collapse, but he also faced severe challenges from the Aramaeans. Ultimately, the Assyrians overextended themselves and again became weaker—until, that is, the reigns of Ashur-Dan II (r. ca. 934–ca. 912 BCE) and Adad-nirari II (r. ca. 911–ca. 891 BCE). Both of these leaders campaigned extensively against the Arameans and managed to push them farther west.

Under Ashurnasirpal II (r. ca. 883–859 BCE), who established Calah (Kalhu; modern Nimrud) as his new capital and launched major campaigns in many different directions, Assyrian imperial power was restored. This king savagely put down Aramaean and Phoenician states to the west and adorned his capital with a huge palace decorated with elaborate reliefs. His successor, Shalmaneser III (r. 858–824 BCE), consolidated previous gains but was nearly defeated by a powerful coalition of Syrians, Israelites, Egyptians, and Arab tribes at the Battle of Qarqar (Karkar) in 853 BCE. Weakened and facing internal rebellion, Assyria once again became unstable.

King Tiglath-pileser III (r. 745–727 BCE), who likely came to power as a usurper, successfully laid the foundations of Assyria's vast empire of the eighth and seventh centuries BCE. He eliminated the threat posed by the Kingdom of Urartu to the north (modern Armenia), invaded Syro-Palestine, and converted cities such as Damascus (Aramaean), Tyre (neo-Hittite), and Byblos (Phoenician) into vassals. Another usurper, Sargon II (r. 721–705 BCE), began building out the empire and decisively defeated another coalition of forces at a second Battle of Qarqar in 720 BCE. Subsequently, he marched through Palestine, deposing local rulers; completed the siege of the Israelite capital of Samaria; and campaigned in eastern Turkey against Midas of Phrygia and Urartu, weakening both of these states and creating a broad frontier. In Babylonia, however, Sargon was less successful, encountering trouble from the Chaldaean chieftain known in the Bible as Merodach-Baladan (Marduk-Baladan). After moving the Assyrian capital to Dur-Sharrukin (modern Khorsabad)—which became known for its splendid palace adorned with reliefs and sculptures of winged human-headed bulls and lions representing deities—Sargon died in battle in 705 BCE while campaigning in the north.

Sargon's son and successor, Sennacherib (r. 705–681 BCE), invaded Syro-Palestine in 701 BCE and purportedly caged the Judean king Hezekiah in Jerusalem. The Assyrian leader demanded harsh terms from Judah, emptying its treasury and laying siege to its fortified cities as well as to several more distant cities (in Philistia and Phoenicia). Hezekiah's daughters were sent as concubines to Sennacherib's new capital, Nineveh. After a revolt in Babylon, the latter city was destroyed (689 BCE), even as internal disorder grew within the Assyrian Empire. Sennacherib was assassinated by two of his sons, and a third son, Esarhaddon, forced his two brothers out of power.

Esarhaddon (r. 680–669 BCE) and his successor, Ashurbanipal (r. 668–627 BCE), succeeded in conquering Egypt but were only able to maintain control of it for about fifteen years (ca. 673–658 BCE). This period, then, represented the height of the Assyrian Empire.

## CULTURE AND SOCIETY

Archaeological findings, along with unearthed texts concerning the Assyrian kings and their activities, conform to the picture presented in the Bible of Assyrians as militarily powerful and brutal toward foreign peoples. In Assyrian relief sculptures and in their annals, one often encounters acts such as maiming, burning, impaling, and flaying captives. The Assyrians used such techniques as a form of psychological warfare designed to instill terror and discourage rebellion. Another infamous method was the mass deportation of subject populations, where deportees were used as slaves to build cities and operate farmlands within the ever-widening Assyrian Empire.

The Assyrian economy centered on agriculture, animal husbandry, and trade. Assyria stood at the crossroads of trade routes that connected central Asia with Anatolia, and its leaders were heavily involved with foreign trade, as their own region lacked many resources needed to support the realm. Much of the Assyrian state existed to enrich the homeland, and little effort was made to economically sustain the outlying conquered territories, so long as they continued to provide their annual tributes. As a result, over time, the economies of these areas went into decline, fomenting rebellion and causing trouble at home for the Assyrians.

The mainstay of Assyrian society was the tribe and the family; it was the goal of every Assyrian man to protect and propagate both. A hierarchical society, Assyrian class structure was based on wealth, political power, and social standing. The king was at the top of the social pyramid, and under him, there were various classes of nobles, government officials, skilled laborers, and unskilled laborers—the latter, including both freemen and slaves. All land belonged to the king, as the representative of the god Ashur on earth; yet, in practice, much of it was controlled by wealthy families, temples, and commercial operators.

The capital cities built by the Assyrian kings, especially Nimrud (Calah) and Nineveh, functioned as sophisticated multilingual urban centers in the first millennium BCE. They contained Aramaean craftsmen and scribes and people of other nationalities as well. While Assyria considered Babylonia a vassal state, it remained dependent on the southern region for much of its resources. Indeed, much of Assyria's cultural heritage came to it by way of Babylonia. The contents of the Library of Ashurbanipal at Nineveh, made up of myths, epics, ritual texts, and divinatory and magical texts written on cuneiform tablets, were derived from Babylonia. The Assyrians also created their own literature, including works like those of Babylonia; in addition, many legal texts, annals, and commercial and administrative documents have survived.

Assyrian art is especially known for its colossal winged bulls and lions, which stood at the entrances of the royal palaces. Also notable, fine bas-reliefs decorated the palace walls, and sets of impressive carved ivories adorned furniture. These ivories feature motifs of Egyptian design that suggest they may have come to Assyria in the form of war booty or tribute. On the stone reliefs, portrayals of Assyrian kings engage in acts such as hunting, honoring the gods, and subjugating foreign peoples. Their level of refinement makes them gems of Assyrian art.

Assyrian religion was polytheistic, like most other religions of the ancient Near East. The paramount god was Ashur, who oversaw the land of Assyria and held supreme power over the other deities. Deities such as Ishtar (love and war), Ninurta (warfare and hunting), Shamash (sun), Adad (storm), and Sin (moon) were each associated with devotional cults and temple complexes. Temples were tower-like structures (ziggurats) maintained by priests and temple officials. Religious ceremonies involved the performance of regular and seasonal rituals and the presentation of offerings. The king was considered the chief priest of the religious cults and was therefore usually present at important ceremonies.

## DEMISE

Under King Ashurbanipal, Assyria arrived at the height of its power. At the same time, it once again became overextended in terms of its resources, and between 652 BCE and 648 BCE, it faced a major civil war. Following the death of Ashurbanipal in 631 BCE, the empire's collapse was only a matter of time. In 616–612 BCE, Assyria was attacked and destroyed by a coalition of Medes (an ancient Iranian people) and Chaldeans, resulting in the destruction of every major Assyrian city. Many of Assyria's former subjects, who had experienced firsthand the harshness and brutality of Assyrian rule, took pleasure in witnessing the demise of the empire.

## RECENT DISCOVERIES AND CURRENT STATUS

The first great discoveries in ancient Mesopotamia took place in the mid-nineteenth century, when the region was still part of the Ottoman Empire. At cities such as Assur, Nimrud, and Nineveh, a number of monumental buildings came to light, most of them decorated with fine works of art. Tens of thousands of cuneiform records were excavated, and new museums in London, Paris, Berlin, and Istanbul loaded up on Assyrian (and Babylonian) objects and texts. Exploration has continued ever since, although political events in Iraq and the wider Middle East have often made such work difficult or impossible.

In the late 1980s, Iraqi archaeologists unearthed the "Nimrud treasure," which contains a great quantity of works of gold, semiprecious stones, ivory, and other materials given to various queens of the ninth century BCE (and buried with them). The pieces were put on display at the Iraqi national museum but then lost during the Persian Gulf War (1990–1991). They were rediscovered, however, in 2003. During the Iraq War (2003–2011), the museum was looted, and many items were lost (though not the Nimrud treasure), even as curators and benefactors around the world sought to relocate many of the institution's holdings. Further, in 2015, parts of Nimrud were bulldozed by the Islamic State on the grounds that the Assyrian remains were idolatrous and un-Islamic. In the following year, the site was retaken by the Iraqi army, but by then, substantial damage had already been done.

For its part, Nineveh appears on the Global Heritage Fund's list of "vanishing" world cultural sites because of threats posed by looting and creeping development. At the same time, new discoveries—tablets, reliefs, and even one whole city, Idu—continue to crop up through the diligent efforts of Assyriologists across the globe.

*Michael Shally-Jensen*

*See also:* Babylon; Hittites; Phoenicians.

## FURTHER READING

Chavalis, Mark W. 2006. *The Ancient Near East: Historical Sources in Translation.* Malden, MA: Blackwell.

Cotterell, Arthur. 2019. *The First Great Powers: Babylon and Assyria*. London: C. Hurst & Co.
Radner, Karen. 2015. *Ancient Assyria: A Very Short Introduction*. Oxford: Oxford University Press.
Rizza, Alfredo. 2007. *The Assyrians and the Babylonians: History and Treasures of an Ancient Civilization*. Vercelli, Italy: White Star.
Snell, Daniel C. 2005. *A Companion to the Ancient Near East*. Malden, MA: Blackwell.

# Athens

Athens built a massive but fleeting empire in the greater Aegean region in the mid-first millennium BCE. Already a large city and burgeoning democracy, Athens hit its stride in the fifth century. After playing a pivotal role in defeating the Persian invasions in the beginning of the century, Athens built a naval empire over the Aegean Sea and beyond. After their leadership proved heavy-handed and exploitative, Sparta and other Greek city-states banded together and overthrew the Athenian Empire at the tail end of the century. Through this time, a multivaried culture blossomed in Athens, featuring key historical figures working in tragedy, comedy, historiography, philosophy, art, and more.

The capital of the present-day nation-state of Greece, Athens remains a thriving Aegean hub, but the remains from antiquity stand above and among the modern city. The Acropolis looms over the city, the temples' vibrant colors now a sun-bleached white. The remains of the Parthenon, not destroyed until 1687, are the largest and most famous structure on the Acropolis. Yet, the Acropolis also features the Erechtheion's Porch of the Caryatids, the Temple of Athena Nike, and the Propylaea, among other ruins. The Temple of Dionysius, where Sophocles's *Antigone* and Aristophanes's *Lysistrata* were originally performed, sits on the slope up to the Acropolis. Around the Acropolis lies the ancient agora (or marketplace), the remains of a massive Temple of Zeus, and Pnyx Hill, where the democracy met.

## INHABITANTS

The Athenians themselves claimed that they were autochthonous, that is, that their ancestors sprung directly from the earth. This myth sprouted from a seedling

---

*Atlantis*

The city of Atlantis was first conceived by the fourth-century BCE author Plato, who used the mythical city as a foil for his own city of Athens. Atlantis was a fictional, exaggerated form of the naval imperialistic tendencies of Athens. In the story, it was a wealthy, powerful city but was eventually swallowed by the sea. Plato uses the story not as the history of a real lost city but as a warning to his fellow Athenians about the nature of their own city. Despite this straightforward origin, people have long believed the city to be real and have sought to locate it at the bottom of various seas. Closely linked with the city's name, the Atlantic Ocean has been a common site for these types of search missions. Others have associated Atlantis with Minoan Crete or the Aegean island of Thera.

*Acropolis* is Greek for "High City." The Athenian Acropolis looms over present-day Athens, including Monastiraki Square, pictured here. The Parthenon, built under the leadership of Pericles in the fifth century BCE, dominates the Acropolis and the skyline now as it did when it was first constructed. (TomasIIII | Dreamstime.com)

of truth: the city of Athens and the surrounding region of Attica did see millennia of constant inhabitation, and when the archaeological records show other areas experiencing periods of destruction and violence—especially ca. 1200 BCE—Attica seems to have been spared. One reason for this is Attica's rocky, mountainous soil, which is relatively less fertile than other regions of mainland Greece. Athena was the patron goddess and namesake of the city, and myths often portray her as active in the city's formation, sometimes alongside other gods popular in Athens, particularly Poseidon and Hephaestion. Cecrops was the mythical first king of Athens and is often portrayed with the tail of a fish or snake. The Attic Greek dialect spoken in Athens was a branch of Ionic Greek, and the Athenians were closely linked with the Ionian Greeks of Asia Minor, whose cities the Athenians take credit for colonizing.

## HISTORICAL BACKGROUND

From the seventh century to the fifth century BCE, Athens expanded the franchise within its male citizen population as well as its influence in the Aegean and wider Mediterranean. Athens is credited as the birthplace of democracy, but this unique government did not come about in one fell swoop; it formed gradually over generations. Little is known of Draco, Athens's first lawgiver of the seventh century, but his name survives in English in the adjective *draconian*, which means "excessively harsh." The Athenians themselves named Solon, the lawgiver of the early sixth century, as the father of democracy. While his reforms were influential in the formation of the Athenian state, it is better to view him as setting the stage for Athens's later democracy. After Athens experienced two generations of tyranny under Pisistratus and his son Hippias, Cleisthenes finally ushered in Athens's democracy in the late sixth century.

Athens rose to become a Greek superpower as a result of its indispensable role in warding off the Persian invasions of the early fifth century. The Athenians defeated a Persian army sent by Darius the Great at Marathon in 490. They then proved pivotal in defeating the much larger invading force led personally by Darius's son and successor, Xerxes. According to the historian Herodotus and others, the Athenian Themistocles persuaded his fellow Athenians to build a navy between the two Persian invasions and then used cunning and deception to catalyze the Battle of Salamis in 480, the Greek naval victory that served as a turning point in the war. The Athenians' contribution to Greek victory and their powerful navy allowed them to seize control of the Aegean Sea over the following five decades. Exploiting their allies and neutral Greek city-states, they transformed the Delian League into an Athenian Empire that ruled the Aegean Sea and beyond. An expedition to Egypt in the 450s failed, but Athens's star rose on. Meanwhile, Ephialtes and Pericles expanded access to democracy for Athenian male citizens.

Athens's meteoric rise in the fifth century put them on a collision course with Sparta, Greece's preeminent power. Athens's growth was in naval power, whereas Sparta retained the strongest land army; yet, the two could still only avoid each other for so long. They fought the long and inconclusive First Peloponnesian War in the middle of the century before signing the Thirty Years' Peace. Before the peace was half complete, with Sparta fearful of Athens's continued expansion, the Second Peloponnesian War—often simply called the Peloponnesian War—commenced. After twenty-seven years of on-again, off-again fighting and an ill-advised Athenian expedition to Sicily, Sparta defeated Athens in 404.

## CULTURE AND SOCIETY

Athens reached a high watermark in Greek literary and intellectual culture in the fifth century BCE. Our views of ancient culture are often shaped by the texts that have survived, and a large amount of luck can go into that process. However, Athens's cultural prowess was highly regarded, even in antiquity; later Greek authors tried to replicate the Attic dialect used by fifth-century Athenians, which therefore became the standard for literary Greek. Before the fifth century, the only major notable Athenian author was Solon, the sixth-century lawgiver who also wrote political and erotic poetry.

The cultural output exploded in the fifth century. All extant Greek tragedy was written by Athenians—namely Aeschylus, Sophocles, and Euripides—during this time. Most surviving Old Comedy was written by the Athenian Aristophanes during this time. Socrates prowled the Athenian agora, creating a turning point in the history of philosophy. Herodotus and Thucydides created the genre of history. The former was from Halicarnassus but spent much time in Athens; the latter was from Athens.

This literary high point coincided with the blossoming of other arts. After the Persians burned the buildings on the Athenian Acropolis during their invasion of 480, Pericles oversaw a massive building program on the Acropolis using funds taken from allies. These temples mostly still stand on the Acropolis today, although they were originally painted with vibrant colors, not whitewashed as we have grown accustomed to seeing them. Phidias, the most famous sculptor of the fifth century, was born in Athens and designed, among other works, the gigantic statue of Athena Parthenos that originally stood in the Parthenon on Athens's Acropolis. In the sixth century, Athens was home to the innovation of red-figure pottery, which displayed red figures against a painted black background. This new style quickly grew more popular than black-figure pottery, and Athens served as its primary exporter.

Athenian society included conflicting ideologies. On the one hand, the ever-expanding democracy gave the people a voice in an unprecedented way. This change coincided with and was accelerated by Athens's shift to naval power. The navy was powered by the labor of the lower classes as rowers, so it was natural that the government would grant them more of a say. On the other hand, elite culture continued to flourish. Thucydides remarked on the vast differences between Sparta and Athens regarding class gaps: Athenians made ostentatious displays of wealth in fashion and architecture, while the Spartans did not. Symposiums, or drinking parties, were popular among the male elite.

## DEMISE

The year 404 BCE is often considered the year Athens fell. Sparta defeated Athens, tore down the Long Walls connecting Athens proper to the sea, and overthrew Athens's democracy. However, the city rebounded quickly. It never restored the influence it held in the fifth century, but it remained an important player in the Aegean world. In 403, Thrasybulus overthrew the so-called Thirty Tyrants, the oligarchic government installed by the Spartans, and restored Athenian democracy. In the 390s, Greece had grown wary of Spartan hegemony, and Athens joined the other major Greek city-states in opposition to Sparta in the Corinthian War. By the end of the decade, Athens had rebuilt the Long Walls.

In 378, to combat Sparta, Athens formed the Second Athenian League with most of the allies that it had exploited in the fifth century. The terms of the league were drawn up to contrast Athens's earlier heavy-handedness; for example, the allies would no longer pay a tribute. However, the league once again established Athens as the naval power of Greece. After Sparta faded, Athens opposed Theban hegemony and the rise of Macedon. However, King Philip II of Macedon defeated the Athenians and a number of other Greek contingents at the Battle of Chaeronea in 338, essentially ending the autonomy of Athens and most other Greek city-states. Philip II and his successor, Alexander the Great, spared Athens from punishment for its opposition to Macedon, as they were eager to wield the Athenian navy for the planned invasion of Persia. It was during this fourth century that philosophy flourished in Athens, with Plato establishing his Academy and Aristotle founding his Lyceum. Though no longer an autonomous city-state, Athens continued to thrive after the fourth century, and it now stands as Greece's most populous city and capital.

## RECENT DISCOVERIES AND CURRENT STATUS

Excavations are ongoing around Athens, including in the ancient agora and on the Acropolis. The city is bursting with antiquities. In 2020 alone, archaeologists unearthed a head from a statue of the god Hermes from under some street pavement; an ancient aqueduct in Athens's port, Piraeus; and a curse tablet in a well. The Athenian Acropolis is a UNESCO World Heritage Site.

*Anthony Vivian*

*See also:* Delphi; Ephesus; Olympia.

## FURTHER READING

Neils, Jenifer, and Dylan Rogers. 2021. *The Cambridge Companion to Ancient Athens*. Cambridge: Cambridge University Press.
Ober, Josiah. 1999. *The Athenian Revolution*. Princeton, NJ: Princeton University Press.
Samons, Loren, II. 2010. *The Cambridge Companion to the Age of Pericles*. Cambridge: Cambridge University Press.
Strassler, Robert B. 1998. *The Landmark Thucydides: A Comprehensive Guide to the Peloponnesian War*. New York: Touchstone.

# Ayutthaya

The city of Ayutthaya became the seat of power and namesake for the Ayutthaya Kingdom, also known as Siam, which thrived from the fourteenth to the eighteenth century CE. The city was built on an island between the Chao Phraya, Pa Sak, and Lopburi Rivers, about fifty miles north of Thailand's current capital, Bangkok. The city grew into a kingdom encompassing the plains surrounding the Chao Phraya River valley, the mountainous regions in the north, and the Malay Peninsula to the south. This kingdom became the territorial—as well as cultural—forerunner to the modern nation-state of Thailand.

Many sites remain from the kingdom's heyday, especially within the erstwhile capital of Ayutthaya itself. Many of these sites are impressive wats, the regional name given to Buddhist temples. Wat Phra Si Sanphet was constructed by King U-thong, the founder of the Ayutthaya Kingdom, in 1350, the first year of his reign, to be his palace within the new capital. When the palace was moved across town a century later, Wat Phra Si Sanphet was transformed into a holy site. Although much of the site was destroyed in 1767, three chedis remain today. Wat Phutthaisawan is another site built by King U-thong; it features a distinctive white prang—or tower—rising from the center of the site. Among the many sites from later in the kingdom's existence is Wat Chaiwatthanaram, built by King Prasat Thong in 1630, to the southwest of Ayutthaya island.

## INHABITANTS

There is no consensus on whether Ayutthaya was inhabited when King U-thong officially established the city in 1350. To avoid an outbreak of smallpox, U-thong moved his court to this site. From whence they came is still debated, but many contend that they came from a nearby city in the Chao Phraya River valley or perhaps from the north. The inhabitants of Ayutthaya called themselves Tai and their kingdom Krung Tai. Westerners called the kingdom Siam and the population Siamese. Today, the individuals from the region are called Thai and their nation Thailand. Like many kingdoms in Southeast Asia, Ayutthaya was broadly influenced by Indian culture, religion, and language. Theravada Buddhism was Ayutthaya's primary religion, and the Thai language shows a large influence from Indian languages.

## HISTORICAL BACKGROUND

King U-thong, also known as King Ramathibodi I, founded the city of Ayutthaya in 1350. There is no scholarly consensus on where exactly he came from or whether the location that came to be known as Ayutthaya was settled beforehand, but many contend that he was the king of another city in the Chao Phraya River valley and moved his kingdom to Ayutthaya island to avoid a raging smallpox epidemic. U-thong named the new city Ayutthaya, after the Buddhist holy, and potentially mythical, city of Ayodhya. In its early history, Ayutthaya was a relatively small regional mandala, or city-state, and featured internal fighting among rival dynasties.

In the fifteenth century, Ayutthaya began to expand its sphere of influence, and its government was reformed. In 1433, Borommarachathirat II, also known as Samphraya, marched on Angkor, in present-day Cambodia, forcing the Khmers to move farther east. Borommatrailokkanat, also known as Trailok, ruled from 1448 to 1488 and was largely responsible for reorganizing and upgrading the kingdom's government. To limit wars of succession, he ended the practice of sending royal princes to govern various cities within the kingdom. He separated out civil and military officials and constructed a new system of ranks. He also published the Chatusadom, the kingdom's constitution.

By the sixteenth century, Ayutthaya had grown into a regional powerhouse and repeatedly clashed with Burma to the west. Portugal was the first European power to make direct contact with Ayutthaya and commenced a trading relationship beginning in 1511. However, it was Ayutthaya's repeated conflicts with the Toungoo dynasty of Burma, known as the Burmese-Siamese Wars, that dominated the kingdom's foreign and domestic affairs in this era. The Burmese successfully captured the capital of Ayutthaya in 1564 and rendered it subordinate to their rule for the following two decades. Naresuan regained independence for Ayutthaya and put the kingdom on the offensive against Burma, for which he has become known as Naresuan the Great.

Ayutthaya continued to thrive in the seventeenth and the first half of the eighteenth centuries. Ayutthaya's involvement in international trade increased, as did influence from external powers. The role of international powers came to a head in the reign of Narai. The growth in trade led to some prosperity; however, many of Narai's Thai subjects began smarting at the heavy influence that outside powers, particularly the French, played within their own government. This dynamic led to the revolution of 1688, in which Phetracha, a hardened nationalist, seized power after Narai's death and expelled all of the foreign powers, allowing only the Dutch to retain trade relations with Ayutthaya. The kingdom experienced one final era of prosperity during the reign of Borommarachathirat V, who ruled from 1733 to 1758.

## CULTURE AND SOCIETY

Ayutthaya featured a rich culture that took on many other types, often showing influences from India. Literature of the period was primarily poetry, that is, written in verse, but it took on many different forms. For example, Lilit poetry specialized in combining multiple different poetic meters, while Nirat poetry was an expression of travel and longing. Many famous works have survived until today. The *Ramakien* is a national epic of Thailand that originated in the Ayutthaya period and was derived from the Sanskrit epic *Ramayana*; portions of the *Ramakien* were often staged, especially at court in Ayutthaya. *Khun Chang Khun Phaen* is a long folktale that centers on a love triangle from around the turn of the seventeenth century. Sculpture from the Ayutthaya period often featured the figure of Buddha and was often made from stone, stucco, or bronze. Religious architecture was famous for its prangs and stupas.

The king sat atop a highly hierarchical society. The royal family and munnai, or court elite, who were exempt from taxes, were under him. Below them were the phrai luang and phrai som, or royal officials and commoners, respectively. The sangra, the Buddhist monastic class, was understood to exist outside of this hierarchy. The government was organized by Chatusadom, which served as the constitution for the Ayutthaya Kingdom as well as some later Thai governments. Chatusadom divided the bureaucracy into military and civilian realms, and within the civilian realm, there were four departments: the police, palace affairs, the treasury, and agriculture. Chatusadom means "Four Pillars," referring to these four civilian ministries.

The society—like the culture—of the kingdom was influenced by India to the west. Theravada Buddhism was the primary religion. Nonetheless, Hinduism and other forms of Buddhism were prevalent, while Islam and Roman Catholicism were also present during certain periods.

## DEMISE

Internal conflict over succession left Ayutthaya weakened and open to attack from its old foes, the Burmese. Burmese forces, now under the Konbaung dynasty, invaded one final time beginning in 1765. They seized the capital of Ayutthaya two years later and razed it to the ground. The capital's wealth of art and literature was looted or destroyed. The Burmese forces left after a few months to deal with an ongoing conflict with the Qing dynasty of China. They left behind a kingdom in shambles and without a capital. Taksin, a former general, was largely able to reunite the kingdom, but with Ayutthaya destroyed, he did so from a new capital at Thonburi, closer to modern-day Bangkok.

## RECENT DISCOVERIES AND CURRENT STATUS

The remains of Ayutthaya are a UNESCO World Heritage Site.

*Anthony Vivian*

*See also:* Angkor; Bagan/Pagan; Borobudur.

## FURTHER READING

Baker, Chris, and Pasuk Phongpaichit. 2017. *A History of Ayutthaya: Siam in the Early Modern World*. Cambridge: Cambridge University Press.
Baker, Chris, and Pasuk Phongpaichit, trans. 2016. *The Palace Law of Ayutthaya and the Thammasat: Law and Kingship in Siam*. Ithaca, NY: Southeast Asia Program Publications.
Miksic, John Norman, and Goh Geok Yian. 2016. *Ancient Southeast Asia*. London: Routledge.
Reid, Anthony. 2015. *A History of Southeast Asia: Critical Crossroads*. Hoboken, NJ: Wiley-Blackwell.

# B

## Baalbek

The city of Baalbek served as an important religious center for multiple different religions in succession. Its name combines the god Baal and the Bekaa Valley, where the city is located. This valley provided an ideal location thanks to its fertility and its placement near the major watershed between the Orontes River to the north and the Leontes River (today known as the Litani) to the south. The city sits about fifty miles inland from the ancient Phoenician port of Byblos on the Mediterranean Sea. The Greeks and Romans also knew the city under a religious name: Heliopolis, or "City of the Sun God."

The ancient ruins are primarily found within the vast and impressive temple complex, which was constructed in the Roman era. The Temple of Jupiter, of which the colossal foundation remains, was the largest temple in the Roman world. Scholars still debate how exactly the inhabitants of Baalbek laid the massive foundational stones. Connected to the Temple of Jupiter is the Temple of Bacchus, which is still relatively intact today. Also nearby is the Temple of Venus. The temple complex has gone through many changes over the eras. It was fortified under the Arabs, who first took the city in the seventh century CE, and it served as a citadel for much of its later existence. Over the years, it has faced destruction from earthquakes and at the hands of humans. Its ruins sit in the middle of modern Baalbek, a small Lebanese city.

---

### *Sodom and Gomorrah*

Sodom and Gomorrah were two cities on the Jordan plain that, according to the Abrahamic religions, were destroyed by God. The cities were said to have been located near the Jordan River and the Dead Sea. The tale of the cities' destruction is first told in Genesis, the opening book of the Hebrew Bible, and then frequently repeated or alluded to later in the Hebrew Bible, in the Christian New Testament, and in the Islamic Qur'an. According to the story, God destroyed the cities with fire and brimstone because of their excessive wickedness, although Abraham tried in vain to spare the cities from God's wrath. Abraham's nephew Lot and Lot's family were found to be the only pious inhabitants and were allowed to escape, provided that they did not look back at their burning city. When Lot's wife glanced back, she was transformed into a pillar of salt, a mineral closely linked with the region surrounding the Dead Sea.

## INHABITANTS

The site at Baalbek shows signs of habitation as old as nine millennia. In the shadows of giant empires, the location was ruled by various local, Near Eastern, and Mediterranean powers throughout the years. The inhabitants cultivated the fertile valley that encompassed the city. The location also acted as a watershed for two major rivers flowing in opposite directions, placing the city in an ideal locale for trade and commerce. But it was the inhabitants' religious devotion—and architectural prowess—that made them world famous.

## HISTORICAL BACKGROUND

The site of Baalbek has been continually inhabited for thousands of years. It may have blossomed into a larger settlement under the Egyptian New Kingdom, which ruled over this part of the Levant in the middle of the second millennium BCE, or the Neo-Assyrian Empire, which controlled the area in the first half of the first millennium BCE. However, it does not appear in any contemporary Egyptian or Assyrian records, at least not as Baalbek.

Baalbek grew into an important religious center that revolved around the worship of a triptych of gods. Chief among them was Baal, or Baal Hadad, a Canaanite sky god. His temple was at the peak of the original tel (or hill), and the name Baalbek is a shortened form of Baal of the Bekaa Valley. The second Canaanite god in Baalbek's original triad was Astarte, a fertility, sexuality, and war goddess who was also Baal's consort. Finally, a youthful male god, who was associated with a mystery cult and was perhaps Baal and Astarte's son, rounded out the trio.

Baalbek thrived under Persian rule after the region was conquered by Cyrus the Great in the late sixth century BCE. In the later fourth century BCE, greater Phoenicia was seized by Alexander the Great, and Baalbek came under Hellenized Greek rule. After Alexander's death, his newly formed empire splintered, and Baalbek was part of various successor kingdoms in turn, including those founded by Ptolemy and Seleucus. The Greeks knew Baalbek as Heliopolis, or "City of the Sun God," and the city became a center for the worship of the Greek sun god Helios, possibly from a connection between the Egyptian god Ra and the city's namesake Baal. Growing more active in the Near East, Rome conquered the region in the 60s BCE.

Architecturally, at least, Baalbek reached its zenith under Roman rule. Pompey first seized control of the region for the Romans, and toward the end of the first century BCE, the Romans established a colony at Baalbek that they named Colonia Julia Augusta Felix Heliopolitana. The construction of the massive Temple of Jupiter, the largest Roman temple ever built, may have begun around then; there is evidence that it was finished around 60 CE. It is still a hotly debated archaeological mystery how the builders were able to move the massive stones of the foundation into place. Dozens of the stones weigh hundreds of tons each, and the three largest have been estimated at upward of a thousand tons each. The Temple of Bacchus, which was later added to the same temple complex, was dubbed the

"Small Temple" next to the colossal Temple of Jupiter, but the name is misleading, as it was itself still larger than the Athenian Parthenon.

The temple complex grew in the following centuries. The Temple of Bacchus, large courts, and a Propylaea—or monumental gate—eventually composed the gigantic temple complex with the Temple of Jupiter, sharing a raised platform. The Temple of Venus was built nearby, although it did not share the same platform, and the Temple of Mercury was constructed on a nearby hill to the southwest. In the latter part of the second century CE, Emperor Septimus Severus bestowed the city with *Ius Italicum*, that is, the highest status possible for provincial municipalities; it granted Roman citizenship to individuals born there. As Christianity spread in the region, Baalbek became a focal point in the growing conflict between pagans and Christians, with Christians such as Gelasinus and Saint Barbara martyred there.

## CULTURE AND SOCIETY

Baalbek's culture and society were greatly affected by the city's status as a religious center, across several different religions throughout the centuries. The oldest cults that we can reconstruct are those of a trio of Canaanite gods. This troika included the goddess Astarte and a youthful male god, but the privileged position in the group was held by the storm god Baal, also known as Hadad. He is perhaps best known from the Baal Cycle, a series of mythological stories featuring Baal. They were written in a cuneiform script in the Ugaritic language and found at Ugarit, a Mediterranean port about 150 miles northwest of Baalbek.

Baalbek offers an interesting case study in the Mediterranean, particularly Roman, practice of appropriating other cultures' religions and mapping others' gods onto one's own. The Greeks first associated Baal, the Canaanite god at the center of Baalbek's religious life, with Helios, the Greek divine personification of the sun, but eventually the Greeks and later the Romans shifted Baal's association to Zeus/Jupiter, a regal sky god like Baal. As in other instances, the Greeks and Romans retained many of the local idiosyncrasies; for example, the connection to the sun was retained by conceptualizing this iteration of the god as Heliopolitan Zeus/Heliopolitan Jupiter. The Romans associated Astarte with Venus, the goddess of sexuality. The Temple of Bacchus may have taken up some of the mystery cults of the third youthful male god; however, the Romans associated this god more with Mercury, for whom they also built a temple at Baalbek.

## DEMISE

The city of Baalbek did not go through a demise so much as a shift away from the paganism that had inspired its monumental temples. Although Emperor Constantine had converted to Christianity and codified tolerance for Christianity within the Roman Empire in the early fourth century CE, religious violence between pagans and Christians continued. Despite its strong pagan roots, the city eventually became primarily Christian, and a church was built within the temple complex. The Arabs conquered Baalbek in the 630s CE, amid their rapid conquest of the Near East. They later fortified the temple complex. Al-Qala, or "the Fortress," as they knew it, became a stronghold during the Middle Ages and proved especially influential amid the Crusades. Many Christians and Muslims refused to believe that pagans had built Baalbek's monumental temples, so they falsely credited them to Solomon, the former king of Israel.

### RECENT DISCOVERIES AND CURRENT STATUS

Baalbek is a UNESCO World Heritage Site. Excavations have been ongoing since the twentieth century, especially of the city's temple complex. In 2014, archaeologists found a massive stone that had been quarried but then abandoned; based on present evidence, this is the world's largest quarried monolith.

*Anthony Vivian*

*See also:* Rome.

### FURTHER READING

Jidejian, Nina. 1975. *Baalbek: Heliopolis: "City of the Sun."* Beirut: Dar el-Machreq Publishers.
Paturel, Simone. 2019. *Baalbek-Heliopolis, the Bekaa, and Berytus from 100 BCE to 400 CE.* Leiden: Brill.
Rawlinson, George. 2020. *History of Phoenicia.* New York: Antiquarius.

## Babylon

The city of Babylon was the capital of the southern Mesopotamian kingdom of Babylonia in the second and first millennia BCE. It stood beside the Euphrates River about fifty-five miles south of modern Baghdad in central Iraq. Babylon first rose to significance as the center of Semitic Amorite civilization. The sixth of the Amorite kings, Hammurabi (r. 1792–1750 BCE), brought what is called the Old Babylonian Empire to its peak; the city functioned as the main commercial center of the Tigris–Euphrates valley.

After the sack of Babylon by the Hittites around 1595 BCE, their allies, the Kassites, installed a succession of kings at Babylon. Like the Amorites before them, the Kassites were not native to Mesopotamia but came from the outside, in this case from what is now northwest Iran. A long transitional era followed Kassite rule, and around 911 BCE, Babylon came under Assyrian control. To put down internal agitation, the Assyrian king Sennacherib (r. 705–681 BCE) completely destroyed Babylon in 689 BCE. The city was rebuilt, however, and soon became the capital of the Chaldeans, a Semitic people who established the Neo-Babylonian (or Chaldean) Empire. Babylon achieved its greatest glory under Nebuchadnezzar II (r. 605–562 BCE), the longest reigning and most powerful monarch of the Chaldean period. The legendary Hanging Gardens of Babylon and the fabulous Ishtar Gate date from this time. The ruins of Nebuchadnezzar's Babylon are spread over some 2,000 acres and represent the largest archaeological site in the Middle East.

> *Garden of Eden*
>
> The Garden of Eden is an ideal paradise described within the Abrahamic religions. Among other mentions in the Hebrew Bible, the place is described in the books of Genesis and Ezekiel. According to these and other biblical depictions, the garden was a utopian paradise created by God and inhabited by the first man and woman, Adam and Eve. The couple is expelled from paradise after Eve, seduced by a snake, tastes the forbidden fruit from the tree of the knowledge of good and evil, thereby committing humankind's original sin. While many scholars and theologians have read the story as allegory, others have taken the Garden of Eden to be a real place on earth and proposed various locations. The story includes elements shared from other Near Eastern and Mediterranean traditions, including a lost utopia, an evil snake, and a woman as the scapegoat.

## INHABITANTS

The Amorites who established the first Babylonian empire were a Semitic-speaking people who arrived in Mesopotamia from Syria. Under their sixth king, Hammurabi, all of Babylonia (including Sumer to the south) was united into a single state; Hammurabi is also noted for his code of laws. With the coming of the Kassites, rule passed to another "foreign" regime that lasted to the twelfth century BCE. Then, under the Middle Babylonian kings, the kingdom was restored to native Mesopotamian rule, but only to about 1000 BCE. Following that, Babylonia was controlled by a string of foreign powers, the most important of which was Assyria, based to the north. The Assyrians, who demanded tribute from the Babylonians, at first ruled from afar, but after 729 BCE, they operated as kings of Babylonia as well as rulers of Assyria. A revolt (626 BCE) against Assyrian control eventually returned Babylonia to independence under the Chaldean dynasty, whose most important king was Nebuchadnezzar II. The Chaldeans were originally from the marshy land at the far southeastern quarter of Mesopotamia, though by the time of their ascension, they had been more or less assimilated into Babylonian society.

## HISTORICAL DEVELOPMENT

West Semitic (Amorite) influence in Mesopotamia emerged around 1900 BCE, adding a new element to the already ancient Sumerian and Babylonian cultures. Wars and intrigues between different Amoritic states led to the victory of Hammurabi (lived ca. 1810–1750 BCE), the sixth king of Babylon's First Dynasty, over his rivals. Hammurabi promulgated his famous code of laws and oversaw an early florescence of Babylonian science and scholarship. Cuneiform was refined, and dictionaries of Sumerian and Akkadian were compiled. Astronomers recorded the movements of the planets and prepared lists of the stars and constellations. Forms of divination and magic were advanced, as were weights and measures. It was the Babylonians who first set out the twenty-four-hour day and the system of counting 360 degrees in a circle.

After Hammurabi's death, decline set in. In 1595 BCE, the Hittite king Mursil I marched from Anatolia and destroyed Babylon. The Hurrians (biblical Horites) and their Indo-Aryan chieftains established the kingdom of Mitanni in the north, while the non-Semitic Kassites invaded Babylonia and destroyed the Amorite dynasty, replacing it with one of their own that lasted nearly 400 years.

Meanwhile, Assyria, taking advantage of the decline of Mitanni, quickly rose to prominence in the northern Tigris valley. Another of Babylon's traditional foes, Elam (in what is now southwestern Iran), also became strong, and its kings repeatedly invaded Babylonia. The capital was sacked by Elamites in 1158 BCE, and the invaders removed many Babylonian monuments, including the famous Code of Hammurabi, to the Elamite capital of Susa.

Babylon was dominated by Assyria from the ninth century until that empire's fall to the Medes in 612 BCE. The Assyrians absorbed Babylonian civilization, and although harsh at times toward the populace, they respected the Babylonian cult of Marduk (biblical Merodach). Tensions between Babylonia and Assyria came to a climax in 689 BCE, when the city of Babylon was destroyed and the Marduk statue carried off to Assyria.

Eventually, the Chaldeans won control of the territory, and Babylonia once again became a significant political power under the sixth-century Chaldean kings, in particular Nebuchadnezzar II (r. 605–562), who erected much of what remains of the city. For three-quarters of a century, Babylon prospered. Nebuchadnezzar achieved victory over the Egyptians at Carchemish on the upper Euphrates River in 605 BCE. As a consequence, Babylonia won control over all Syria and Palestine to the Egyptian border. Nevertheless, the act for which Nebuchadnezzar is best known is his destruction of Judah and Jerusalem, in 587 BCE, and the consequent captivity of the Jews. In addition, he rebuilt the Temple of Marduk in Babylon and constructed the Hanging Gardens, one of the Seven Wonders of the Ancient World. (Virtually nothing of them remains today.)

## CULTURE AND SOCIETY

Babylonia was situated at the nexus of important trade routes and derived much of its cultural and historical significance from that. For much of its existence, Babylon controlled an expanse of the Tigris River extending from Assyria to the Persian Gulf. In the Euphrates River, on the other hand, the Babylonians found access to the West. Eastern access—to the Zagros Mountains and Iran—was in the form of a caravan route. Babylon not only functioned as the political capital but also as the major religious center. In time, it became one of the most populous cities of the ancient Near East, renowned for its architectural marvels. These included the great walls that surrounded the city; a massive ziggurat, or pyramidal structure, known as Etemenanki; its imposing gates and decorated temples; and the legendary Hanging Gardens, a series of luxuriously planted terraces, the whole of which was the size, it was said, of a mountain.

The city under Nebuchadnezzar featured three overlapping walls and measured about eleven miles in circumference. On the east bank of the Euphrates stood the Temple of Marduk, from the time of Hammurabi, along with the seven-level ziggurat Etemenanki; it has long been associated in popular consciousness with the biblical Tower of Babel, and some scholars have conjectured that the authors of Genesis were likely familiar with it from the time of the Jewish captivity. In any case, north of the temple was a processional route lined with walls decorated with animals that led through the Ishtar Gate, which features blue and yellow glazed brickwork with animal figures in relief. Northwest of the processional way stood Nebuchadnezzar's palace, with its 250 rooms, five courtyards, and a nearly 100-foot entry arch. Vaulted structures at its northwest corner may be remains of the Hanging Gardens.

The Babylonians relied on a network of irrigation canals for agriculture, something that had been in place since at least 5000 BCE and carefully maintained over the centuries. Food staples included barley and farro (wheat) for bread, sesame for oil, and onions and marrow squash, among other vegetables. Dates were eaten in place of other fruits and sugar, and date palm logs were used in building. Meat was a key part of the diet, and cattle, goats, fowl, and sheep were raised for this purpose as well as for products such as milk, hides, and wool. Fish were eaten as well.

A number of product areas were traded, ranging from agricultural commodities to textiles. Although crafts were a regular part of both domestic life and the marketplace, a lack of raw materials required artisans to import their supplies from neighboring areas. Industries included cabinetmaking, gem cutting, and metalworking. Articles of commerce and trade were transported either by donkey or, after about the twelfth century BCE, camel.

Behind the operations of Babylonian economic life lay the important institution of bookkeeping, which originated during the Third Dynasty of Ur (about 2000 BCE) when a simple but adequate system of double entry was developed. Beyond bookkeeping, the Babylonians also compiled royal histories, religious texts, and other documents using cuneiform with clay tablets.

The chief god of Babylon was Marduk. He was probably originally a minor Sumerian deity but was made supreme when the Amorites established the First Dynasty of Babylon about 1830 BCE. The chief gods of the early city-states of Uruk, Eridu, and Nippur had been Anu (god of heaven), Ea (god of the waters), and Enlil (god of the earth), but the kings of Babylon wanted a paramount god of their own and thus substituted Marduk for Enlil in the story of creation—which they wrote in Akkadian as an epic poem known as the *Enuma elish* ("When on high"), after its opening words.

## DEMISE

In 539 BCE, Babylon was taken without a struggle by the Persians under Cyrus the Great. For a time, it continued as a vassal state, but after a last revolt in 514 BCE against Darius the Great, the city's walls were destroyed. During his campaign of conquest, Alexander the Great planned to make Babylon the capital of his eastern empire, but after his death in 323 BCE, Babylon soon lost importance. Henceforth, it continued life merely as a province in a succession of empires: Seleucid, Parthian, and Sassanian (312 BCE–650 CE). Nevertheless, the world owes a great debt to ancient Babylonian civilization, which through its influence on Hebrew and Greek cultures contributed enormously to the development of Western civilization.

## RECENT DISCOVERIES AND CURRENT STATUS

Babylon was first excavated in 1811, although the principal early investigations were done by Hormuzd Rassam for the British Museum in 1879–1882 and Robert Koldewey for the German Oriental Society between 1899 and 1917. Other institutions have also recovered materials from the site, and in the late twentieth century, the Iraq Department of Antiquities carried out some restoration work.

Following the Persian Gulf War of 1990–1991, the Iraqi dictator Saddam Hussein began construction of a modern marble palace overlooking the ruins and had plans to install cable cars. His plans were scotched with the start, in 2003, of the Iraq War. Babylon was the site of a military base used by the U.S.-led coalition forces and appears to have suffered damage. In 2010, archaeologists and preservationists began to repair and restore Babylon's treasures; they also began excavating new sites in the area. A refurbished modern museum opened in Babylon in January 2011. Later that year, scholars discovered the oldest known representation of the ziggurat of Old Babylon carved on a black stone; it dates from 604 to 562 BCE, the time of Nebuchadnezzar II. Many of the clay tablets recovered from the site in recent decades remain untranslated.

In 2019, the remains of Babylon were declared a UNESCO World Heritage Site.

*Michael Shally-Jensen*

*See also:* Assyrians; Hittites; Persepolis; Susa; Ur.

## FURTHER READING

Cotterell, Arthur. 2019. *The First Great Powers: Babylon and Assyria*. London: C. Hurst & Co.
Leick, Gwendolyn. 2003. *The Babylonians*. New York: Routledge.
Radner, Karen. 2020. *Babylon: A Short History*. New York: Bloomsbury Academic.

## Bagan/Pagan

Pagan flourished on the east bank of the Irrawaddy River in Upper Burma, particularly thriving in the eleventh through the thirteenth centuries CE. As the English spelling has shifted from Pagan to Bagan, this entry uses Pagan when referring to the historical site and Bagan when discussing the present-day city. Expansive plains dominate the area. The Arakan Mountains shield the region from the monsoons of coastal Burma, leaving Bagan and its environs in a relatively dry climate. Today, Old Bagan rests in what is called the Bagan Archaeological Zone, an eight-by-five-mile area bordering the Irrawaddy River.

The Bagan plains house an estimated 2,200 temples, pagodas, and other structures that have survived since the height of the Pagan Empire. Although less than a quarter of the estimated 10,000 that once stood, their number, size, and variety have become world famous. The largest cluster is situated in the Bagan Archaeological Zone. Among other impressive structures, Dhammayangyi Temple is the largest temple in Bagan; Shwesandaw Pagoda is the tallest pagoda; and Ananda Temple is one of the most famous and esteemed temples from the Pagan Empire.

## INHABITANTS

There are still many scholarly disagreements on early Pagan and its original inhabitants. The Burmese chronicles, a broad collection of texts primarily detailing the monarchic history of Burma, date the founding of the Pagan Kingdom to the second century CE. While there is no firm agreement on the exact date, the standard chronology places the founding in the year 107. According to these chronicles, Thamoddarit founded the city in that year, fulfilling a prophecy that the Buddha himself gave: Visiting the location of Pagan, the Buddha proclaimed that a great city would be founded there 651 years later, that is, the year 107. Thamoddarit and the other Pagan kings are considered legendary.

Although it has been over eight centuries since the height of the Pagan Empire, the ruins still dot the landscape. Over 2,200 pagodas and other structures still populate the local skyline.
(© Rfoxphoto | Dreamstime.com)

Although modern scholars dispute the historicity of these chronicles, there is no definite consensus on the founding of Pagan. One influential theory holds that the Mranma, then a part of the Nanzhao Kingdom, founded Pagan in the ninth century CE. The later chronicles then appropriated the legendary history of the Pyu peoples, who had lived in the region around Pagan since the early first millennium, as their own. The Mranma inhabitants of Pagan incorporated diverse peoples and cultures into their budding kingdom, including the Pyu, Mon, and others.

## HISTORICAL BACKGROUND

Although the Burmese chronicles date the founding of Pagan to the second century CE, modern scholars contend that the city was not founded until later, with many pointing to a date in the ninth century. According to this theory, the Mranma people (also known as the Bamar and Burmese) migrated south from the Nanzhao Kingdom and established the settlement along the Irrawaddy River. The region then housed several major settlements of the Pyu people. The nascent Pagan settlement then received further waves of Mranma migrating south. The Mranma adopted much from the Pyu's local Buddhist culture. Over the next couple of centuries, the Burmese fortified their new city and further developed agricultural irrigation systems. The first outside mention of Pagan comes from Chinese records of the Song dynasty in 1004.

While the city of Pagan had been growing steadily, a major acceleration came with the coronation of Anawrahta in 1044. He inherited a small kingdom and immediately set about reforming the economy and military. He had canals cut and weirs built to turn the once dry plains into ideal rice producing regions. His reforms turned the kingdom into a regional powerhouse, and he set his sights outward. He expanded his state by conquering lands, especially to the north and south. It is during Anawrahta's reign that most historians contend the Pagan Empire began. He is also looked at as a forefather of the nation of Myanmar, the first to unite the region and control an approximation of the present-day nation-state.

Anawrahta's successful reign initiated what is considered the golden age of the Pagan Empire, which would last for two centuries. Kyansittha ruled the empire at the turn of the twelfth century, and he is credited with melting the new empire's different cultures into one Burmese national identity. His successor, Alaungsithu, also known simply as Sithu, standardized weights and measures and vastly improved the empire's infrastructure. He strengthened his empire's ties to various wide-ranging trade networks and monetized the Pagan economy.

The Pagan Empire reached its administrative, martial, and territorial apex under the reign of Narapatisithu, also known as Sithu II. During his reign at the turn of the thirteenth century, Burmese culture fully blossomed. The Burmese script superseded that of the Pyu and Mon to become the primary script of the empire. Relatedly, at this time, writings in the Burmese script first started openly using the term *Mranma* to denote and self-identify a distinct group. Narapatisithu instituted military and administrative changes that survived not only him but the entire Pagan Empire.

## CULTURE AND SOCIETY

The Pagan Empire included a rich diversity of cultures. Up to and throughout the empire's existence, Upper Burma hosted an array of peoples, of whom the Mranma—or Burmese—were one. The Pyu and Mon constituted two other prominent cultures, among many. The Burmese script was derived from that of either the Pyu or Mon. Writing was primarily restricted to the court and the clergy. The Mranma associated themselves closely with the Pyu, but beginning in the reign of Narapatisithu at the turn of the thirteenth century, the Mranma began distinguishing themselves as a distinct group more and more.

Many different religions—befitting the many different cultures—flourished within the territory of the Pagan Empire, but Theravada Buddhism took up a primary importance beginning in the reign of Anawrahta. In the mid-eleventh century, Anawrahta transformed Pagan from a local kingdom into a regional empire; his conversion from Tantric Buddhism to Theravada Buddhism established the latter as the primary religion of the court until the late twelfth century, when Mahayana Buddhism gained ascendancy. The religious architecture of the Pagan Empire has become world famous; roughly 2,200 temples and other religious structures have survived to this day. The temples fall into two major groups: pagodas (also known as stupas) and hollow temples.

The Pagan Empire had a hierarchical society with the king and his family at the peak and the majority of individuals as commoners. While the Pagan Empire took part in extensive trade networks, agriculture was the cornerstone of its economy. As advances in the irrigation systems increased the amounts of rice production, the empire gained wealth, influence, and territory. An estimated 200,000 individuals inhabited the city of Pagan at its peak in population, right before the Mongol invasions of the late thirteenth century.

## DEMISE

After Narapatisithu's death in 1211, the Pagan Empire continued on for decades. Despite the momentum of the previous centuries, problems surfaced even before the Mongol invasions in the latter part of the thirteenth century. Individuals living in the empire had a religious incentive to donate their lands to the Buddhist community; however, this left the government overseeing an increasing amount of untaxable land. Narathihapate, the final king to rule over an intact Pagan Empire, faced revolts in the empire's western and southern regions upon his ascension in 1256. Kublai Khan and the Mongols demanded tribute from the Pagan Empire, but Narathihapate refused. The Mongols invaded the empire twice, first in 1277 and then again in 1287. Although the invasions themselves did not directly overthrow the country, they revealed the weakness of Pagan control, and the Pagan Empire splintered as a result.

## RECENT DISCOVERIES AND CURRENT STATUS

The Bagan Archaeological Zone is a UNESCO World Heritage Site hosting thousands of remains from the height of the Pagan period. After a 2016 earthquake, the Zamini Project, a research group at the University of Cape Town that specializes in cultural heritage sites, worked with local Myanmarese officials to document a dozen monuments in Bagan.

*Anthony Vivian*

*See also:* Angkor; Ayutthaya; Borobudur.

## FURTHER READING

Aung-Thwin, Michael. 1985. *Pagan: The Origins of Modern Burma.* Honolulu: University of Hawaii Press.

Miksic, John Norman, and Goh Geok Yian. 2016. *Ancient Southeast Asia*. London: Routledge.
Reid, Anthony. 2015. *A History of Southeast Asia: Critical Crossroads*. Hoboken, NJ: Wiley-Blackwell.
Strachan, Paul. 1990. *Imperial Pagan: Art and Architecture of Burma*. Honolulu: University of Hawaii Press.

# Borobudur

Built in central Java in what is today Indonesia, Borobudur is the world's largest Buddhist temple. Constructed in the ninth century CE, it flourished for up to five centuries and then was abandoned and forgotten by all but the Javanese locals as it was covered by jungle growth and volcanic ash. The temple occupies the Kedu Plain, a particularly fertile site that has long been sacred to the Javanese. The plain sits between the Sundoro, Sumbing, Merbabu, and Merapi volcanoes, in the Progo River valley. The site is about 24 miles from the modern city of Yogyakarta and a little over 300 miles from the modern Indonesian capital of Jakarta.

Borobudur is one in a triptych of temples that were built concurrently and in a straight line, with the much smaller Pawon and Mendut Temples being the other two. Scholars agree that the temples must have been built to complement one

### Jakarta

The bustling megacity of Jakarta, Indonesia, is sinking faster than any other city on earth.

Located on the northwestern coast of the island of Java, the region that today hosts Jakarta has been inhabited for millennia. Buni culture flourished in the area at the end of the first millennium BCE and the beginning of the first millennium CE. In the fourth century CE, the old port of Jakarta, named Sunda Kelapa, was established, and it was a part of two local Hindu kingdoms, first the Taruma Kingdom and then the Sunda Kingdom. From roughly the seventh to the thirteenth century, while nominally part of the Sunda Kingdom, the port was controlled by Srivijaya, a Buddhist kingdom based on the neighboring island of Sumatra. In the sixteenth century, the Banten sultanate, an Islamic kingdom, dominated northwest Java, including the port, now renamed Jayakarta, a name that later morphed into Jakarta. The Dutch established imperial dominance of the region in the seventeenth century; they knew the city as Batavia. Following World War II, Indonesia won its independence, and Jakarta became its capital. Its long, diverse history has produced an eclectic, vibrant, and bustling Pacific metropolis.

Jakarta faces the same rising sea that opposes all coastal cities. However, Jakarta is confronted with an additional, unique challenge. While other cities around the world are sinking, none have been descending as quickly as Jakarta. The city has been growing at a phenomenal rate, and this massive urban development dovetails with the related trend of land subsidence, that is, the removal of groundwater and the ground sinkage that results. All told, Jakarta has been sinking at the rapid rate of around four inches per year. The city is already facing frequent flooding, which will grow worse with the passage of time. Reacting to this alarming trend, Indonesia has been planning to relocate its capital from Jakarta to Kalimantan, on the island of Borneo, since 2019.

Borobudur's square terraces act as the foundation for the upper three circular terraces. These upper platforms house the monuments' seventy-two perforated stupas. (Leonid Krichmara/Dreamstime.com)

another and were probably included within the same ceremonies. Borobudur consists of a series of massive square terraces topped with three circular platforms. These platforms house seventy-two perforated stupas, each housing its own Buddha statue. A central dome sits in the middle of the top platform. Built in a mix of local Javanese and imported Indian styles, the massive structure includes over 2,600 bas-reliefs and over 500 Buddha statues and covers an estimated 27,125 square feet. The Shailendra dynasty constructed it in the ninth century CE, and it was long a Buddhist pilgrimage destination before its abandonment.

## INHABITANTS

As a temple, Borobudur did not have any direct inhabitants, despite its monumental size. Those who used the site from its outset were Mahayana Buddhists. The temple was built by the Shailendra dynasty of the Medang Kingdom, probably during the reigns of Dharanindra, Samaragrawira, and Samaratungga, who ruled in the late eighth and early ninth centuries. It became an important destination for Buddhist pilgrims from near and far. Scholars are not in agreement on what exact ceremonies were performed at the site, but most agree that the ceremonies probably incorporated the nearby temples of Mendut and Pawon, which were built at the same time and in a straight line with Borobudur. The ceremonies almost certainly culminated at Borobudur, which is far more massive and splendid than the other two temples, and included an ascent up the various levels, past the many Buddha sculptures and narratives in bas-relief.

## HISTORICAL BACKGROUND

Borobudur was built in the ninth century by the Shailendra dynasty of the Medang Kingdom. Also known as the Mataram Kingdom, the Medang Kingdom was a Hindu-Buddhist state located on the island of Java in modern-day Indonesia. The origins of the Shailendra dynasty are murky. There are currently three theories as to where the dynasty came from. Some contend that the dynasty originated where it later flourished: the island of Java. Others posit a genesis on the neighboring island of Sumatra. Still others contend that the Shailendras sailed to Java from Kalinga, a region of eastern India, to flee local pressures there.

Some seventh-century inscriptions may pertain to the Shailendra dynasty, yet it is the eighth century that provides the first clear evidence of both the Shailendra dynasty and the Medang Kingdom. Java experienced waves of religious and cultural influence from the Indian subcontinent, first Hinduism and then Buddhism. The Shailendra dynasty practiced Mahayana Buddhism and built Mahayana Buddhist temples, including Borobudur. In line with the lack of clarity regarding the dynasty's original location, there is no consensus on whether the dynasty replaced a different Hindu dynasty or was originally Hindu and then converted.

The styles of Borobudur's many reliefs help us date the temple's construction. This does not give us an exact date, but it is likely that Dharanindra began the planning of the temple and perhaps oversaw the beginning of its construction. Dharanindra, also known as King Indra, was a powerful martial king who ruled Srivijaya on the neighboring island of Sumatra as well as much of Java from ca. 775 to 800. Pawon Temple and Mendut Temple were constructed contemporaneously with Borobudur, and since they are much smaller, they may have been completed or nearly completed by Dharanindra. Borobudur was not completed in his lifetime; construction continued under his successors: Samaragrawira, who ruled ca. 800–812, and Samaratungga, who reigned ca. 812–833. Epigraphic evidence shines a little light on their lives. The latter is named on an inscription dated to 824 for building a tomb for his predecessor, Dharanindra.

Borobudur was built when the Medang Kingdom and Shailendra dynasty were at their pinnacle of power. After Samaratungga died, there was a conflict over succession. Rakai Pikatan retained the throne in central Java, and Balaputra moved to Srivijaya and ruled parts of Sumatra from there. In the early tenth century, the Javanese line moved from central to eastern Java, but the conflict between the Medang Kingdom on Java and Srivijaya only intensified. Around 990, the Javanese invaded Srivijaya, compelling the rulers of the latter to pursue an alliance with the Song dynasty of China for defensive aid. The fighting lasted into the next century, but Srivijaya was able to fend off the invasion. They, in turn, supported a revolt on Java that led to a sacking of the capital and the downfall of the Medang Kingdom. After a brief power vacuum, the kingdom of Kahuripan consolidated the former Medang territory.

## CULTURE AND SOCIETY

Borobudur marks a high watermark for medieval Javanese and Indonesian culture. Its gigantic magnitude has been embellished with hundreds of Buddha statues and thousands of bas-reliefs. It served as a Mahayana Buddhist temple, combining local Javanese and imported Indian architecture and art. Though intricate in design and replete with massive amounts of fine art, the temple is fundamentally a step pyramid, a type of building found in many ancient cultures, including the Austronesian culture that had inhabited Java for centuries before the building of Borobudur. In Buddhist architectural terms, the temple constitutes one massive stupa and appears as a mandala from a bird's eye view.

The temple incorporates a plethora of art meant to be enjoyed as one ascends the multiple terraces. The more than 500 Buddha statues greet visitors from niches on the square levels and from within perforated stupas on the upper circular levels. All the statues portray Buddha similarly seated with legs crossed; however, they feature five distinct mudras, or hand positions. Of the original statues, hundreds are damaged, and dozens are completely missing, victims of looting. The thousands of bas-reliefs provide a spectacular variety and a detailed glimpse at life in ninth-century Java. They tell lengthy narratives, eleven in all, the longest of which includes 372 panels. They combine scenes of everyday life on Java with scenes from Buddhist mythology. It is by comparing the artistic style of these reliefs to others elsewhere that scholars have been able to date the temple.

## DEMISE

Borobudur, once a crowning achievement of the thriving Medang Kingdom, eventually fell into disuse and was all but forgotten by the outside world for centuries. A number of factors led to the temple's abandonment. In the tenth century, the Medang Kingdom moved eastward, away from Borobudur. This decreased but did not halt pilgrimages to and ceremonies at the site. Natural disasters plagued the region, from earthquakes to volcanic eruptions. Finally, when most of the Javanese people converted to Islam in the fifteenth century, the Buddhist temple fell out of use and was largely overtaken by the verdant jungle and layered with volcanic ash. The site was still known among the locals but increasingly became associated with bad luck and misfortune, as attested by eighteenth-century Javanese chronicles.

The temple's rediscovery by European colonial powers marked not an end to the site's demise but a continuation. Hearing rumors of the colossal temple in the jungle, Thomas Stamford Raffles, a British lieutenant governor stationed in the region, sent Dutch explorer Hermann Cornelius and 200 men to attempt to locate the site in 1814. They succeeded in finding the site and made the wider world aware of the existence of Borobudur. This led to a century or so of damaging looting, both official and unofficial. Christiaan Lodewijk Hartman, an early excavator of the site, is rumored to have stolen a large Buddha statue from the temple's now empty main stupa. King Chulalongkorn of Siam visited the site and left with eight cartloads of sculptures. The rampant theft, coupled with centuries of exposure to natural disasters, left the temple in danger of toppling. Luckily, twentieth-century restorations and more restrictive measures against looting have since brought some security to the site.

## RECENT DISCOVERIES AND CURRENT STATUS

Borobudur has been listed as a UNESCO World Heritage Site since 1991. In addition to its role as an active tourist attraction, the temple has taken on religious rituals more in line with its original intended use. It has once again become a popular pilgrimage site for practicing Buddhists. Every year on Vesak, a holiday on the full moon of May or June that celebrates the birth, enlightenment, and death of the Buddha, Indonesian Buddhists worship at Borobudur. The ceremonies begin at the nearby and contemporaneously built temples of Mendut and Pawon and culminate at Borobudur.

*Anthony Vivian*

*See also:* Angkor; Ayutthaya; Bagan/Pagan.

## FURTHER READING

Adams, Kathleen M. 2020. *Indonesia: History, Heritage, Culture.* Ann Arbor, MI: Association for Asian Studies.

Miksic, John N. 2017. *Borobudur: Golden Tales of the Buddhas.* North Clarendon, VT: Tuttle Publishing.

Miksic, John Norman, and Goh Geok Yian. 2016. *Ancient Southeast Asia.* London: Routledge.

Reid, Anthony. 2015. *A History of Southeast Asia: Critical Crossroads.* Hoboken, NJ: Wiley-Blackwell.

# C

## Cahokia

Cahokia is a complex of prehistoric earthworks and other structures built by Native Americans of the Mississippian cultural tradition between about 1000 CE and 1250 CE. It is located near the Mississippi River in what is now southwest Illinois, across from St. Louis, Missouri. The largest prehistoric site north of Mexico, Cahokia features the 100-foot-high, 15-acre-square Monks Mound, the largest human-constructed earthen mound in North America. In its original state, Monks Mound consisted of a series of four stepped terraces. Each of the four levels had temples used for ceremonial purposes. Cahokia as a whole spread out over 5 square miles and was made up of 100 smaller earthen mounds along with various residential units.

When active, Cahokia represented the main settlement within a political chiefdom—that is, an assortment of smaller villages headed by minor chiefs linked to the center and the paramount chief through patronage and tribute. Surrounding Cahokia's core was a wooden palisade featuring regularly spaced redoubts that likely served a defensive function. Population estimates for Cahokia at its height range from 5,000 to 15,000 inhabitants.

Mississippian culture, a North American Indian culture that existed in the southeastern portion of the continent, particularly in the major river valleys, flourished between 800 CE and about 1550 CE. One of the most elaborate civilizations to appear in North America, it left its mark as far north as the upper Mississippi and Ohio River valleys, as far south as what is now northern Georgia and central Alabama, and as far west as the Trinity River in modern-day Texas. Although mound-building is one activity associated with Native Mississippian culture, other cultures, such as the earlier Hopewell tradition (100 BCE–500 CE) of the midwestern region, also erected mounds and similar earthen structures.

### INHABITANTS

The Indigenous peoples of the Mississippian tradition were linguistically diverse but culturally similar. They drew on the abundant water resources in the region to produce corn, beans, and squash on a scale sufficient to create surpluses. A hierarchical society developed to manage and distribute these stores. Known especially for their large towns featuring great earthen temples and burial mounds, Mississippian groups were commonly organized into chiefdoms. Among the largest were the Apalachee (in northwestern Florida), the Tuscaloosa (in south central Alabama), and the Cofitachequi (in north central South Carolina). The inhabitants

### New Orleans

New Orleans's location and low elevation make it a prime target for rising sea levels and increasingly intense hurricane seasons.

Jean-Baptiste Le Moyne de Bienville founded New Orleans on Chitimacha territory for the French Mississippi Company in 1718. The city and region remained under French or Spanish control until the young United States bought it as part of the Louisiana Purchase in 1803. The final battle of the War of 1812 was fought there in early 1815. At the mouth of the Mississippi River, New Orleans played a pivotal role in regional trade, including the slave trade of the antebellum South. In the year after the Confederacy lost the Civil War, white rioters killed dozens of Black freedmen in the bloody New Orleans Riots. The city later played a central role within the civil rights movement.

New Orleans's eclectic history has fostered a vibrant, singular culture. Jazz music was born in New Orleans around the turn of the twentieth century. New Orleans cuisine is world renowned for its rich mix of Cajun, French, Caribbean, and other influences. People come from all over the world to celebrate the raucous party at Mardi Gras every spring.

New Orleans has already faced climate issues for decades. Six major hurricanes caused flooding in the city throughout the twentieth century. In August 2005, Hurricane Katrina revealed a glimpse at a potential future, killing over 1,800 people while flooding and destroying much of the city. Beyond hurricanes, New Orleans will be one of the earliest global locations to feel the effects of a rising sea level. The city already sits slightly below sea level, and the Mississippi River is slowly but steadily eroding Louisiana's coastline. In the meantime, the locals continue to sell hurricanes—strong, fruity rum drinks—to tourists enjoying Bourbon Street.

---

of Cahokia at its apex probably represented a mix of related ethnic groups rather than a long-enduring populace of a singular identity.

Given the existence of pyramid-shaped temple complexes and hierarchical relationships among central settlements and satellite communities, there has been some speculation about the Mississippians possibly being influenced by cultural traditions from Mexico and Central America. Sculptures from Cahokia and other sites likewise suggest the possibility of a Mesoamerican link of some sort. The prospect is intriguing, but the connection has not been proved.

## HISTORICAL BACKGROUND

It appears that Cahokia was settled around 700 CE, shortly after the introduction of maize (corn) cultivation and the concomitant drawing away from a nomadic lifestyle. The original name of the village is not known; the name *Cahokia* derives from another people (an Illiniwek tribe) that arrived in the 1600s, long after Cahokia's demise.

The village grew to more than 1,000 inhabitants between the 900s and the early 1000s. According to the archaeological evidence, buildings and shrines were constructed by 1050. Shortly thereafter, rows of family residences came to surround the town's various communal plazas. The latter served as gathering places for ceremonies and games. Farm fields spread out in all directions in the outskirts of the settlement.

The community reached its peak size and complexity between 1050 and 1100, when the population shot up and new villages were established in the nearby countryside. It is possible that the combined population of the center and its periphery reached up to 50,000 people at this time, rivaling comparable urban sites in Mesoamerica. Such assessments are difficult to make with certainty, however.

## CULTURE AND SOCIETY

The many mounds at Cahokia functioned as burial plots as well as symbolic representations of the connection between earth and sky. The largest of the mounds, Monks Mound, rises to a height of nearly 100 feet (about ten stories) through a series of massive terraces and sits next to an expansive plaza in the center of the town. The mound acquired its name from scholars who observed a group of seventeenth-century monks gardening near the structure and living in the vicinity.

Over time, the Cahokians enlarged the mounds by adding layers of earth. Because earth was sacred in the Cahokian religion, the building activity likely carried religious overtones. Religious symbols found throughout the site suggest that the Cahokians revered the four cardinal directions along with the sun, moon, and stars, in addition to the gods and goddesses of the earth and sky. Cahokia could well have served as a religious center for a vast expanse of the Mississippian region, although sites such as Moundville (in Alabama) and Etowah (in Georgia) are impressive in their own right and may have operated in much the same way in their respective areas.

Cahokian society was somewhat hierarchical and based on areas of specialization, such as priest-leader, warrior, farmer, or laborer. Cahokia probably was not as rigidly stratified as most of its Mesoamerican cousins. It likely operated, instead, as a village community—albeit one of increasing size and complexity as it aged. While Cahokian leaders clearly inherited considerable power and wealth, both leaders and nonleaders enjoyed a solid diet and normal health, unlike some of their Mesoamerican counterparts. Luxury items and other craft goods were produced using shell, stone, copper, clay, and wood, but residents at all levels of society seem to have possessed objects of value. High-ranking members were buried with well-crafted prestige goods, such as mica and copper artifacts, along with their human retinues. For example, one burial featured a soft bed of tens of thousands of shell beads arranged in the shape of a bird; another contained the remains of a mass sacrifice: fifty-three Mississippian "maidens."

Cahokian artifacts represent outstanding examples of prehistoric Native American crafts. They include carved figurines, decorated pots, well-worked arrowheads, and pipes used for smoking. One notable sculpture is of a figure playing chunkey, a Cahokian game similar to horseshoes but employing spears and disks. Among the images depicted in Cahokian art are the corn mother, the sun disk, the human hand, weeping eyes, arrows flanked by semicircles, and the four winds of the universe. Illustrations of exotic bird people and animal deities have been found in related Mississippian sites. Materials used in some objects came from remote locations: researchers have identified conch shells from the Gulf of Mexico and mica from North Carolina in necklaces and other jewelry. Beads and mineral paints containing copper from the shores of Lake Superior have been identified, as have rocks from the Missouri Ozarks used as ax-heads and other tools. Effigy jars have been found with depictions of human faces, often bearing painted designs.

## DEMISE

According to research, just fifty years after Cahokia's peak (ca. 1150), the smaller "suburban" settlements surrounding it were starting to be abandoned, and people were beginning to construct a wooden wall around the city center. By 1250, as few as 2,000 people remained at Cahokia, and by 1400, the city was completely deserted. Archaeologists believe that climate change may have played a role in depleting needed resources or otherwise impacting the locale. Social unrest or war with external groups could also have contributed to the city's decline. Ultimately, the fate of the prehistoric Cahokians and their community remains something of a mystery.

By the time of the arrival of Europeans in the sixteenth century, classic Mississippian culture as a whole was in decline. Hernando de Soto and his soldiers entered the southernmost region in 1539 and delivered a blow to the Mississippians through warfare, pillaging, and the spread of disease. Following de Soto's incursion, groups of related upland peoples, including the Caddo and the Creek, emerged as significant forces.

## RECENT DISCOVERIES AND CURRENT STATUS

Cahokia has been studied extensively since the nineteenth century; by the 1920s, excavations had revealed many of its main structures. Archaeologists working in the western portion of the site in the 1960s, and again in the 1980s, discovered the foundations of large wooden posts arranged in a pattern and collectively named "Woodhenge." Originally, Woodhenge consisted of seventy-two cedar posts in a large circle around a center post. The structure was a solar calendar: the center post aligned with specific outer posts during sunrise and sunset at certain times of year (equinoxes and solstices). It may also have served religious purposes.

More recently, researchers have found (1) that women, as well as men, sometimes received high-status burials; (2) that flooding around 1150 may have contributed to Cahokia's collapse; and, more speculatively; (3) that as much as one-third of Cahokia's inhabitants may have been immigrants who spoke different languages and followed different social and religious traditions (the last is based on osteological evidence and isotopic analysis of human remains). Research at the site, and at other Mississippian centers, continues today.

Cahokia was made a UNESCO World Heritage Site in 1982. By then, large sections of the surrounding area had been destroyed by the expansion of East St. Louis. The central portion of the site, however, is preserved as a state park.

Visitors may view what remains of the earthworks there and tour the adjacent interpretive center.

*Michael Shally-Jensen*

*See also:* Maya; Tenochtitlán; Tula.

## FURTHER READING

Alt, Susan. 2018. *Cahokia's Complexities: Ceremonies and Politics of the First Mississippian Farmers.* Tuscaloosa: University of Alabama Press.
Chappell, Sally A. Kitt. 2002. *Cahokia: Mirror of the Cosmos.* Chicago: University of Chicago Press.
Fagan, Brian. 2011. *The First North Americans.* New York: Thames & Hudson.
Pauketat, Timothy R. 2009. *Cahokia: Ancient America's Great City on the Mississippi.* New York: Viking.
Young, Biloine W., and Melvin L. Fowler. 2000. *Cahokia: The Great Native American Metropolis.* Urbana: University of Illinois Press.

# Carthage

A city located on the northeastern coast of present-day Tunisia, in North Africa, Carthage was an important center of Phoenician culture (ca. 800–146 BCE) and later a major Roman outpost (ca. 146 BCE–439 CE) in the western Mediterranean. Through trade, the Phoenicians of Carthage helped advance the economies and cultures of the ancient Mediterranean world. In their struggles against Greece and Rome, the Carthaginians established themselves as a formidable force worthy of emulation by others. As a Roman city, Carthage was second only to Rome as an imperial capital in the west. Under the Romans, the city also became a significant center in early Christianity.

## INHABITANTS

Most early writings on Carthage are from the sixth century BCE or later and hail from hostile Greek and Roman sources that do not give full credence to Carthaginian culture. We do know that Carthage was founded sometime around 800 BCE (814 BCE is the traditional date) by Phoenicians, a Semitic seafaring people whose homeland was the narrow coastal strip of the eastern Mediterranean. The principal Phoenician cities in the second and first millennia BCE were Byblos, Sidon, and Tyre, the latter being particularly important as the home of Carthage's legendary founding figure. Known as Elissa, or Dido to the Greeks, in the legend, she is said to have fled to the site of Carthage after the murder of her husband in Tyre. She bought land from the Libyan Berbers and marked out a citadel, which became Carthage.

The Phoenicians who settled Carthage began in the eighth century BCE to found trading posts in North Africa, western Sicily, Sardinia, the Balearic Islands, and southern Spain (Cádiz). Phoenicia itself came under Assyrian control and was ravaged by Assyrian kings in the late 700s and early 600s BCE. The city of Tyre was besieged by Nebuchadnezzar II of Babylon in the years 586–573 BCE. After

Tunis, the present-day capital of Tunisia, has grown around the ruins of ancient Carthage. The Phoenician port once dominated the western and central Mediterranean. (Valery Bareta | Dreamstime.com)

580, Carthage led Phoenician settlements on Sicily in resisting Greek aggression. It also moved to consolidate control of Sardinia. By then, Carthage was the largest and strongest Phoenician city and the center of an emerging Carthaginian Empire.

Carthage under Rome was a fairly cosmopolitan place. It was the capital of the province of Africa Proconsularis and had a diverse population that included Phoenicians, Romans (or so-called Roman Africans), Berbers, Greeks, Spaniards, and others, along with a growing population of Christians. The latter were primarily of Phoenician and Roman African descent; the famed religious scholar Saint Augustine (Augustine of Hippo; 354–430 CE) is probably the best-known member of the latter group.

## HISTORICAL DEVELOPMENT

The emergence of the Carthaginian Empire inevitably produced conflict with Greece and then Rome. A powerful Carthaginian naval fleet protected the capital while mercenary armies made up of Numidians (Algerians), Libyans, and Spaniards were employed for military operations on land. Although the Phoenician settlement in western Sicily was preserved in the face of Greek pressure, the Phoenicians were never able to secure the entirety of the island. (Wars were fought there in 480 and 410–409 BCE.)

Ultimately, the threat from Greece was eliminated when the Peloponnesian War erupted (431–404 BCE) and Athenians fought Spartans in a self-destructive conflict. As Greek power waned, the rise of Rome presented the Phoenicians with a new enemy. Roman leaders were determined to control the Mediterranean from north to south and from east to west. Three wars between Rome and Carthage were fought on this account.

In the First Punic War (264–241 BCE), Carthage's navy lost several major sea battles while still inflicting harm on its Roman counterpart. In the aftermath, the

Phoenicians agreed to relinquish Sicily. After the war, the Carthaginian mercenaries revolted because of nonpayment of debt for their services; this conflict broke out in 240 BCE and lasted for forty months, placing a strain on Phoenician resources. Meanwhile, in 238 BCE, the Romans seized Sardinia and Corsica from Carthage. An effort by Carthage to expand in Spain caused concern in Rome, and the Second Punic War (218–201 BCE) erupted. This conflict produced a brilliant Carthaginian general, Hannibal, who surprised Rome by marching across southern Gaul to the Po Valley to invade the Italian peninsula in 217. Hannibal won every battle of this campaign, but he was less successful in getting Rome's subjects to revolt against the capital. He returned home during a truce and was defeated at Zama, in North Africa, in 202. The postwar settlement saw the loss of Carthage's navy along with the Phoenicians' overseas possessions. The Third Punic War (149–146 BCE) took place because imperial Rome wished to be done with Carthage once and for all. The city was invaded, the population slaughtered or removed, and the buildings torched or flattened.

A hundred years later, the Romans rebuilt the city for their own purposes, drawing on its location as a key trading and military port. Carthage was now the capital of the Roman province of Africa Proconsularis, and it soon became as wealthy and substantial as its ruined predecessor. It featured Roman baths, a theater, a long aqueduct, and other notable structures. On the city's outskirts, wheat was grown to supply the Roman populace. By the second century CE, Christianity had gained a foothold in the city. In fact, Carthage became the seat of a bishopric; the Donatist heresy of the fourth century arose because of a dispute over elections to that office. Saint Augustine, a central figure in the early church, received his higher education at Carthage; in his *Confessions* (397–400 CE), he describes the bustling life of the city.

## CULTURE AND SOCIETY

Carthage was renowned for trade, as were the Phoenicians generally. Ships from Carthage not only carried goods to and fro throughout the Mediterranean, but Carthaginian pack trains (using mules and camels) traversed overland routes to distribute and receive goods. The city's exports included textiles, olive oil, wine, pottery, and livestock. Traders took payment in silver, spices, gold, silk, ivory, slaves, and various luxury items. The Carthaginians were among the first to use money of no value in and of itself—symbols stamped on pieces of leather—that could then be redeemed for silver, gold, or other valuables. Coinage, too, was used. By decree, all Carthaginian territories were closed to outside traders; the latter could be killed as pirates if caught. By treaties with Rome (509 and 348 BCE) and other states, foreigners were only permitted to trade in Carthage itself.

Before the third century BCE, Carthage's government consisted of a king, a senate (made up of aristocrats), and a popular assembly. The kingship, though perhaps originally hereditary, was for most of this period elective and for a term of life. Beginning in the 200s BCE, the king was replaced by two chief magistrates (*shophets*; Latin, *suffetes*), who were elected annually from among the aristocracy, and by elected career generals who had proved their effectiveness. Senate membership was for life and involved decisions regarding the important business of the day. The assembly, on the other hand, only became involved in matters of war and peace or of other issues left unresolved by the other institutions of government.

The Carthaginians relied on a standing army during times of conflict but also hired teams of mercenaries. They typically preferred negotiation and bribery to armed conflict as a means of settling political disputes. Nevertheless, they excelled at naval warfare, and their warships were superbly built. In addition, domesticated elephants were used in land battles to frighten or trample the enemy. Hannibal became a living legend for bringing elephants with him as he crossed the Alps into Italy, although most of them died as a result. The Carthaginians also excelled in fortifications and succeeded in making Carthage almost impregnable—until the Romans became committed to its destruction.

The Carthaginians worshipped deities such as Baal Hammon (male), Tanit (female), and Melqart (male), the protector of the city. A fourth deity, Eshmun (male), was a god of wealth and health. In times of crisis, human sacrifice, especially of the firstborn, was practiced. Carthaginian art, however, was not highly dramatic; it mainly copied design elements from Egypt and Greece.

As elsewhere in the ancient Mediterranean, women in Carthage were veiled and secluded. Not averse to enjoying luxury, the Carthaginians strove to dress their women in fine fabrics and adorn them with spectacular jewelry; the ideal was that of a beautiful, alluring individual who nonetheless followed the dictates of her father or husband. At the same time, women were known to be influencers in government affairs and were able to leave their mark in society. In the final hours of Carthage under Phoenician rule, the city's lead general pleaded with the attacking Romans for his life; but his wife, denouncing his meekness, chose to leap with her young sons into the fires of the collapsing city.

## DEMISE

With the Western Roman Empire in sharp decline, in 429 CE, the Vandals under King Gaiseric invaded North Africa from Spain. They occupied Numidia in 435 and proceeded northeastward to Carthage in 439, taking the city and introducing there the heretical cult of Arianism (a nontrinitarian Christian doctrine). The city's commercial life and cultural development largely ceased. Owing to Vandal neglect and mismanagement, Emperor Justinian I of Constantinople sought to recapture Carthage for the Byzantines. He succeeded in doing so in 534 through the efforts of one general, Belisarius. However, further religious disputes in the city stymied attempts to revive it. In 697, Carthage fell to Arabs rushing across North Africa from Egypt to spread the new faith of Islam. The new arrivals set about destroying, burning, and looting the city and then took up residence in the nearby town of Tunis (soon to be a major city in its own right).

## RECENT DISCOVERIES AND CURRENT STATUS

Carthage today remains a tourist attraction and an important archaeological site, even though much of it has lain in ruins for over a millennium (or over two millennia, in the case of Phoenician Carthage). The outline of the great harbor can still be seen as well as the ruins of the homes and palaces from the time of the Carthaginian Empire. Carthage was named a UNESCO World Heritage Site in 1979, one of the first sites to be so honored.

A debate over how common child sacrifices were in pre-Roman Carthage or, indeed, *whether* such sacrifices took place (given that it was mostly Greek and Roman authors who described them) seemed to be settled recently when an archaeological team from Oxford University found solid evidence of the practice. In fact, the researchers estimate that up to twenty-five victims a year were sacrificed (*Archaeology* 2014).

*Michael Shally-Jensen*

*See also:* Constantinople; Phoenicians; Rome.

**Further Reading**

*Archaeology.* 2014. "Study Concludes Child Sacrifice Took Place in Ancient Carthage." January 23, 2014. https://www.archaeology.org/news/1759-140123-carthage-tophet-sacrifice
Hoyos, B. D. 2010. *The Carthaginians.* New York: Routledge.
Lancel, Serge. 1995. *Carthage: A History.* Cambridge, MA: Blackwell.
López-Ruiz, Carolina, and Brian R. Doak, eds. 2019. *The Oxford Handbook of the Phoenician and Punic Mediterranean.* New York: Oxford University Press.
Miles, Richard. 2011. *Carthage Must Be Destroyed: The Rise and Fall of an Ancient Civilization.* New York: Viking.
Pilkington, Nathan. 2019. *The Carthaginian Empire.* Lanham, MD: Lexington Books.

# Chan Chan

Chan Chan is the largest adobe city in South America and the second largest in the world. Occupied by the Chimú people of Peru between about 900 and 1470 CE, the city was built at the mouth of the Río Moche, which allowed the Chimú to use irrigation to enrich their farmlands and create wealth from an abundant food supply.

Among its most distinctive features, Chan Chan has ten royal palaces set within walls. Each palace has double walls, in fact, sometimes thirty feet high, along

---

*El Dorado*

El Dorado, or the Golden One, is a fabled city of gold said to be in what is today Colombia. The myth began as a Spanish legend about the Muisca people, also known as the Chibcha people. This group inhabited the Andes highlands in the central region of present-day Colombia. A kernel of inspiration for the story may have been that the Muisca were skilled in creating golden crafts. El Dorado first referred to a golden man, that is, the *zipa*—or leader—of the Muisca people, who was supposedly covered in gold dust before leaping into Lake Guatavita at his coronation ceremony. The fable grew rapidly among the invading Spanish, who were eager for tales of gold and other riches. Soon El Dorado referred not to a man but to a golden city and then a golden empire. Many expeditions went out in search of the city, usually led by Spaniards or Englishmen. None were successful.

with labyrinthine interiors and a single entrance (to enhance protection). The exterior walls are decorated with repeating patterns, often mimicking those found in regional wall textiles. Similar buildings have been found at other sites within the Chimor Empire, the capital of which was Chan Chan.

The city also contains various functional structures, such as administrative buildings, storage locations, and burial chambers. As Chan Chan expanded, more artisan homes and work spaces were built as well as more storage locations.

## INHABITANTS

Not a great deal is known about the Chimú people. However, we do know that following the conquest of the Chimor Empire by the Inca in the fifteenth century, the Inca incorporated some features of Chimú culture into their own, including aspects of its political structure and irrigation techniques. When the Spanish arrived some fifty years after Chimor's defeat, they were able to gather some information from the remaining Chimú. They believed that the Chimor Empire had grown out of the remains of the Moche culture (100–700 CE), which archaeological research later confirmed.

The Chimú people of Peru built and occupied Chan Chan, the second-largest adobe city on the planet, from ca. 900 to 1470 CE. The archaeological remains of the city bear witness to a complex and stratified society. (Corel)

At its peak, the city covered twenty square kilometers and was home to more than 30,000 people, with an estimated 20,000 being craftspeople, both men and women. Many of the fine materials used in creating Chimú objects were taken from conquered cities. Some of the craftspeople may have also been forcibly relocated as the palaces expanded, indicating a clear social hierarchy.

## HISTORICAL BACKGROUND

From around 900 CE to the 1470s CE, the Chimor Empire was a major power in the culture and history of South America. Its capital city was Chan Chan, located on the coast around three miles from modern-day Trujillo, Peru. The city was known for its crafts. Producing unique pottery and beautiful metalwork, artisans (both men and women) frequently worked with gold, silver, brass, and copper as well as clay and other materials.

The people of Chimor, the Chimú, were agricultural. Unlike the Inca and other South American cultures, they held their moon goddess as the most important deity in the pantheon. They expanded through conquest until approximately 1470 CE, when they were conquered, in turn, by the Inca Empire. The Inca kept few records of the cultures they conquered and absorbed, but some information about the Chimor Empire has remained.

## CULTURE AND SOCIETY

While the Chimú were skilled in many different types of crafts, their distinctive black pottery is perhaps the most notable. In fact, the spread of this pottery style across the area has helped archaeologists determine how the Chimor Empire expanded. The empire covered the Lambayeque, or Sicán, people and also took control of the La Leche Valley. Before their conquest by the Inca, the Chimú controlled over 800 miles along the coast of Peru.

There is evidence that the people of Chan Chan lived in a stratified society. The high walls built around the various palaces at the site and the different types of housing occupied by artisans are viewed as evidence of this. There are different theories on the nature of the palaces: one idea is that while leadership may have been inherited, property was retained within the lineage, and thus a new king was often required to go out and create his own wealth and prosperity. Some experts suggest that this may also be a reason behind the Chimor pattern of conquest.

Unlike many cultures in the South American civilizations, the Chimú worshipped Si, their moon goddess and the most important god in the pantheon. They believed the moon was linked to crop growth, weather patterns, and fertility; the moon also appeared during the day and night, demonstrating its strength. The sun god, Jiang, and the sea god, Ni, were worshipped as well, but they were both considered less powerful. Sacrifices of crops, fabric, and children were made to the moon goddess. The Chimú believed that children who were sacrificed would become gods in their own right.

## DEMISE

The Inca, in control of an even more powerful South American state, had begun to expand their territory in 1438, slowly moving up and down the western coast of South America. They eventually covered parts of modern-day Peru, Ecuador, Bolivia, Columbia, Chile, and some of Argentina. When the Inca conquered an area, they generally removed local leaders and installed their own family members. This ensured loyalty to the Inca.

In 1470, the Inca arrived in Chan Chan, and the city was quickly conquered by Topa Inca Yupanqui. After that, the Chimor Empire fell into sharp decline. Chan Chan was no longer a center for trade or commerce in the area, as those functions were moved toward major Inca cities. There is evidence, however, that the Inca took various cultural elements from the Chimú to use in their own society, such as crafting techniques and aspects of political organization.

By 1532, when the Spanish conquistador Francisco Pizarro arrived in Peru, the city of Chan Chan had been largely abandoned. Written records, however, tell of the high walls and the hundreds of thousands of pesos' worth of gold that was recovered from the storerooms. The Spaniards extracted all the precious metal they could from the city and left the rest to the elements.

## RECENT DISCOVERIES AND CURRENT STATUS

In 2018, two notable architectural discoveries were made in Chan Chan. First, three statues were found in the corridor leading into the city. The figures represented in them were probably considered by the Chimú to be guardians of the city. Similar figures seem to have been used as markers for the tombs of important personages in Chimú history.

Archaeologists also uncovered a site where more than 100 children between ages eight and twelve and more than 200 young llamas had been sacrificed. This was probably carried out sometime between 1400 and 1450 CE, according to researchers. It is believed that an event of this scale is unprecedented in the history of pre-Columbian civilizations in the area and may have signaled a grim attempt to gain control of a desperate situation.

Modern Peruvian conservation efforts are being made to preserve some of the mud friezes and other key elements of Chan Chan. Some of the adobe work can be hardened with a mixture of distilled water and cactus juice, helping it better withstand weather elements; other works have been photographed and then covered. Some observers have suggested that the best solution for Chan Chan may be a large roof that could protect its adobe structures from damaging rainstorms, although such a solution would be comparatively difficult to implement.

Today, the city of Chan Chan has been designated a UNESCO World Heritage Site, and conservation efforts are ongoing. The biggest threat to the remains of Chan Chan is erosion from heavy rains; as climate change accelerates, the damage is becoming more severe.

*Michael Shally-Jensen*

*See also:* Machu Picchu; Moche Culture.

## FURTHER READING

Hathaway, Bruce. 2009. "Endangered Site: Chan Chan, Peru." *Smithsonian* magazine, March 2009. https://www.smithsonianmag.com/travel/endangered-site-chan-chan-peru-51748031/

Keatinge, Richard W., ed. 1988. *Peruvian Prehistory: An Overview of Pre-Inca and Inca Society.* New York: Cambridge University Press.

Mosely, Michael E. 2001. *The Inca and Their Ancestors.* Rev. ed. New York: Thames & Hudson.

Mosely, Michael E., and Kent C. Day, eds. 1982. *Chan Chan: Andean Desert City.* Albuquerque, NM: School for Advanced Research.

# Chang'an

Nestled into a fertile valley among the mountainous region of what is today central China, Chang'an sits just south of the Wei River before it issues into the larger Yellow River. This ideal location played a part in the city's influence and stability and is responsible for its name: *Chang'an* translates to "Perpetual Peace." Merchants and travelers coming from the West knew Chang'an as the end of the Silk Road. Similarly, when traveling to the Silk Road from the regions around either Beijing or Shanghai, one must travel through Chang'an.

Today, the modern city of Xi'an has superseded Chang'an. Some vestiges of the ancient city remain among and just beyond the bustling streets of Xi'an. The Giant Wild Goose Pagoda, a large Buddhist tower dating to the Tang dynasty, still stands in the middle of the city. The tomb of the Han emperor Jingdi is stationed just outside of town, as is the famous Terracotta Army, which was built as part of a necropolis for Qin Shi Huang, the first emperor of a unified China, before the founding of Chang'an.

## INHABITANTS

The fertile region along the Wei River that would later house Chang'an has been inhabited since at least the Neolithic period. The region immediately surrounding Chang'an housed two major capitals before Chang'an's founding. The twin city Fenghao—originally two distinct settlements, Feng and Hao—was located just southwest of what would be Chang'an and served as the capital of the Western Zhou dynasty from the eleventh to the eighth century BCE. Xianyang, located just north of the Wei River, became the capital of Qin in 350 BCE, during the Warring States period, and later of newly formed China when Qin Shi Huang first unified it in 221 BCE. Two decades later, Emperor Liu Bang, the founder of the Han dynasty, appointed Xiao He to oversee the construction of a new capital, Chang'an. This original iteration of Chang'an featured the Changle and Weiyang Palaces; approximately 146,000 people inhabited the city as of its founding in 195 BCE.

## HISTORICAL BACKGROUND

Chang'an served as the capital of the Western Han dynasty for the majority of its more than two-century rule. Xiao He designed the new city of Chang'an for Liu Bang, the founder of the Han dynasty in the beginning of the second century BCE. With the emperor originally put off by the magnitude of the new construction, Xiao He defended the grandeur as a necessary projection of the emperor's power. The emperor forcibly relocated many of his subjects to the region. His son, Emperor Hui, built the walls of Chang'an. Several generations later, Emperor Wu oversaw a third phase of construction, adding several more large palace complexes to the city. While the start of the Silk Road had long been in the surrounding region, it was during the this Western Han period that Chang'an became the official beginning of this important trade route. In 23 CE, a peasant revolt besieged and took Chang'an, and the rebels killed Emperor Wang Mang, officially ending the Western Han era. The capital was moved east to Luoyang under the Eastern Han. In 190, the throne was seized by Dong Zhuo, and the capital was moved back to Chang'an. However, this proved short-lived, and the capital was shifted back to Luoyang upon Dong Zhuo's death in 196.

Chang'an once again became the seat of power under the Sui and Tang dynasties. Before this, it was intermittently the capital of smaller kingdoms: the Western Jin, Former Zhao, Former and Later Qin, Western Wit, and Northern Zhou. Emperor Wen, the founder of the Sui dynasty, deemed Han-era Chang'an too small and resolved to break new ground for his own capital. Just south of Han Chang'an, Emperor Wen initiated construction on a new fortified capital in 582. He named it Daxing, which translates to "Great Prosperity." Although the Sui dynasty would be short-lived, encompassing the rule of two emperors over less than four decades, Wen's Daxing lived on as the seat of power under the subsequent Tang dynasty.

Li Yuan, the founder of the Tang dynasty, retained Daxing as his own capital, but in 618, the first year of his reign, he renamed it Chang'an, the same name as the former Han capital located immediately to the north. This new iteration of the city, built under the Sui and further developed under the Tang, was nearly a perfect fortified rectangle, except for Daming Palace protruding out of the northern border and part of Furong Garden sticking out of the southern border. Imperial buildings and two marketplaces, one in the west and the other in the east, stood out among an otherwise perfect grid. The avenues were especially wide, and the wall protecting the exterior of the city measured eighteen feet. As the regional metropolis, Chang'an was a plump target for enemies of the Tang dynasty, and it was occupied by various rebels and rivals in 756, 763, 783, and 881 before falling for good in 904.

## CULTURE AND SOCIETY

Because Chang'an flourished across centuries, it produced a vibrant and evolving culture and society. From the Han period, Chang'an became a center for philosophical thinking. The schools of Legalism and Huang-Lao dualism were influential alongside Confucianism in the early centuries of the Han dynasty. Around the turn of the first century BCE, Emperor Wu made Confucianism the official state doctrine. Dong Zhongshu, a member of the court, crafted this particular strain of Confucianism and is thought to be largely responsible for Emperor Wu's policy. Under the Han, philosophical and scientific tests flourished, and Chinese historiography came into its own.

Centuries later, Chang'an experienced a cultural highpoint under the Tang dynasty. Confucianism continued to flourish, and Taoism and Buddhism also held a broad influence. The Tang era is often understood as the golden age of Chinese literature. This culture was centered in Chang'an. Poetry blossomed, and nearly 50,000 poems have survived. Meanwhile, the classical prose movement shifted some writers' thinking beyond poetry. Fiction thrived, as did nonfiction in the form of historiography and encyclopedias. The production of other forms of art accompanied the boom in literature, with painting, pottery, sculpture, and music being particularly popular.

By the Tang era, Chang'an was by some accounts the largest city in the world. It was notably cosmopolitan and included populations from many non-Chinese Asian peoples. Throughout its history, Chang'an housed a particularly hierarchical society, with one's rank influencing most aspects of day-to-day life. In Tang Chang'an, one's status determined what material and color of clothing one could wear. Light blue was reserved for high-ranking officials; dark blue was for the next grade down, followed by light green, and so on. The position of one's dwelling likewise depended on the person's status, with locations nearer the city's central avenue reserved for those of higher ranks.

## DEMISE

After a series of uprisings and rebellions, the Tang dynasty wielded a weakened version of its former glory by the second half of the ninth century. Huang Chao, a salt smuggler, led a rebellion against the Tang dynasty in the 870s. His army wreaked havoc around Tang Ching before conquering Chang'an, and Huang Chao declared himself emperor in 881. Although the Tang deposed Huang Chao a few years later, their rule never really recovered. With Tang power in disarray, the warlord Zhu Wen seized control of Chang'an. He ordered the capital to be moved to Luoyang to the east in 904. Since many of the buildings were made of wood, much of the capital was physically removed and transported to Luoyang. Zhu Wen ruled for a few years behind the scenes before officially declaring himself emperor, the first of the Later Liang dynasty. Meanwhile, what remained of Chang'an fell into disrepair and was soon overgrown.

## RECENT DISCOVERIES AND CURRENT STATUS

Excavations run by the Chinese Institute of Archaeology of the Chinese Academy of Social Sciences (CASS) have been ongoing since 1956. Underground tunnels as well as a major imperial thoroughfare by the Zhicheng Gate dating back to the Han period were found in the first decade of the 2000s. The ancient city is part of the UNESCO World Heritage Site named Silk Roads: The Routes Network of Chang'an–Tianshan Corridor.

*Anthony Vivian*

*See also:* Kyoto; Xianyang.

## FURTHER READING

Cotterell, Arthur. 2007. *The Imperial Capitals of China: An Inside View of the Celestial Empire*. London: Pimlico.
Feng, Linda Rui. 2015. *City of Marvel and Transformation: Changan and Narratives of Experience in Tang Dynasty China*. Honolulu: University of Hawaii Press.
West, Keith. 1946. *The Three Blossoms of Chang-an*. New York: Macmillan.

Xiong, Victor Cunrui. 2000. *Sui-Tang Chang'an: A Study in the Urban History of Medieval China*. Ann Arbor: University of Michigan Center for Chinese Studies.

# Chavín de Huántar

The ancient site of Chavín de Huántar lies between the eastern and western Andes in an area over 10,000 feet high. The site, which seems to have been of ceremonial or religious significance, is situated at the confluence of two rivers: the Mosna and the Huanchecsa. It has been carbon dated to sometime before 1200 BCE, although it seems to have been most active between about 900 BCE and 400 BCE. Chavín de Huántar displays impressive architectural constructions that show both a dedication to craftsmanship and a religious devotion on the part of the inhabitants.

The site is dominated by a group of monumental stone mounds, the pieces of which have been carefully fitted together and polished to present brilliant facades. The two main mounds are called the Old Temple and the New Temple. There is also a large sunken rectangular plaza and some lesser structures. Dozens of stone carvings on slabs and other forms that once decorated the temples are also present. Chavín de Huántar is considered one of the most important archaeological sites in South American prehistory.

## INHABITANTS

Although archaeologists refer to the Chavín people as being responsible for the building of Chavín de Huántar, relatively little is known about the people themselves. Historians do not even know what the Chavín called themselves; they are simply referred to by the name of what appears to have been their greatest monument. Some experts believe that Chavín culture may have begun as a religious cult with priests as leaders; then it slowly transformed into a more expansive civilization as it drew in surrounding populations and flourished over time.

Beyond that, we only know that the Chavín were an Amerindian people who employed iconography in their art but did not have a writing system. Archaeologists

---

**Z**

The Lost City of Z is a fabled city hidden deep in the jungles of the Amazon basin, an area that has long been inhabited by Indigenous peoples. The supposed city was named Z by the British explorer Percy Fawcett, with whom the search for the lost city is inextricably linked. Convinced of the city's existence, Fawcett conducted multiple expeditions in the 1910s and 1920s in search of it, pausing to return to Europe to serve in World War I. In 1925, Fawcett set out with a small team, including his oldest son, never to be seen again. The story has been made popular by writer David Grann, first as a magazine article and then as a book, which has been adapted into a movie. Many believed Fawcett may have been inspired by Indigenous accounts of the ruins of Kuhikugu, a sprawling archaeological site by the Xingu River that once housed an advanced civilization of tens of thousands of inhabitants.

High in the Andes, the site of Chavín de Huántar was active in the first two millennia BCE. It served religious and ceremonial purposes through temple complexes such as this one. (Maria Luisa Lopez Estivill | Dreamstime.com)

believe that they were an agricultural people who domesticated animals and used irrigation to farm in areas that otherwise were less hospitable to agriculture. They are sometimes cited as creating the first distinctive and recognizable Peruvian art style. Their crafts included gold work, unique forms of incised black pottery, and detailed textiles. They evidently traded with people from as far away as Ecuador and the south central highlands of Peru.

## HISTORICAL BACKGROUND

The art and architecture of Chavín de Huántar may have been inspired by earlier Peruvian cultures on the coast, in the jungle, and in the highlands. The site itself was built over a few centuries and incorporated several building phases. Some researchers think that Chavín was something of a "mother culture" to the Peruvian and South American cultures, indicating that forms of iconography, religious beliefs, and other elements started with the Chavín and were transmitted across time and place to succeeding cultures. Others have suggested that the situation is more complex: while a Chavín influence can be seen throughout the region, it is possible that Chavín society incorporated elements from surrounding cultures rather than merely disseminated them unidirectionally.

There is no question that the Chavín society was a crucial pre-Columbian influence on Peru and the surrounding areas. How that influence waxed and waned is still a matter of discussion.

The site has several distinct buildings that were created over the 700 years during which it was most active as a religious site. There are various names for the different sections of the site; these have evolved somewhat as more have been uncovered through excavation and restoration at the site. The Old Temple and the New Temple are the best known; beyond that, there are circular and square plazas, north and south platforms, and the so-called Tello obelisk. These different areas and structures were created over time as the site evolved, though most construction had been completed by around 500 BCE. Construction materials included local stone for many sections of the buildings, but they also included black limestone and granite, neither of which were found locally. Researchers point to this quarried stone as evidence of the site's importance in terms of social hierarchy. Leaders would have needed to organize workers to bring stone from distant quarries to complete the work.

## CULTURAL AND SOCIETY

Unlike many ancient cities, Chavín de Huántar does not appear to have been fully occupied on a regular basis; instead, it seems to have served as a pilgrimage site for residents living throughout the region. The iconography at the site incorporates elements found along the coast of Peru; whether those images were brought to Chavín de Huántar or taken from it is difficult to tell, but it seems likely that, as a pilgrimage location, it also became home to a significant degree of cultural exchange. The site is also located in one of the few passages through the Andes from the jungle to the desert coast, meaning that it was likely used by populations whose members traveled between the two areas.

The Circular Plaza at Chavín de Huántar was an open-air space that is believed to have ritual importance; its primary purpose may have been simply to enter the oldest temple. Over time, however, temples were constructed around it; this led to the U-shaped structure that is commonly called the Old Temple.

The Old Temple contains many passageways and has internal galleries and structures filled with figures of jaguars, caimans, and other sacred animals. At the very center of the Old Temple is the Lanzón, a granite stella (carved stone) assumed to be the primary deity of the Chavín people. The Lanzón is just one of the many anthropomorphized jaguar figures that are tied to Chavín; some experts hold that this culture may have held the roots to later jaguar cults.

The New Temple contains similar galleries and another Lanzón figure, this time holding shells demonstrating the balance between male and female energies.

There are no windows in any of the temples, which means that worshippers would have been led through the galleries in the dark or with torchlight. There are, however, smaller tunnels running through the structures that allow air to pass through. While researchers do not yet fully understand the purpose of these air conduits, some acoustic effects have been noted: a strong wind, for example, can make a sound that might be interpreted as the snarl of a jaguar. To some extent, the sounds from inside could carry out into the plazas, letting the worshippers hear, as it were, the voice of their god. This is another reason why some see Chavín de Huántar as not just a place of worship but as an oracle site where believers might have obtained messages about their situations and prospects.

## DEMISE

According to the archaeological evidence, somewhere between 400 BCE and 200 BCE, a slow decline and social upheaval took place. Data from the surrounding areas suggests that Chavín culture at large was beginning to decline at the same time. Eventually, the large temples were abandoned, and the areas of worship were replaced with villages and agricultural lands. Stones and carvings were salvaged for use in building homes through the 1940s. Peruvian archaeologist Julio Tello had completed his initial study and restoration of the site by that time. Later excavations performed during the 1960s and 1970s uncovered some new areas of the plaza and additional domestic areas outside the main complex.

## RECENT DISCOVERIES AND CURRENT STATUS

Work is under way today to continue the preservation of the original Chavín de Huántar site. Post-Chavín materials are being removed, allowing the original reliefs and structures to become visible. As stabilization of the site unfolded, researchers from the Global Heritage Fund found Chavín artifacts in local homes, storage areas, and tool sheds. The site was added as a UNESCO World Heritage Site in 1985. Flooding has damaged many of the galleries and the artifacts they contained, and earthquakes have threatened the foundation of the site itself. Landslides have also been a problem.

What is certain is that Chavín society, with Chavín de Huántar as its hub, had a significant influence on the pre-Columbian societies of Peru. The motifs and crafting techniques that the Chavín people cultivated are visible in many subsequent cultures, demonstrating that the site was a place of cultural exchange and value throughout its relatively short existence in the highlands.

*Michael Shally-Jensen*

*See also:* Chan Chan; Machu Picchu; Moche Culture.

## FURTHER READING

Burger, Richard L. 1992. *Chavín and the Origins of Andean Civilization.* New York: Thames & Hudson.
Fux, Peter, ed. 2013. *Chavín: Peru's Enigmatic Temple in the Andes.* Zurich: Sheidegger & Spiess; Museum Rietberg.
Silverman, Helaine. 2004. *Andean Archaeology.* Malden, MA: Blackwell.
UNESCO. n.d. "Chavín (Archaeological Site)." Accessed October 27, 2019. https://whc.unesco.org/en/list/330/

# Constantinople

The city known as Constantinople ("City of Constantine") was originally a small colony founded by Greek merchants in the seventh century BCE. In the fourth century CE, it was refounded by the Roman emperor Constantine and gained new cultural and political importance. Renamed in honor of the emperor, Constantinople became the capital of a new Christian Roman Empire and later the Byzantine Empire. During this period, the city acted as the center of church and secular politics until its fall to the Ottoman Turks in 1453. Several emperors intended to leave their mark on the city, and as a result, many famous monuments, art, and architecture survive from Constantinople's heyday.

Located on a peninsula at the border of Europe and Asia, Constantinople lay along the Bosporus strait that links the Black Sea to the Sea of Marmara. The city had an easily defensible position with the sea protecting it on two sides and strong land fortifications on another. It also had a deepwater harbor, known as the Golden Horn, that made the city a nexus for trade networks.

## INHABITANTS

Recognizing the advantages of the site's harbor, Greek colonists from Megara founded the city of Byzantium in the seventh century BCE. Little is conclusively known about this early period, but it is clear that the colony was built on the west side of the strait because of its strategic location and the fertile land suitable for agriculture. The Chalcedonians had also previously built their own city on the eastern side of the strait.

During the Greco-Persian Wars of the early fifth century BCE, Byzantium changed hands between the Greeks and the Persians several times, ultimately falling under Greek control. Byzantium played an important role during the Peloponnesian War between Athens and Sparta because it helped supply grain to Athens through the strait. The Spartan control of the city proved crucial in the course of the war, stopping the flow of grain to Athens and pressuring the city to surrender to Sparta in 404 BCE.

Philip II of Macedon besieged the city in the fourth century BCE before it was fully annexed by his son Alexander the Great on his way eastward to campaign against the Persians. Byzantium had relative independence under the successors of Alexander and in the subsequent Roman period. It remained a source of wealth from trade and as a waypoint for the Roman army heading east. The Roman emperor Septimius Severus razed the city in 196 CE as punishment for supporting one of his rivals to the throne, but it was rebuilt soon afterward.

## HISTORICAL BACKGROUND

After the division of the empire into four administrative regions under Emperor Diocletian in the late third century, Milan had supplanted Rome as the imperial center in the West. Constantine envisioned a similar benefit to having an imperial residence in the East, closer to the empire's frontier. The site of Constantinople held many advantages: the city was near the frequent sites of Roman military campaigns in the lower Danube and the Euphrates and could act as a hub of trade and travel. Material goods and people would pass through the city as it connected western Europe, the Near East, and the Balkans.

Constantine attributed his choice of Byzantium as the new city's site to divine inspiration, as he did with many of his other decisions. But the city was not necessarily intended to be a new Christian city or a rival to Rome. Rather, Constantine envisioned a city meant to celebrate himself and his reign. The city's formal dedication as Constantinople came in 330 CE with a procession and the erection of a porphyry column with a statue of Constantine as Apollo on top. The emperor collected other pieces of art from across the empire to decorate his new city, including the Serpent Column from Delphi, an Augustan victory monument from Nicopolis, and an Egyptian obelisk.

After Constantine's death in 337, Constantinople continued to expand. The population increased from the late fourth century to its height of approximately half a million in the sixth century. This period witnessed new construction in the city. The initial foundations of the Hagia Sophia (the Church of Holy Wisdom) were laid in the fourth century, and it was subsequently rebuilt twice by later emperors. The water supply was also a continual concern of the emperors, who funded the construction of cisterns and aqueducts in the city. And Emperor Theodosius II (r. 402–450) constructed a university and fortified the walls around the city.

The reign of Justinian (r. 527–565) and his wife, Theodora, was a period of great change in the city. In addition to expanding the empire back into Italy, Justinian oversaw the codification of Roman law into the Justinian Codex. A pivotal event during Justinian's reign was the Nika revolt, in which rival circus factions destroyed much of the city, resulting in the deaths of 30,000 people. Following the riots, Justinian saw an opportunity to rebuild parts of the city, including the Hagia Sophia, the version of which stands to this day. In 541, an epidemic of the black plague moved through the city, killing at least 100,000 people.

## CULTURE AND SOCIETY

Christianity played a major role in Constantinople over the course of its history. The emperor styled himself as God's representative on earth, and he wielded his power as a result. He also exercised much influence on church affairs, organizing councils of bishops to settle debates of doctrine and maintaining religious unity. Though traditional Roman religion (paganism) remained vibrant for at least a century after Constantine's reign, it was the large number of churches constructed in the city that cemented its Christian image. Sources for the history of the city record the names of 485 churches.

The most impressive church, and still standing today, is the Hagia Sophia. This church of Justinian was built on an enormous scale, with its main dome 105 feet in diameter; it is decorated with elaborate mosaics within. The public square that contained the Hagia Sophia also included the Imperial Palace and the Hippodrome, creating a nexus for the emperor's religious and political duties. Other churches built during the reign of Justinian include the Church of Saints Sergius and Bacchus, the Church of St. Irene, and the Church of the Holy Apostles.

Constantinople was famous for its production of magnificent art, including jewelry, portraits, illustrations for books and manuscripts, and religious icons. The iconoclast controversy (725–843 CE) centered on the role of art in Christianity and the religious use of sacred images. Religious officials felt that this traditional use was an orthodox practice, while some emperors and patriarchs believed that it promoted idolatry. The end of the ban on religious art resulted in a popular style of art that flourished in Byzantine monasteries from the ninth to the twelfth century.

Another important cultural contribution of the Byzantines was the preservation of classical works from Greek and Roman antiquity. Byzantine scholars compiled and transmitted these works to the West, ultimately playing a part in the cultural resurgence of the renaissance.

## DEMISE

Following the reign of Justinian, Constantinople experienced periods of resurgence but mostly a series of setbacks until its capture by the Ottoman Turks. Emperor Leo III (r. 717–741) repelled an invasion of Arabs into the city, and Basil I (r. 867–886 CE) rebuilt much of the city, including several churches and an Imperial Palace. But the Fourth Crusade (1202–1204 CE) precipitated the collapse of the Byzantine Empire.

Infighting and conspiracies in the imperial court as well as negative relations with the West, including the destruction of the Italian quarter of the city during the so-called Massacre of the Latins in 1182, influenced the Crusaders' desire to raid and pillage Constantinople. The city was plundered, with monuments and churches desecrated. This occupation of the city by a foreign power contributed to Constantinople's slow decline and eventual fall to the Turks in 1453.

## RECENT DISCOVERIES AND CURRENT STATUS

The city of Constantinople is today known as Istanbul, the most populous city in Turkey. The Hagia Sophia was converted into a mosque in 1453, and in 1985, it was included among the city's other historical monuments as part of the UNESCO World Heritage Site called the Historic Areas of Istanbul. In 2020, President Recep Tayyip Erdoğan decided to again designate the Hagia Sophia a mosque. Though the Hagia Sophia remains open to visitors, this decision proved controversial.

*Chris Bingley*

*See also:* Pergamon; Rome.

## FURTHER READING

Harris, Jonathan. 2017. *Constantinople: Capital of Byzantium*. 2nd ed. London: Bloomsbury.
Herrin, Judith. 2008. *Byzantium: The Surprising Life of a Medieval Empire*. Princeton, NJ: Princeton University Press.
Mango, Cyril. 1986. "The Development of Constantinople as an Urban Centre," 117–136 in *The 17th International Byzantine Congress, Major Papers*. New Rochelle, NY: Caratzas.
Potter, David. 2012. *Constantine the Emperor*. Oxford: Oxford University Press.

# Ctesiphon

On the east bank of the winding Tigris River sits Ctesiphon, the erstwhile capital of the Parthian and Sassanian iterations of the Persian Empire. When Ctesiphon was founded in the second century BCE, it was constructed among already ancient ruins. Since the third millennium BCE, some of the world's earliest cities had populated Mesopotamia, or "Land between the Rivers," meaning the Tigris and Euphrates Rivers in present-day Iraq. Although Ctesiphon was not technically between the rivers, its proximity to this already ancient and still thriving urban hotspot was among the reasons that the Parthians and Sassanians utilized it for their capital.

Mithridates I of Parthia built Ctesiphon less than twenty miles from the ancient city of Sippar and about fifty miles from the ancient metropolis of Babylon. The new city was directly across the Tigris River from Seleucia, which was not as ancient as some of its neighbors but still centuries old by the second century BCE. The site of Ctesiphon is also only about twenty miles from the modern-day capital of Baghdad. The only major structure from Ctesiphon still partially standing is Taq Kasra, the Sassanid-era palace complex. Taq Kasra's impressively massive standing arch has become world famous.

## INHABITANTS

Mithridates I of Parthia founded Ctesiphon across the Tigris River from Seleucia, a Hellenistic trading hub for the Seleucid Empire. According to Strabo, Ctesiphon's settlement first began as a military encampment, when Persian soldiers balked at the idea of stationing among the Greek inhabitants of Seleucia. Whether or not this anecdote is true, it is clear that Ctesiphon was founded to give the Parthians a fresh Persian start in a region that already had millennia of history.

The Parthian dynasty came from northern Iran, in the region southeast of the Caspian Sea. However, the Parthians made serious strides to position themselves as the heirs of the Achaemenid dynasty of centuries prior, who originated in the Fars region, or south central Iran. For instance, Mithridates I, founder of the city, took on the Achaemenid title "King of Kings." Despite Ctesiphon originating as a deliberately Persian city within Mesopotamia, it soon grew to incorporate Seleucia and developed a wealth of additional neighborhoods that included a diverse population.

## HISTORICAL BACKGROUND

The Parthian Kingdom had already existed for decades when Mithridates I, the founder of Ctesiphon, took the throne and transformed Parthia into an empire. Throughout its early years, the kingdom remained relatively small, perched just north of the sweeping Seleucid Empire on the southeast coast of the Caspian Sea. The Seleucid Empire, the regional superpower, often meddled with Parthian affairs. Upon his coronation, after winning victories in the east, Mithridates turned the tables on the Seleucids. He conquered Media, Mesopotamia, and Persis and incorporated them into his budding empire. The conquest of Mesopotamia, in particular, shifted the empire's center of gravity westward. Mithridates set up royal capitals at Ecbatana, where he and his successors spent their summers, and Seleucia. Moreover, across the Tigris River from Seleucia, Mithridates founded Ctesiphon, which connected his new capital to the majority of his empire.

Ctesiphon grew in importance through the end of the second and first centuries CE. King Orodes II officially shifted his Mesopotamian residence from Seleucia to Ctesiphon, across the Tigris River, in ca. 58 BCE. The latter would continue to grow in importance and eventually incorporated Seleucia and other local settlements into a single urban space. Besides being a seat of Parthian royalty, the city rose in status thanks to its role as a major trade hub along both the Silk Road and the Tigris River.

The expanding Parthian and Roman Empires inevitably came into conflict. The Parthians took a decisive early victory at the Battle of Carrhae in 53 BCE, killing tens of thousands of the Roman invading force, including their commander, Crassus. However, Rome gained the upper hand and focused much of its retaliatory energy on Ctesiphon. The Romans sacked the Parthian capital three times in the second century CE, leaving it and the wider Parthian Empire a shell of its former self.

Although the Romans were pesky antagonists to the Parthians' West, it was the Iranian Sassanids who overthrew the Parthian Empire. Ardashir I, whose family originally came from the Fars region of Iran, defeated the Parthians in 224, established the Sassanid dynasty, and formed the Sassanid Empire. He (and his successors) generally tried to distance themselves from their Parthian predecessors. Nevertheless, two years after defeating them, he followed their lead in making Ctesiphon his official capital. The newly minted Sassanid capital held off its first Roman onslaught under Severus Alexander in 233. However, the Romans succeeded in capturing the Sassanid capital in 283 and 299. After the final Roman takeover, the Sassanid emperor Narses ceded some of his western territories to the Romans in exchange for his capital city.

Despite these early Roman captures of Ctesiphon, the Sassanid Empire soon flourished, as did its capital. In the fourth century, the empire thrived under the reign of Shapur II, who sat on the throne for an astounding seven decades. He revitalized the Sassanid military and expanded the empire's borders. Then, after a lull, the empire went through another period of resurgence and prosperity in the sixth and early seventh centuries. The city of Ctesiphon blossomed as well. The court resided in the White Palace, which stood in the old city. Among many other new neighborhoods, Asbanbar grew to the south of the city, which included Taq Kasra. Across the Tigris, near Seleucia, which had become part of Ctesiphon proper, the neighborhood of Veh-Ardashir developed. This section of town became popular among religious minorities, especially Jews and Christians.

## CULTURE AND SOCIETY

Ctesiphon featured a revitalization of Persian culture and society among a heterogeneous mix of other regional influences. The Seleucid Empire, the Parthians' successors, Hellenized Iran and the surrounding lands. The Parthians, by contrast, cultivated their Persian roots, codifying the use of the Parthian language. They repeatedly sought to evoke the Achaemenids, who ruled the first Persian Empire of centuries past. Nevertheless, the Parthians retained some Hellenistic ties, calling themselves Philhellenes, or "Friends of the Greeks."

The Sassanids went further in prioritizing Persian culture over Greek and other cultures at Ctesiphon. The Sassanid dynasty originated from Fars, the same region of Iran that the Achaemenids came from, and the Sassanids emphasized their ties to Persia's first empire to an even greater extent than the Parthians. Zoroastrianism, Iran's ancient religion, found new influence under their Sassanid patrons; Bahram II and some other kings went so far as to restrict and discriminate against religious minorities. Many see the Sassanid era as the height and culmination of pre-Islamic Iranian culture. The broad Middle Persian corpus, also known as Pahlavi literature, after its script, was composed in this period; Ctesiphon became a hub for science and the arts. In addition to its Persian culture, the capital's status as a trading center produced a society filled with a wide array of Near Eastern and Mediterranean cultures.

## DEMISE

Ctesiphon was at the height of its influence on the eve of its demise. Under Khosrow II, in the early seventh century CE, the Sassanid Empire reached the zenith of its territorial extent, and its capital city was likewise thriving. However, an ongoing war with the Byzantine Empire to the west had left both powers with depleted resources and vulnerable to the Arabs, who had just been united under Islam. The latter expanded out from the Arabian Peninsula at lightning speed.

Less than a decade after Muhammad had returned to Mecca, Arab forces were marching on the Sassanid capital of Ctesiphon, over 800 miles away. After defeating Sassanid forces at the Battle of al-Qādisiyyah in 636, Arab forces took Ctesiphon, which was mostly deserted after the flight of the royal court. Neither the Sassanid Empire nor Ctesiphon would recover. The Arabs inhabited the city for some time, converting part of Taq Kasra into a mosque. However, they chose other cities in Mesopotamia to develop into political and economic centers of power. As these neighboring cities grew in influence, Ctesiphon faded. This trend accelerated when the Abbasids founded Baghdad to be their capital in 762, only about twenty miles north of Ctesiphon.

## RECENT DISCOVERIES AND CURRENT STATUS

Ctesiphon experienced much damage during a battle between Ottomans and invading British troops during World War I. Major excavations occurred under the supervision of Germans in the 1920s and 1930s and Italians in the 1960s and 1970s. The United States' twenty-first-century Iraq War and its aftermath have so far hindered any major attempts at further excavation.

*Anthony Vivian*

*See also:* Babylon; Persepolis; Rome.

## FURTHER READING

Daryaee, Touraj. 2008. *Sasanian Persia: The Rise and Fall of an Empire.* New York: I. B. Tauris.

Daryaee, Touraj. 2011. *The Oxford Handbook of Iranian History*. Oxford: Oxford University Press.
Katouzian, H. 2010. *The Persians: Ancient, Mediaeval, and Modern Iran*. New Haven, CT: Yale University Press.
Yarshater, E., ed. 1983. *The Cambridge History of Iran*. Vol. 3, *The Seleucid, Parthian and Sasanid Periods*. Cambridge: Cambridge University Press.

# Cyrene

Cyrene was a Greek colony on the Libyan coast that blossomed into a Mediterranean trading hub. Colonists from Thera (present-day Santorini) first established the city in the seventh century BCE at the height of Greek colonization of the Mediterranean and Black Seas. The city became famous for its export of silphium, an important, but now extinct, crop used in ancient Mediterranean medicine and cuisine. After a stint of autonomy for Cyrene, the Persian Empire, Greek Ptolemaic dynasty, and Roman Empire ruled the city in turn.

As a major Mediterranean trading center, Cyrene mixed Greek, Roman, and other Mediterranean influences with local Libyan ones to create a society and culture distinct from the surrounding North African civilizations in Carthage and Egypt. The city boasted a rich philosophical life. It has been considered by many to be the birthplace of the philosophical school of hedonism, and it also served as an integral part of early Christianity. A number of different factors, not least among them the extinction of silphium, led to the city's downfall in the third and fourth centuries CE, but impressive ruins remain to this day.

## INHABITANTS

The region around Cyrene had been inhabited by local Libyans stretching back into prehistory. The city itself was founded by Greek colonists from the island of Thera, present-day Santorini. The Greek historian Herodotus asserts that a group of Therans under the leadership of Battus settled Cyrene under instructions from the oracle of Apollo at Delphi. Sailing in two ships, they first settled on an island off the Libyan coast and then a mainland location called Aziris before finally establishing themselves at Cyrene. In the generations that followed, additional Greek colonists would arrive, making the city the most important Greek settlement in the entire region.

## HISTORICAL BACKGROUND

Cyrene flourished as a powerful North African city and trading center for almost a thousand years. Greek colonists first settled in Cyrene in 630 BCE, according to Herodotus. Under the third king, Battus the Blessed, the population ballooned with waves of new colonists, as the Cyrenians offered tracts of land to additional settlers willing to make the journey. They were successful in clashes with local Libyans as well as with Egyptians to the east. Silphium was a large factor in the city's continued rise. Native to the region around Cyrene, this crop was

Cyrene was once an important Greek colony on the coast of northern Africa. The erstwhile trading center and philosophical hub now stands in ruins. (Global Heritage Fund)

in high demand around the Mediterranean and became such a major export for the city that it was featured on their coinage.

In 525, a few decades before the Greco-Persian Wars of the early fifth century and immediately after the Persian conquest of Egypt, Arcesilaus III, the king of Cyrene and the surrounding region, forged an alliance with Persia, and his domain served as a Persian satrapy. In the mid-fifth century, the city remained under Persian control but transformed from a monarchy to a republic. After Alexander the Great toppled the Persian Empire and then died, control over the republic of Cyrene fell to Ptolemaic Egypt, one of the successor kingdoms. Cyrene was one of the far-flung locations to receive Buddhist missionaries sent from India by Ashoka the Great in the third century. First appointed governor of Cyrene for the Ptolemaic Kingdom, Magas was able to pull his province free from its control in 276. After his successor, Demetrius the Handsome, was assassinated amid court intrigues, a republic survived for three years before the Ptolemaic Kingdom reincorporated Cyrene in 246.

Upon his death in 96, Ptolemy Apion, the Ptolemaic leader of Cyrene, granted control of the region to the Roman Republic, and the Romans formally made it a province in 74, decades before doing the same to neighboring Egypt. More court intrigue, according to Plutarch, led to Aretaphila, a local woman, deposing two Cyrenian tyrants in the mid-first century. The city continued to play the role of regional power under Roman rule for centuries.

The Jewish revolt of the early second century CE caused major unrest in the region. Facing worsening treatment under the Romans, the Jewish community of Cyrene revolted, and the ensuing bloodshed led to social, economic, and demographic upheaval that long outlasted the event. The emperor Hadrian attempted to restore the city, and it survived for more than two centuries but as a diminished version of its former self.

## CULTURE AND SOCIETY

Cyrene was a Mediterranean trading hub that fused Greek, Persian, and Roman influences with local North African ones. The city became known for a specific strain of Greek philosophy known as hedonism and was also renowned for its art and close connections to early Christian culture.

Aristippus of Cyrene, a pupil of Socrates, founded the Cyrenaic School of Philosophy in the fourth century BCE. Intrigued by Socrates's reputation, Aristippus traveled to Athens and followed Socrates until the latter's execution in 399. The school of thought that Aristippus set in motion was very different from that of his teacher: Aristippus believed the purpose of life was to extract pleasure out of all circumstances. His hedonism was not a call to surrender to one's every impulse but to maintain control and find pleasure in both prosperity and adversity. After he moved back to Cyrene, he taught philosophy to his daughter Arete, who in turn taught her son Aristippus the Younger. The younger Aristippus formalized the Cyrenaic School, which influenced and was eventually superseded by Epicurean hedonism.

Other culture beyond philosophy flourished throughout Cyrene's long history. Many sculptures and other pieces of art from Cyrene have survived. The *Venus of Cyrene* and the *Apollo of Cyrene* are two noteworthy Roman-era works. The latter was looted by Sir Robert Murdoch Smith in the nineteenth century and currently resides in the British Museum along with a trove of other Cyrenian sculptures and artifacts stolen by Smith. Eratosthenes, famous for many mathematical and scholarly innovations, including accurately measuring the circumference of the globe, was born in Cyrene, as was the Greek poet Callimachus.

Cyrene was closely linked with early Christianity. The Gospels of Matthew, Mark, and Luke place Simon of Cyrene at Christ's crucifixion, saying the Romans forced him to bear the cross immediately before the event. Cyrene and Jerusalem's connections across the southeastern Mediterranean account for the fact that individuals from Cyrene bespeckle the New Testament. Many important Christian figures for the first centuries CE were likewise Cyrenians, including Mark the Evangelist.

## DEMISE

Social unrest, economic factors, and natural disasters led to Cyrene's demise in the second through the fourth centuries CE. Although the region's Jewish revolt ended in 117, its economic and social effects were felt for decades. Silphium, Cyrene's most important export, was overharvested to extinction. In fact, despite its widespread use and popularity in the ancient world, historians still debate silphium's plant species. The disappearance of the plant stunted Cyrene's economy as well as its status among Mediterranean trading powers. Conflicts with Libyans of the interior increased in ferocity. Finally, two major earthquakes decimated the city. The first earthquake struck in 262. Although the Romans, in particular Emperor Claudius Gothicus, set about restoring the city, it never returned to its former glory. The second earthquake, a century later in 365, rang the death knell for this once powerful city. When the historian Ammianus Marcellinus visited in the fourth century, he described the city as "deserted."

## RECENT DISCOVERIES AND CURRENT STATUS

The archaeological remains of Cyrene are a UNESCO World Heritage Site. With recent civil unrest in Libya, Cyrene has been on UNESCO's List of World Heritage in Danger since 2016.

*Anthony Vivian*

*See also:* Athens; Carthage; Phoenicians.

## FURTHER READING

Lampe, Kurt. 2014. *The Birth of Hedonism: The Cyrenaic Philosophers and Pleasure as a Way of Life*. Princeton, NJ: Princeton University Press.

Mathisen, Ralph W. 2020. *Ancient Mediterranean Civilizations: From Prehistory to 640 CE*. Oxford: Oxford University Press.

Strassler, Robert B. 2009. *The Landmark Herodotus: The Histories*. New York: Anchor Books.

# D

## Deir el-Bahri/Djeser-Djeseru

Near the Egyptian Valley of the Kings, the remains of a funerary monument called Djeser-Djeseru, dedicated to one of the few—and great—women pharaohs of Egypt, Hatshepsut, stand at a mortuary complex known as Deir el-Bahri. The story of Djeser-Djeseru is the story of Hatshepsut, although one can also learn about Egyptian burial rites and Egyptian culture and history in general from the study of this site.

Hatshepsut, whose name means "first among noble women," came to power in approximately 1458 BCE as regent to her stepson, Thutmose III. She continued to rule in Egypt for many years after Thutmose came of age, crowning herself pharaoh and undertaking building projects and military campaigns to demonstrate her legitimacy as a leader. While she appears to have been respected in her time—her temple being so beloved that other royal figures wanted their own monuments nearby, resulting in the creation of the Valley of the Kings and Valley of the Queens—Hatshepsut's name was erased from all monuments and history after her death. Her existence was only uncovered when Jean-François Champollion, famous for his work in deciphering the Rosetta Stone, was unable to reconcile hieroglyphs that referred to a female ruler with statuary that depicted a male one. While Hatshepsut is not as famous as Cleopatra, she was a formidable figure and is often considered the most successful female ruler in the ancient world.

### INHABITANTS

Egypt had a long and glorious history behind it by the time the New Kingdom era arose with the founding of the Eighteenth Dynasty around 1540 BCE. The Egyptians always had one of the most static and firmly stratified societies in existence. The place of women in this society was well defined. Although a small number managed to become pharaohs, most were excluded from prominent roles. Their status was largely based on their family. At the same time, Egyptian religion, with its numerous gods and goddesses, fostered a certain degree of respect for female figures among the populace.

In her own time, Hatshepsut seems to have been well regarded as a ruler. Having a female regent was not uncommon when a young child came into power, but having her openly retain power was a new event. Although ancient Egyptian society had some level of equality for high-status women, as they could become priests and scribes as well as builders of great works and monuments, few assumed high-level political roles, and even fewer had established themselves as independent rulers.

In Egyptian mythology, the god Osiris ruled with Isis as his consort. Since Egyptians believed that their land was a mirror of the celestial world, women were similarly designed to be consorts, not rulers. Historians, however, point out that there is no way Hatshepsut could have taken on as many building projects and military campaigns as she did if she had not had access to substantial wealth, respect, and influence.

## HISTORICAL BACKGROUND

The pharaohs of the early New Kingdom involved Egypt in international affairs on a greater scale than their predecessors had. Hatshepsut opened new trade routes to the Land of Punt (around the Horn of Africa), made expeditions to Byblos and the Sinai Peninsula, and likely launched military campaigns in Nubia and Canaan.

Hatshepsut was the daughter of Thutmose I. As was traditional for Egyptian royal families, Hatshepsut was married at some point to her half brother, Thutmose II. The couple had a daughter, Neferu-Ra, and Thutmose also fathered a son with one of his lesser wives. That son was designated heir. When Thutmose II died around 1479 BCE, his son was still very young; therefore, as was typical, Hatshepsut became his regent until he came of age.

During the time of her marriage, Hatshepsut was also declared the God's Wife of Amun at Thebes, the capital. Amun was the most popular god in the city, and being named his wife—an upper-class woman who helped with the high priest's duties—gave a woman the power to dictate certain policies. In fact, the God's Wife often held more power than the queen herself.

Seven years into her reign as regent, Hatshepsut was therefore able to change policies and declare that she could be made pharaoh. She said that she was a demigoddess, the daughter of Amun, who had impregnated her mother. She also had reliefs constructed throughout the city that showed her as her father's coruler, legitimizing her status as a ruler. Given the beautiful building projects completed during her reign, it is unlikely that Hatshepsut's declaration of herself as pharaoh caused any kind of civil unrest; Thutmose III was made one of her generals and seems to have been content with that position for at least some time. Around 1457 BCE, Thutmose III led the Egyptian armies to end a rebellion in Kadesh; at this point, Hatshepsut disappears from the historical record.

## CULTURE AND SOCIETY

In Egypt, the state controlled the production and distribution of both food supplies and manufactured goods. Indeed, such control was one of the government's most important functions, as it allowed it to demand loyalty in the bureaucratic ranks and to infiltrate other aspects of life not under its direct control. The state maintained large granaries and warehouses, which it used to provide for the people when times were bad.

Although Egyptian society was stratified, some upward mobility was possible, especially in the New Kingdom. Immigrants, including Blacks from Nubia, and women could find opportunity to enhance their social status. A middle class consisting of scribes, lower-order priests, and various court functionaries was expanded during the New Kingdom with the addition of a corps of professional soldiers along with more people working as merchants, artisans, and farmers.

One commonly thinks of the Egyptians as building great monuments out of a sense of vanity. While this may be true to a degree, building projects were also a matter of social stability. When the Nile flooded, building projects were essential employment for many people; contrary to popular belief, monuments and temples were built by paid workers, not by slaves, and builders had fairly high status in society. Temples were also considered a statement of national unity and an expression of *ma'at*, the harmony or balance that was at the core of Egyptian culture. The Temple of Hatshepsut, Deir el-Bahri, is considered one of the most beautiful examples of Egyptian architecture and is one of the most frequently visited monuments in Egypt.

Hatshepsut was a great admirer of Mentuhotep II's (r. 2061–2010 BCE) temple; his tomb was carved into the cliff wall directly behind the temple. She had her own temple and tomb designed the same way and had it placed right next to the older temple, in case any observer might miss the similarity. Every element of Mentuhotep's temple was incorporated into Hatshepsut's, but the execution for hers was more elaborate and more graceful. A long ramp led up to the temple's second level, distinguished by lush gardens and reflecting pools. The tomb of Senenmut, the temple's designer who seems to have been the tutor of Hatshepsut's daughter and may have been Hatshepsut's lover, was placed on the ramp leading to the temple's third level. The three levels of the temple were all designed to preserve the crucial Egyptian belief in symmetry and harmony. Reliefs showed both Hatshepsut's colonnade to Punt (a land near the Horn of Africa) and her divine conception. The final level of the temple was built into the cliff itself and included chapels for the Royal Cult, the Solar Cult, and the Sanctuary of Amun.

## DEMISE

Hatshepsut ruled for over twenty years and left as her main legacy a massive funerary structure, or temple. There is no clear evidence of any ill will between Hatshepsut and her stepson, but the signs are there. When Hatshepsut disappeared from official writings, Thutmose III took the extreme measure of having the start of his reign backdated to the time when Hatshepsut took power. Her name and face were removed from all public monuments; notably, however, the stories of her life and victories as depicted within her temple were left untouched. The Egyptians believed that individuals could only continue their journey to the afterlife if they were remembered; having Hatshepsut completely erased from memory would thus have destroyed her ability to move into the next world. It seems that Thutmose may only have wanted to claim her works as his own and to remove from the record any evidence of a strong female ruler. In any case, Hatshepsut remained unknown to later generations until the archaeologists who discovered her tomb began to make sense of the hieroglyphs that related her story.

## RECENT DISCOVERIES AND CURRENT STATUS

Hatshepsut was not buried in her mortuary temple but rather in the nearby Valley of the Kings. Her mummy was discovered in the holdings of the Egyptian

Museum in 2006. Based on an examination of the mummy, it appears that the most successful female pharaoh died at approximately the age of fifty due to an abscess that followed a tooth extraction. This offers further evidence that there were no bad feelings between Hatshepsut and her stepson regarding her rule.

More recently, a stone chest was discovered within the royal cemetery at Deir el-Bahri. It was a common practice for pharaohs to be reburied when their tombs had been robbed or needed to be restored. The chest was inscribed with the name of Thutmose II, Hatshepsut's husband, and was also located near the tomb of Thutmose III.

*Michael Shally-Jensen*

*See also:* Abydos; Thebes.

**FURTHER READING**

Cooney, Kara. 2018. *When Women Ruled the World: Six Queens of Egypt.* Washington, DC: National Geographic.
Roehrig, Catherine, Renee Dreyfus, and Cathleen A. Keller, eds. 2005. *Hatshepsut: From Queen to Pharaoh.* New York: Metropolitan Museum of Art.
Shaw, Ian, ed. 2004. *Oxford History of Ancient Egypt.* New York: Oxford University Press.
Wilkinson, Toby. 2013. *The Rise and Fall of Ancient Egypt.* New York: Random House.

# Delphi

Delphi hosted a sanctuary and oracle to the Greek god Apollo and served as a religious and political hub through centuries of Greek history. The site stood in the mountainous region of central Greece, just north of the Gulf of Corinth. The Greeks considered Delphi the "navel of the earth," that is, the center of the universe. During the ancient oracular readings, a priestess of Apollo would enter a trance and make utterances, supposedly possessed by the god; these utterances were then translated and transcribed by priests. Some have suggested that a natural leak of ethylene or a similar gas helped induce these trances. The site was at times the most influential religious site in all of Greece, acting as a unifying institution for the disparate Greek city-states and drawing travelers from across Greece and beyond.

The site today features beautiful ruins among a picturesque mountain setting. The large Temple of Apollo dominates the former sacred precinct. The ruins are those of the third iteration of this temple, which was built in the fourth century BCE. Many treasuries, set up by various city-states of Greece, dot the landscape. The Tholos of Delphi is one of the more recognizable structures of the site: the round sanctuary was dedicated to Athena Pronoia ("Forethinking Athena"). A large open-air theater sits in the precinct's northwest corner, where the audience members had a sweeping view of the location's other structures. Although not part of the sacred precinct, a gymnasium, stadium, and hippodrome were located nearby.

## INHABITANTS

The site of Delphi was inhabited from the mid-second millennium and early on served as an important religious site. Priests and priestesses lived in the vicinity,

> **Hollow Earth**
>
> Several ancient cultures believed in a hollow earth. In some of these traditions, such as Greek Hades and Jewish Sheol, the underworld is the place where souls go after death. Edmond Halley, a renowned British scientist, first proposed the modern theory of a hollow earth in 1692. Halley and his fellow Hollow Earthers believed that the earth's crust was a hollow shell surrounding two smaller shells as well as an inner core. Halley first set forth the theory to account for unexplainable compass readings as well as the aurora borealis. Although Charles Hutton's Schiehallion experiment disproved the theory in 1740, it had major proponents well into the nineteenth century. Despite the fact that it has long been dismissed as a scientific theory, a hollow earth still features in subterranean fiction, a thriving subgenre of science fiction.

but at any given time, the location was filled with pilgrims who were there to consult the oracle and visit the sacred precinct. This was particularly true during festivals and events, such as the quadrennial Pythian Games. Various groups controlled Delphi throughout its history, and these groups exercised some control over the site's priests, priestesses, and pilgrims. These groups included Kirrha, the Delphic Amphictyonic League, Phocis, the Macedonians, and others.

## HISTORICAL BACKGROUND

The Greeks' most important oracle was at Delphi, and the space was among the most influential of all of Greece's religious sites for the whole of Greek history. Four so-called Sacred Wars were fought over control of the important location, and the oracle was sought out by countless Greeks and others, including some of the most important historical figures of these eras.

Centuries before the site was dedicated to Apollo, Delphi was a sanctuary devoted to worship of the goddess Gaia, or Mother Earth. Some accounts place the foundation of the location back in the fifteenth century BCE. It was at this stage that the site's close association with snakes formed. Before it took on the name Delphi, it was known as Pytho, which is where the English word *python* comes from. Sometime around 800 BCE—roughly the same time that the Greek alphabet began to be used and Greek society was seeing wide changes in general—the site was rededicated to Apollo. At this early stage, access to the sanctuary became controlled by the town of Kirrha, just south of Delphi on the Corinthian Gulf.

The Sacred Wars were four distinct conflicts across three centuries fought to some degree or another over control of Delphi. The First Sacred War saw Kirrha's control of Delphi challenged and eventually seized by the Amphictyonic League in the early sixth century BCE. Although the sanctuary was technically autonomous by this point, Kirrha could still control the flow of pilgrims to and from the religious site. The Amphictyonic League, a conglomeration of local powers, defeated Kirrha and took over stewardship of the oracle. After their victory, the league established the Pythian Games, the quadrennial Panhellenic games only second in prestige to the Olympic Games. The Pythian Games featured competitions in music, writing, and painting as well as athletic contests.

The Amphictyonic League continued to look over Delphi for over a century uncontested before the nearby city-state of Phocis seized control in the mid-fifth century BCE. The Second Sacred War quickly expanded into a wider conflict, embroiling the two regional superpowers, Athens and Sparta. The war ended with the Athenian-backed Phocians in charge of Delphi, but their power slowly melted away in the proceeding years. In the mid-fourth century, the Third Sacred War also entangled Greece's major powers in a conflict ostensibly between the Amphictyonic League and Phocis. Philip II distinguished Macedon as a major player within the region in helping the Amphictyonic League secure victory. Philip II likewise used the Fourth Sacred War to his advantage. This conflict over control of Delphic land culminated in the Battle of Chaeronea and Macedon's hegemony over Greece.

Throughout these conflicts, Delphi continued to receive a heavy influx of pilgrims who sought out the oracle of Apollo. The narratives of concurrent historians are littered with famous leaders soliciting the advice of Apollo and the oracle's often ambiguous responses. The site's pilgrims ranged from Lycurgus, the early Spartan lawgiver, and Croesus, the sixth-century BCE king of Lydia, to countless less famous others who have not been recorded in history books. Delphi's wide network and broad influence continued through the Hellenistic era and into the Roman era, as Delphi continued to play central religious, cultural, and political roles within the Greek world.

## **CULTURE AND SOCIETY**

The worship of Apollo was at the center of Delphic culture and society. Pilgrims traveled from all over Greece and beyond to consult the god's oracle. Other divine oracles existed around the Greek world, but none as prevalent as Delphi's oracle of Apollo. On certain days of the calendar, pilgrims were able to put a question to the Pythia, the priestess through whom Apollo spoke. Her response, which she gave while in a trance, would be incomprehensible to the pilgrims, but the priests would translate it into a more understandable answer in hexameters—a specific poetic meter. Even these more accessible answers were often ambiguous. For example, Croesus, the wealthy king of Lydia, was told that if he attacked the Persians, a great empire would fall. The flow of pilgrims and their accompanying donations—as well as the quadrennial Pythian Games—dominated life at Delphi.

The institution of Delphi also played a major role in the culture and society of the Greek world in general. Many famous works of literature feature the oracle and sanctuary. The Homeric Hymn to Apollo details the mythological founding of the sanctuary. Tragic playwrights, such as Aeschylus and Euripides, often centered Delphi in their tragedies. Historians narrated the famous events in Greek history that featured or were impacted by the oracle; Herodotus, in particular, seemed fascinated with the double-edged power of these divine interventions. Beyond the numerous instances when an oracle's response influenced major events in world history, Delphi was a powerful and lucrative institution, control of which sparked the four so-called Sacred Wars. Finally, the widespread and commonplace reverence for Delphi—similar to that for the city of Olympia and the Olympic Games—acted as a unifying force in the otherwise disparate Greek world.

## DEMISE

Delphi, with its vital religious sanctuary and oracle, thrived for over a millennium before falling victim to the spread of Christianity. Beginning in the second century BCE, the Romans occupied Greece, incorporating it into their expanding empire. On the one hand, Roman forces under Sulla and Nero ransacked the wealthy sanctuary of Delphi in the first century BCE and first century CE, respectively. On the other hand, the Romans had long accepted Delphi's status as an important oracle and holy site. Therefore, for a time, the flow of pilgrims, the Pythian Games, and the overall reverence for Delphi carried on under the Romans as it had under the control of the Greeks. However, the rise of Christianity and the subsequent conversion of the Roman Empire eventually clashed with the status of Delphi. This sanctuary, like other formerly prominent pagan sites, faced violence and destruction in the persecution of pagans under the Christian Roman Empire. Finally, in the late fourth century CE, Emperor Theodosius I permanently closed the sanctuary.

## RECENT DISCOVERIES AND CURRENT STATUS

Excavations on the erstwhile sanctuary have been ongoing since the late nineteenth century. Delphi has been a UNESCO World Heritage Site since 1987.

*Anthony Vivian*

*See also:* Athens; Olympia; Rome.

## FURTHER READING

Kindt, Julia. 2016. *Revisiting Delphi: Religion and Storytelling in Ancient Greece*. Cambridge: Cambridge University Press.
Morgan, Catherine. 1990. *Athletes and Oracles: The Transformation of Olympia and Delphi in the Eighth Century BC*. Cambridge: Cambridge University Press.
Scott, Michael. 2010. *Delphi and Olympia: The Spatial Politics of Panhellenism in the Archaic and Classical Periods*. Cambridge: Cambridge University Press.
Scott, Michael. 2014. *Delphi: A History of the Center of the Ancient World*. Princeton, NJ: Princeton University Press.

# E

## Easter Island

Easter Island, also known as Rapa Nui in the local language, is a Polynesian island in the southeastern Pacific Ocean. Only sixty-three square miles, the island is about the size of Washington, DC. With its closest inhabited neighbor over 1,000 miles of ocean away, it is the second most remote inhabited place on earth after the Atlantic archipelago Tristan da Cunha. A volcanic island formed from three volcanoes, Easter Island has a tropical rain forest climate; however, much of its forests have disappeared, which played a role in its society's demise. Experiencing an average high of seventy-five degrees Fahrenheit, it rains year-round and has a particularly wet season from March to September.

Easter Island is world famous for its moai. The people of Easter Island constructed these monolithic statues from tuff and other stone materials in the first half of the second millennium CE. The statues are large humanlike figures with oversized heads, squat bodies, wide noses, and deep-cut eye slits. On average, their height is more than double life-sized at around thirteen feet, and their average weight is a remarkable fourteen tons. Over 900 moai have survived until today. Although they were toppled in the late second millennium CE, many have been restored to their original upright position.

### INHABITANTS

Rapa Nui is the local name of both Easter Island itself as well as the people who have inhabited it. The first settlers were a culmination of Austronesian expansion.

---

### Mu

Mu was a proposed lost continent first claimed to have existed in the Atlantic Ocean and then in the Pacific. In the nineteenth century, Charles Étienne Brasseur de Bourbourg, a French archaeologist, first mentioned the continent while unsuccessfully attempting to translate the Mayan text now known as the Madrid Codex. He believed the text spoke of Mu, a continent submerged by the sea. Augustus Le Plongeon associated the continent of Mu with the city of Atlantis, which originated in ancient Greek literature. Le Plongeon depicted Mu as an Atlantic continent of great antiquity, whose descendants became both the ancient Egyptians as well as the ancient Maya. In the early twentieth century, the myth of the lost continent of Mu continued to be proliferated, although it began to become associated with the Pacific Ocean. One of the key proponents of this new iteration of Mu was James Churchward, who wrote multiple books on the subject.

Having originated on Taiwan, the Austronesians settled much of the Indian and Pacific Oceans. Easter Island marks the easternmost settlement of the Austronesians, whose other settlements ranged for thousands of miles to the west. Their language, also called Rapa Nui, encompasses an eastern branch of the Polynesian language tree. Most scholars place their arrival at around 1200 CE, although some contend they arrived as early as 300 BCE. The Rapa Nui have inhabited the island continually ever since, although the island has been occupied and ruled by outside powers since the nineteenth century.

## HISTORICAL BACKGROUND

Millennia before a group of their descendants first approached Easter Island, the Austronesian peoples were already exploring the southwestern Pacific Ocean. They first set out from Taiwan sometime before 3000 BCE. The invention of outrigger boats—vessels with outriggers attached to one or both lateral sides for stability—allowed the Austronesians to more safely explore the seas and become expert navigators. Some Austronesians branched westward, eventually making it as far as Madagascar, off the southeastern coast of Africa. Those who branched eastward spread to settle almost the entire southern Pacific.

The first islands that the Austronesians settled were already inhabited upon their arrival. In these locations, there was typically some degree of integration between Austronesians and other peoples. However, as Austronesians ventured farther from the Asian mainland, they eventually came upon islands yet to be visited by humans. As far as we can tell, they were the first to settle all of the islands in what is today known as Polynesia. Austronesians first entered Polynesia in the last couple of centuries of the first millennium CE and went on to settle islands as far as Hawaii in the north, New Zealand in the south, and Easter Island in the east.

A group of Austronesians first settled Easter Island around 1200 BCE, although some scholars argue they arrived earlier. They were probably traveling from the Pitcairn Islands, the Gambier Islands, or the Marquesas Islands, which range from about 1,200 to 2,000 miles away. Hotu Matu'a was the legendary founder and first chief, and according to tradition, the first settlement was located on Anakena, a beach on the northern shore of the island. The settlement on Easter Island, the easternmost of the many Polynesian settlements, primed its inhabitants to go even farther east. They frequented the uninhabitable Isla Salas y Gómez, 240 miles to the east, from which they collected eggs and young birds. They may very well have had contact and traded with communities in South America; it is highly unlikely that they were unaware of the continent given their seafaring and navigational prowess. Some point to the sweet potato (which originated in South America and ended up on Easter Island and other Polynesian settlements) as evidence of this contact, but other theories have been put forward to explain this root vegetable's spread.

On Easter Island itself, the Rapa Nui—which is what the inhabitants of Easter Island called themselves—thrived for centuries. At its height, the island of sixty-three square miles housed a population of approximately 15,000 individuals. From the time they first settled the island up through the next few centuries, the inhabitants executed an impressive building program, constructing and transporting

A moai looks out over the Pacific Ocean. It features a distinctive oversized head and deep-cut eye slits. (Larry Portmann | Dreamstime.com)

hundreds of moai, stone representations of Rapa Nui ancestors. These statues average fourteen tons, rendering their transportation around the island an impressive feat. Even before the arrival of European and South American outsiders in the eighteenth century, society on Easter Island had peaked and begun to decline. Deforestation had reduced the island's resources, leading to civil strife.

## CULTURE AND SOCIETY

Easter Island's culture has become famous for its moai, but it also features an array of other art. The moai—large humanlike figures with enlarged heads—were carved from stone, usually tuff but also basalt, trachyte, or red scoria. Their eyes were made of coral with obsidian or red scoria pupils. They are massive monolithic blocks, averaging thirteen feet in height and weighing fourteen tons. After the carvers formed the moai in the quarries, individuals then transported the statues elsewhere on the island, where they were stood on ahu, stone platforms or pedestals made to support and exhibit the statues. Of those moved from the quarries, the vast majority were placed on the island's perimeter. As representations of deified ancestors, the statues faced inland, overlooking the island's living inhabitants.

Other art forms likewise flourished. Wood was a diminishing commodity on Easter Island, but highly elaborate wood carvings have survived, including a style of slender figurines distinctive to Easter Island. Ornate petroglyphs, or rock engravings, proliferated. Rongorongo, a script unique to the island, survives on a handful of wooden tablets and, perhaps, in a few petroglyphs. However, it has yet to be deciphered, and some contend it may be a form of proto-writing as opposed to a developed writing system. The inhabitants of Easter Island cultivated bananas and root vegetables such as sweet potato, yam, taro, and cassava. They also raised chickens and fished the surrounding seas. The deforestation of the island decreased the rainfall and hindered their ability to support a large population.

## DEMISE

By the time the people of Easter Island first came in contact with non-Polynesian peoples in the eighteenth century, their society had already been in decline from an earlier peak, a process exacerbated by European and South American intervention. Deforestation led to precipitous population fall: from a population of approximately 15,000 in the mid-second millennium CE, the society dwindled to less than one-fifth of that by the time of European contact in the eighteenth century. Multiple factors led to this. The population had ballooned to a point where it could not be easily sustained. The introduction of Polynesian rats had adversely affected the forest's ecosystem. And, finally, the decrease of island foliage had led to a decrease in rainfall from the lack of condensation, which, in turn, caused a greater decrease in foliage and a vicious cycle of deforestation. The depletion in resources brought about civil strife and violence among the inhabitants of the island.

When Europeans first made contact with the inhabitants of the Easter Island, the construction of the moai had long since ceased, a sign of the society's decline; however, most of the statues were still standing upright. In the following centuries, all of the moai would be toppled over, a sign of the island's loss of autonomy and further demise. Eleven or possibly more have been removed from the island. Slave traders decimated the island's populations. Christian missionaries converted those who remained, devastating the Rapa Nui culture that had survived. It is not known who exactly toppled all of the moai, but in recent years, a restoration process has begun, with dozens now standing back on their platforms.

## RECENT DISCOVERIES AND CURRENT STATUS

Rapa Nui National Park on Easter Island is a UNESCO World Heritage Site. Restorations of the island's moai and other Rapa Nui sites are ongoing.

*Anthony Vivian*

*See also:* Indigenous Australian Cultures; Lapita People.

## FURTHER READING

Cardinali, Sonia Haoa, Kathleen B. Ingersoll, Daniel W. Ingersoll Jr., and Christopher M. Stevenson, eds. 2019. *Cultural and Environmental Change on Rapa Nui*. London: Routledge.
Fischer, Steven Roger. 2006. *Island at the End of the World: The Turbulent History of Easter Island*. London: Reaktion Books.

Kjellgren, Eric. 2001. *Splendid Isolation: Art of Easter Island*. New York: Metropolitan Museum of Art.

van Tilburg, Jo Anne. 1994. *Easter Island: Archaeology, Ecology and Culture*. Washington, DC: Smithsonian Institution Press.

# Ephesus

Located on the west coast of Asia Minor (modern-day Turkey), Ephesus was built at the mouth of the Caÿster River. It flourished as a Greek port city in the fifth and fourth centuries BCE and later as a Roman city during the imperial period. During its long history, the city changed locations several times but remained an important center for trade. Due to the silting of the river, however, the city was no longer viable as a port and was eventually abandoned in the medieval period. It is remarkably well preserved today and includes a massive ancient theater, among other monuments.

In addition to its economic influence, Ephesus was also a cultural and religious hub. The city's Temple of Artemis was a massive structure and deemed one of the Seven Wonders of the Ancient World. And Ephesus was the site of a burgeoning Christian community, visited by Paul the Apostle in the first century and the site of anti-pagan violence after the spread of Christianity.

## INHABITANTS

The original settlement of Ephesus was by groups Indigenous to Asia Minor, including the Anatolians and Carians, and evidence for its occupation date back to around 6000 BCE. The site of the Greek city of Ephesus was occupied from at least the Bronze Age but grew in status when the migrations of Ionian Greeks began around 1200 BCE. According to Greek mythology, the city was founded by the Athenian prince Androclos in the eleventh century BCE after consulting the Oracle at Delphi. This myth may have some basis in reality, as the Ionians are believed to have originated in Attica before settling in Asia Minor. One of four traditional Greek tribal groups, the Ionians spoke and wrote in the Ionic dialect of Ancient Greek and settled the central coast of Asia Minor, a region that would come to be known as Ionia.

During this early period, Ephesus was periodically ruled by tyrants. The Cimmerians, a people originally from the Caucasus, attacked and destroyed much of the city in 650 BCE. The Lydians took over the region in 560 BCE, and under the control of King Croesus, the city experienced an influx of wealth and prosperity. Croesus enlarged the city's size, contributed to the construction of monuments, and increased the population.

## HISTORICAL BACKGROUND

The Lydians were conquered by the Persians in 547 BCE, but Ephesus remained relatively autonomous in the sixth and fifth centuries BCE. The city was momentarily a member of the Delian League, an association of Greek city-states led by Athens, but revolted around 412 BCE to side with Sparta. The city's status fluctuated in the ensuing years under both Spartan and Persian control and finally came under Macedonian rule when Alexander the Great conquered the region in 333 BCE.

Ephesus again operated as an autonomous trade hub until the death of Alexander. Following the ensuing disintegration of the Macedonian Empire, Lysimachus came to rule Ephesus. In 290, this Macedonian general resettled the city to a new location two miles southwest. Lysimachus brought in new colonists from nearby Ionian cities and renamed the city Arsineia, after his wife, Arsinoe. The name did not stick, and after the death of Lysimachus, the city's residents reverted its name back to Ephesus.

During the Hellenistic period, Ephesus was at its most prosperous. It was under the control of Pergamum, a client state of the Romans, until 133 BCE. In that year, King Attalus of Pergamon died and left the city to Rome in his will. In 88 BCE, Mithridates of Pontus rebelled against Rome, leading to the sack of Ephesus by the Roman general Sulla. Aside from this brief period under the control of Mithridates, the city stayed under Roman control for the remainder of its existence.

In the first century BCE, Ephesus was a prominent trade hub and singled out by Emperor Augustus to be the seat of Rome's government in the province of Asia. During this time, a triumphal arch and impressive aqueduct were built, embellishments that spoke to its important status. Ephesus experienced damage from an earthquake in 17 CE but continued as an economic center in the region.

## CULTURE AND SOCIETY

Ephesus had a vibrant culture with a large population that spoke to its importance in the region. From its large theater, which could hold an audience of around 25,000 people, we can estimate that the city's population was around 250,000 at its height. It was a center of philosophy and learning throughout its history, home to the pre-Socratic philosopher Heraclitus as well as the Library of Celsus. Built in the second century CE, this library was the third largest in antiquity.

The city's most impressive monument was the temple dedicated to the goddess Artemis (the Artemision), deemed one of the Seven Wonders of the Ancient World by ancient writers. Artemis had a special relationship with Ephesus, as the Ephesians believed that her birthplace was near the city, and the grand temple constructed to her is one of the most impressive of the ancient world. In its largest iteration, the temple measured roughly 425 by 225 feet and contained 127 columns. Its frieze depicted scenes of Amazons, who were sheltered at Ephesus according to Greek mythology. The temple contained a wooden cult statue of Artemis, presumably depicted covered in eggs, suggesting her role as a fertility goddess.

The temple went through several stages of rebuilding during its long history. The earliest version dates to the Bronze Age but was destroyed by a flood in the seventh century BCE. The temple was then rebuilt around 550 BCE and again destroyed by arson in 356 BCE. When Alexander the Great passed through Ephesus, he offered to pay for the temple's construction. But the Ephesians refused, wishing to rebuild it through their own funding and initiative.

Ephesus also played a prominent role in early Christianity. Mary, the mother of Jesus, and Saint John are both said to have retired in Ephesus. And the Cave of

Seven Sleepers is an important site near the city where a group of Christian martyrs hid to escape persecution. Paul the Apostle spent three years in Ephesus, founding a church and expanding the city's sizable population of Christians, and his Letter to the Ephesians is included as part of the New Testament. In 57 CE, however, he was met with resistance by a group of vendors who sold small souvenir statues of Artemis. These statues were a lucrative business, and the vendors saw Paul and his teachings as a threat. Paul decided to leave Ephesus after this event.

## DEMISE

Ephesus was sacked by the Goths in the third century CE but continued to be a site of imperial patronage. For example, in the fourth century, Emperor Constantine constructed a new public bath, and Emperor Arcadius rebuilt the street from the theater to the harbor. Emperor Theodosius (r. 379–395), however, instituted anti-pagan policies and closed temples and schools in the city. Christians destroyed the Temple of Artemis, an act indirectly sanctioned by the emperor.

Ephesus still continued to be a site of cultural importance in this later period. Imperial officials periodically organized meetings of clergy to work out issues of orthodoxy and church doctrine. At the Council of Ephesus in 431, the teachings of Nestorius were declared heresy, while the cult of the Virgin Theotokos ("Godbearer") was found suitable. In addition, Emperor Justinian built the Basilica of Saint John in Ephesus in the sixth century.

The slow silting of the harbor eventually led to the city's decline and to a steady decrease in population. Ephesus was a relatively small town by the time it was captured by Seljuk Turks in 1090. Despite a short period of resurgence under the Turks, who stationed a naval force in the nearby harbor, the city was ultimately abandoned after the fourteenth century.

## RECENT DISCOVERIES AND CURRENT STATUS

Located three miles inland from the Aegean coast due to the silting of the harbor since it was abandoned, Ephesus is today a UNESCO World Heritage Site.

*Chris Bingley*

See also: Athens; Constantinople; Rome.

## FURTHER READING

Foss, Clive. 1979. *Ephesus after Antiquity: A Late Antique, Byzantine, and Turkish City.* Cambridge: Cambridge University Press.
Jones, A. H. M. 1940. *The Greek City: From Alexander to Justinian.* Oxford: Oxford University Press.
Koester, Helmut, ed. 2004. *Ephesos, Metropolis of Asia: An Interdisciplinary Approach to Its Archaeology, Religion, and Culture.* Cambridge, MA: Harvard University Press.
Meeks, Wayne. 1983. *The First Urban Christians: The Social World of the Apostle Paul.* New Haven, CT: Yale University Press.

# G

## Giza

The pyramids of Giza may be one of the most famous monuments in the world. They are deeply associated with Egypt around the world and are the last remaining "wonders" of the original Seven Wonders of the Ancient World. Both scholars and the general public have been fascinated by the pyramids for hundreds of years. Common questions include, How were they constructed? For what purpose? And, what does the overall complex at Giza represent?

The three main pyramids at Giza, along with the equally well-known Great Sphinx of Giza, were built during the Old Kingdom era (ca. 2686–2181 BCE) by pharaohs of the Fourth Dynasty. Some consider this period to have been the golden age of ancient Egypt.

### INHABITANTS

The pyramids at Giza were built over several decades by three different Egyptian pharaohs; the origin of the Sphinx is still a matter of intense scholarly debate. It is often thought that the pyramids were built by slaves, but archaeological evidence makes it clear that this was not the case. During the time of construction, around 2400 and 2500 BCE, the geography of Egypt differed markedly from what it is today. Giza was not sandy desert; rather, the area was fertile farmland, and Egypt was an agricultural community. About two months out of the year, the Nile River flooded the area so thoroughly that the farmers could not work. During that time, the pharaohs kept them fed in exchange for completing immense building projects. This practice likely began before the pyramids and continued through the end of the Ptolemaic dynasty (305–30 BCE), when the country was occupied by Rome.

Archaeologists have uncovered vast worker complexes around the Giza pyramids that offer clear evidence that the workers lived nearby to facilitate construction. The number of animal bones buried nearby indicate that the workers were well fed, and the graves of workers have skeletons that show expertly mended bones; the workers had access to medical care and were probably well treated, despite stories to the contrary.

### HISTORICAL BACKGROUND

Egypt during the Old Kingdom (ca. 2575–2130 BCE) represented an age of economic prosperity, social stasis, and technical innovation. The Egyptians of this

The Pyramid of Khufu is the oldest and largest of all of the pyramids in Egypt. Constructed in the mid-third millennium BCE, the pyramid, together with the Pyramids of Khafre and Menkaure, is one of the three Great Pyramids of Giza. (Jupiterimages)

period maintained some trade with Syria and other parts of Western Asia, but there do not appear to have been extensive contacts between Egypt and Mesopotamia. Such contacts do not seem to have greatly influenced Egyptian culture, as it maintained its own unique style.

Some of Egypt's earliest pharaohs built pyramids designed as tombs and places of devotion, but not on the scale that the Fourth Dynasty rulers did. All of the Old Kingdom pharaohs erected monuments to symbolize their wealth and renown. Reverence for the pharaoh was virtually absolute, as his (or her) person was considered divine. Monuments to the pharaohs indicated their importance to the world and their legacy for future generations. Giza, in fact, was never a city per se but merely a necropolis—that is, a place to bury the dead and honor them by means of monumental funerary structures. It was literally a "city of the dead," the meaning of *necropolis*.

There are three major pyramids (and associated pyramid complexes) at Giza, each constructed by a different pharaoh. All of the main structures are aligned precisely along east–west lines. The Great Pyramid of Khufu stands 481 feet high, is constructed of approximately 2.3 million limestone and granite blocks, and was completed around 2560 BCE. The next tallest, Khafre's pyramid, stands 448 feet high, has fewer blocks than Khufu's but contains some blocks weighing nearly 100 tons, and was completed around 2530. The Great Sphinx—a lion's body with a pharaoh's head—belongs to Khufu's pyramid complex; it is 240 feet long and 66 feet high. Finally, Menkaure's pyramid is 204 feet tall and was completed in about 2510 BCE.

## CULTURE AND SOCIETY

Modern scholars have debated for decades about how the Great Pyramid (Khufu's pyramid), with its thousands of tons of stone, could have been constructed. While many details about the pyramid's design are preserved, there are hardly any records of the technology used to move the stones. This could possibly mean that the method was so common as to not require mention, or it could mean, simply, that those records have not survived or have not yet been located.

The principal methods thought to have been used in constructing the pyramids are ramps built along the sides of the main structure or a pully system that ran through parts of the interior or unfinished areas of the pyramid, perhaps both. Neither method seems entirely feasible to some researchers, as the weight of the stones and the amount of friction involved, even with the use of wooden pallets or sand as a lubricant, would seem prohibitive. Questions remain, too, about how the massive stones were cut at the quarry and how they were transported to the building site. For cutting tools, the ancient Egyptians would have been limited to copper or bronze—both malleable metals—along with stone and wood. And transporting the rough-cut stone would have been as difficult as cutting it. To this day, many questions regarding Egyptian construction techniques remain unanswered.

It has long been assumed that the pyramids were designed as tombs for their pharaohs, yet some researchers have cast doubt on this use—at least in the case of Giza. No human remains have been found within the pyramids, causing some observers to speculate that the structures may have had some other religious or metaphysical purpose. On the other hand, looting and desecration of tombs was common in earlier times; grave robbing was one of the few crimes that could lead to capital punishment. It is quite possible, even likely, that the pharaohs were entombed within their pyramids, only to have their bodies (and grave goods) removed or desecrated later.

The Egyptians believed that their earthly world was a mirror of the celestial one and that to live happily in the afterlife, one needed to be remembered in this world. Constructing giant stone monuments would have been a way to achieve this. In addition, many smaller pyramids dedicated to lesser figures have been found in recent decades, suggesting that pharaohs were not the only ones who hoped to live on.

## DEMISE

The seemingly changeless world of the Old Kingdom ended around 2130 BCE, owing to several different factors. There were rivalries among the nobles in the provinces. There was the economic strain resulting from the many enormous building projects. And there were the inevitable crop failures that left the society depleted and dissatisfied. With the breakdown of central authority, a transition period opened that saw provincial governors vying among themselves for power. It was not until around 2055 BCE, when Mentuhotep II conquered Lower Egypt and reunited the country, that peace began to return. (Yet, unification took another twenty-five years to solidify, thus starting the Middle Kingdom period.)

As for the pyramids at Giza, although they are still standing, they have suffered heavily in the thousands of years since they were built. The pyramids were originally covered with a polished limestone facade that was such a bright white that the sun gleaming off it was blinding. By now, however, virtually all of the limestone surface has fallen away or been removed; much of it was used in later construction projects in Cairo. Simple erosion and time have caused significant damage to the stone structures. The pharaoh Ramesses the Great took an interest in the Giza pyramids during his reign, about a thousand years after the pyramids had been built; he had a small temple constructed in front of the Sphinx to honor his predecessors' legacy. Ramesses's fourth son, Khaemweset, never ruled Egypt but was dedicated to preserving the Giza site over time.

When the Romans occupied Egypt, interest in the great monuments faded. The Romans' focus was Alexandria, the cosmopolitan city where trade and agriculture flourished. It was not until Napoleon's campaign in Egypt in the late eighteenth century that European scholars and scientists became aware of the pyramids and other Egyptian monuments. Egyptology became a popular subject, and both professional and amateur archaeologists began to search the sands for historical artifacts. Early archaeologists, however, were often no better than grave robbers themselves; some Europeans were said to have smashed any artifacts they found that they did not intend to send back to their university or museum.

Flinders Petrie, often thought of as the first modern archaeologist, worked in Egypt from the late 1800s to the early 1900s. He was the first to fully excavate the Great Pyramid of Giza, along with many other monuments in Egypt. Because of his work, modern students know more about the pyramids than they ever otherwise would.

## RECENT DISCOVERIES AND CURRENT STATUS

As noted, constructing the pyramids entailed moving huge quantities of stone. Little knowledge had accrued regarding the details of this process until 2013, when a cache of papyrus documents discovered in the Egyptian desert near the Red Sea was found to include the journal of an official named Merer, who was involved in transporting limestone along the Nile River. The journal describes the process of building of the Great Pyramid at Giza. Researchers have learned that, rather than transporting the limestone blocks overland, workers transported them along the Nile River. It seems that some ancient canals were used along with transport boats. It is likely that the blocks were then transported to the construction site by wooden sleds, with wet sand placed in front of the sled to reduce friction. Researchers also discovered that the water table below Giza would have been much higher when the pyramids were constructed, thus allowing easier access to water throughout the transport and building process.

While the Giza pyramids are undoubtedly the most famous, they were not the first pyramids in Egypt. Khufu's father tried several times to build a successful pyramid but never managed to get the angles right; the Red Pyramid and the Bent Pyramid are both examples of his attempts. Near the Bent Pyramid, archaeologists have found evidence of a structure that dates back to the Thirteenth Dynasty, well after Khufu and his sons were building their pyramids. This structure appears to have been the burial chamber of a royal princess, but the archaeologists have struggled to find out more about her, as the name on the coffin has been badly damaged. Erasing someone's name was thought to be the worst thing one could do to an enemy, as their name needed to be spoken for the person to reach the afterlife. Egyptophiles have said that if they can decipher and speak the princess's name, the ancient Egyptians will know she has achieved immortality.

Giza was made a UNESCO World Heritage Site in 1979. It remains one of the most heavily visited sites in the world, and the main threats to it come from excessive tourist traffic together with the ravages of time and the elements.

*Michael Shally-Jensen*

*See also:* Memphis and Saqqara.

## FURTHER READING

Hawass, Zahi. 1998. *The Secrets of the Sphinx: Restoration Past and Present.* Cairo: American University in Cairo Press.
Romer, John. 2013. *A History of Ancient Egypt: From the First Farmers to the Great Pyramid.* New York: Thomas Dunne Books.
Taylor, John. 2014. *The Great Pyramid: Why Was It Built—and Who Built It?* New York: Cambridge University Press.
Thompson, Jason. 2015. *Wonderful Things: A History of Egyptology.* Cairo: American University in Cairo Press.

## Granada

Today, Granada is both a modern city and the name of a province in southeastern Spain. The city is situated on the Genil River, at the foot of the Sierra Nevada mountains, about 120 miles southeast of Córdoba, the onetime capital of Muslim-era Al-Andalus (Andalusia). Granada, too, was the capital of the former Moorish kingdom of Granada, which is sometimes called Upper Andalusia. Indeed, it was the last stronghold of the Moors—the Muslims of Iberia—in Western Europe. The city attracts many tourists, who come to see its Moorish antiquities and famous buildings. It is perhaps best known as the site of the great palace the Alhambra.

### INHABITANTS

The label *Moor* (*Moro*, in Spanish) derives from *Mauretania*, the Roman name for a region in Northwest Africa that stretched from the western half of present-day Algeria to northern Morocco and the Atlantic Ocean (and not to be confused with the present-day nation of Mauritania). As early Islam swept across North Africa, it brought under its wing the Berbers of this region. It was a Berber-majority "Moorish" army that invaded Spain in 711, pushing the Visigoths further north into the peninsula. Between then and the time of the Christian reconquest of the area in the fifteenth century, the Moors were the dominant political and military force, establishing grand courts and building spectacular architectural works. The center of Moorish civilization was southern Spain, or Al-Andalus, and it was there that the so-called Moorish style of art and architecture developed before spreading northward and also back into North Africa.

> **Tartessos**
>
> Unlike many other mythic cities discussed in this volume, Tartessos appears to have been a historical settlement; however, we mainly know about it through its ancient mythologized form. It was a port city that controlled the swath of land that surrounded it on the southern Iberian Peninsula, west of the Strait of Gibraltar. It was a prosperous trading hub, specializing in the exportation of tin. As a necessary and relatively hard-to-find component of bronze, tin was an important and lucrative trading material in the Bronze Age and beyond. Tartessos was a part of Mediterranean trade networks that also included the Phoenicians, Greeks, and others. To the Greeks, Tartessos was outside of the Strait of Gibraltar—or as they knew it, the Pillars of Heracles—which rendered it exotic and mystical. Tartessos has been falsely identified as the historical site for the mythical city of Atlantis.

Iberian Christians who lived under Moorish rule were called Mozarabs; they spoke the Arabic-influenced vernacular language of Andalusia and adopted elements of Arabic culture, yet they remained unconverted to Islam. A Sephardic Jewish population was also present in the province and featured prominently in Granada.

## HISTORICAL BACKGROUND

In ancient times, Granada was a small Iberian settlement and later a Roman town; it did not become historically significant until it came under the influence of the Moors. Egged on by Arab invaders of the Umayyad caliphate, the Berbers accepted Islam and formed a large army to bring the new faith to the Iberian Peninsula. They founded an emirate in Córdoba in 756, which later was expanded into a caliphate (929–1031) separate from the main caliphate (then under the Abbasids) in Baghdad. Many Iberian Christians of the Eastern Visigothic tradition at first lived peacefully under the Islamic rulers. This is attested by the Byzantine and Visigothic elements visible in one of the most important Umayyad monuments, the Great Mosque of Córdoba (begun in 785); the mosque followed the traditional Islamic plan but employed reused Roman columns to support elaborate horseshoe-shaped arches that were later decorated by craftsmen working in a new syncretic style. Also from the tenth century, on the outskirts of Córdoba, the Medina Azahara, an expansive, richly decorated, fortified palace-city, served as the caliphate's headquarters.

The Moors made Granada into a notable city as well. Between 1031 and 1090, it was ruled by a local dynasty, the Zirids. Around the same time, the Córdoban caliphate began to break up into warring factions. During the late eleventh and early twelfth centuries, two Berber dynasties known for their warlike tendencies and religious fervor held power, successively, in North Africa and Spain. Granada fell to the Almoravids in 1090, who restored a centralized Moorish government; numerous palaces were constructed under their rule. In the twelfth century the Almohads, an even more aggressive and fanatical religious faction, established themselves across North Africa and far into Spain.

Almohad attacks on Christian cities persisted into the early thirteenth century. By then, Granada was a sizable urban center protected by the Alcazaba citadel and an elaborate system of walls. After the Battle of Al-Uqab (or the Battle of Las Navas de Tolosa) in 1212, the Almohads fell to Christian forces, and Granada passed to the Nasrid dynasty, the last Moorish Muslim rulers in the region. The Nasrids reigned for 250 years and built the great palace of the Alhambra and other structures. The city was heavily fortified and had twenty towers in the surrounding area to defend it from attack. During the reign of Mohammed V (1354–1391), Granada reached its peak. Beginning in the latter part of the fifteenth century, it faced challenges from feuding families and began to weaken.

## CULTURE AND SOCIETY

Granada's population was a mixture of Arabs, Berbers, and Iberians (Spaniards) and three faiths: Islam, Judaism, and Christianity. Each group lived in its own quarter in the city, a standard arrangement in medieval times.

The Nasrid palace-city known as the Alhambra, dating from the fourteenth century, is the most renowned of Moorish architectural works, with its spacious gardens, attractive colonnaded courts, and spectacular vaulted halls. It and most of the structures around it on Alhambra hill were built by the Granadan Moors between 1238 and 1358; however, Emperor Charles V (Charles I of Spain, r. 1516–1556) built a palace adjoining the Alhambra.

The name *Alhambra* means "red" (or "the red" in Arabic); it refers to the sun-dried bricks used to build the original citadel, known as the Alcazaba. As seen today, only the citadel's outer walls, towers, and ramparts are visible. The adjacent palace of the Alhambra, entered through the Gate of Judgment, features a series of halls, courtyards, and galleries. One of the most impressive spaces is the Hall of the Ambassadors, a throne room for sultans. Another is the Court of the Lions, a large open space with a fine alabaster basin and fountain. Then there is the Hall of the Abencerrajes (derived from the name of a legendary sultan), crowned with an elaborate honeycombed dome, standing next to the Hall of the Two Sisters, so named because of the pair of white marble slabs that form its foundation. The Court of the Myrtles is notable for its long central pond skirted by plantings of myrtle. Of the outlying buildings, the Generalife, a thirteenth-century structure used as a summer palace by the sultans, is the most famous.

Granada also features numerous buildings of note erected by Christian leaders after the conquest of the city in 1492. Moorish influence nevertheless continued thereafter, with a variety of city gates, churches, synagogues, palaces, and castles displaying the so-called Mudéjar (postconquest) style in regions as far apart as Andalusia, Castile, and Aragon. The region can be said to exemplify a medieval form of multiculturalism, even as ethnic differences and enmities were apparent.

## DEMISE

Granada was the last city held by the Moors of Spain. In 1492, it fell to the Christian armies of Ferdinand and Isabella, who jointly ruled a now united Spain.

Jews and Muslims were expelled by the Crown, and Granada was made part of the Kingdom of Castile. The original Moorish town suffered during this transition, as new churches, monasteries, and other Christian edifices arose. In the end, however, Granada experienced decline under its Christian overseers. The city was especially impacted by the loss of residents following the Crown's expulsion of the Moriscos—Spanish Moors who converted to Christianity but never were trusted by the government—in 1610. It was not until the nineteenth century that the city again began to prosper in a new, more modern era.

### RECENT DISCOVERIES AND CURRENT STATUS

The Alhambra palace, together with the gardens of the Generalife (the summer residence) and the medieval Albaycín quarter, became a UNESCO World Heritage Site in 1984. Other notable sites in the city include the renaissance cathedral (begun 1523), with the tombs of Ferdinand of Aragon and Isabella of Castile, and the palace (unfinished) of their grandson Charles V of the Holy Roman Empire. The University of Granada was chartered in 1531 and remains a public university today. A new Mosque of Granada, overlooking the Alhambra, was inaugurated in 2003.

Historical research continues to fill out details of Moorish culture in Spain. Researchers recently made a 3D rendering of the medieval warlord Ali Atar's Nasrid sword to preserve the artifact digitally as well as physically. Atar, Lord of Zagra, was the father-in-law of the sultan of Granada, King Boabdil, the last sultan of the Nasrid dynasty. The sword was taken after the ninety-year-old Atar's death at the Battle of Lucena, in Córdoba, in 1483.

*Michael Shally-Jensen*

*See also:* Carthage; Rome; Syracuse.

### FURTHER READING

Constable, Olivia Remie. 2018. *To Live Like a Moor: Christian Perceptions of Muslim Identity in Medieval and Early Modern Spain.* Philadelphia: University of Pennsylvania Press.
Flood, Timothy. 2019. *Rulers and Realms in Medieval Iberia, 711–1492.* Jefferson, NC: McFarland & Co.
Irwin, Robert. 2004. *The Alhambra.* Cambridge, MA: Harvard University Press.
Nash, Elizabeth. 2005. *Seville, Córdoba, and Granada: A Cultural History.* New York: Oxford University Press.

## Great Zimbabwe

Today, Great Zimbabwe consists of impressive stone ruins in southern Zimbabwe, but in its day, it was an important religious and trading center that flourished from about 1100 to 1450 CE. The site is situated seventeen miles southeast of Masvingo. The size of the ruins and their relatively good state of preservation distinguish them from most others in this region of Africa. Nevertheless, they are part of an assortment of early Shona states and kingdoms whose leaders erected walled settlements across Zimbabwe, Botswana, Mozambique, and Transvaal.

The main structure is known as the Great Enclosure. It is made up of an elliptically shaped freestanding outer wall of granite blocks more than 800 feet in circumference and up to 32 feet high. It encloses the remains of several huts, associated compounds, and a conical tower, which may have been a grain bin as well as a symbol of chieftainship. Three entrances are present and partly reveal the wall's great thickness—up to 20 feet. The compelling curvature of the wall echoes the contours of other elements at the site and is often remarked on by visitors. The neatly arranged granite bricks, or slabs, were locally sourced and, once sized, laid in regular courses using no mortar to hold them together. The wall inclines slightly inward to provide stability and strength.

Inside the main wall is a second wall, 350 feet long, that runs parallel with the circuit wall, separated by only 3 to 4 feet; the two structures thus form a long, curving passage. The corridor widens into a semi-enclosed area, popularly called the Sacred Enclosure, where the conical tower can be found, a 30-foot-high tapering cone of solid masonry with a base diameter of about 18 feet.

Another feature of the site is the Hill Complex, a boulder-covered hill some 300 feet above the Sacred Enclosure. Steep stone steps lead up to and through crevices in the rock precipices, on top of which are large parapet walls of great strength.

Below both main structures is an area known as the Valley Ruins, which features a number of remains of smaller stone buildings and clay houses and walls.

The name *Zimbabwe* is generally assumed to be a Bantu term meaning "houses of stone" or "venerated houses." Other lesser *zimbabwes* dot the region. The modern Republic of Zimbabwe takes its name from such ruins, with particular reference to Great Zimbabwe.

## INHABITANTS

The Hill Complex has yielded evidence of up to five occupation periods. The earliest, made up of simple Iron Age farmers, flourished in the fourth century CE. Of chief interest in later periods, the Karanga peoples (a Shona subgroup) settled at the hill site about 950 and built the first stone-walled enclosures there some fifty years later. As their trading activities increased, Zimbabwean society became more complex and was led by prominent chiefs, who erected the imposing elliptical walls and other structures for their protection. The walled enclosures were originally filled with earth-and-clay (*daga*) "huts" or houses. Over the centuries, their reconstruction caused rising levels of debris, in some cases up to several feet thick. This made it necessary to occasionally raise the height of associated wall structures. At its peak, about 15,000 people lived around the stone buildings, spread over an area of over 1,800 acres. At different periods, various Shona tribes rose and fell in prominence. There was likely a marked division of labor and differences of status between men and women.

## HISTORICAL BACKGROUND

The age and origin of Great Zimbabwe have only slowly come into view, after a century and a half of excavation and research. Archaeological assessment was hindered by the depredations of early English gold hunters, who were prompted by reports from medieval Arab chroniclers concerning ancient gold mining at the site. One early theory was that the buildings were erected by Phoenician prospectors sometime between 2000 BCE and the early Christian era. Another was that Great Zimbabwe was the legendary city of Ophir, the site of King Solomon's mines. A third, put forth by the German geologist Carl Mauch in the 1870s, was that the structures had originally housed the biblical Queen of Sheba; Mauch went so far as to claim that they replicated the queen's palace in Jerusalem. (Sheba also played a role in the founding myth of another African empire, namely, Aksum in Ethiopia.)

All these theories were overturned by subsequent scientific excavations, which definitively showed that Great Zimbabwe was of native origin and of premedieval and medieval age. The underlying premise of all such bogus cultural histories was that unsophisticated African peoples lacked the ability to create such impressive structures; therefore, the site must have been designed and built by civilized foreigners. These types of racist myths persisted even after the colonial era. Indeed, Rhodesia, under white rule (prior to its becoming Zimbabwe), perpetuated them through censorship and deliberate distortion of the evidence.

At Great Zimbabwe, sustained occupation began around the fourth century CE by people using iron and living in pole-and-*daga* huts, but without stone walling. These people were replaced in the ninth century by new settlers responsible for the earliest examples of granite walling. The great stone monuments were not begun and maintained until the 1200s or 1300s, as trade networks expanded and wealth grew.

## CULTURE AND SOCIETY

Zimbabwe's inhabitants were involved in cattle husbandry, crop cultivation, and the exploitation of trade routes. They bartered gold and copper from local mines with traders from the East African coast. The wealth so produced allowed the rulers of Great Zimbabwe to extend their influence over a very large area, between the Zambezi River in the north to the Limpopo River in the south (i.e., much of the territory of modern Zimbabwe). Fine metal ornaments of African origin as well as imported glass beads and Chinese porcelain have been recovered at the site. Thus, Zimbabwe was an integral part of a much larger economic system that connected Southern Africa to far distant states.

Oral traditions as well as evidence from material culture suggest that Zimbabwe was an important ritual center associated with ancestor worship and rainmaking. Some structures feature double entrances, one for humans and the other for spirits. Besides facilitating rain, fertility, and good harvests, spirits had a hand in selecting and ratifying rulers. Carved clan symbols are among the artifacts with likely ritual significance that have been found in the Hill Complex, such as soapstone birds perched on pillars. Their design was later drawn on to fashion the Zimbabwean national emblem (which appears on the state flag).

## DEMISE

Great Zimbabwe's decline around 1450 had to do with ongoing ecological change and environmental degradation: an ever-growing population depleted life-sustaining resources and the availability of arable land, while a drier climate reduced the length of the growing season and altered the landscape generally. Competition from rival states also played a part. Rulers eventually abandoned the site and moved the inhabitants northward, closer to the Zambezi River. By the nineteenth century, the territory of the Kingdom of Zimbabwe was populated by the Ndebele people and subsequently taken over by the British South Africa Company, after which it became Southern Rhodesia and, ultimately, Zimbabwe.

## RECENT DISCOVERIES AND CURRENT STATUS

Work in the 1970s and 1980s served to stabilize endangered structures, obtain radiocarbon dates, and turn up selected new artifacts, among them coins imported from the port of Kilwa on Tanzania's Swahili Coast. In the 1990s and early 2000s, further efforts enhanced the picture of the rise and demise of Zimbabwean culture and the nature of daily life. More recently, some scholars working in related sites have suggested that distinctions of social status and the building of protective walls may have emerged 200 years earlier than had been thought.

Great Zimbabwe was designated a UNESCO World Heritage Site in 1986.

*Michael Shally-Jensen*

*See also:* Aksum; Kilwa.

## FURTHER READING

Ehret, Christophe. 2016. *The Civilizations of Africa: A History to 1800.* 2nd ed. Charlottesville: University of Virginia Press.

Le Quellec, Jean-Loïc. 2016. *The White Lady and Atlantis Ophir and Great Zimbabwe: Investigations of an Archaeological Myth.* Translated by Paul Bahn. Oxford: Archaeopress Publishing.

Vogel, Joseph O. 1994. *Great Zimbabwe: The Iron Age in South Central Africa.* New York: Garland.

# H

## Harappa and Mohenjo-Daro

Harappa and Mohenjo-Daro were the two largest cities of the Indus valley civilization, also known as the Harappan civilization, which flourished in and around present-day Pakistan. Mohenjo-Daro sits on the west bank of the Indus River about 300 miles upriver from where it issues into the Indian Ocean and about 17 miles south of the modern town of Larkana. The now seasonal Ghaggar-Hakra River west of Mohenjo-Daro was more active while the city was flourishing. The two rivers encompassed the city within a fertile midriver floodplain. The builders constructed the city on a high point that would loom above floods during the wet season, though the long centuries have left the site eroded and partially covered in silt. The ancient city once covered a little over a square mile.

Harappa is more than 400 miles northeast of Mohenjo-Daro, farther up into the Indus River valley. It is adjacent to the present-day village of Harappa, from which it got its name, and sixteen miles southwest of the town of Sahiwal. The ancient city of Harappa was built on the southern bank of the Ravi River, one of the Indus River's tributaries. It is a little less than fifty miles north of the Sutlej River, another Indus tributary. Excavations have been occurring longer at Harappa than at Mohenjo-Daro. The ancient city is estimated to have covered a little more than half of a square mile, rendering it about half the size of Mohenjo-Daro downriver.

### INHABITANTS

There is still much we do not know about the inhabitants of Harappa and Mohenjo-Daro. Mehrgarh was a neolithic site in the Indus River valley that some have seen as a predecessor to the Indus valley civilization. The inhabitants of Harappa and Mohenjo-Daro relied on agriculture, animal husbandry, and trade, but they decided to forgo rural settlements to live in these major urban centers that were largely unprecedented in magnitude. They had a distinctive script, but as it has not yet been deciphered, we are not certain what language they spoke. Some have posited that it was in the Dravidian family of languages, which still exist today, mostly in southern India and Sri Lanka. We do not know much of their religion. Some inscriptions seem to depict gods. Unlike the other two major Early Bronze Age settlements of Egypt and Mesopotamia, no known temples have been excavated. They may have worshipped outside or in buildings also used for other purposes.

## HISTORICAL BACKGROUND

The ancient cities of Harappa and Mohenjo-Daro constitute the two major urban centers of what we today call the Indus valley civilization. This civilization is thought to have existed from around 3300 to 1300 BCE, with a so-called mature phase, or high point, from 2600 to 1900 BCE. The Indus valley region, therefore, cradled one of the three earliest world civilization centers, along with two other river-based, fertile regions: Mesopotamia and Egypt. However, the Indus valley civilization covered a broader area than these other civilization centers. It is sometimes called the Harrapan civilization, after the site of Harappa. This is not because Harappa was the largest settlement—Mohenjo-Daro holds that distinction—but because it was the first site excavated.

The so-called Early Harappan Phase began around 3300 BCE. The population migrated more and more from the surrounding mountainous regions to the river valleys surrounding the Indus River and its tributaries. These early inhabitants cultivated peas, sesame, cotton, and other crops, and they domesticated a number of animals. Trade networks built up both within the Indus valley and with neighboring regions. Finally, these early Harappans developed metallurgy, gaining the ability to produce bronze, copper, lead, and tin. Eventually, the predictable floods, produced by the seasonal monsoons upriver, allowed the population to swell.

The Mature Harappan Phase, the high point of the Indus valley civilization, began around 2600 BCE and brought early cities and societal complexities to the region. The construction of Mohenjo-Daro and Harappa, like other urban centers

The Harrapan society is one of the oldest on earth. The extensive archaeological remains bear witness to their advanced drainage system. (Faysalkhalid | Dreamstime.com)

in the Indus valley civilization, have been dated to around the twenty-sixth century BCE. The cities are remarkably similar in nature. They are both planned cites built to form a grid, and they both feature an upper city—sometimes dubbed an acropolis or citadel—and lower city. Fortifications have been found at both sites, including walls at Harappa and guard towers at Mohenjo-Daro. Other settlements in the Indus valley civilization share these many similar characteristics, although they are smaller in size. Based on current excavations, Mohenjo-Daro grew to become the largest and most sophisticated city of the Indus valley civilization.

One of the most advanced features of Mohenjo-Daro, Harappa, and other locations from this civilization was their control of water. Ample wells provided drinking water for the inhabitants, while sophisticated sewage and drainage systems removed wastewater. Covered drains in private houses as well as in public places like streets could carry wastewater away. There is also evidence of baths, both public baths and baths in a few private residences. One advantage these cities had was their planned nature, which allowed urban designers to account for wells and drainage as they built the rest of the city. This is far easier than trying to add sufficient wells or sophisticated drainage systems to already built cities. As far as the present evidence shows, these urban centers boasted the world's first citywide drainage systems.

There is still a debate over just how centralized the leadership of the Indus valley civilization was. On the one hand, Mohenjo-Daro, Harappa, and other sites show remarkable similarities in their planned constructions. This suggests some sort of central leadership overseeing and coordinating the similar construction projects. Mohenjo-Daro has been put forward as a possible capital, as it is the largest of the settlements and sits in a relatively central location within the civilization. On the other hand, the Indus valley civilization stretched over a sweeping amount of territory, covering most of present-day Pakistan and parts of India and Afghanistan, making it considerably larger than the other two Early Bronze Age civilizations in Mesopotamia and Egypt. Some doubt that a centralized government could exert any serious control over such a wide span in the third millennium BCE.

## CULTURE AND SOCIETY

The peoples of Harappa, Mohenjo-Daro, and the other major settlements of the Indus valley civilization boasted a vibrant culture. Many artifacts have survived, made of stone, terra-cotta, bronze, and gold. Some of the more common pieces include seals, painted pottery, and statuettes. The four-and-a-half-inch Dancing Girl is a famous bronze statuette from Mohenjo-Daro dated roughly to the turn of the second millennium BCE.

Many artifacts, especially seals, contain intriguing inscriptions. The more than 4,000 inscriptions feature over 400 distinct symbols, known collectively as the Indus script or the Harappan script. Since most inscriptions are very short and none contain a second language, the Indus script has yet to be deciphered. Some have posited that it is not a complete writing system but includes symbols for certain clans, gods, and the like, but others have dismissed this theory. Some see the Indus script as a predecessor of the Brahmi script; others classify it as a Dravidian language.

Harrapan society depended on agriculture, animal husbandry, and extensive trade networks. Despite their advanced urban well and drainage systems, the settlements of the Indus valley civilization do not seem to have employed irrigation systems while farming, instead depending on the seasonal flooding of the regions' river system. Inhabitants of these settlements domesticated many types of animals, including water buffalos. Mohenjo-Daro may have been the location from where worldwide chicken domestication spread. Individuals from Harappa, Mohenjo-Daro, and the wider Indus valley civilization were avid traders. They particularly traded with Mesopotamian ports via the Indian Ocean and Persian Gulf.

## DEMISE

The Indus valley civilization began to decline around 1900 BCE and ceased to exist by 1300 BCE. Evidence suggests that Mohenjo-Daro was abandoned soon after the time when the entire civilization began its decline in 1900 BCE. Harappa, meanwhile, went into decline around the same time and was abandoned around 1300 BCE. Several theories have been put forward in attempts to explain the downfall of this civilization; the truth is likely some combination of them. Climate change seems to have played an influential role. The settlements relied on their rivers' seasonal floods, and scientists have shown a general increase in aridity, including a decrease in the monsoons upriver, in the second millennium BCE. Others have posited that the introduction of other cultures—such as the Cemetery H culture and the Aryans, among others—in the region may have overtaken the Indus valley civilization, possibly violently. Finally, some argue that decline is the wrong conceptualization and that the inhabitants of Mohenjo-Daro, Harappa, and other Indus valley settlements simply migrated to more rural settlements or to the rising civilizations in the East.

## RECENT DISCOVERIES AND CURRENT STATUS

Mohenjo-Daro is a UNESCO World Heritage Site, while Harappa is on UNESCO's Tentative List. Pakistan has submitted Harappa to become a World Heritage Site, but it is still under consideration. Harappa was rediscovered in the nineteenth century and has been excavated intermittently since. Excavations at Mohenjo-Daro began in earnest in the 1920s.

*Anthony Vivian*

*See also:* Babylon; Memphis and Saqqara; Thebes; Ur.

## FURTHER READING

Coningham, Robin, and Ruth Young. 2015. *The Archaeology of South Asia: From the Indus to Asoka, c. 6500 BCE–200 CE*. Cambridge: Cambridge University Press.
Habib, Irfan. 2015. *The Indus Civilization*. New Delhi: Tulika Books.
McIntosh, Jane. 2001. *A Peaceful Realm: The Rise and Fall of the Indus Civilization*. Boulder, CO: Westview Press.
Rao, Shikaripura Ranganatha. 1991. *Dawn and Devolution of the Indus Civilisation*. New Delhi: Aditya Prakashan.

# Hittites

The Hittites were an Indo-European (i.e., non-Semitic) people who played an important role in the Near East in the second millennium BCE. Their capital was Hattusa, in central Anatolia (Turkey), about 125 miles east of modern-day Ankara, near the present Turkish village of Boğazköy. The Hittites did battle with the Hurrians, the Egyptians, and the Assyrians while building a lasting culture or their own.

Hattusa was the center of Hittite rule from about 1600 BCE to 1200 BCE. At its height, the city covered over 400 acres. Its archaeological remains include a central citadel, with its royal and administrative buildings; five temple complexes spread out over the area; and a massive defensive wall famous for its great stone gates, one of them protected by a pair of sculpted lions and the other by a pair of massive sphinxes.

## INHABITANTS

The Hittites are a people mentioned in the Bible. They seem to have originally been migrant pastoralists living above the Black Sea. When they migrated into Anatolia, around 2300 BCE, the region was already occupied by another people (Hattians), whom the Hittites eventually absorbed. By about 1750 BCE, the Hittites had established a kingdom in central Anatolia. It flourished as a powerful empire in the fourteenth and thirteenth centuries BCE before being destroyed, probably by the so-called Sea Peoples.

## HISTORICAL BACKGROUND

Hittite history is divided into two periods, the Old Kingdom and the New Kingdom, or the Hittite Empire.

The founder of the Hittite Old Kingdom, according to ancient sources, was a man named Labarna, who is said to have set up his sons as governors of several conquered territories. Labarna's successor, Hattusili I (r. ca. 1680–1650 BCE), is credited with erecting the fortress city of Hattusa as the kingdom's capital. In the "Annals" of Hattusili I, it is related that the king made forays into northwestern Syria and eastward across the Euphrates River to the land called Arzawa, seeking control of trade routes. He was, however, largely frustrated by opposing forces. His son and successor, Mursili I (r. ca. 1620–1590 BCE), launched similar campaigns and achieved greater success, destroying Babylon (1595 BCE) and defeating the Hurrians on his march home.

Mursili's assassination a few years after his return, however, brought a period of chaos, insurrection, and power struggles. The Hittites lost possession of their territory in Anatolia and Syria. A leader named Telipinu, author of the valuable historical source *The Proclamation of Telipinu*, gained the throne around 1525 BCE and won back a measure of order. His reign is sometimes considered the start of a middle period in which Hittite strength waned and that of the Hurrians to the south and the Egyptians in the Levantine coastal region increased.

It was under Tudhaliya I, beginning about 1450 BCE, that Hittite power was restored and a new empire established. Tudhaliya I opened the southeastern routes to Syria and checked the Hurrian state of Mitanni. His reign, however, was followed by another period of decline. Tudhaliya's successors were unable to defend the Hittite heartland against repeated attacks from multiple directions.

In 1380 BCE, one of the greatest of Hittite kings, Suppiluliuma, recovered Isuwa (the upper Euphrates), destroyed Mitanni, and subjected northern Syria—specifically, the city-state of Carchemish—to Hittite rule. Egypt, too, nearly fell under Hittite political influence. The widow of Tutankhamen, Ankhesenamun, invited Suppiluliuma to send one of his sons to be her new husband, but the young man was murdered en route, ending the budding alliance.

Hittite expansion into western Anatolia took place under Mursili II, who reigned from about 1345 to 1310 BCE. Mursili kept a tight rein on the empire, even as Egypt renewed its interest in northern Syria. A great battle between the Egyptians under Ramesses II and the Hittites under Muwatalli II (r. ca. 1310–1294 BCE) unfolded at Kadesh (Qadesh, in modern Syria) about 1274 BCE. The Egyptian advance was put down, and under Hattusili III (r. ca. 1289–1265 BCE), a treaty was eventually signed between the two empires. In Anatolia itself, however, a number of vassal states began to reassert their independence. The previously weak Assyrians claimed Mitanni and moved into territory once controlled by the Hittites. Additional regional forces also arose to challenge Hittite power in the thirteenth century BCE. For example, the Ahhiyawa—which may be the Hittite term for the Achaeans, or Greeks—threatened Hittite power in far western Anatolia.

## CULTURE AND SOCIETY

The Hittites established the first known instance of an Indo-European kingdom, which went on to encompass vassal states within an imperial system. The empire's political organization was based largely on forms first developed in the Old Kingdom. Throughout the later empire, vassal kings, provincial governors, local officials, and the heads of various protectorates were linked through formal tribute requirements to the great king residing in Hattusa. Although the Hittite king was understood to be part of a powerful human clan, he also embodied the gods' will and was deified after death. After his death, the queen would remain in office, even after the king himself had been replaced. During his lifetime, the king served as a priest, judge, and military leader as well.

The power and influence exercised by the Hittites was largely owing to their military strength. As with many of their contemporaries, the Hittites relied heavily on the horse-drawn chariot. However, unlike the Egyptians, who used chariots as maneuverable platforms from which they fired arrows, the Hittites employed chariots as part of a mass formation designed to directly assault and demolish enemy lines. Hittite infantry troops also often proved superior to those of their enemies, particularly when it came to traveling over long distances in difficult terrain or in darkness; the element of surprise was often on their side.

The Hittite legal system recognized the rights and responsibilities of slaves. Nevertheless, slaves were commodities that could be bought and sold, and runaway slaves were expected to be returned to their masters. Slaves could be married to free persons, though in the case of a free woman marrying a slave, the woman sank in rank to the slave's level (this was not so in the case of a free man marrying a slave).

Perhaps the most striking feature of Hittite architecture is the use of huge defensive walls, notably around the city of Hattusa and its inner citadel. The same kind of massing can be seen in the design of temples in the capital and at other sites in the region. Relief sculptures decorated selected walls and gates, but the level of refinement in these sculptures is not as great as that in some of the Hittites' contemporaries. A comparable directness can be seen on royal seals, in statues, and on pottery reliefs. Much of the pottery, in fact, is unornamented. The most compelling examples are vessels in the shape of animals, especially bulls—a symbol of power.

The scribes of the Hittite Empire were familiar with Sumerian, Assyrian, and Babylonian texts and to a lesser extent with Egyptian works. Hittite culture thus represented something of a cosmopolitan approach to life in the ancient Near East. This is evidenced in the thousands of cuneiform tablets uncovered in the ruins of Hattusa. The Hittites left a fairly large body of native mythological tales as well as translations of foreign epics (Hurrian, Canaanite, and Babylonian). In the annals of the Hittite kings, the authors demonstrate an ability to go beyond simple chronology to present events as part of a narrative, involving cause and effect and the use of the past to comprehend the meaning of the present.

Hittite religion centered on a pantheon made up of hundreds of deities, many of them associated with particular localities in Anatolia. One of the paramount deities was the sun goddess Arinna, protectress of the royal dynasty. Her consort was the weather god of Hatti, from pre-Hittite times. In the later empire, strong Hurrian influence appeared with the worship of the goddess Hepat and the god Teshub; she was associated with the sun goddess and he with the weather god.

## DEMISE

It is not completely clear what caused the fall of the Hittite capital, Hattusa. Invaders from the west, usually identified with the Sea Peoples in Egyptian sources, were likely the catalyst for its end. The invading force cut off the northwestern trade route, destroyed Arzawa, and eventually cut off the southeastern route. Under such pressure, what remained of Hittite power was weakened and finally destroyed. Hattusa itself was ravaged by enemies from the northern hills, and by 1180 BCE, the empire was no more.

The Hittite presence did not end with the fall of Hattusa, however. Various successor dynasties set up at Tarhuntassa (location indeterminate) and at Carchemish on the upper Euphrates. Smaller so-called neo-Hittite states continued in southeast Anatolia and Syria for at least the next 500 years (ca. 700 BCE). These states were often in conflict with rival Aramean states, before both they and the Aramean states were absorbed into the Assyrian Empire. Passages from the Bible (2 Samuel and 1–2 Kings) that mention the "sons of Heth" likely refer to the neo-Hittite states of Syria. The Indo-European languages of Anatolia survived even longer in Lydia, Lycia, and Cilicia (all in the far west or south).

## RECENT DISCOVERIES AND CURRENT STATUS

Archaeologists began excavations at Hattusa in 1906, when the German researcher Hugo Winckler (who worked in both 1906–1907 and 1911–1912) uncovered a royal archive of about 10,000 cuneiform tablets. Since then, numerous Anatolian sites have been found to contain objects and inscriptions from the Hittite period. Today, the preserved archival material at Boğazköy, Turkey, represents the major source of information about Hittite history and culture.

Hattusa was made a UNESCO World Heritage Site in 1986. For decades, a pair of the most impressive stone sphinxes from the site were separated, one held by Germany and the other by Turkey. In 2011, however, the pair were reunited when Germany agreed to return its sphinx in exchange for continued access to archaeological sites in Turkey.

In 2013, an Israeli research team reported that a devastating drought could have been at the root of the regional turmoil surrounding the Hittites' demise. The team examined pollen grains in soil cores dating as far back as 3,500 BCE and found that between 1250 and 1100 BCE, evidence of oaks and pines associated with well-watered land virtually disappeared. The theory may help explain similar collapses experienced by Egyptian and Mycenaean cultures at that time (a phenomenon known as the Bronze Age collapse).

*Michael Shally-Jensen*

*See also:* Amarna; Babylon; Thebes.

## FURTHER READING

Bryce, Trevor. 2002. *Life and Society in the Hittite World*. New York: Oxford University Press.
Bryce, Trevor. 2019. *Warriors of Anatolia: A Concise History of the Hittites*. New York: Bloomsbury Academic.
Collins, Billie Jean. 2007. *The Hittites and Their World*. Atlanta: Society of Biblical Literature.
Macqueen, J. G. 1986. *The Hittites and Their Contemporaries in Asia Minor*. New York: Thames & Hudson.

## Ife

The town of Ife (pronounced ee'-fay; also called Ilé-Ifè) in southwestern Nigeria was the seat of an influential Yoruba kingdom from the eleventh to the seventeenth century CE. The best-known early urban center in the Nigerian forest, Ife is described in Yoruba traditions as the place where the world was created. Today, it remains important in Yoruba religious life as the location of many ancient shrines that are maintained by the *oni*, the ruler of Ife.

Ife is also known for the many striking art objects in copper alloy, terra-cotta, and stone uncovered there by researchers. The most notable are naturalistic portrait heads of ancient kings, cast in metal by the lost-wax process and dating from the twelfth to the fourteenth century. Scholars have suggested that these heads were probably attached to wooden figures representing dead leaders and used in secondary burial ceremonies. The modern settlement of Ife is located on top of the ancient site, making archaeological investigation a challenge.

### *Lagos*

The large and quickly growing metropolis of Lagos, Nigeria, stands at risk of extreme heat, rising sea levels, and saltwater intrusion.

Lagos spans from Lagos Island to other islands in Lagos Lagoon and the mainland, just off the Atlantic coast; the name *Lagos* comes from the Portuguese word for "Lakes." Lagos Island was settled by the Awori, a subset of the Yoruba people who have inhabited this region of West Africa, by the fifteenth century. The powerful Oyo Empire, also known as the Benin Empire, conquered the island and surrounding regions in the sixteenth century and called the city Eko, which remains its name to this day in the local Yoruba language. The region was plagued by European imperialism and the Atlantic slave trade. Even under the pretense of abolishing the slave trade, the British advanced their own material interests in the region and took control of the region for two centuries. In 1960, Nigeria gained its independence, and Lagos, long the capital of the British colony of Nigeria, became its capital. Although the capital has since moved to Abuja, Lagos remains the region's economic and cultural powerhouse, famous in particular for its music, nightlife, and film industries.

Lagos faces a climate battle on multiple fronts. Located near the equator, Lagos has a hot and humid climate, which stands to grow more dangerous as the globe warms. Built near sea level, Lagos is also confronted with the perils of a rising sea. While Lagos will face flooding and other typical symptoms of a rising sea, this trend presents an added danger for Lagos. The city is surrounded by fresh water at near sea level. As the sea levels rise, these lakes and other bodies of fresh water are in danger of saltwater intrusion, threatening the drinking supply of Lagos's massive and still growing population.

## INHABITANTS

The Yoruba are one of Nigeria's three largest ethnic groups. Their language, with its many dialects, belongs to the Volta-Niger subgroup of African languages. Yorubaland is now and has been in the past divided politically into distinct kingdoms, each centered on a capital city or town and headed by a hereditary king (*oni* or *oba*). Ife was the earliest of these and—besides developing into a thriving, sophisticated state—was remarkable for the centrality of its women in the area of trade. Ife society placed importance on seniority over gender; thus, women were not necessarily subordinate to men but rather controlled much of their own affairs and participated in trade and other areas of social life. Most Yoruba men were farmers, growing yams, corn, and millet as staples. Craftsmen worked in ironsmithing, leatherworking, glassmaking, bronze casting, and ivory and wood carving. Though some Yoruba were Muslims, belief in their traditional religion remained strong.

Ife was and is the sacred city of the Yoruba people, where, according to tradition, the god Oduduwa created the earth and established himself as *oni* (king). All later *oni* (or *oba*) are traditionally believed to be descended from the mythological ruler of Ife, the most important Yoruba cult center.

## HISTORICAL BACKGROUND

Both Yoruba legend and archaeological evidence suggest that people settled at the site of Ife during the last decades of the first millennium CE. By the eleventh century, it was a powerful kingdom ruled by a divine king. Its influence reached beyond Yorubaland, particularly in the areas of trade and artistic accomplishment. Beyond this, many details of this period of West African history are absent.

At its height, Ife operated as a large walled city with several large stone buildings, including a palace, workshops, and shrines. Some of the city's streets and courtyards were paved with potsherds and quartz pebbles. Courtyards featured shrines or altars consisting of low semicircular structures with central spaces for pottery vessels or other religious objects. Most houses were made of clay, or clay and wood, and thus disintegrated centuries ago.

With the arrival of the Portuguese in coastal Nigeria in the late fifteenth century, the written record regarding West African forest kingdoms commences, and the historical picture begins to change as a result of the encounter. The Europeans made use of existing trade networks and relied on coastal African traders as middlemen in trading with peoples of the interior—including trade involving enslaved people. European accounts and African oral traditions from this time describe a number of other states in the region, such as Asante (in modern Ghana), Dahomey (in the Republic of Benin), and Oyo (in Nigeria). The European presence created new opportunities and altered existing political realities for these states.

The Kingdom of Oyo was founded by the Yoruba people in the late 1400s or early 1500s. It was centered to the north of Ife in a drier, more open grassland area in what is called the western savanna. In the 1600s and 1700s, it became the most powerful state in West Africa, reaching its peak in about 1750, when it gained wealth by providing slaves to European traders on the Guinea coast (or Slave

Coast, as it was known). Oyo controlled a loosely knit empire that extended from the border of the Kingdom of Benin in the east, to the Kingdom of Dahomey in the west, and from the Niger River to the Atlantic Ocean in the south.

## CULTURE AND SOCIETY

Ife is widely known for its art, particularly the portrait sculptures that date back to the twelfth century and after. Ife bronzes, created by the lost-wax process, and terra-cotta heads rank with the world's finest naturalistic art and are highly valued by museums.

Ife art, centering on divine kingship, includes scores of ceramic heads, animals, and other ritual forms plus about thirty copper alloy or bronze-like pieces. These are mostly hollow cast heads, many featuring fine parallel score lines suggesting scarification patterns. Although somewhat idealized, the Ife heads are compellingly naturalistic and exquisitely executed. Many seem to be portraits modeled after living persons. There are also some castings of ceremonial objects along with a few half and full figures. The figures likely represent the *oni*, while the other objects relate to religious belief and rituals attending kingship.

With the demise of Ife, the center of casting shifted not to Oyo but to Kingdom of Benin, which comprised a mix of Edo, Itsekiri, Esan, Igbo, Yoruba, and other peoples. Benin bronzes were a product of the same lost-wax techniques but were more stylized than their naturalistic Yoruba predecessors.

## DEMISE

The holy city of Ife could not sustain itself in the face of the Portuguese presence and the rise of newer, more powerful kingdoms in the region. In a way, however, the Oyo Kingdom represented an extension of Ife, in that it had reportedly been founded by the last-born son of the same mythical being, Oduduwa, who had founded Ife.

Oyo itself began to fall apart in the late 1700s. By 1821, its *oni*'s authority was restricted to the area around the capital at Katunga, or Old Oyo. The city was destroyed by the Fulani ruler of Ilorin in 1837. A new capital was built to the south on the site of the present city of Oyo, but the wider kingdom was no more.

## RECENT DISCOVERIES AND CURRENT STATUS

Modern Ife betrays few signs of its glorious past. However, a museum on the grounds of the *oni*'s palace features many examples of Ife art. The Nigerian National Museum in Lagos houses a fine Ife copper mask and other works. In 2017, archaeologists discovered a large cache of 1,000-year-old glass beads in Ife that likely were used for decorative purposes, possibly including the adornment of the great metal heads.

*Michael Shally-Jensen*

*See also:* Timbuktu.

## FURTHER READING

*Archaeology*. 2017. "Evidence of 1,000-Year-Old Glass Production Found in Nigeria." June 13, 2017. https://www.archaeology.org/news/5654-170613-west-africa-glass-beads
Blier, Suzanne Preston. 2015. *Art and Risk in Ancient Yoruba: Ife History, Power, and Identity, c. 1300*. Cambridge: Cambridge University Press.
Drewal, Henry John. 2009. *Dynasty and Divinity: Ife Art in Ancient Nigeria*. Seattle: Museum for African Art.
Olupona, Jacob K. 2011. *City of 201 Gods: Ilé-Ifè in Time, Space, and the Imagination*. Berkeley: University of California Press.

## Indigenous Australian Cultures

The Indigenous Australian cultures are a diverse tapestry of peoples who have inhabited the continent of Australia for tens of thousands of years. The expansive landmass covers almost three million square miles, and the various cultures have adapted to the multifarious climates therein. Deserts and plateaus span most of the western and central regions. Tropical rain forests occupy the north of the continent, while a fertile plain stretches across the southeast. The Australian Alps, also in the southeast, receive large amounts of natural snow annually and are snow-capped for most of the year. In addition to the Australian continent, Indigenous Australian peoples have inhabited Tasmania, the large island off Australia's southeast shore, as well as various small islands to the continent's east and north. The Torres Strait Islands, however, which fall between Australia and New Guinea, are home to a group of Indigenous people different from Aboriginal Australians.

Indigenous Australian art still fills the landscape, standing testament to these cultures' heyday before British colonization. Rock art comprises the most famous and prevalent type. Made by painting or engraving, this art form transcends the many cultural differences, appearing across the continent and ranging in age from tens of thousands of years old to relatively recent. Stone arrangements are another common form of Indigenous Australian art found throughout the continent. These typically feature stones laid out in horizontal patterns, and some seem to have played roles within religious ceremonies.

### INHABITANTS

The people who have made up the Indigenous Australian cultures arrived to the continent over 50,000 years ago. Upon arriving either from New Guinea or the northwest, they spread across Australia and branched off into many different groups. The same peoples seem to have inhabited the continent for tens of thousands of years with little integration from the outside world. They inhabited the entire continent and surrounding islands and developed into hundreds of different cultures. One way to track the diversity of the Indigenous Australian cultures is through their many languages: These cultures included at least 250 different language families with 800 different individual dialects. Most peoples had nomadic or seminomadic lives, although some developed agriculture and lived in settled communities. The territories of these different peoples varied in size, with inland and desert peoples tending to inhabit greater swaths of territory and coastal regions typically showing more diversity.

*Sydney*

Extreme heat, rising sea levels, and increased risk of fire all threaten Sydney in the twenty-first century and beyond.

In the eighteenth century, the Cadigal people, an Aboriginal Australian group, inhabited the region around the natural harbor known today as Sydney Cove. In early 1788, the so-called First Fleet—a prison convoy—arrived and founded the colony of Sydney, the first British colony on Australia. Like the rest of the continent, the region of Sydney witnessed plenty of violence inflicted on the Aboriginal inhabitants by the British settlers. In particular, the Hawkesbury and Nepean Wars raged at the turn of the nineteenth century in Western Sydney. Sydney transformed from its humble beginnings as a prison colony to a world-renowned metropolis. One big era of advancement was during World War II, as Australia played a major role in the fight against Japan, and afterward, when the city experienced a major population boom. The famous Sydney Opera House first opened its doors in 1973, and since the 1970s, Sydney has grown into a cosmopolitan economic and cultural hub.

Sydney faces a range of different climate challenges in the coming decades. The Parramatta River and the Georges River, both of which are in fact estuaries, will see increased flooding as the sea levels rise, as will other parts of the sprawling coastal city. Sydney already experiences hot summers, commonly topping 100 degrees Fahrenheit in the summer months. As temperatures increase, future heatwaves stand to test residents' capacity to withstand extreme heat. Experts predict this increasing heat will be coupled with less precipitation, which will leave Sydney and the surrounding region more open to droughts and fires. Already, bushfires often threaten the city with swift damage and poor air quality.

## HISTORICAL BACKGROUND

Humans first arrived in Australia an astounding 50,000–70,000 years ago. Remains found in Australia are the oldest that have been found so far outside of Africa, the birthplace of the human race. Therefore, these remains are the oldest hard evidence we have for early migrations outside of Africa. At this time in earth's history, the sea levels were significantly lower than they are now, and Australia was consequently larger than it is today and connected by land to both New Guinea and Tasmania. Nevertheless, the first inhabitants of the continent would still have had to arrive by sea. Scholars debate the route they took, but whether they came from the north or the northwest, their sea journey made them the oldest human seafarers for which we have hard evidence. Scholars likewise disagree on whether that first migration was responsible for the entire Indigenous population. It used to be thought that three waves of migration took place. While some continue to support this argument, the leading theory today holds that the future population arrived in one mass migration, with perhaps as many as thousands of people coming at once.

While several archaeological sites bear witness to the presence of early humans on Australia, the remains at Madjedbebe, in the far north of the continent, are the oldest; analysts have measured them to be approximately 65,000 years old. Although not quite as old as those found at Madjedbebe, other early remains have been found around the continent. Mungo Man, named after Lake Mungo in southeastern Australia, where he was found, embodies the oldest human remains found on the continent at roughly 40,000 years old. Perhaps about 35,000 years ago, migrants coming south from Australia settled Tasmania when it was still attached

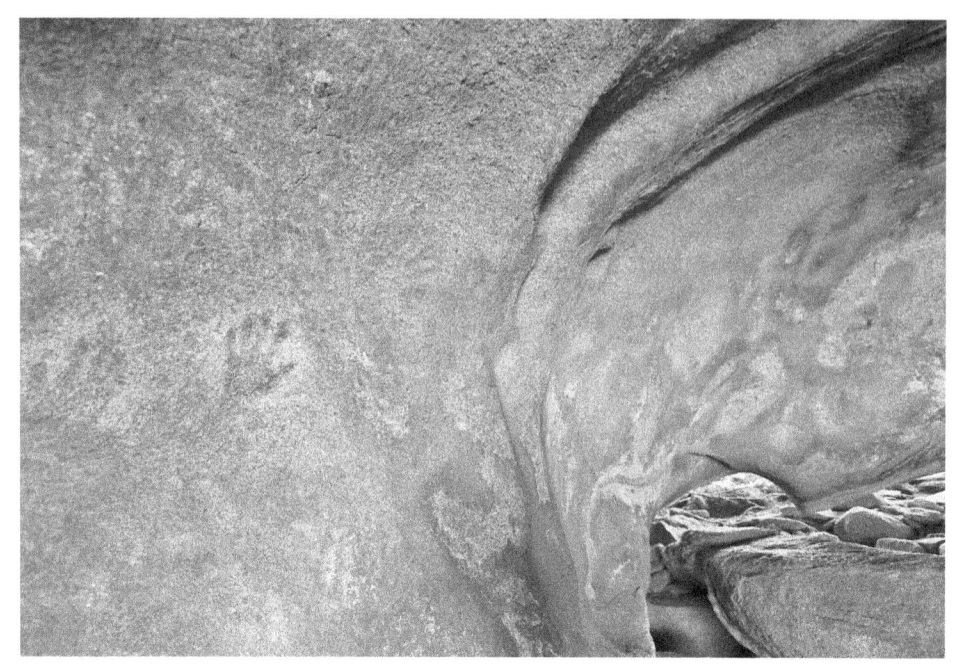

The diverse and widespread Indigenous cave paintings across Australia speak to the rich diversity of Indigenous Australian culture. This painting resides in Mulkas Cave in Western Australia. (Rafael Ben Ari | Dreamstime.com)

to the southeast of the continent. At the beginning of the first millennium BCE, the land bridge between Tasmania and Australia disappeared, leaving the Indigenous cultures of Tasmania isolated from those on Australia proper. Roughly a couple hundred years later, the Torres Strait submerged the land bridge between Australia and New Guinea, severely limiting contact between Australians and the outside world. The Torres Strait Islands were subsequently settled by separate Indigenous peoples migrating from the north.

Although the Indigenous Australian cultures seem to have flourished mostly in isolation from the outside world, there appears to have been at least minimal integration with outsiders. Scholars point to a period roughly 4,000 years ago when some contact with the outside world seems to have occurred. It was at this time that the dingo was first introduced to the continent. Some researchers have pointed to potential origins in India for the dingo; others have suggested that it came to Australia as part of the Austronesian expansion that would eventually reach much of the Indian and Pacific Oceans, including New Guinea and New Zealand. Either way, the introduction of this new species, coupled with linguistic and archaeological evidence, point to this period as a point of some degree of interaction between northern Australians and the outside world.

## CULTURE AND SOCIETY

The cultures of the Indigenous Australian peoples are as richly diverse as the different peoples themselves. Indigenous Australians are perhaps best known for their cave paintings. These murals often held spiritual significance. They appear across multiple regions and encompass various styles, from geometric patterns to naturalistic figures. Some of the more famous sites of cave paintings include Quinkan Country, in the northeast of the continent, as well as the Kimberley and Murujuga in Western Australia. Other types of art proliferated among the Indigenous Australian cultures, including stone arrangements, wood carving, and textiles.

The societies likewise varied from region to region and from people to people. Most of the societies were at least partially nomadic, with their members living as hunter-gatherers. Fish and other forms of seafood were popular around the coasts. Some regions developed agriculture, and members of these societies lived in settlements. Australian megafauna—or large animals—populated the continent in the early years of Indigenous habitation and provided game for the various peoples before most of these species went extinct. Although belief systems varied among the different societies, commonalities existed across the continent, including a reverence for nature and a mythology known in English as Dreamtime or the Dreaming.

## DEMISE

The British arrived in Australia at the end of the eighteenth century, and over the following centuries, they carried out a genocide on the Indigenous Australian peoples. The continent's first British settlement was a penal colony. After the American Revolution, Great Britain could no longer send its convicts to what had been the thirteen colonies, so it set out to found a penal colony in southeastern Australia, first arriving in 1788. An immediate result of their settlement was the spread of European diseases through the Indigenous populations. Smallpox, in particular, devastated local populations. Some scholars have suggested that the disease was intentionally spread, like it had been by European colonists elsewhere in the world, but hard evidence for this claim has yet to be found.

After the first colony, several others followed in short succession in the early nineteenth century. The colonizers perpetrated hundreds of massacres against the local populations. The so-called Frontier Wars took the lives of tens of thousands of Indigenous Australians. In the 1820s and 1830s, British settlers killed nearly the entire Indigenous Tasmanian population. From the late nineteenth century up into the 1970s, Indigenous children were systemically stolen from their parents by settler governments and church missions in an attempt to eradicate the Indigenous Australian cultures. Despite the violence and genocide, many of the cultures have persisted to this day.

## RECENT DISCOVERIES AND CURRENT STATUS

Five sites from Indigenous Australian cultures are UNESCO World Heritage Sites: Budj Bim Cultural Landscape, Kakadu National Park, Tasmanian Wilderness, Uluru-Kata Tjuta National Park, and Willandra Lakes Region. While these locations have received global recognition, hundreds of sites from across the continent speak to the heritage of the Indigenous Australian cultures. These include archaeological excavations as well as sites of Indigenous art, particularly cave paintings.

*Anthony Vivian*

*See also:* Easter Island; Lapita People.

**FURTHER READING**

Cane, Scott. 2014. *First Footprints: The Epic Story of the First Australians*. London: Allen & Unwin.

Flood, Josephine. 2006. *The Original Australians: Story of the Aboriginal People*. London: Allen & Unwin.

Isaacs, Jennifer. 2006. *Australian Dreaming: 40,000 Years of Aboriginal History*. London: New Holland Publishing Australia Pty Ltd.

Jupp, James, ed. 2001. *The Australian People: An Encyclopedia of the Nation, Its People and Their Origins*. Cambridge: Cambridge University Press.

# Iroquois Confederacy

The Iroquois Confederacy was a league of Iroquoian-speaking North American Indian peoples that existed from the late sixteenth century CE to the late eighteenth century. Originally composed of the Seneca, Cayuga, Onondaga, Oneida, and Mohawk, the confederacy was joined by the Tuscarora as the sixth member in the early eighteenth century. These Native nations occupied a territory that took up much of what is now upstate New York (from the Mohawk Valley through the Finger Lakes region). Other Iroquoian nations not belonging to the league occupied territories in what are now southern Ontario (in the case of the Huron) and northern Pennsylvania (the Susquehannock).

The Iroquois had the most effectively organized tribal alliance anywhere north of Mexico at the time the French explorer Samuel de Champlain contacted them in the early seventeenth century. The purpose of the confederacy was to maintain peaceful relations among the member nations and present a united front against foreign tribes and, later, whites.

Given the makeup and operation of the confederacy, with its somewhat democratic representation and its deliberative decision-making process, some historians have argued that the Iroquois Confederacy may have served as a model for the drafters of the American Articles of Confederation (which employs the term "league of friendship" in describing relations between the states)—or perhaps even the U.S. Constitution. Other scholars dispute such a connection, saying that the evidence is thin and the similarities superficial.

## INHABITANTS

The Iroquois, or *Haudenosaunee* ("People of the Longhouse"), were a group of Native American peoples living in eastern North America, generally south and east of the Great Lakes. The Iroquoian language family includes other tribes, such as the Cherokee, who otherwise are not part of Iroquoian culture.

The Iroquois sustained themselves through horticulture. Their principal crops, known as the "Three Sisters," were maize, beans, and squash. These were grown on floodplains, in natural clearings, and in forest areas cleared by burning. Men organized work crews and cleared the land, and the women came together to plant, hoe, and harvest crops. Maize (corn) was prepared manually by grinding it with wooden pestles in deep mortars. Food was usually boiled in clay pots, though some foods, such as berries and mushrooms, were eaten as is and added variety to the diet.

In the fall and early winter, Iroquois families hunted game by using bows and arrows, snares, and nets. Fishing was a principal occupation in the spring and summer. In both cases, the Iroquois might travel considerable distances to visit good hunting and fishing sites. Home, however, was always the longhouse—or rather a group of longhouses—which was sometimes surrounded by wooden palisades. Iroquoian villages stayed put for years or decades, but villagers eventually relocated to take advantage of shifting resources.

The confederacy, also called the Five (or Six) Nations, was a prominent part of political life. Each member nation had a name referring to its place within the whole, symbolized by the longhouse. The Mohawk were "guardians of the eastern door," the Oneida protected the northern wall, the Cayuga held the southern wall, the Seneca watched the western door, and the Onondaga, near the center, were "keepers of the council fire."

The confederacy had a total of fifty chiefs, or sachems, drawn from the villages and clans of member tribes. The number of sachems took account of population and influence: there were fourteen from the Onondaga, ten from the Cayuga, nine each from the Oneida and Mohawk, and eight from the Seneca. The sachems were civil leaders who stood apart, to some extent, from military war chiefs. The council of the confederacy was not convened on a regular basis but as the need arose. It had the power to receive representatives from other nations, to arbitrate intertribal conflicts, and to decide on peace or war with a tribe. It could not, however, intervene in the affairs of individual member tribes.

## HISTORICAL BACKGROUND

Exactly when the Five Nations confederacy was founded is not known. Some historians suggest that it probably arose in the early sixteenth century. In Iroquois legend, the league is said to have been founded by Deganawidah, a leader of divine status. He persuaded the original Five Nations to stop fighting among themselves and to give up cannibalism. Ethnohistorians regard the confederacy's formation as a defensive response to warfare with the neighboring Huron and other Algonquian-speaking tribes. The prophet Hiawatha (flourished ca. 1550), who was Deganawidah's earthly spokesman, traveled among the five tribes in an attempt to unify them in a political alliance. He ultimately succeeded, and the tribes came together in what proved to be a powerful diplomatic and military force—until its eventual collapse during the American Revolution.

By the sixteenth and seventeenth centuries, warfare had become a major feature of Iroquois life. This was partly owing to the fact that the European nations on the continent enlisted the support of the Iroquois tribes in their fights for territory and to gain control of the fur trade. It is likely, too, that as the various Iroquois tribes sought to gain an edge in the fur trade, animosities grew. Most of the

Five Nations became allies of the British against the French, but some tribal groups, mainly from the Mohawk and Onondaga, converted to Catholicism and sided with the French. Many of these Catholic Iroquois settled along the St. Lawrence River and fought against the Five Nations, which declared them traitors. Iroquois influence was strong in the region and did much to limit French power, while it facilitated British expansion in the form of forts and settlements.

In Iroquois culture, sporadic warfare and raiding against tribes outside the confederacy allowed young Iroquois warriors to earn prestige and honor. In earlier times, conquest of territory and gaining economic and political advantage were of lesser importance. Eventually, however, in dealing with the British and French, and later the British and the colonists, leaders in the confederacy strategically used opposing interests to their own advantage, playing off parties against one another and subjugating neighboring tribes for economic and territorial gains. Before its collapse in the late eighteenth century, the Iroquois Confederacy controlled areas far to the south and west of its traditional homeland.

## CULTURE AND SOCIETY

The basic unit of Iroquois society was the family, traced through the female line. Family units, in turn, were organized into clans, which cut across tribal lines and determined marital relations. Each clan was named after an animal (Bear, Deer, Turtle, Wolf, etc.), and the number of clans varied with each tribe. The Cayuga had ten, the Seneca and Onondaga nine each, the Tuscarora eight, and the Mohawk and Oneida three each. Each clan had civil chiefs who were elected to the tribal council, but only certain clans possessed hereditary titles that enabled them to elect representatives (sachems) to the league council. Because women inherited all titles and descent was traced through them, they held an important place in the authority structure, although all negotiations were conducted by male officials.

There was never a single Five Nations army, as the council served only as a deliberative body. War chiefs, such as the well-known figures Cornplanter and Joseph Brant, were chosen for their personal courage and ability; their tenure lasted only for the duration of each war. According to convention, no member tribe could go to war without the entire confederacy's approval; occasionally, however, some tribes did engage in private warfare. Weapons included the bow and arrow, clubs, and shields of wood or bark; body armor made of wooden slats tied with cord was often used. After the arrival of the Europeans, iron tomahawks and firearms were employed. The Iroquois were accomplished in the use of ambush and surprise in battle. By the end of the seventeenth century, the Iroquois defended their larger settlements by constructing log palisades and surrounding them with ditches and earthworks.

The confederacy was modeled after existing family, clan, and community institutions; its aim was both to unite its members through symbolic social and kinship relationships and to maintain the independence of individual tribes. Major decisions on the council were reached through unanimity, thus compensating for the otherwise unequal tribal representation. An individual sachem could be challenged through a type of impeachment proceeding initiated by his lineage's headwoman.

Council members were responsible for keeping the internal peace, representing the Five Nations to outsiders, and coordinating tribal activities in unified warfare against nonmembers.

## DEMISE

During the American Revolution, with its disruption of the status quo, the Iroquois Confederacy elected to permit each member tribe to decide its own allegiance. All the tribes except the Oneida and about half of the Tuscarora chose to ally with the British. Yet, by this time, losses due to warfare and disease had so seriously impacted the Iroquois, while the Europeans strength only increased, that the Iroquois never could regain their former preeminent status.

One of the central tenets of Iroquois culture was that the land was sacred and therefore not to be sold to whites. This belief was widely accepted and is still maintained among some contemporary Iroquois. Yet, despite the strength of the belief, the Iroquois sold some lands through treaties in 1784 and 1794. Subsequently, various treaty violations, fraudulent sales, and great social and economic changes resulted in the Iroquois losing most of their lands. Today, they own about 80,000 acres, mainly in the form of reservations.

After the collapse of the Iroquois Confederacy and the loss of their lands in the aftermath of the American Revolution, the Iroquois religion was revitalized and transformed by the prophet Handsome Lake, or Sganyodaiyo. In 1799, he experienced a series of visions, which he put down in a set of 100 commandments known as *Gaihwiyo* ("Good Word"). The so-called Code of Handsome Lake included traditional Indian dances and ceremonies to be carried out along with injunctions against liquor and witchcraft.

## RECENT DISCOVERIES AND CURRENT STATUS

Scholars estimate that at the end of the seventeenth century, there were about 16,000 Iroquois in the Five Nations. A sharp population decline occurred in the eighteenth century, and by 1774, the Six Nations were estimated to contain 10,000 to 12,500 individuals. Although the Iroquois population increased in later centuries, Iroquois nations also became more dispersed as people left the reservations and mixed with the general society. Still, Iroquois traditions continue to be honored by ceremonial societies today, and a number of Iroquois heritage museums are open to the public.

In 2012, the Archaeological Conservancy, a U.S.-based nonprofit organization that acquires and preserves sites, purchased the sites of two sixteenth-century Cayuga villages in New York's Finger Lakes region. One of the villages shows signs of having been surrounded by a wooden palisade that may have been constructed during a time of conflict with outside groups or with members of the Iroquois Confederacy. The second site contains traces of longhouses.

*Michael Shally-Jensen*

*See also:* Cahokia.

## FURTHER READING

Aquila, Richard. 1997. *The Iroquois Restoration: Iroquois Diplomacy on the Colonial Frontier, 1701–1754*. Lincoln: University of Nebraska Press.

Fenton, William N. 2010. *The Great Law and the Longhouse: A Political History of the Iroquois Confederacy*. Norman: University of Oklahoma Press.

Jennings, Francis, and William N. Fenton, eds. 1995. *The History and Culture of Iroquois Diplomacy*. Syracuse, NY: Syracuse University Press.

Richter, Daniel K. 2016. *Trade, Land, Power: The Struggle for Eastern North America*. Philadelphia: University of Pennsylvania Press.

Taylor, Alan. 2006. *The Divided Ground: Indians, Settlers, and the Northern Borderland of the American Revolution*. New York: Knopf.

# K

## Kilwa

Kilwa is a small island in the Indian Ocean off the coast of Tanzania in Eastern Africa. Separated from the mainland by a narrow channel, Kilwa has a deep harbor sheltered by coral reefs, making it a good transport point for use by small boats. Historically, it was the seat of an important Muslim sultanate, established in 975 CE and maintained by a variety of sovereigns over a 500-year period. Kilwa's wealth and power, based on the gold and slave trades, contributed to the prominence of the Swahili coast during the medieval and early modern periods in the region.

An assortment of ruins of different types, sizes, and ages echo Kilwa's history. An expansive palace, military bastions with massive walls, and two large mosques date to the sultanate. Portuguese occupiers in the early sixteenth century left a fort, as did conquering Omani forces in the late seventeenth century. On nearby Songo Mnara, a related seaport of the same era, there are vestiges of palaces, mosques, and a lighthouse. Ibn Battuta, a noted Muslim traveler of the fourteenth century, wrote of Kilwa, "[It] is one of the most beautiful and well-constructed cities in the world. The whole of it is elegantly built."

### INHABITANTS

The Swahili kingdoms were set along the coasts of modern Somalia, Kenya, Tanzania, and Mozambique. The main city-states included Malindi, Mombasa, Lamu, Kilwa, Mogadishu, Zanzibar, and, far to the south, Sofala. The Bantu had resided in these communities since around 800 CE. Additional waves of immigrants—Arabs, Persians, and Indians—arrived in the eleventh and twelfth centuries and intermixed with the Africans. Many of the original inhabitants converted to Islam as a result of trade and communication with the Arabian Peninsula and the spread of Islam generally. The culture that developed in these cities was thus a blend of Bantu and Islamic. The main language was Swahili, which means "people of the coast"; it also came to be a lingua franca throughout much of East Africa, as it incorporated a large number of Arabic and other words into its corpus.

### HISTORICAL BACKGROUND

On the eastern seaboard, Swahili civilization thrived because of its intermediary position between the gold and ivory producers of the interior and the sea traders of the Indian Ocean. Products of the southern hinterland were collected at thriving centers such as Great Zimbabwe and carried by porters to east coast seaports. Towns there began to feature mosques and houses built of local coral limestone. Arguably the greatest of the many Swahili city-states was Kilwa. It was situated on two adjacent islands, Kilwa and Songo Mnara, that were united around 1200 under the rule of Abi bin Hasan—of the Persian Shirazi dynasty. The principal town, Kilwa Kisiwani, was constructed during his reign, and Kilwa also became the first kingdom in East Africa to mint coins. A successor dynasty, the Mahdali, held power from the late thirteenth to the late fifteenth century. The Mahdali rebuilt much of the city in stone, augmented its Great Mosque, and erected a fine palace and emporium.

Arabian and Indian trading ships as well as local dhows—a type of small sailing vessel traditionally used in the Red Sea and Indian Ocean (and called a *mtepe* in Swahili)—plied their trade throughout the medieval period. The Swahili coast became a major center of international commerce, exporting gold, ivory, enslaved people, and other items and importing cotton cloth, porcelain, glassware, and beads—some of which were used as barter to obtain more gold and trade goods.

These coastal emporiums were sited on islands not only for trading purposes but also for defensive reasons. Their fortified coastal sections acted to repel would-be invaders from the sea, and their grand architecture served to signal the eminence of their leaders and Swahili civilization generally.

## CULTURE AND SOCIETY

Before the arrival of the Europeans in the 1500s, the city-states of East Africa formed a central part of an expansive Muslim commercial network. By the mid-thirteenth century, the Muslims had consolidated their commercial and political influence across the Indian Ocean and beyond. Kilwa and the other Swahili towns sustained Muslim control in the western arc of this trading empire while also acting as a link between Islam and the native peoples of Africa.

Based on surviving accounts, the Swahili were prosperous and comfortable. As noted, the renowned Berber traveler Ibn Battuta, visiting the coast in the fourteenth century, remarked on the beauty of Kilwa and also reported on the lavish dress and domestic arrangements at Mogadishu along with large meals of rice and ghee with side dishes of stewed meats, fish, and vegetables. Later, Portuguese explorers also noted the riches of Kilwa, commenting on women adorned with gold and silver jewelry.

Swahili society was organized into three main classes: (1) the sultan and his family, along with high-ranking officials and prosperous merchants; (2) a professional or artisan class made up of skilled craftspeople, minor government officials, ship captains, and the like; and (3) a lower class consisting of farmers and laborers as well as servants and slaves. East African women were generally subordinate to men, although they had important rights concerning marriage, the practice (or not) of polygamy, and so on. At its height, Kilwa was home to at least 12,000 inhabitants.

## DEMISE

Kilwa was still very prosperous when the Portuguese entered its port in 1497, with their large, canon-bearing sailing vessels, to demand that it yield and pay tribute to the new arrivals. Although their initial foray did not play out, the Portuguese returned in 1505 with a greater armada to lay siege to the city. They bombarded and sacked the town and stayed on as occupiers until 1512. Trade was constricted, and Kilwa went into decline.

In the sixteenth century, a migration by the Zimba people of central Africa ravaged the coast, virtually wiping out Kilwa and devastating Mombasa. Only when another Bantu group attacked the Zimba at Malindi did the Zimba cease their warring.

In the seventeenth century, Islamic fleets from Oman, on the Persian Gulf, arrived and established their principal base on the island of Zanzibar. The Omani built forts, took over the existing trade routes, and promoted the slave trade. The French and Persian Gulf kingdoms, in particular, purchased large numbers of slaves from East Africa.

## RECENT DISCOVERIES AND CURRENT STATUS

Kilwa and Songo Mnara are, together, a UNESCO World Heritage Site. They were placed on the list of such sites in danger of experiencing damage or decline in 2004 but were removed in 2014. New excavations at both sites, begun in 2009, have continued to add details of daily life and historical change.

*Michael Shally-Jensen*

*See also:* Great Zimbabwe.

## FURTHER READING

Chittick, H. Neville. 1974. *Kilwa: An Islamic Trading City on the East African Coast.* Nairobi: British Institute in East Africa.
Fauvelle-Aymar, François-Xavier. 2018. *The Golden Rhinoceros: Histories of the African Middle Ages.* Princeton, NJ: Princeton University Press.
Maxon, Robert M. 2009. *East Africa: An Introductory History.* 3rd ed. Morgantown: West Virginia University Press.

# Knossos

Knossos flourished as the most powerful city on the island of Crete through the Bronze Age and the primary superpower of the Aegean Sea during the mid-second millennium BCE. The city was the largest and most complex attestation of Minoan culture, the Bronze Age civilization that dominated Crete and wielded a wide influence beyond the island. Crete is a long, mountainous island that stretches horizontally across the southern border of the Aegean Sea. Knossos is located in the north central region of the island, just about three miles from the northern coast.

The ruins of Knossos center around the large palace complex. More extensive than a mere residence for the royal family, this massive structure boasted an estimated 1,300 rooms and towered as high as five stories in some places. The complex had four large gates facing north, south, east, and west and included an array of residential, communal, administrative, and storage rooms. Among the standout features of the ruins are a number of colorful and intriguing frescoes. Many

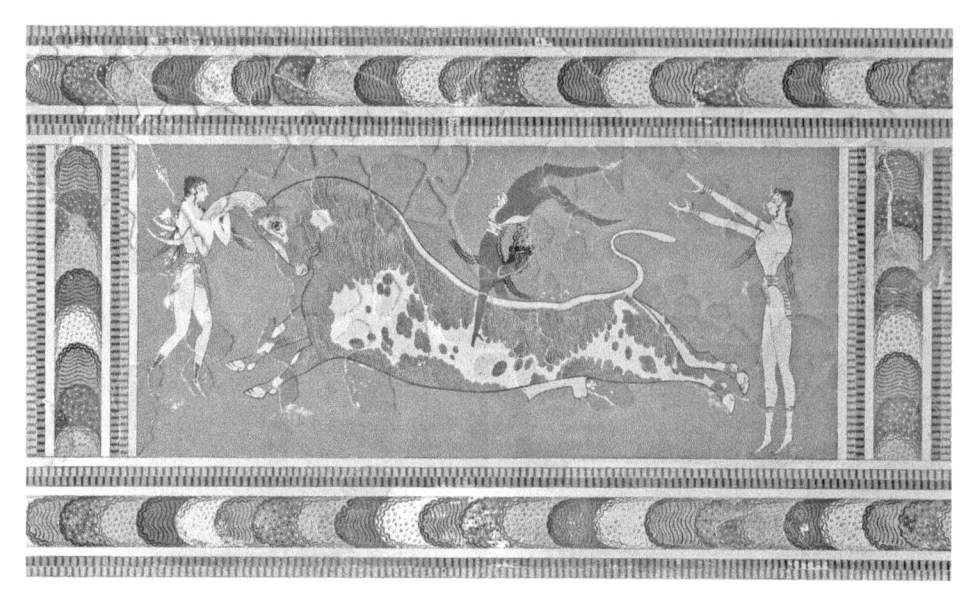

The Bull-Leaping Fresco, shown in its reconstructed form here, originally dates to the mid-fifteenth century BCE and is among the most noteworthy pieces of Minonan art. Note the difference between the original fragments and the painted reconstruction. (Xiaoma | Dreamstime.com)

frescoes and buildings of the palace in situ are not remains from antiquity but early twentieth-century CE restorations.

## INHABITANTS

Knossos was the largest settlement of the Minoan people, who prospered on Bronze Age Crete and the surrounding islands. At its height in the mid-second millennium BCE, Knossos was the regional metropolis, showcasing a population and diversity not seen in the rest of the Aegean. After much debate, we are still not sure how to categorize the Minoan language. Linear A, which presumably denotes it, has yet to be deciphered. The leading candidates are the Indo-European and Semitic family trees. The inhabitants worshipped a polytheistic pantheon centered on a mother goddess. The current leading theory on the government at Knossos is that it was a theocracy, infusing Minoan religion into its administration.

## HISTORICAL BACKGROUND

The site of Knossos shows a long and varied inhabitation long before the onset of the Minoan era for which it is famous. Kephala, the hill on which Knossos was built, shows signs of settlement as early as 7000 BCE. At this very early stage, inhabitants lived in wattle-and-daub housing; tools and carved figurines have been found among this earliest stratum. The hill appears to have experienced uninterrupted inhabitation through the millennia of the Neolithic period. The wattle-and-daub housing was eventually replaced by mud bricks. Around the fourth millennium BCE, the population ballooned. The so-called Great House, too large to be a simple residence, served as a precursor to the two later iterations of the Minoan centralized palace.

What we call the Minoan civilization began with the onset of the Bronze Age in Crete, in the late fourth millennium BCE. Both the population and the society's complexity continued to increase through the third millennium BCE. In the early second millennium, around 1900 BCE, the inhabitants built vast palace complexes in Knossos as well as in some other Cretan cities, namely Phaistos, Malia, and Zakros. We call them palace complexes as opposed to palaces because they were far larger than palaces and fulfilled administrative and religious functions as well as residential functions. These complexes across Crete were destroyed around 1700 BCE. The two leading theories as to how they were ruined are a large earthquake and an invasion from the Greek mainland.

In the seventeenth century BCE, the Minoans quickly rebuilt the various palace complexes soon after their destruction. The subsequent period, ca. 1650–ca. 1450 BCE, that featured this second iteration of palace complexes marked the height of Minoan society and culture. During this time, the Minoans utilized Linear A, a written script yet to be deciphered by linguists, most likely to keep track of administrative affairs. The palace complex at Knossos was considerably larger than the others at Phaistos, Malia, and Zakros, yet this era's artifacts show an island-wide uniformity, leading some to suggest that Knossos was the capital of a unified Crete. All of the palaces featured large central courts that undoubtedly fulfilled a range of communal and administrative functions.

The Minoan people wielded influence well beyond Crete. Herodotus and Thucydides, later Greek historians, credited King Minos of Knossos—who gives the Minoan culture its name—with controlling a thalassocracy over the Aegean Sea. This dovetails with King Minos's portrait in later mythology as a powerful but cruel king. These later accounts should be viewed warily, however. Even the historians were, at best, depicting an amalgamation of various Knossian kings; it has been suggested that *Minos* was a Cretan word or honorific for kings. The survival of Minoan wares and other artifacts throughout the Aegean and around the eastern Mediterranean displays, at the very least, extensive commercial contact. Akrotiri, a well-preserved settlement on Thera (present-day Santorini), features Linear A inscriptions and Minoan art, confirming a direct Minoan influence on the island. The nature of the Minoan presence on the other Aegean islands and shorelines is a matter of scholarly debate.

## CULTURE AND SOCIETY

Knossos served as the epicenter of Minoan society and culture, which extended across Crete and beyond. The palace complexes at Knossos and the other major Minoan sites reveal an intricate and hierarchal society. Linear A, a Minoan script yet to be deciphered, appears to have kept track of administrative business. The palace complexes were fitted with giant storerooms to house large vessels of grain, oil, and wine and smaller areas to protect valuables, revealing the society's ability to amass wealth and resources. Much of this wealth was accumulated through trade; the Minoans kept up extensive trading relationships with the Mycenaeans on mainland Greece as well as the Egyptians.

Minoan art flourished in many forms, from frescoes and sculptures to pottery and jewelry. Minoan painting, which has survived on frescoes and pottery, commonly featured humans, animals, and natural scenes, with a particular emphasis on ocean life. In wider Minoan culture, bulls, serpents, and labryses (two-headed axes) bore sacred significance. A fresco found at the palace complex of Knossos shows an athlete leaping over a massive bull, leading to speculation that Minoan contests or festivals staged such bull leaping events. In the mid-second millennium BCE, the Minoans exported culture throughout the region. Minoan art and wares were popular throughout the Aegean, and Mycenaean art (on the Greek mainland) and Cycladic art (on the Cycladic islands of the Aegean) show substantial Minoan influence during this time period.

Knossos and the height of Minoan culture figured deeply into the culture of generations of later Greeks. The Athenians, whose broad surviving literature renders them more knowable to modern readers than their peers, often depicted King Minos of Knossos as a prominent foil for Athens. Describing the various naval powers who ruled over the Aegean Sea, the historian Thucydides starts with King Minos and ends with the Athenians. The king features in mythology as the cruel antagonist to Athenian heroes such as Theseus and Daedalus. These stories usually feature Minos's son, the Minotaur: a half man and half bull monster that lives in a labyrinth under Knossos's palace complex.

## DEMISE

Minoan society began to collapse throughout Crete around 1450 BCE, with the city of Knossos holding out the longest, until around 1375 BCE. It had long been believed that the massive volcanic eruption of Thera (present-day Santorini), which buried and preserved the settlement of Akrotiri, was also responsible for the downfall of Minoan civilization on Crete. However, more analysis has shown that the dates do not exactly align with the eruption, which occurred in the late sixteenth century BCE, fifty years or a little more before the downfall of Minoan society on Crete. Most scholars now believe that an attack from the Mycenaeans, who inhabited major cities on mainland Greece, around 1450 BCE sparked the fall of Minoan society. Knossos, Crete's largest city, held out for the longest but eventually fell as well. The evidence for this explanation resides in a period of Mycenaean occupation of the major Minoan cities of Crete immediately following the collapse of Minoan society. After the Mycenaean occupation and a period of abandonment, Knossos was resettled around the turn of the first millennium BCE.

## RECENT DISCOVERIES AND CURRENT STATUS

Knossos's rediscovery by Arthur Evans at the turn of the twentieth century rendered it one of the most important archaeological sites in the entire Mediterranean, a status that it still carries today. It is also one of the more controversial remains of the Mediterranean. Evans eschewed conservation, the primary objective of later archaeology, for restoration. He and his team rebuilt the throne room, the colossal north entrance, and various other parts of the palace complex, and they added to and painted over frescoes. Much of their work is among the most popular tourist attractions today, but it is only a little over a century old.

*Anthony Vivian*

*See also:* Athens; Mycenae.

**FURTHER READING**

Castleden, Rodney. 1993. *Minoans: Life in Bronze Age Crete.* London: Routledge.
Scarre, Chris, and Rebecca Stefoff. 2003. *The Palace of Minos at Knossos: Digging for the Past.* Oxford: Oxford University Press.
Shelmerdine, Cynthia W. 2008. *The Cambridge Companion to the Aegean Bronze Age.* Cambridge: Cambridge University Press.
Watrous, L. Vance. 2021. *Minoan Crete: An Introduction.* Cambridge: Cambridge University Press.

# Kyoto

Kyoto, known historically as Heian and Heian-kyo, served as the seat of the Japanese emperor for over a millennium (794–1869 CE). A medieval metropolis, Kyoto grew to become the largest city in Japan and held that distinction until the late sixteenth century, when it was overtaken by Osaka and Edo (present-day Tokyo). It sits in a valley just northeast of the modern hub of Osaka, about thirty-five miles from Osaka Bay. The Katsura and Kamo Rivers run north to south through the valley before meeting up with the Yodo River and issuing into the bay. Lake Biwa, a large lake covering about 260 square miles, sits northeast of the city. Together, Osaka and Kyoto comprise the second-largest urban sprawl in present-day Japan behind the Tokyo/Yokohama urban space a little over 250 miles to the northeast.

The palaces and temples of Kyoto's heyday stand among a bustling modern city. As of 2010, Kyoto remained the seventh-largest city in Japan. The city limits include the prosperous city as well as spacious and mountainous forests to the north. In the center of the urban portion, the Imperial Palace stands just north of the modern business district. Many Shinto shrines and Buddhist temples from centuries past still populate the city. Among these, the Shingon Buddhist temple Toji boasts several buildings, including a five-story pagoda, and was constructed shortly after Kyoto was founded. Kinkaku-ji is a famous Zen Buddhist temple that was originally built around the turn of the fifteenth century.

## INHABITANTS

The area around Kyoto has been inhabited since the Paleolithic period. Kyoto was founded as a planned city in the eighth century to be the new capital for the Japanese emperor. It was immediately filled with administrators of the imperial court as well as a number of other tradespeople and quickly grew to become the largest city in Japan. The palace loomed over the city along its northern border. As a result, the wealthiest and most influential inhabitants lived in the north central neighborhood, in the closest proximity to the palace. In the city's early years, this included members of the powerful Fujiwara clan, among others. Meanwhile, the city's poorest inhabitants, who could not afford to live in the original city proper, set up homes just east of the city along the Kamo River, stretching the city in that direction.

## HISTORICAL BACKGROUND

Emperor Kammu, the fiftieth emperor of Japan, moved the capital from Nara to Heian, known today as Kyoto, at the end of the eighth century. His first choice for his new capital was not Heian but Nagaoka, about twenty miles north of Nara. His stated reason was Nagaoka's more ready access to water transportation. Nagaoka was, indeed, closer to the Yodo River system; however, many believe that the emperor had ulterior motives. Buddhism had been in Japan for a while, but emperors in the eighth century began actively promoting it and granted the Buddhist clergy large authority. Many contend that Emperor Kammu wished to move his palace and court away from the Buddhist clergy's base of power at Nara and the political machinations that took place there. A year after the capital moved to Nagaoka, the official who recommended the new site and oversaw the move was assassinated. Many were implicated, including the crown prince, and the emperor decided to move the capital again in 794 to Heian ("Tranquility and Peace"), ten miles northeast of Nagaoka.

Just like the old capital of Nara, the new capital at Heian, or Heian-kyo ("Tranquility and Peace Capital"), seems to have been modeled after the Chinese capital of Chang'an. The palace, which was most likely the first portion of Heian built, sits in the center of the northern border of the originally rectangular city. The city as a whole covered almost ten square miles. Its main thoroughfare, a broad avenue, stretches south from the center of the palace, dividing the remainder of the city into eastern and western halves. The design allowed the palace to be seen from the remainder of the city, particularly from the main avenue. Both the eastern and western halves have their own market. The Kamo River flowed along the city's eastern border and provided water transport for people and goods. In addition, two canals were cut through the city. The primary difference between the new Japanese capital and Chang'an, its Chinese model, was that Heian was not walled.

The next four centuries, known today as the Heian period, featured a mix of thriving imperial culture and decreasing imperial power. Future generations looked back to the Heian period as the pinnacle of imperial Japanese culture. One of the reasons for this was that this period saw the development of a more distinctive Japanese national identity. With upheaval in China at the end of the ninth century, Japanese missions to China ceased, and Chinese influence on Japanese culture waned. This created space for a flourish of Japanese national culture, especially at the imperial court. Nevertheless, the court's influence waned throughout this same time period. In the early Heian period, the Fujiwara clan increased its power through political machinations and intermarriage with the imperial family and largely held sway over the imperial court. Although the Fujiwara's power eventually faded, the strength of regional military leaders began to rise at the expense of the emperor's power.

The rise in the influence of regional military leaders eventually led to the outright rule of shogunates from 1185 to 1869, the period sometimes known as feudal Japan. Over these centuries, although the emperor remained the nominal head of state in Heian-kyo, shoguns—military dictators—served as the actual rulers, sometimes operating out of Heian-kyo but often not. Minamoto no Yoritomo was the first shogun and largely responsible for negotiating the initial relationship with the imperial court whereby the court would continue to exist and be nominally in charge but would officially recognize the shogunate—a *bakufu*, or "tent government," in Japanese. Yoritomo set up his tent government in Kamakura, less than forty miles from modern Tokyo, and the next century and a half of Japanese history is known as the Kamakura shogunate.

For a brief period in the fourteenth century (1333–1336), Emperor Go-Daigo restored himself and the imperial court to power. Having enlisted the help of General Ashikaga Takauji, he toppled the Kamakura shogunate. However, his rule proved unpopular, and Ashikaga declared himself shogun, retaining Heian-kyo as his own base of operations. The capital city was largely razed during the Onin War of the fifteenth century, as the country descended into civil unrest and balkanization that lasted until the turn of the seventeenth century. In 1603, the Tokugawa shogunate gained ascendancy and ruled from Edo, modern-day Tokyo. After Emperor Meiji again restored the imperial court to power in 1868, he officially moved the court from Heian to Tokyo, ending Heian's nearly eleven-century run as the seat of the Japanese emperor.

## CULTURE AND SOCIETY

Although Kyoto's society continued to develop over the years, the first centuries of the city's existence—the so-called Heian period—proved formative in its cultural identity. It was during this period that contact with China decreased and Chinese influence in Japan faded. A more distinctive Japanese culture began to assert itself. Kana, or syllabaries, developed, moving the physical form of the Japanese written language away from the Chinese script. The poets Sei Shōnagon, Murasaki Shikibu, and Ki no Tsurayuki (the first two of whom were women) flourished during the Heian period. Religion, both native Shinto and Buddhism imported from India via China, played a large role in shaping Kyoto's culture as well as its society. As Japan's capital and the largest city on the island for much of its existence, the city is home to impressive architectural feats, many of which are religious in nature. Of the sites that the nation of Japan has labeled National Treasures, an impressive one-fifth reside in Kyoto.

## DEMISE

Although Kyoto served as capital for more than a millennium, its power ebbed and flowed, and the city faced many setbacks before its status was finally demoted in the nineteenth century. Toward the end of the twelfth century, Kyoto went from being the actual capital to the nominal capital. For the next seven centuries, the imperial court remained in Kyoto, but shogunates, sometimes based in Kyoto but not often, held the real power. The Onin War (1467–1477) proved devastating to Kyoto, as the capital was largely destroyed in the fighting.

Finally, in 1869, Emperor Meiji moved his imperial court from Kyoto to Edo. He gave Edo the name Tokyo ("Eastern Capital") and Kyoto, formally Heinan, briefly became Saikyo ("Western Capital") before taking on the name Kyoto ("Capital City"). The new name reflected the fact that although Kyoto was no longer the official seat of the emperor, the millennium that it served as capital solidified its status as Japan's honorary and cultural capital. Emperor Meiji's change in capital city, therefore, did not represent a demise for Kyoto so much as a shift in function.

## RECENT DISCOVERIES AND CURRENT STATUS

A group of monuments from the long period when Kyoto was the seat of the Japanese emperor are collectively a UNESCO World Heritage Site titled Historic Monuments of Ancient Kyoto (Kyoto, Uji and Otsu Cities). These seventeen monuments include secular and religious—both Shinto and Buddhist—sites.

*Anthony Vivian*

See also: Chang'an.

## FURTHER READING

Dougill, John. 2006. *Kyoto: A Cultural History*. Oxford: Oxford University Press.
Fiévé, Nicolas, and Paul Waley. 2003. *Japanese Capitals in Historical Perspective: Place, Power and Memory in Kyoto, Edo and Tokyo*. London: Routledge.
Lone, John. 2000. *Old Kyoto: A Short Social History*. Oxford: Oxford University Press.
Stavros, Matthew. 2016. *Kyoto: An Urban History of Japan's Premodern Capital*. Honolulu: University of Hawaii Press.

# L

## La Tène Celtic Culture

Neuchâtel, Switzerland, is home to an important archaeological site dating from the late Iron Age (450–50 BCE). Excavations conducted there from 1907 to 1917 revealed two timber causeways and other structural remains. In the shallow waters of Lake Neuchâtel, researchers found over 2,500 relics, ranging from chariots, coins, and chalices to iron swords, axes, scythes, and other objects. Many of them display the abstract spiral designs associated with the European Celts. In fact, Neuchâtel is considered one of the key centers of an era in Celtic prehistory referred to as La Tène (pronounced lah-TEN), after the archaeological site on the northeastern end of the lake. The site is believed to have been a major ceremonial center within the Celtic world and, as such, is something of an archetype of this phase of Celtic civilization.

### INHABITANTS

Although many people today, particularly in the British Isles and the United States, think of Celtic culture as being synonymous with ancient Irish, Scottish, and Welsh traditions, continental Europe was in fact home to a great population of Celts for centuries before the Roman era. Most historians hold that the inhabitants of the La Tène site were Celts and that they were one and the same with those whom Greek and Roman literary records refer to as "Keltoi" or "Celtae."

The Celts, however, were less a monolithic people than a collection of related ethnic groups that spoke an ancient Celtic language and shared cultural similarities. They are regarded as the ancestors of later peoples on the western fringe of Europe, including the modern Irish, Welsh, and Bretons. Information about the Celts comes from ancient written sources; from accounts from the early medieval period; from linguistic evidence, such as place names and the occasional inscription; from archaeological finds; and, more recently, from genetic research.

Other notable La Tène cultural sites include Bliesbruck-Reinheim, on the German-French border; Mont Beuvray and Vix, in France; Donnersberg, Manching, and Waldalgesheim, in Germany; and Sandberg, Austria. Use of the term *Celts* in relation to the British Isles is ambiguous and subject to debate; some writers use it (arguably incorrectly) in connection with ancient Stone Age sites such as Stonehenge, while others use it to refer to developments in early medieval history (i.e., Gaelic culture). Most scholars tend to restrict its use to pre-Roman Iron Age cultures.

> **Buyan**
>
> Buyan is a magical island in Slavic folklore that can vanish and reappear at will. Perun, the Slavic all-powerful sky god, is credited with creating the island. Traditions vary, but Buyan is often associated with natural forces: the Northern, Western, and Eastern winds—three brothers in Slavic lore—are said to reside there and the Zoryas, themselves sisters and solar goddesses. The mystical oak tree, which is the Slavic version of the Indo-European world tree, grows on Buyan. Koschei the Deathless hid his soul on the island to retain his immortality. The mystical location has inspired depictions for centuries. It appears in the medieval Russian *Dove Book* and was one of the locations for Nikolai Rimsky-Korsakov's *Tale of Tsar Saltan*. Today, it lends its name to entities ranging from a class of Russian naval ships to an island within a liquid methane sea on Saturn's moon of Titan. Some connect Buyan to Rügen, the Baltic island off the shore of Germany.

## HISTORICAL BACKGROUND

The Iron Age in Western Europe was preceded by the Bronze Age and was the last era in European prehistory before the Hellenistic and Roman eras. It is conventionally divided into an earlier period (700–450 BCE), named for a cemetery site at Hallstatt in Austria, and a later period (450–50 BCE), named for the La Tène site in Switzerland. Each period is associated with particular patterns of settlement and forms of cultural expression, such as architecture, metal industry, pottery styles, human burials, and, as far as they can be ascertained, economy and social structure. There is some disagreement, however, about the uniformity of La Tène culture, with some scholars emphasizing differences between locales and styles rather than similarities.

La Tène culture is thought to have developed when Celtic traders and warriors came into contact with Greek and Etruscan influences from south of the Alps. The culture grew and spread into eastern France, Switzerland, Austria, southwestern Germany, large areas of central Europe, and selected parts of the British Isles. The site of La Tène was mainly occupied between 275 and 60 BCE, even though the larger culture it represents was more extensive in both time and geographical spread.

While bronze objects continued to be made and traded in the Iron Age, after about 450 BCE, ironworking began to reach a new level of artisanship. Well-crafted iron long swords—and many of them—marked the existence of a warrior society. Some Celtic groups lived in hill forts, such as that at Heuneburg, in southern Germany, from an early period, while others did not (even as they defended themselves). Celts also served as mercenaries in the armies of a number of Mediterranean states. These people were familiar with horse-drawn chariots, the minting of coins, the potter's wheel, and highly stylized art forms that combined Northern European, Mediterranean, and possibly even Steppe (or nomadic) elements. One of the more striking features of La Tène culture was the unique, elaborate decoration of many of the objects—the swirling patterns that rework animal, plant, and spiral designs into forms widely recognized as "Celtic."

> **Ys**
>
> Ys was a mythical city that once thrived on the peninsula of Brittany before being swallowed by the sea. The city's name comes from the local Breton phrase for "Low City," and many associate the city with Brittany's Baie de Douarnenez. The oldest extant version of story comes from the early seventeenth century, with many more iterations, often with slight variations, appearing in the following centuries. The tale of the city's destruction features Gradlon, a semi-mythical king, and Dahut, his daughter. Some versions have Dahut as an irreverent or immoral daughter; others take it further and depict her as a witch. The princess takes the keys to Ys's dike and floods the city. On horseback, Gradlon saves his daughter from the sinking city only to have her fall to her death. The fable weaves anxieties over the sea and flooding with male insecurities over femininity and the family bloodline.

## CULTURE AND SOCIETY

In both ancient and medieval written sources, the Celts are depicted as a warlike people noted for their bravery in battle. The main political group was the tribe, which was made up of both nobles and commoners. Some works describe a graded series of ranks within society and point to the importance of patrons and clients. The former provided protection and status in exchange for loyalty and service. In the earlier centuries, power and authority within the tribe was more fluid and constantly tested based on claims of kinship, material wealth, success in battle, and the number of one's clients. In later centuries, the head of the tribe, the king, enjoyed more or less universal allegiance and may have even allowed the election of magistrates and councillors. The latter would include those endowed with special skills or knowledge: bards, seers, and Druids, that is, guardians of sacred knowledge.

Two defining features of Celtic society were the concepts of honor and rank. Although high status was accorded to those with the right background or significant achievements in war, it was also possible to gain rank through the development of valuable skills, such as expertise in poetry, law, prophecy, music, or craftwork. Honor accrued to those with high status, and yet each individual had an "honor price," or, essentially, a level of compensation to be paid if the person were harmed or defamed. Oaths, too, were important within this system, and the oath of a person having a high honor price outweighed that of a lesser individual.

The archaeological record generally backs up this picture. Richly furnished burials have been found that contained two-wheeled chariots, gold and bronze objects, and imported Mediterranean items. The inhabitants of these graves were clearly kings or nobles. In general, men were buried with their weapons—shield, spear, and sword—and women were buried with their ornaments, especially brooches, bracelets, and torcs (neck rings). In La Tène itself, female items and domestic material are far less evident than weapons and other metalwork. Fine drinking cups are also well represented, indicating that feasting and drinking were important to the Celts. (The classical authors bemoaned the Celts' habit of drinking undiluted wine, unpalatable according to the norm in the Mediterranean world at the time.) Evidence of human sacrifice in and around La Tène suggests a public religious function for the site.

Celtic religion entailed belief in a number of different gods, some of them specific to individual tribes. There was Epona, an equine goddess; Sucellus, god of the hammer; Cernunnos, "wearer of deer's antlers"; and Lug, god of art and war (especially in his later expression in Irish mythology). Temple worship appears not to have been widespread; rather, the individual's relationship to the gods was personal. The details of the religion are not particularly well known, in part because the Celts had no system of writing and left only a few inscriptions in Latin and Etruscan late in their history.

## DEMISE

La Tène Celtic culture is said to have ended with the Roman conquest of Gaul (Western Europe) between 58 and 50 BCE. By this time, the culture had changed considerably, with fortified settlements appearing at major trading points, temple construction on the increase, and homes for elites receiving extra protection. The Celts were not entirely eliminated as a people but were forced to adapt to new circumstances and merge with other peoples and cultures. Celtic religion, customs, and art, however, were able to survive in regions that remained outside the Pax Romana, such as Ireland and Scotland. This is ultimately what formed the basis of the flourishing Gaelic culture in that region as well as the popular Celtic revival of the late nineteenth and early twentieth centuries, with its heightened interest in Celtic art, Gaelic literature, and early song and dance. Another Celtic revival took place during the New Age era of the 1980s, and a Gaelic revival movement remains strong today in Ireland, Wales, and Scotland.

## RECENT DISCOVERIES AND CURRENT STATUS

The latest archaeological finds relating to the La Tène phase of Celtic culture add details to our understanding without fundamentally altering the consensus view. A number of additional burials have been uncovered, including, in 2013, a large necropolis (cemetery) in northern France; it largely confirms the importance of warriors within the society.

Today, La Tène is a small holiday resort. The Laténium museum, in Neuchâtel, focuses on the prehistory of the region, especially La Tène culture.

*Michael Shally-Jensen*

*See also:* Rome; Stonehenge.

## FURTHER READING

Cunliffe, Barry W. 2003. *The Celts: A Very Short Introduction.* New York: Oxford University Press.

Farley, Julia, and Fraser Hunter, eds. 2015. *Celts: Art and Identity.* London: British Museum Press.

Haywood, John. 2004. *The Celts: Bronze Age to New Age.* New York: Pearson Longman.

Jones, Prudence, and Nigel Pennick. 1995. *A History of Pagan Europe.* New York: Routledge.

# Lapita People

The Lapita people were the earliest settlers of a large swath of the southwestern Pacific. Part of the broad Austronesian expansion, the Lapita people flourished ca. 2000–ca. 500 BCE. Much connected these people, despite the long distances between their islands; the most readily apparent connection in the archaeological record is their distinct pottery. They produced unique decorations on their earthenware using some sort of serrated stamp. Their islands of settlement ranged from the Bismarck Archipelago in the northwest to the Solomon Islands, New Caledonia, Vanuatu, Fiji, Wallis, Futuna, and finally to Tonga and Samoa in the east. They are called the Lapita people based on the archaeological type site of Lapita, which was discovered in 1952 near the village of Kone, on the west coast of New Caledonia's Grand Terre island. Since then, over 200 hundred additional sites have been found, allowing us to better delineate the wide swath of their territory.

## INHABITANTS

The Lapita people were a part of the eastward Austronesian expansion. These skilled seafarers and explorers originated from the island of Taiwan. They first set out from Taiwan before 3000 BCE and eventually went on to settle enormous sweeps of the Indian and Pacific Oceans. The Lapita spoke a Proto-Oceanic language, a branch of the wider Austronesian language family. There are opposing theories on the route(s) the Lapita took from Taiwan to get to their eventual homelands. Unfortunately, much of the debate on the identification of the different Austronesian peoples has for centuries been tied up with problematic colonial European views on race.

## HISTORICAL BACKGROUND

The Austronesians developed outrigger ships, which have a float—or outrigger—fastened to one or both lateral sides of the main hull. This technological innovation,

---

*Terra Australis*

Terra Australis, meaning "South Land," was a large continent assumed to be in the Southern Hemisphere. The proposed continent has ancient roots and was popular until navigation of the globe precluded its existence. Cicero discussed a southern land in his famous *Dream of Scipio*, in the first century BCE. The geographer Ptolemy more formally proposed a southern continent in the second century CE. It was important to him and others that the landmass of the Southern Hemisphere matched that of the Northern Hemisphere for the sake of symmetry. The idea was largely accepted for centuries, and Terra Australis began appearing on globes and maps in the fifteenth century CE. As the earth was navigated, the idea began to fall out of favor; however, the proposed continent still appeared on maps through the eighteenth century. The continents of Australia (which shares a Latin root with Terra Australis) and Antarctica proved the existence of southern continents previously unknown to much of the world; however, they proved much smaller than what Terra Australis had been assumed to be.

still utilized today by their descendants and others, greatly stabilizes the seafaring craft, especially amid choppy or stormy seas. This allowed the Austronesians to become experts at navigating and traversing the open seas and oceans. The technology helped spark an explosion of Austronesian exploration and settlement.

Sometime before 3000 BCE, Austronesian explorers originally set out from Taiwan. They first settled in the Philippines, and from there, some moved on to Indonesia and Malaysia. In almost all of the locations where the early Austronesian peoples arrived, they came upon inhabitants already living there, with whom they integrated. Some Austronesian peoples traveled east or northeast to the small islands of what is today known as Micronesia. Others traveled west to the Indian Ocean, eventually making it as far as Madagascar, off the southeast coast of Africa.

One branch of these diffuse movements of Austronesians, the Lapita people, first lived in the Bismarck Archipelago, which lies just north of New Guinea. They are distinguished from other Austronesian peoples by their unique pottery, an analysis of which allows their movements to be tracked across the Pacific. As the archaeological record currently stands, they first began producing this pottery on the Bismarck Archipelago in the early to mid-second millennium BCE. Around 1200 BCE, they seem to have picked up and migrated to the southeast: at this time, their pottery first appeared on the Solomon Islands and stopped being produced on the Bismarck Archipelago. In both of these locations, the Lapita lived among other non-Austronesian peoples, who had inhabited these islands for tens of thousands of years.

As the Lapita people migrated farther southeast from the Solomon Islands, they were likely the first settlers on most if not all of their new islands. Shortly after the time they appeared on the Solomon Islands in the late second millennium BCE, they also settled Vanuatu, New Caledonia, and Fiji. From there, they appear to have been the earliest humans to have settled or even entered what is today known as Polynesia, the broad—that is, tens of millions of square miles—sweep of the Pacific west of Fiji. They settled in Wallis, Futuna, Samoa, and Tonga in the early first millennium. Non-Lapita Austronesian peoples explored farther: north to Hawaii, south to New Zealand, and east to Tahiti, Easter Island, and probably South America. Perhaps, these explorers were related to or descended from the Lapita, but Lapita-style ceramics—as far as the present evidence shows—did not make it farther than the western Polynesian islands of Samoa and Tonga.

This cast of a pot sherd exhibits a geometric design indicative of Lapita culture. Artifacts like this have allowed historians to track the group's movement across the Pacific. (The Metropolitan Museum of Art, New York. Rogers Fund, 1980. www.metmuseum.org)

## CULTURE AND SOCIETY

The material record offers us a firsthand look at the Lapita people. The stylized pottery that has allowed us to track their movements across the Pacific was a fired earthenware. They used a serrated tool to stamp geometric and—less often—figurative designs into their bowls, pots, and beakers. Their ware was bifurcated, with plain, undecorated pottery found among the famously decorative vessels and sherds. As the Lapita people expanded eastward and the centuries progressed, the designs simplified. After Lapita ceramics ceased being produced, it was replaced with other forms of decorative ware, which is sometimes labeled post-Lapita pottery.

The archaeological record offers us much information on this ancient society beyond their pottery. We know that they domesticated dogs, pigs, and chickens and cultivated yams, taro, breadfruit, bananas, and coconuts. They also fished and gathered shellfish. Their diffuse expansion is the strongest possible testament to their immense seafaring and navigation prowess. They practiced tattooing; in fact, the word *tattoo* comes from the Samoan language, a successor of the language that the Lapita spoke. Their tattoo designs likely resembled that of their Polynesian descendants and were, perhaps, related to some of the patterns found on Lapita pottery.

## DEMISE

The Lapita people did not face a demise so much as an evolution in ceramics style. By the end of the first millennium BCE, all of the many sites that had at one point produced Lapita pottery stopped doing so, and the specific serrated stamped designs disappear from the material record. Other decorative ceramic styles proliferated instead, including those with decorative incisions or impressions. However, the people producing and using the pottery continued to flourish. The many branches of the broad Austronesian expansion blossomed for centuries. Thousands of miles to the west, Austronesians settled Madagascar in the mid-first millennium CE. The Pacific Austronesians, perhaps descendants of the Lapita people, made it as far as Hawaii, New Zealand, and Easter Island by the early second millennium CE.

## RECENT DISCOVERIES AND CURRENT STATUS

Ever since the Lapita site near the village of Kone in New Caledonia was first excavated in 1952, archaeologists have been busy locating and analyzing additional sites that have Lapita-style pottery and, therefore, a shared culture. Over 200 such sites have been identified, and excavations and analyses are ongoing. The broad scope of the different sites offers researchers a clearer understanding of the Lapita people's existence over the first and second millennia CE and across thousands of miles.

*Anthony Vivian*

*See also:* Easter Island; Indigenous Australian Cultures.

## FURTHER READING

Bellwood, Peter. 1978. *Man's Conquest of the Pacific*. London: Collins.
Chiu, Scarlett, and Christophe Sand. 2013. *From Southeast Asia to the Pacific: Archaeological Perspectives on the Austronesian Expansion and the Lapita Cultural Complex*. Taipei: Center for Archaeological Studies, Research Center for Humanities and Social Sciences, Academia Sinica.
Clark, G., A. Anderson, and T. Vunidilo, eds. 2000. *The Archaeology of Lapita Dispersal in Oceania: Papers from the 4th Lapita Conference*. Canberra: Pandanus Books.
Kirch, Patrick Vinton. 1997. *The Lapita Peoples: Ancestors of the Oceanic World*. Oxford: Blackwell.

# M

## Machu Picchu

At its height, the Inca Empire spanned a region extending from the northern border of modern-day Ecuador to an area south of Santiago, Chile. The empire included some twelve million people and used almost 25,000 miles of roads to connect cities and smaller communities throughout this vast area. Machu Picchu, a fifteenth-century CE Inca city built into the side of a mountain in the Eastern Cordillera of southern Peru, has been considered one of the New Seven Wonders of the World. Although of great importance to the Inca people, it was remote enough as to have gone undiscovered by the Spanish when they conquered the Incas in the mid-1500s; it was never plundered or destroyed by the conquistadors. In fact, Machu Picchu did not come to world attention until 1911, when the Yale archaeologist Hiram Bingham became the first Euro-American to lay eyes on it.

Machu Picchu is set in the middle of a mountain forest on the eastern side of the Andes Mountains. Its terraces, stairways, and walls are designed to blend in seamlessly with the natural location. The buildings in this citadel city are exceptionally well made, having held up against earthquakes and landslides as well as the elements. With its placement on a cloud-covered ridge amid taller peaks, Machu Picchu has long inspired modern visitors with its ethereal feel and fascinating history.

## INHABITANTS

Machu Picchu serves to reinforce the understanding that Inca society was highly stratified. The highest tiers of the citadel were reserved for royalty; the lower tiers were occupied by workers and other members of the peasant class. As impressive as it was architecturally, the city was not especially large: roughly 500 to 750 people lived in its rooms and temples, which appear to be carved out of the rock but are actually neatly sculpted constructions.

Archaeologists believe, based on skeletal evidence, that the Inca were not the only people to live in Machu Picchu. People of other ethnicities from different parts of the empire may have come to live in this city high up in the Andes.

Some small farming was probably done on the mountain, as various large terraced areas are present. It is unlikely, however, that sufficient crops could have been grown there to support the city's entire population; rather, food supplies must have been brought up from the surrounding areas.

While archaeologists have uncovered some information about who lived at Machu Picchu, they have less information about why, exactly, they might have lived there. Even today, although a good deal is known about Inca religion, culture,

> *Rio de Janeiro*
>
> The famed bustling metropolis of Rio de Janeiro, Brazil, faces multiple climate challenges.
>
> The region that would become Rio de Janeiro was inhabited by a number of peoples before the Portuguese arrived, including the Puri, Tupi, Botocudo, and Maxakalí. The Portuguese first arrived in the vicinity on New Year's Day 1502; the name *Rio de Janeiro* means "January River" in Portuguese. In the eighteenth century, gold and diamonds were discovered in the area, vaulting Rio de Janeiro past other Brazilian ports in importance. The city became the American capital for the Portuguese Empire in 1763 and then home of the Portuguese royal family, who were fleeing from Napoleon's forces, from 1815 to 1822. On September 7, 1822, Brazil won its independence from Portugal, and Rio served as the capital to an independent Brazil until 1960.
>
> Rio de Janeiro has long been a cultural hub. From the time of its independence until well into the twentieth century, Rio hosted a thriving literary scene that has featured such heavyweights as Machado de Assis. The music and theater scenes have likewise flourished. Rio, like much of the rest of Brazil, is crazy for soccer; global stars such as Romário and Ronaldo were born there.
>
> Rio de Janeiro exists in a hot and humid climate that will get hotter in the coming years. In fact, thanks to the rapid deforestation of the area surrounding the urban center, Rio is currently warming at a faster rate than the rest of the globe. Like other coastal cities, Rio de Janeiro is on the front lines of the fight against rising sea levels. Experts also warn that the proliferation of disease, sparked by flooding, extreme heat, and other climatic changes, will be a—if not *the*—major climate challenge for the city.

and society, many aspects of Inca civilization remain obscure and continue to be explored by scholars. The problem is compounded by the fact that, unlike the major Mesoamerican societies of this period, the Inca had no system of writing.

## HISTORICAL BACKGROUND

Machu Picchu seems to have been built between 1438 and 1471, during the rule of King Pachacuti. It conforms to other projects erected under this leader but stands out in its level of refinement. The main structure is indeed something of a wonder, built from granite blocks, without mortar, and with such tight fits between the stones that a knife blade cannot be inserted between them. The complex is made up of dwellings, storehouses, temples, and palaces. Overall, the site appears to have been a religious center used for ceremonies. It is also surrounded by a moat, though experts believe that the moat's purpose was to provide cultural isolation, not military protection.

Machu Picchu was barely a hundred years old when the Spanish entered the region and forced the Inca to defend themselves. In so doing, the Inca warriors did not retreat to Machu Picchu but instead took up a position at Vilcabamba, leaving Machu Picchu essentially unattended. However, the finer points of the Inca's movements through the area before and after the colonial encounter remain subject to debate.

When Hiram Bingham came upon Machu Picchu, he believed he had found the legendary Lost City of the Incas, where, according to early colonial chronicles, the last of the Inca leaders had held their ground against the Spanish conquistadors. Although Bingham had indeed discovered a lost city, it was not the one he thought it was. The last capital defended by the Inca, Vilcabamba, was also encountered by Bingham, but he misidentified it. Bingham's belief about Machu Picchu being the legendary Lost City remained with him until his death in the mid-1950s. It was not until the late twentieth century that explorers showed that Vilcabamba was likely the Lost City mentioned in the early texts and that Machu Picchu was essentially unknown when Bingham "discovered" it.

## CULTURE AND SOCIETY

The "purpose" of Machu Picchu as a city has been debated by archaeologists, and the picture has changed over time. Bingham's original belief that he had located the city defended by the Inca against the Spanish led researchers in the early twentieth century to view the site as a citadel—that is, a military structure designed to withstand powerful attacks. Subsequently, that view was modified. The "citadel," as it is still sometimes called, is made up of several different sectors: farming zones, residential districts, a sacred area, and royal districts. Modern scholars believe that the location may have been a convent for religious leaders, a home for one of the leaders of the Inca, or perhaps a place for the wealthy to visit when they wanted to escape the bustle and noise of city life. While there is no firm consensus, few today hold that Machu Picchu was strictly a military citadel.

Two of the more famous monuments in Machu Picchu are the Temple of the Sun and the Intihuatana stone. The Temple of the Sun is considered to have been a place for the Inca people to worship the sun god, Viracocha, their creator and the most important deity in their pantheon. Windows inside the structure were constructed to view the summer and winter solstices and possibly the stars. The Intihuatana stone is thought to be a solar calendar.

The Inca possessed a highly developed political and administrative system. When they conquered a city, they would leave a militia behind to guard against insurrection. They would also move individuals from their homeland to another city to keep them from revolting. The Inca are known for practicing human sacrifice as well—particularly the sacrifice of children. They seem to have believed that children would be deified after death owing to their sacrifice.

## DEMISE

Since there is no record of Machu Picchu in the Spanish documentation of the time, it is difficult to understand exactly what happened to the remote location. Most scholars believe that smallpox, one of the most common diseases transmitted by Europeans to the Indigenous cultures in the Americas, may have infected the inhabitants of Machu Picchu. As smallpox was extremely lethal to Indigenous peoples, an infection would have spread quickly and been devastating to the populace. Because of its relative remoteness and the way it blends into the natural scenery, the city might well have been left abandoned for centuries until European and American explorers began searching the Andes for ancient ruins.

## RECENT DISCOVERIES AND CURRENT STATUS

Tourism is the main "purpose" of Machu Picchu today, and tourism dollars help support not only the local economy but also ongoing preservation efforts at the site. Heavy tourist traffic poses a threat, however, even though no vehicles are allowed and one must walk to the site from far below. Other major threats to Machu Picchu include extreme weather and landslides.

During the original exploration of Machu Picchu in the early twentieth century, artifacts were sent back to Yale University. In recent years, the Peruvian government has become increasingly insistent that these artifacts be returned to their homeland. At first, Yale sent back only a selection of the items. Peru's demands escalated, however, and in 2008, it sued the U.S. government over the matter. Subsequently, President Barack Obama intervened and facilitated the return of the material.

Machu Picchu was declared a UNESCO World Heritage Site in 1983.

*Michael Shally-Jensen*

*See also:* Chavín de Huántar; Nazca.

## FURTHER READING

Alconini, Sonia, and R. Alvan Covey, eds. 2018. *The Oxford Handbook of the Incas.* New York: Oxford University Press.
MacQuarrie, Kim. 2007. *The Last Days of the Incas.* New York: Simon and Schuster.
Morris, Craig. 2011. *The Incas: Lords of the Four Quarters.* New York: Thames & Hudson.
Rice, Mark. 2018. *Making Machu Picchu: The Politics of Tourism in the Twentieth Century.* Chapel Hill: University of North Carolina Press.

# Madurai

The Vaigai River cuts through the center of Madurai, an ancient city in what is now the Tamil Nadu province of southern India. Hills and mountains rise to the north and west. The sea is a little less than 70 miles to the east and to the south, and the southern tip of India is only about 150 miles to the south. The city sits on a flat, fertile plain in what is classified as a tropical savanna climate. The temperatures can be scorching, with highs averaging above ninety degrees Fahrenheit for most of the year. The dry season lasts about twice as long as the wet season.

The abundant historical sites live in and among the vibrant modern city of Madurai, which hosts a population of over a million people. Arulmigu Meenakshi Sundareshwarar Temple, also known simply as Meenakshi Temple, rises south of the Vaigai River. Built at the turn of the thirteenth century CE, the massive Hindu temple is the city's most famous site. Only two miles to the southeast stands

> ### Seven Pagodas
>
> The Seven Pagodas—or the Seven Pagodas of Mahabalipuram—denote what some have supposed to have been a once magnificent building program at Mahabalipuram, known to locals as Mamallapuram. The seventh-century CE Shore Temple, named for its location directly on the coast of the Bay of Bengal, still stands today with its two towers. According to legend, the site originally totaled Seven Pagodas, or holy structures, with the remaining pagodas having supposedly been swallowed by the sea. Mahabali, the ancient Hindu king, is credited with founding Mahabalipuram at the site where his great-grandfather Hiranyakashipu was killed by the god Vishnu for failing to pay him due respect. Mahabalipuram has long fascinated and been visited by Europeans, including Marco Polo, who mentioned the Seven Pagodas in the thirteenth century. Ever since the tsunami that struck the region in 2004 briefly retracted the sea and seemed to reveal ancient ruins to eyewitnesses, there has been a renewed interest in the shore off Mahabalipuram and the story of the Seven Pagodas.

another site of renown, Thirumalai Nayak Palace. This seventeenth-century structure was home to the Nayaks of Madurai after they broke off from the Vijayanagar Empire.

## INHABITANTS

Although a rich diversity of peoples have lived in Madurai over the centuries, it is primarily known as a cultural hub of the Tamil people. Today, the Tamils live across southern India and Sri Lanka. The Tamil language spoken in Madurai is a part of the Dravidian family of languages. Historically, Madurai was the power base of the Pandya dynasty, one of the Tamil regions' three major dynasties. Although the city underwent multiple periods of Muslim leadership, it is predominately Hindu and has been seen as a hub of Hindu worship and intellectualism for millennia.

## HISTORICAL BACKGROUND

The history of Madurai stretches back at least until the third century BCE. The city appears in Kautilya's Sanskrit treatise *Arthashastra* and is also identified in Sangam literature as the capital of the Pandyas. The city's reputation, even in this early stage, reached far beyond India and Indian literature. Megasthenes, a Greek ethnographer, is said to have visited and written about Madurai (though some claim he instead visited Mathura, in northern India). Other ancient Mediterranean authors have mentioned Madura, including, Pliny the Younger, Ptolemy Claudius, and Strabo.

The early period of Madurai's history is known today as the Sangam period, which ranged from ca. 300 BCE (or before) to ca. 300 CE. Later literature describes three Sangam academies, the last of which occurred at Madurai. These academies were assemblies of Tamil scholars and poets that supposedly lasted for centuries. Although the narratives depicting these academies are steeped in legend, and some features are undoubtedly exaggerated, their widespread prevalence and

Colorful carvings of gods and goddesses adorn the walls of the seventeenth-century Meenakshi Temple in Madurai, India. (Travel Pictures Gallery)

acceptance in later literature indicate that aspects of this history must be true. This shows that Madurai was known as a scholarly and cultural hotspot even at this early stage.

During the Sangam period, three dynasties ruled the Tamil regions, which roughly correspond to southern India; these dynasties were the Pandya, the Chola, and the Chera. Each had its ancestral portion of the region, and the Pandyas were based in Madurai. Following the Sangam period, the Kalabhra dynasty ruled over the Tamil regions from ca. 300 to ca. 600. We know less about this period because of the relative lack of literature. Much of our information comes from a long inscription from the eighth century, and some even go as far as to contend that Kalabhra rule is all or largely legend.

Around the turn of the seventh century, King Kadungon ended the Kalabhra dynasty and brought the Pandyas back to power; they were once again centered in their ancestral capital of Madurai. Sendan, Arikesari, and other later kings then expanded their land until the Pandyas controlled all of southern India, except for a strip of land down the west coast. They ruled Madurai until 920, when the city was swallowed up by the rapidly expanding Chola Empire. At their empire's height, the Cholas exerted influence over the southern and eastern portions of the Indian peninsula, half of Sri Lanka, and many sites around the Bay of Bengal.

The Pandyas came back to power in Madurai in the early thirteenth century and ruled over an empire centered in the city for a little over a century. Many look to this century as the height of Madurai's long existence. King Kulasekara Pandya oversaw the construction of the renowned Meenakshi Temple during this period. The empire flourished politically, territorially, and culturally until the early fourteenth century. At that point, the city briefly came under the control of the Delhi sultanate, a Muslim empire ruled by a dynasty of Turkic origin. The Madurai sultanate then separated from this larger empire but retained Muslim rule over the city until the Hindu Vijayanagar Empire captured Madurai in 1371.

The Vijayanagar Empire ruled over Madurai and the rest of southern India for the majority of the next two centuries. This empire thrived in part by decentralizing authority: they appointed Nayaks (governors) who were required to pay tribute to the empire but wielded a considerable amount of autonomy to rule their various regions. In the mid-sixteenth century, the Madurai Nayaks seceded from the Vijayanagar Empire and ruled as completely autonomous rulers until the eighteenth century. Finally, the Nawabs of the Carnatic, a Muslim sultanate, ruled the city and region for several decades before the onset of British colonial rule.

## CULTURE AND SOCIETY

Madurai has been a cultural and intellectual hub for millennia. In the Sangam era, the city hosted the third and final Sangam academy, where all extant Sangam—or ancient Tamil—literature outside of *Tolkāppiyam* was reportedly written. While this may be an oversimplification, there is little doubt that many of the thousands of Sangam-era poems were written in Madurai. As the centuries progressed and Madurai cycled through different leaders, it retained its status as a cultural focal point. Although other religions were present, the city thrived as a center of Hinduism. Different strands of Hinduism dominated the local scene: At first, Shaivism flourished, which was later supplemented by Saivism and Vaishnavism. The city became renowned for its Hindu architecture, especially but not limited to the breath-taking Meenakshi Temple.

Over the centuries, Madurai's society underwent vast changes, but many constants remained. The Vaigai River feeds the surrounding lands, rendering them fertile, and the inhabitants of Madurai have utilized these lands for agricultural production, particularly as rice paddies. Although agriculture was the foundation of the city's economy, Madurai was also a major trading center, connected via nearby ports to the maritime Silk Road. The city boasted trading connections as far away as the Mediterranean Sea as far back as the first centuries BCE. The region was known to the outside world for its exquisite pearls.

## DEMISE

Madurai's long history included many different regimes. The city was ruled by local Pandyas, neighboring Cholas, a sultanate based in Delhi, and many others. However, up through the eighteenth century, the city had always been ruled by powers based somewhere on the Indian subcontinent. This reality came to an end with an influx of European colonial presence in India. After asserting increasing influence in the region for decades, the British East Indian Company took over direct control of Madurai in 1801 and ruled the city until the end of World War II. Nevertheless, the city remained a religious, cultural, and intellectual hub throughout the British colonial period and beyond.

## RECENT DISCOVERIES AND CURRENT STATUS

Historical structures fill the modern bustling city of Madurai. Among the most famous sites are the seventeenth-century Tirumalai Nayak Palace and two Vishnu temples: Koodal Azhagar Temple and Alagar Koyil. The most famous site, however, is the thirteenth-century temple to Parvati and Shiva: Meenakshi Temple. This spacious temple remains a center for community, hosting festivals every month of the year. The most famous festival held there is Meenakshi Thirukalyanam, the springtime wedding festival that brings in over a million people annually. Madurai remains the cultural hub that it was in antiquity. With its bustling nightlife, it has earned itself the name *Thoonga Nagaram*, or "Sleepless City."

*Anthony Vivian*

*See also:* Vijayanagara.

## FURTHER READING

Nilakanta Sastri, K. A. 2000. *A History of South India: From Prehistoric Times to the Fall of Vijayanagar*. Oxford: Oxford University Press.

Singh, Upinder. 2008. *A History of Ancient and Early Medieval India: From the Stone Age to the 12th Century*. New Delhi: Pearson Education India.

Srinivasa Iyengar, P. T. 2019. *History of the Tamils from the Earliest Times to 600 A.D.* Chennai: MJP Publishers.

Velappan, D., and C. A. Sham Shankar. 2019. *Economic History of Tamil Nadu: 200 B.C.– 2000 A.D.* Chennai: MJP Publishers.

## Maya

Maya culture, which flourished between 250 and 900 CE, was based in what is today southern Mexico, Guatemala, Belize, El Salvador, and western Honduras. For centuries before this Classic period of their history, the Indigenous Maya people were settled agriculturalists who made a living through the production of maize (corn), beans, cocoa, and other crops. Yet, they also ultimately became determined warriors who established dominance over a vast area of Central America. They engaged in rapid urbanization, building major civic centers, such as Tikal, Copán, Palenque, Caracol, Bonampak, Chichén Itzá, and Uxmal. These centers were less part of a uniform empire than constituent members of an aggregate political bloc within which they both cooperated and competed with each other.

It was belief in the gods, and faith in their kings (and queens) as divine rulers, that aided the expansion of Maya political power and fostered the growth of a complex hierarchical society. It was also this faith that produced elaborate temple pyramids, great decorated palaces, brilliant painted murals, and other remarkable

> **Ciudad Blanca**
>
> Ciudad Blanca, or the "White City," is a legendary city of great wealth on Honduras's Mosquito Coast. This region extends across most of Nicaragua's Caribbean coast up into Honduras and was the historical region of the Mosquito Kingdom. Replete with dense rainforests, this area is far less accessible than Honduras's or Nicaragua's western regions. Stories of a grand, isolated city originated in local folklore and spread like wildfire among European and North American imperialists, who were eager to loot the region for its wealth and resources. Although the name Ciudad Blanca did not come into use until the twentieth century, Hernán Cortés received word of wealthy cities in the area and futilely sought them out in the sixteenth century. Aviator Charles Lindbergh is credited with coining the name, having witnessed a large white city in the area from the sky. In 1939, Thomas Morde claimed to have found the City of the Monkey God, which he claimed to be the same city, and the search and speculation has only ramped up through the twentieth and early twenty-first centuries.

works of art and architecture. The Maya studied the stars and planets and created a detailed calendar system. They also recorded their mythology, folklore, customs, and historic achievements in illustrated codices written in a hieroglyphic script—although only a few of these survive today.

## INHABITANTS

At around the time that the great northern city of Teotihuacán arose, Maya civilization began to develop on the Yucatán Peninsula of southern Mexico and Central America. The area eventually controlled by the Maya was divided into districts, each dominated by an urban center that maintained authority over its populace and surrounding towns and villages. These city centers varied in size and impact. One of the largest, Tikal, oversaw a territory of fifty square miles and housed a population of 40,000–60,000; it featured a temple that soared 212 feet in the air—the tallest pre-Columbian structure in the Western Hemisphere. Other centers were of comparable size or somewhat smaller, while the total population of the Maya cultural sphere could have been as high as four or five million.

The primary sites were religious and ceremonial centers run by a hereditary elite consisting of priests, rulers, high officials, and skilled artisans. Adjacent towns and villages were home to farmers, soldiers, lesser bureaucrats, simple craftspeople, and unskilled laborers. The lives of the latter group differed significantly from those of the ruling class. In fact, skeletal remains found in royal tombs and peasant graves show that the nobility were of a taller stature than farmer-laborers—no doubt as a result of better nutrition. Maya women sometimes rose to political prominence: two women leaders (Kan Ik, 583–604; and Zac Kuk, 612–615) ruled at Palenque, and women occasionally held high positions at other centers, too. The Mayan language, which is still spoken today, featured a number of regional dialects.

## HISTORICAL BACKGROUND

The beginnings of Maya culture date from about 1000 BCE with the introduction of pottery. The earliest Maya were farmers living in small villages. By the so-called Late Preclassic period (300 BCE–250 CE), one starts to see greater cultural complexity as evidenced by early temple structures with stuccoed and painted facades, built by commoners at the behest of Maya rulers. This period is also noted for the development of long-distance trade in such items as jade and obsidian. Stylistic elements in building and sculpture, which show affinities to Olmec art, begin to appear in far-flung sites.

The Classic period (250–900 CE) can be defined, among other ways, as the time when the Maya erected stelae, or carved monuments, with dates in the Maya calendar system. The stelae are stone slabs, each with a representation of an important Maya person (usually a ruler) on one side and hieroglyphic writing and dates on the other side. The stelae were erected in front of temples and palaces in the central areas of the cities for public viewing and recounted significant events in a ruler's life. Most of the other identifying features of Maya civilization, including pyramids, hieroglyphic writing, elaborate tombs, polychrome pottery, and urbanism, make their appearance during this period.

The height of Maya civilization was during the Late Classic period (600–900 CE), when building efforts, population, and artistic endeavors reached their peaks. The high population densities in the cities increasingly taxed the Maya farmers, who provided labor to construct the Maya temples and palaces and food for the city dwellers. These temples were situated on large pyramidal bases; adjacent to them were multiroomed palaces, carved stelae, large open plazas, ballcourts (where ceremonial games were played using hard rubber balls), raised causeways, and houses of varying sizes. Excavations at sites such as Palenque and Tikal have revealed elaborate tombs inside some of the pyramids and beneath certain palaces. Limestone was the most common building material, cut and carved without the use of metal tools.

There is evidence that other Mesoamerican groups both influenced and were possibly influenced by the Maya. The Olmec were clear predecessors, informing all aspects of the culture. Also, the great central Mexican urban center of Teotihuacán probably had an effect on the development of Classic Maya civilization. Other centers, such as Monte Albán (home of Zapotec culture), may have had a similar relationship.

## CULTURE AND SOCIETY

Maya painting, pottery, and sculpture share some clear resemblances to, and yet are markedly different from, those of most of their neighbors. The Classic Maya style is generally more elaborate and complex, featuring scenes of nobles, for example, accompanied by their ancestral deities and with inscriptions describing the events. Maya painting tends to be naturalistic, depicting real persons and events; the great murals at Bonampak, for instance, relate the story of a Maya raid and the capture and sacrifice of prisoners. Other Maya works, such as sculptures of the gods, can be highly stylized, with certain features, gestures, and colors signifying the individual subject and the type of act involved.

The impressive stone stairways on the pyramids at Tikal and elsewhere symbolized the divine road that one took from the land of humanity and the earth to that of the gods and the heavens. The supreme deity, often depicted as a snake, was Itzamna, creator of the world and lord of fire. Another powerful figure was Bolon Dzacab, or K'awiil, god of lightning, fertility, and maize; he is recognizable by his large rodlike nose and smoking "cigar" or stone celt sticking out from his forehead. No one today quite understands what such symbology means; in general, Maya imagery is filled with mysteries. The Maya did worship the feathered serpent god known as Kukulcán (or, to the Aztecs, Quetzalcoatl), which also appears in the mythology and iconography of Teotihuacán. The Maya world was one of symbolic divisions and subdivisions. The four directions were prominent, each one associated with a particular color, plant, and bird. There were specific numbered layers to the cosmos and the underworld. The latter was ruled by a jaguar god, who thrived on blood. Sacrifices—human and animal—to him and other gods were routine, as were torture and self-mutilation. These acts functioned as grim forms of ritual appeasement.

The Maya writing system was based on a set of 850 characters representing objects, concepts, and sounds. Using it, they recorded historical information, religious subject matter, and astronomical data. The Maya calendar was based on different cycles, including a 365-day solar year, a 360-day lunar year, a 584-day Venusian year, and a 260-day ceremonial year revolving around ritual activities. Not all of the Maya glyphs have been deciphered.

Besides worshipping the gods and erecting monumental buildings in their honor, the Maya made ceramics, jewelry, and cotton textiles, which they exported to other peoples of Mesoamerica in exchange for goods. Ancestor worship played a role throughout the society, as did the tracing of lineages—to a particular deity, in the case of elites. Maya warlords launched military campaigns with the guidance of divine sponsors, as often to capture prisoners for sacrifice and slavery as to acquire new territory. Thus, as with most any highly complex culture, Maya culture had its alluring aspects as well as its repulsions.

## DEMISE

Between about 800 and 900 CE, Classic Maya civilization collapsed. The construction of monumental works ceased, and most sites became virtually emptied out of inhabitants. The cause of such a rapid collapse has long been debated by specialists. Among the many theories that have been advanced are overpopulation, overuse of the soil, natural disasters, climatic changes, disease, crop infestations, peasant revolts, and invasions. None of these explanations has proved to be satisfactory on its own. Rather, scholars today have concluded that the collapse was probably due to multiple overlapping causes, heightened by increasing population, socioeconomic difficulties, ecological change, and political failure.

Overpopulation and ecological strain brought on by extensive clearing of the rain forest and overuse of the land for agriculture were key precipitating factors.

In addition, warfare between cities and cultures within the same region was endemic during the Late Classic period. Although a few smaller cities survived into the subsequent Postclassic period (900–1500 CE), the locus of power, such as it was, shifted to the northern Maya lowlands of the Yucatán Peninsula, while Maya groups living in the southern lowlands returned to their rural agrarian way of life.

The region as a whole never fully recovered, and even today, it remains lightly populated. Except for tourist sites such as Tikal and related civic centers, the ancient lands are mostly covered by jungle growth.

## RECENT DISCOVERIES AND CURRENT STATUS

Some controversy exists over the status of relations between the Maya and the Toltec, who became the new power in the region with the Maya's demise. The city of Chichén Itzá, in particular, raises questions that have been debated. Many scholars have assumed that Chichén Itzá was a Maya center that was later architecturally reworked by the Toltec who came to inhabit it. But recent dating efforts raise the prospect that the Maya there may have employed Toltec styles in finishing the city. This suggests that the two peoples may have interacted more closely than previously thought.

Another fruitful area of research in recent years has been the use of satellite imagery and scanning technology. In the first decade of the twenty-first century, archaeologists discovered a number of new structures hidden from sight by thick jungle growth through the use of satellite images. At least one pyramid and a number of other stone works were found buried under centuries of vegetal growth and decay. More recently, the scanning technology known as lidar (light detection and ranging) was used to reveal hundreds of hidden ruins near existing Maya sites in Guatemala and a number of entirely new sites in Mexico. The discoveries suggest that Maya civilization may have been home to hundreds of thousands more people than had previously been thought.

Several of the larger Maya centers have been designated as UNESCO World Heritage Sites: Tikal (1979), Copán (1980), Palenque (1987), Chichén Itzá (1988), Uxmal (1996), and Calakmul (2002). Most are well maintained and suffer not from neglect but from growing tourist traffic.

*Michael Shally-Jensen*

*See also:* Monte Albán; Olmecs; Teotihuacán; Tula.

## FURTHER READING

Coe, Michael, and Stephen D. Houston. 2015. *The Maya*. 9th ed. New York: Thames & Hudson.

Houston, Stephen D., and Takeshi Inomata. 2009. *The Classic Maya*. New York: Cambridge University Press.

Miller, Mary Ellen, and Megan E. O'Neil. 2014. *Maya Art and Architecture*. 2nd ed. New York: Thames & Hudson.

## Memphis and Saqqara

Memphis was the capital of ancient Egypt during the Old Kingdom period (ca. 2686–2181 BCE). This is sometimes referred to as the "Age of the Pyramids" because the famous pyramids at Giza were constructed during this time. While the Giza pyramids are notable for their precise stone fitting and their mysterious method of construction, they were not the first pyramids built in Egypt. At Saqqara (or Sakkara), near the capital city of Memphis (which lies about twenty-three miles south of present-day Cairo), the architect Imhotep built the Great Step Pyramid. This was constructed around 2630 BCE at the request of Djoser, a king from the Third Dynasty. Saqqara was a necropolis for the city of Memphis, and the Step Pyramid was its crowning glory.

### INHABITANTS

As early as 5000 BCE, people in the Nile River valley had a well-developed culture around food crops and domesticated animals. Given the near total absence of rainfall, such agricultural development was only possible through reliance on irrigation. Canals were built that required a great deal of labor and social cooperation, and this in turn fostered the growth of a centralized government with an authoritarian system of rule.

The nature of farm labor in Egypt did not change much over the course of the country's long history. In working the fields, the Egyptians used wooden plows pulled by oxen. The great majority of farm workers did not own their own land but were compelled to labor on the large estates of the nobility. Most such laborers were sharecroppers who received a proportion of the harvest as pay, with most of the bulk of the accrued wealth going to the landowners as well as to the government in the form of taxes.

In time, Egyptian villages came to be ordered around two central political systems: the delta area was known as Lower Egypt, and the southern region farther upstream along the Nile was called Upper Egypt.

Memphis became the cultural and economic center of Old Kingdom Egypt. In this era, the rulers living there sought to create monuments and burial grounds for themselves close by. (Prior to this time, officials and royalty were buried at Abydos, farther south in Upper Egypt.) With Djoser's placement of the Step Pyramid at Saqqara, the site's status was raised, and the Step Pyramid became the first truly massive pyramid tomb built for an Egyptian pharaoh.

### HISTORICAL BACKGROUND

It was the legendary southern king Menes (also known as Narmer) who, around 3050 BCE, first united the "two Egypts" by conquering the northern region and making it part of a single national monarchy. At that time, Menes also established a new city, later called Memphis, as the capital of the unitary kingdom.

By about 2700 BCE, the kings of the Old Kingdom had greatly expanded the central government. They began to construct the famous pyramids of Egypt. King

Djoser, founder of the Third Dynasty, constructed the first pyramid, which was the Step Pyramid at Saqqara. The Fourth Dynasty king Khufu and his successors were responsible for the better-known Giza pyramids. The king, or pharaoh, was considered a divine being, having powers that were essentially limitless.

While previous rulers and builders in Memphis had used mud bricks in their creations, when Imhotep designed a monument for King Djoser, he wanted it to be something that would withstand the ravages of time. He designed a stone pyramid standing at the center of a complex of temples. This basic design was followed, to one degree or another, in every subsequent funerary project carried out in ancient Egypt.

The Step Pyramid is actually a stack of *mastabas*, or platforms. There are six platform layers, or tiers, the uppermost of which stands 205 feet high. Compared with previous mud brick projects, the immense amount of labor required to create the pyramid represented a major change. Many scholars consider this a sign that the central government had gained more control over both the populace and the available material supplies than had previously been the case.

## CULTURE AND SOCIETY

As creators of one of the earliest human civilizations, the ancient Egyptians brought both practical knowledge and religious vision to bear to produce some of the world's greatest achievements. They built large cities, vast irrigation projects, gigantic pyramids, and beautiful temples, and they cultivated a written, hieroglyphic language using paper-like papyrus sheaves.

For several hundred years, between about 2950 BCE and 2180 BCE, Memphis was the busy capital of Egypt. It rested at a crucial position at the mouth of the Nile and was a port city. A significant number of workshops, warehouses, and factories were centered in the city, and they supplied food and goods throughout the kingdom. The god of Ptah, the deity of creation and artworks, was a primary focus, and he was considered the father of Imhotep, the sage designer who built the Step Pyramid.

As their monarchic power became increasingly centralized, the kings of Egypt faced few restrictions on their authority to establish and enforce laws, even as priests and nobles maintained considerable political influence in the royal court. The king's high officials were called viziers, and they served as judges and tax collectors, opening them up to corrupt influences and earning them little love among the populace. At the local level, the country was divided into forty-two provinces called nomes. Each nome had an official, the nomarch, to administer daily affairs.

Memphis is the Greek name of the Old Kingdom capital; the Egyptians themselves referred to Memphis as Hiku-Ptah and later as Inbu-Hedj (White Walls) due to its mud brick and painted walls. By the end of the Old Kingdom, it was called Men-nefer ("The Enduring and Beautiful").

While the Step Pyramid is closely associated with Djoser and contains his burial chamber, the design by Imhotep was quite innovative; there is evidence that the structure was redesigned and reconstructed several times, presumably as

Imhotep gained experience with the building method. His methods were perfected later in the Giza pyramids, yet the basic idea of layered stone, a square base, and inward-angled walls was his creation. However, Imhotep almost certainly took his own inspiration from a mastaba found in Saqqara itself.

Under the pyramid, there is a network of passageways, burial chambers for the pharaoh and his family members, and space for the storage of goods that would be used in the afterlife. The walls are decorated with reliefs showing the pharaoh participating in different crucial activities. Djoser's body was never recovered from the tomb, however; evidently the chambers were robbed in the years that followed the pharaoh's death and burial.

## DEMISE

Memphis was the central city in ancient Egypt through the Third through Sixth Dynasties. As time passed, the concept of a central government seems to have lost its hold over ancient Egyptian society. The priesthood had gained more power. Ironically, this seems to have been due to the same societal practices that caused so many temples and tombs to be built in the Saqqara area. The priesthood gave power to local officials, and small communities began to consider the central government irrelevant. Starting around 2181 BCE, Egypt experienced a period of great social unrest. A severe drought caused extreme famine, and without the strong central government, there was no ability to alleviate the suffering. Some scholars also point to the death of Pharaoh Pepi II as a factor; he had outlived all his potential successors and left no heir to the throne, thus contributing to the political chaos.

Whether the Old Kingdom, centered at Memphis, ended suddenly or simply transitioned into the next phase of Egyptian history is a matter of scholastic debate. Regardless of how the transition occurred, the Egyptian dynasties that followed had a different, more complex relationship with the priesthood, religion generally, and the design of funerary monuments and other building works. By the time of the Eleventh Dynasty, near the end of the third millennium, the Egyptian capital had moved to Thebes.

## RECENT DISCOVERIES AND CURRENT STATUS

Saqqara was designated a UNESCO World Heritage Site in 1979. While there had been exploration of the area in the 1840s, it was not until the 1970s that modern scientific exploration of the site began. Since then, several major discoveries have come to light from the various burial chambers and from sites nearby.

In 2011, a dog catacomb was discovered within the necropolis; almost eight million mummies of animals were found. Researchers believe that the animals may have been placed there to send the prayers of their owners to the gods. Then, in 2020, researchers uncovered a burial shaft that contained wooden and stone figures designed to assist their owners in the afterlife.

Another recent discovery occurred in 2018 and has been called a one-of-a-kind find for Egyptologists. A tomb was located far down a ridge that had been buried;

it appears to have escaped the attention of looters, something virtually unheard of. The tomb may have belonged to a high priest, his wife, and his family.

A number of these recent discoveries in the area have occurred because of ongoing restoration efforts at the Step Pyramid and nearby locations. It is hoped that such restoration work safely preserves the ancient sites and perhaps continue to reveal artifacts that escaped discovery by looters in times past.

*Michael Shally-Jensen*

*See also:* Abydos; Giza; Thebes.

## FURTHER READING

James, Peter. 2018. *Saving the Pyramids: Twenty-First-Century Engineering and Egypt's Ancient Monuments.* Cardiff: University of Wales Press.
Romer, John. 2017. *A History of Ancient Egypt.* Vol. 2, *From the Great Pyramid to the Fall of the Middle Kingdom.* New York: Thomas Dunne Books/St. Martin's Press.
Street, Francesca. 2020. "Mummies Discovered in Burial Shaft in Egypt." CNN, April 28, 2020. https://www.cnn.com/travel/article/ancient-egypt-discoveries-saqqara/index.html
Wilkinson, Toby A. H. 2001. *Early Dynastic Egypt.* New York: Routledge.

# Meroë

Meroë (pronounced mehr′-oh-ee) was the capital of the ancient Nubian kingdom of Kush (Cush), which was located to the south of the Egyptian heartland. The city's remains are located on the east bank of the Nile River, in present-day northern Sudan. The kings of Kush ruled there from the mid-sixth century BCE until the mid-fourth century CE. The site is best known for its impressive collection of Nubian pyramids, each exhibiting the distinctive steep, narrow profile identifying them as such.

## INHABITANTS

The Kingdom of Kush was the earliest of the Black African states to develop a civilization that competed with Egypt, even as it was strongly influenced by Egypt and maintained close contact with it for long periods. The region known as Nubia bordered Egypt to the south and extended beyond the banks of the Nile into desert areas to the east and west. The Kushite kingdom was centered on the Nile and extended from an area just north of the second cataract, near present-day Abu Simbel (by the Egypt-Sudan border), to an area to the south where the White Nile and Blue Nile meet, near modern-day Khartoum. The Kushites were bordered to the south by the ancient Ethiopians, to the east by the Beja (or Blemmyes), and to the west by nomadic desert tribes.

## HISTORICAL BACKGROUND

Meroë initially served as a secondary city to the Kushite capital of Napata, farther north. The kings of Napata rose to great prominence, succeeding in

Over eighty pyramids filled the ancient skyline of Meroë. The pyramids were constructed of mud brick and feature a distinctive steep and narrow style. (Maurice Brand | Dreamstime.com)

conquering Egypt during a period of weakness and ruling it as pharaohs of the Twenty-Fifth Dynasty (ca. 725–657 BCE); the Kushites were the famed "Black pharaohs" of that era. Meroë began to increase in importance near the end of this period as a result of the Assyrian takeover of the Egyptian cities of Memphis, Thebes, and other areas. Meroë had a good supply of iron ore and the wood charcoal needed to smelt it; the metal was used by the Kushite leaders to provide arms against the Assyrians. Nevertheless, the Assyrians managed to drive the Kushites from Egypt and threaten Napata, causing the Nubians to settle on Meroë as their new southern capital.

## CULTURE AND SOCIETY

The prosperity and longevity of the Kingdom of Kush may be attributed in part to Meroë's role as a major manufacturer of iron: its products were in great demand, even beyond the Nile region. The city also produced cotton textiles and served as a trade center along routes that stretched from the northeast coast of Africa inland and linked to the cities of Egypt in the north.

Meroë was a stratified society in which royals and government officials occupied the top tier, followed by merchants, skilled artisans, laborers, farmers, servants, and, probably, slaves.

Despite strong Egyptian influence, which is most evident in the pyramidal royal tombs and other architecture, Kush retained its own gods and language and developed its own script. Excavations reveal that the city featured royal palaces, temples to the gods Amon and Isis, domestic buildings, and a central water system as well as about eighty pyramids of varying sizes (averaging about sixty-five feet high). The pyramids were made of mud brick and, unlike those of Egypt, contained no internal passages or hidden tombs; rather, the deceased's remains were placed inside a tomb set in the ground (or bedrock), and the pyramid was constructed above it. A number of these burial sites were found to contain hoards of gold jewelry and other artifacts.

The Meroitic period of Nubian history is marked by a deemphasis of the Egyptian themes that characterized the previous Napatan period. Egyptian-style artifacts became less common as distinctive Indigenous styles arose. While the Kushites sometimes employed Egyptian hieroglyphs in their writing, Egyptian was not their primary language. Various inscriptions (primarily in Egyptian) make reference to campaigns against the eastern Beja, visits to cities and temples, construction works, and festive occasions.

## DEMISE

By the late first century BCE, the Roman Empire had extended its influence into Egypt, and the inhabitants of Kush came into contact with the powerful new rulers of the Mediterranean world. Relations between the Romans and Kushites were fairly strained, however.

As described by the Greek geographer and historian Strabo, in around 25 BCE, the governor of Egypt, Gaius Petronius, launched a punitive expedition against Kush, resulting in the sacking of the city of Napata. Within a couple of years, the Kushites moved a large force north to retaliate. Whether they succeeded or not is not known, but the Romans ultimately refrained from further conquest and never occupied the kingdom. They seem to have decided that overtaking Kush was not worth the effort involved. A famous symbol of the encounter is a bronze head of Emperor Augustus that was hacked off a Roman statue in Lower Egypt and brought home by the Meroites. (It is now in the British Museum.)

Subsequently, more building activity took place in Kush; these new works included the temple to Amon at Meroë and a temple to the lion-headed warrior god Apedemak at Naqa to the south. The Kushites believed that Apedemak brought them victory in war and helped them keep their enemies at bay.

The African kingdom of Kush flourished for nearly 1,000 years, and Meroë was at the heart of the kingdom for much of that time. Beginning in the second century CE, however, Kush as a whole fell into decline. Pyramid construction reflects this: the later cemetery structures are notably smaller than their predecessors. In the mid-fourth century CE, the kingdom was conquered by Ezana of Axum (Ethiopia), who brought Christianity to the area.

## RECENT DISCOVERIES AND CURRENT STATUS

Intensive archaeological excavations conducted over two centuries at Meroë and the surrounding Kushite lands have produced a wealth of findings, but the interpretation of materials is ongoing. The Meroitic language, for one, was long considered largely untranslatable, until in the 1990s some progress was finally achieved by examining funerary monuments. A recent (2018) find at Sedeinga, some 400 miles from Meroë, consists of a cache of additional Meroitic funerary texts, thus adding to our understanding of the language. A cemetery at Sedeinga also contains miniature pyramids, some of them barely two feet wide. The discovery suggests that outside the capital, the Kushites honored not only deceased royalty but also less illustrious citizens and family members.

In 2011, a few archaeological sites associated with the Kingdom of Kush were declared UNESCO World Heritage Sites. These include the city of Meroë and the nearby religious sites of Naqa and Musawwarat es-Sufra.

*Michael Shally-Jensen*

*See also:* Abu Simbel; Rome; Thebes.

**FURTHER READING**

*Archaeology.* 2018. "Cache of Meroitic Texts Recovered in Sudan." April 11, 2018. https://www.archaeology.org/news/6539-180411-sudan-meroitic-texts

Fisher, Marjorie M., ed. 2012. *Ancient Nubia: African Kingdoms on the Nile.* Cairo and New York: American University in Cairo Press.

Powell, Eric A. 2013. "Miniature Pyramids of Sudan." *Archaeology*, July/August 2013. https://www.archaeology.org/issues/95-1307/features/940-sedeinga-necropolis-sudan-meroe-nubia

Welsby, Derek A. 1998. *The Kingdom of Kush: The Napatan and Meroitic Empires.* Princeton, NJ: Markus Weiner.

# Moche Culture

The Moche people lived in what is now Peru—specifically, on the north coast—between about 100 and 700 CE. They left behind adobe brick pyramids, some of the most complex and beautiful pottery from the ancient world, and a history of ritual battle and human sacrifice. We know relatively little, however, about how the Moche lived on a day-to-day basis or what ultimately caused their demise, but the picture has begun to fill in in recent years. Some experts believe that elements of Moche culture evolved into that of the later Chimú (Chimor state); others think that the Moche were defeated by adverse weather events that produced social instability. Because the Moche themselves left no written record, archaeologists must rely on the material evidence. Among the key Moche sites are Sipán and San José de Moro, but others are scattered throughout the Moche River valley.

## INHABITANTS

Most of what we know about the Moche people comes from their artwork, primarily the images adorning their pottery. Common themes include craftwork, hunting, warfare, human sacrifice, and sexual acts. It is thought that Moche priests or priestesses took on the aura of gods in sacrificing prisoners for the collective good and that part of the ritual act was the drinking of the victim's blood. Sexual scenes shown on pottery usually display more ceremonialism than physical action,

### Guayaquil

Flooding and other dangers loom ahead for Guayaquil, Ecuador's primary port city.

The area that would later house Guayaquil was inhabited by Indigenous Ecuadorians for millennia. Among others, the Chorrera people flourished in the region for parts of the first two millennia BCE, as did the Manteño-Huancavilca people beginning in the first millennium CE. The Inca Empire controlled the area briefly in the fifteenth and sixteenth centuries. The Spanish established the city of Guayaquil in 1538 on the site of a local village, and the city became an influential port and trading post in the Spanish Pacific world.

In 1820, Guayaquil was the first Ecuadorian location to rebel from Spain, catalyzing its neighbors. The city hosted a consequential meeting between José de San Martín and Simón Bolívar, the two great liberators of much of South America. After a short stint as a part of Gran Colombia, Guayaquil and the remainder of Ecuador broke off to form its own republic in 1830. Today, the city is home to roughly three million people and remains an important port and trading hub responsible for most of Ecuador's international trade. Host of a vibrant cultural scene, Guayaquil has long been known for its literary and fine art scenes.

Guayaquil faces a confluence of challenges stemming from climate change. As the local climate is projected to get drier and hotter, Guayaquil will be at a greater risk of fire and drought. The city stands near a major fault line, creating an ongoing risk of earthquakes. Yet, the largest and most immediate risk for Guayaquil is flooding. The city already experiences frequent flooding in the wet season, which is January to April. Agricultural development has reduced the Guayas River's natural drainage, and the frequency and intensity of these floods only stand to increase with the rising sea level.

---

suggesting a religious or mythological aspect. Other themes found in Moche art include burials and boat travel, likewise seemingly mythologized.

Moche culture was most certainly based on agriculture. The people lived on the desert side of the Andes and used advanced systems of irrigation to create farmable land; indeed, there are still remnants left of their irrigation system today. The Moche also fished the ocean using reed boats and nets, hunted deer and small animals in the valleys and hills, and raised llamas for wool.

Another notable activity of the Moche was the building of large adobe pyramids, or *huacas*. The two best-known structures of this kind are Huaca del Sol and Huaca de la Luna—temples of the sun and the moon, respectively. These huacas were built with mud bricks and originally painted with rich murals; the sun and elements, however, have eroded most of the paintings after more than a thousand years. While there are other signs of Moche huacas in the area, few survived the looting and destruction carried out by the Spanish in the fifteenth and sixteenth centuries; some huacas appear to have contained gold and other valuable items, all of which were predictably stolen.

## HISTORICAL BACKGROUND

While archaeologists generally agree that the Moche period begins around 100 CE, opinions differ somewhat about how long the society survived. The end of Moche culture is usually dated to between 700 and 800 CE; some scholars, however, recognize a late Moche period extending to 900 or even 1200 CE. These scholars argue that the later Moche culture, which flourished on the other side of the Paijan desert to the south, indicate a different timeline for the Moche's fall. Reasons why a northern group may have died out but a southern group survived are not clear.

The Huaca del Sol took some 600 years to construct and thus shows several different phases in its construction. Toward the end of their dominance in the region, the Moche appear to have shifted from the use of more traditional adobe methods of construction to a chamber-and-fill approach—or the filling of open spaces behind or between walls with sand or gravel instead of building them out using solid material. While this may have been more convenient in the desert climate, it would not have held up as well during heavy rains and may have contributed in its own way to the dissolution of Moche culture.

## CULTURE AND SOCIETY

The Moche left no written record of their civilization, so what is known about them is based on interpretations of their art on the records created by other groups—particularly the Spanish, even though Moche society had long since passed out of existence by the time the conquistadors arrived—and on interpretations of the archaeological findings.

There is no doubt that the Moche were a technically advanced society. Their pottery shows signs of both careful crafting and mass production. Their irrigation system may have been more expansive than what currently exists in Peru. And they created fine works of art and massive adobe structures.

In addition to scenes on pottery, researchers have found physical evidence that the Moche may have practiced human sacrifice. Remains have been uncovered that carry clear marks of sacrificial cuts in them and appear to have been buried in mud. This could have happened only when the ground was very wet, of course, leading some experts to argue that the Moche conducted rites to welcome or encourage rain. For the Moche, living in an arid climate, regular rains would have been crucial to keeping the irrigation systems flowing and their crops watered.

It is thought that women may have played a significant role in Moche society. Moche pottery, which was usually decorated with a red-orange paint over a cream-colored slip, commonly shows various scenes of animal and human activity, but among them are a significant number of examples of women. Women are shown going about daily tasks, such as caring for children, but are also sometimes portrayed as shamans or religious leaders. This has led some researchers to suggest that there could have been a high-ranking priestess class among the Moche, or even perhaps a female political leader. That idea was recently bolstered by a notable mummy find (see "Recent Discoveries and Current Status").

## DEMISE

It is difficult to know exactly what led to Moche society's fading from the scene. One generally accepted idea concerns the onset of adverse weather conditions between 530 and 590 CE. Ice core samples from the Andes and elsewhere show that during that time, a period of about three decades of high rain volume was followed by another three decades of significant drought. For an agricultural society, such a scenario could obviously spell disaster. Intense weather over such a long period of time may have disrupted the Moche way of life and caused political and social unrest. Intense weather could also have affected their buildings and caused them to rethink their methods.

As noted, some researchers maintain that what remained of Moche society was transformed into what we know as the Chimú civilization. There is evidence that the Chimú may have occupied some of the remaining Moche buildings after the Moche's decline.

## RECENT DISCOVERIES AND CURRENT STATUS

Several interesting discoveries from the Moche area have been made recently. The first is a spectacular mummy, dubbed the Lady of Cao, found in a Moche huaca in 2005. She had been buried in a type of chamber reserved for elite members of society and was surrounded by valuable objects—both ceremonial and military—and covered with tattoos. Clearly, she must have been a priestess or other powerful member of Moche society.

In 2001, researchers found tombs containing fine textiles, metalwork, and ceramics in a huaca in the southern Moche area. These tombs were dated to the earliest Moche period and, interestingly, also contained the skeletons of people who were more than six feet tall. The archaeologists conducting the excavations noted that these individuals represent the tallest people they had ever seen entombed in South America.

As for the physical sites left behind by the Moche, only regional conservation efforts exist at this time. Some organizations have been working to have the two primary temple locations designated as UNESCO World Heritage Sites, but so far these efforts have been unsuccessful.

*Michael Shally-Jensen*

See also: Chan Chan.

## FURTHER READING

Benson, Elizabeth P. 2012. *The Worlds of the Moche on the North Coast of Peru.* Austin: University of Texas Press.
Bourget, Steve. 2016. *Sacrifice, Violence, and Ideology among the Moche: The Rise of Social Complexity in Ancient Peru.* Austin: University of Texas Press.
Malpass, Michael A. 2016. *Ancient People of the Andes.* Ithaca, NY: Cornell University Press.
Stone, Rebecca. 2012. *The Art of the Andes: From Chavín to Inca.* 3rd ed. London: Thames & Hudson.

# Mongol Empire

Genghis Khan (ca. 1162–1227 CE) and his successors built one of the largest empires in human history. It encompassed much of modern-day China, Korea, the

Middle East, and Russia. In some areas, the empire's rule lasted a hundred years or more; in others, it was shorter lived. The span of time between the proclamation of Genghis as *khagan*, or great khan, of the Mongols in 1206 CE and the period marked by the Russian defeat of the Mongols at Kulikovo in 1380, following the collapse of their Yuan dynasty in China (in 1368), includes the most impressive and important events of the famous Mongol Empire. Although aftershocks of Mongolian power persisted into the fifteenth century, most notably in the life of Timur (Tamerlane) and the Golden Horde, these were less significant upheavals than those occurring during the height of the empire.

## INHABITANTS

Central Asia has long been occupied by a variety of peoples, two of the most important of which are Turkic- and Mongolic-speaking populations who traditionally supported themselves by pastoral nomadism. They roamed across vast areas to graze their animals and extracted meat and milk from them for sustenance. "Mongol" itself was not actually a designation for the many tribes living on the Mongolian Plateau until the twelfth century CE and the rise of Genghis Khan. Before that, the different Mongolian, Turkish, and other communities of Inner Asia often fought among themselves, formed shifting alliances, and occasionally made raids into the more settled lands to the south. At times, strong leaders arose who brought together powerful tribal groupings to found states or dynasties in the steppes; they sometimes even established rule over parts of China or South Asia. The empires of the Huns in the fifth century CE, for example, and of the Seljuk Turks in the eleventh century were of this variety; they were also, typically, short-lived. During the seventy-five-year reign of Genghis Khan and his immediate successors, all of China, central Asia, Iran, Iraq, and most of Russia fell to Mongol rule.

The great military advantage of the Mongols was their mobility. They were brilliant cavalrymen and made good use of signal flags and the reflex bow, which they loaded and fired on the hoof. They could travel hundreds of miles in a few days, living on what they carried with them on their steeds. Mongol warriors were known for their violence, slaughtering or enslaving all who resisted; and they used

---

*Xanadu/Shangdu*

Xanadu, known to locals as Shangdu, was a real historical city within Inner Mongolia; however, it has since been mythologized. In the thirteenth century, the historical city served as the summer capital for Kublai Khan, founder of the Yuan dynasty, which was the successor state of the sprawling Mongol Empire that ruled over China. The city was conquered by the Ming dynasty the following century and later abandoned. Marco Polo visited the city in the 1270s, while Kublai Khan was still in power. His detailed description set in motion the city's transformation to the realm of myth. A local account of the city comes from Toghon Temur, the Yuan emperor of the following century, lamenting the loss of the city to the Ming dynasty. In 1797, Samuel Taylor Coleridge dozed off while reading old descriptions of the city. Inspired by an opium-induced dream, he penned the famous poem "Kubla Khan," completing the mythologizing of Xanadu.

psychological warfare as well, spreading stories of the horrors awaiting those who dared to oppose them. Genghis himself disliked foreign cities and preferred to leave them in ruins, their inhabitants killed or subjugated. Not surprisingly, the Mongols, with some exceptions, were poor administrators, allowing many of the lands of their empire to fall into disarray shortly after gaining control of them.

## HISTORICAL BACKGROUND

According to the oldest surviving literary work in the Mongolian language, *The Secret History of the Mongols* (composed sometime after the death of Genghis in 1227), the Mongol people date to a time when heaven instructed a blue-gray wolf and his wife, a fallow deer, to mate. Their son, Batachikan, was the first human ancestor of Genghis Khan. In ancient Chinese sources, the first mention of a people living on the steppelands north of China is in the eighth century BCE. (Archaeological evidence goes back further.) In ancient and medieval times, Mongolia was inhabited by a variety of nomadic peoples, including the Xiongnu (possible ancestors of the Huns), the Orkhon (Orhun) Turks, and the Uighurs. Early in the thirteenth century CE, Genghis Khan united the tribes of this area, and the people came to be known as Mongols. From his newly built capital of Karakorum, he rapidly expanded the Mongol Empire. At the time of Genghis's death in 1227, it extended from the Yellow Sea in the east to the Caspian Sea in the west and from Siberia in the north to Tibet in the southwest.

After the death of Genghis, the Mongol Empire was divided among his sons. By the late thirteenth century, there were four separate khanates (kingdoms): (1) the empire of Kublai Khan, who established the short-lived but notable Yuan dynasty (1279–1368) of China; (2) the Ilkhanid dynasty in Iran (known to the Mongols as Hülegü Ulus); (3) the Chagatai khanate in Turkistan; and (4) the khanate of the Golden Horde (Ulug Ulus), founded by Batu Khan in southern Russia.

Genghis Khan had been happy to live in a tent. It was his third son and successor, Ogedai, who established the imperial capital, Karakorum, in 1235. However, when Kublai moved the capital to Beijing in 1260, Karakorum was essentially abandoned. The city was well described by the European explorer William of Rubruck around that time, and it was finally destroyed by the Chinese in 1388. Kublai Khan's summer residence, Xanadu, was in turn described by Marco Polo, whose account inspired the English poet Samuel Taylor Coleridge to compose his immortal *Kubla Khan: or, A Vision in a Dream* (1816). Kublai was a wise and effective ruler who unified China after 150 years of discord and built up its wealth and reputation as a medieval power. At the same time, the move to Beijing weakened the Mongolian imperial project in other regions.

## CULTURE AND SOCIETY

Traditional Mongolian nomadic culture included modest "urban" centers, even before the establishment of Karakorum and the spread of the empire in the thirteenth century. The steppe nomads of Mongolia had long maintained a relationship with the settled farmers on the other side of the Great Wall of China, among other areas. The bulk of the Mongol population was made up of *arats*, or livestock-herding nomads who lived in tents and owed fealty to the high-born princes, who demanded goods and services in exchange for protection. In theory, the noble class traced its ancestry to Genghis Khan. In addition to the various khanates, or kingdoms, there were smaller territorial units overseen by princes and governors. There were also serfs or peasants called *khamjilgas*. The society as a whole was essentially feudal in form.

Classical Mongolian literature was rich in oral epics and other spoken forms, and some historical writing and legal codification developed as well. Genghis's famous *Yasa*, or code of laws, was an impressive compilation. Unfortunately, much of the old literature has been lost or is known in fragments only to specialists.

One Mongolian sport attributed to Genghis is the *zegeteaba*, or great hunt; it was a kind of war game made up of maneuvers and martial demonstrations. Other traditional sports were Mongolian wrestling, archery, and horse racing, all of which have to some extent survived.

After 1586, Tibetan Buddhism spread through Mongolia, and the Tibetan language along with Buddhist literature and art styles came into widespread use. Chinese merchants supplied the manufactured goods needed by the nomads, including Buddhist icons and artifacts. Chinese language and education became more common, especially among the princes, and Chinese literature and drama were cultivated.

## DEMISE

The Chinese expelled the last emperor of the Yuan dynasty residing in China in 1368. A remnant of the dynasty claiming rightful rule in China continued in Mongolia until the death of Ligdan Khan in 1634.

In the west, the Mongols under Batu withdrew from Eastern Europe in 1242 and settled in the southern Russian steppe. They continued their traditional way of life there and intermingled with the nomadic Turkish population. The resulting Turko-Mongolian ethnic community became the Tatars of Russian history, their khanate being known as the Golden Horde. Its capital was Sarai, in the lower Volga River region.

The Russian princes of the forest region north of the steppe served the Mongols as vassals. In time, however, the princes of Moscow and their city became increasingly important. By 1340, when the long-reigning Uzbeg (Öz Beg) Khan died, the Russians were threatening the Golden Horde in Sarai and surrounding areas. At the Battle of Kulikovo, in 1380, the Mongols were defeated by the Russians.

In the fourteenth century, the Persian and Turkistan khanates were taken over by the Turko-Mongol leader Timur (also known as Tamerlane; 1336–1405). He claimed descent from Genghis Khan, yet he was a Muslim and sought to build a new empire through the use of both the sword and Islamic symbols and language. Armies under Timur destroyed Sarai and the trading and political center of Astrakhan in 1395–1396. By then, the Mongol states had broken up, and the Mongols were repopulating their homeland in the steppes of eastern central Asia. It was the end of a once vast and somewhat inglorious empire.

There is one other conqueror of note who claimed descent from Genghis Khan as well as from Timur: Babur (1483–1530), founder of the Moghul Empire in India. From present-day Uzbekistan, where he is still celebrated as a cultural hero, Babur was steeped in Persian culture and introduced it, with lasting effects, to the subcontinent.

### RECENT DISCOVERIES AND CURRENT STATUS

The remains of the Mongol capital at Karakorum were only positively identified as such in 1889. Systematic excavation of the site began in the 1930s and 1940s, when Ogedai's palace, much degraded, was uncovered. Today, visitors can only see a few scattered remnants of medieval structures along with parts of a roughly contemporaneous Buddhist monastery. The surrounding Orkhun Valley of central Mongolia was declared a UNESCO World Heritage Site in 2004 to commemorate traditional Mongolian culture.

Xanadu (or as it is now styled, Shangdu), Kublai Khan's summer residence in Beijing, was destroyed by the Ming army in 1369. Some remains of it were identified in the late nineteenth century, but most of the city is gone today. Nevertheless, the location was declared a UNESCO World Heritage Site in 2012. A few small artifacts have been retrieved in recent years, but nothing that sheds light on the place beyond what was already known of it from medieval written sources.

*Michael Shally-Jensen*

*See also:* Mughal Empire.

### FURTHER READING

Jackson, Peter. 2017. *The Mongols and the Islamic World: From Conquest to Conversion.* New Haven, CT: Yale University Press.
Lane, George. 2018. *A Short History of the Mongols.* London: I. B. Tauris.
Man, John. 2014. *The Mongol Empire: Genghis Khan, His Heirs and the Founding of Modern China.* London: Bantam Press.
McLynn, Frank. 2015. *Genghis Khan: His Conquests, His Empire, His Legacy.* Boston: Da Capo Press.
Rossabi, Morris. 2009. *Kublai Khan: His Life and Times.* Berkeley: University of California Press.

## Monte Albán

Monte Albán (pronounced mohn'-tay ahl-bahn'), located just west of present-day Oaxaca City in southern Mexico, was the center of Zapotec civilization. Situated atop a high ridge that made it easier to defend, the city flourished for a thousand years between 200 BCE and 750 CE. Monte Albán's artistic works, particularly the intriguing *danzante* ("dancer") carvings of the early period, show Olmec

Monte Albán was the heart of the Zapotec civilization. Its cityscape featured pyramid-temples, among other structures. (Jesus Eloy Ramos Lara | Dreamstime.com)

influence. Glyphs from the site represent some of the earliest known writing and calendar usage in Mesoamerica.

The city included pyramid temples, palaces, decorated tombs, a ballcourt, and what seems to have been an astronomical observatory. Relief carvings and hieroglyphic texts, only some of which have been deciphered, appear to focus on military exploits and tales of conquest. The lower slopes of the city were terraced and held adobe dwellings sufficient to house a population of around 25,000.

## INHABITANTS

Monte Albán civilization developed in Mesoamerica at a time when two other major civilizations were also present in the region: Teotihuacán to the north of Monte Albán and the Maya civilization centered on the Yucatán Peninsula to the east. All three were distinct Indigenous societies and yet culturally were not entirely dissimilar.

The Zapotec people of Monte Albán spoke a language (Zapotec) that is still spoken, with modifications, by their descendants today. Monte Albán society had two basic classes: (1) farmers, artisans, and others, who formed the class of commoners, and (2) the hereditary elite, who were born into privileged positions and were responsible for maintaining religious traditions and conducting political affairs. Outside Monte Albán, there were a few smaller Zapotec towns whose residents brought the total population of the state to over 50,000 at its height, between 200 and 500 CE.

## HISTORICAL BACKGROUND

During the period from about 500 to 300 BCE, ancient Olmec civilization, centered in the eastern gulf region, spread west and south. It served as a base for the great civilizations of the Maya of lowland southeast Mexico, the Zapotec at Monte Albán, and the mixed population settled at Teotihuacán in the Valley of Mexico. Founded as early as 500 BCE, within the next hundred years, Monte Albán had a small civic-ceremonial center with stone temple platforms and a growing resident population. By 200 BCE, the town had become the most prominent center in the Zapotec territory, and over the next 300 to 400 years, it came to dominate the area surrounding the Central Valleys of Oaxaca.

While there are clear indications that Monte Albán maintained ties with the larger city of Teotihuacán, and occasionally fought wars against it, Monte Albán maintained its independence despite its smaller size. Indeed, sometime after 200 CE, the two states apparently arranged a truce whereby each agreed not to attack the other. Thus, even as Teotihuacán grew into a regional powerhouse, Monte Albán was generally left to its own affairs.

## CULTURE AND SOCIETY

At its height, Monte Albán displayed all the characteristics of a full-fledged state: it had an official religion that all were required to follow, public buildings related to that religion, a professional ruling class that administered a centralized government, and the means to levy taxes, wage wars, and demand tribute from subsidiary polities. Throughout its history, Monte Albán periodically engaged in warfare, whether it was to subdue groups adjacent to the city in the Oaxaca Valley or to continue state expansion through the conquest of more distant groups.

Monte Albán's main ceremonial center contained temples and other structures erected on massive platforms that enclosed a great plaza. Temple buildings, ceremonial altars, and the plaza itself were used for religious rites, including human sacrifice. The monumental proportions of the buildings and ancillary structures (such as stairways) gave the center a grandeur that is still visible today. One building, Building J (the "Observatory"), is thought to have been aligned with the bright star Capella; it also, unusually, has uneven sides. Another structure, in the shape of an I, was a ballcourt. Competitive games, possibly with teams from the outside, were played there. The remains of a palace complex are also visible. Defensive walls surrounded parts of the city center, where elites and some artisans lived while most commoners resided outside on the hill slopes below.

A variety of tombs cut into rock, some containing frescoes, have been found at or near the core site. One pyramid tomb features figures resembling dancers (*danzantes*) in low stone relief and exhibiting strong Olmec influence. While termed *danzantes* by early European viewers, the figures more likely represented sacrificial captives of war; their display thus constituted something of a rogue's gallery of conquered enemies. Some of these images, as well as other stone carvings, have glyphs that represent the earliest examples of writing in the New World, although a few glyphs found at Olmec sites may predate them. The Zapotec also carved jade figures and fashioned large clay urns representing persons or figures sporting elaborate headdresses.

Religious worship centered on an array of deities, many of them concerned with fertility, crops, and rain. The chief deity was the god of rain and lightning, Cocijo. The Zapotec sought the support of their deities through offerings and sacrifices, both animal and human. Priests communicated with ancestors and deities through rituals and chants and through the use of psychoactive substances such as mushrooms. Church and state were not separate in Zapotec culture but rather acted as two sides of the same coin.

## DEMISE

Monte Albán society changed significantly after about 700 CE. Instead of a highly centralized state with tight control coming from the top of the social and administrative hierarchy, it appears that in this late period, control shifted to smaller local polities and territories. The population of Monte Albán proper dropped to only around 5,000, for reasons not entirely understood. There was likely internal dissension, as leaders fought with one another, and possibly also a decline in the availability of food or problems with the distribution of water, which was based on wells and irrigation channels. It is also possible that the parallel decline of Monte Albán's erstwhile rival, Teotihuacán, played a role: with no potential threat or competitor to face, the Zapotecs had little reason to maintain an elaborate capital set up as a defensive center and based on the exaction of tribute. In any case, after 750, Monte Albán was largely abandoned. Some Mixtec groups used the site for their own tombs, leaving jewels and ornaments of gold, silver, jade, and other precious materials.

## RECENT DISCOVERIES AND CURRENT STATUS

Excavation and restoration efforts have been conducted at Monte Albán for several decades now. The site, together with colonial Oaxaca, was designated a UNESCO World Heritage Site in 1987. In 1999, several of its buildings suffered modest damage from an earthquake. Today, the primary threat is from ongoing urban growth in the area.

Detailed laser scanning of some of the site's buildings began in 2009. In 2012, a brightly painted stone figure from 1,200 years ago was found in a tomb at the Zapotec "suburb" of Atzompa. Speculation is that it represented either the person buried there or his ancestor. Four years later, a find at another suburb, Dainzú-Macuilxochitl, suggested to scholars that during Monte Albán's decline, priests were conducting "private" religious rituals designed to promote their own lineages rather than the health of the wider society.

*Michael Shally-Jensen*

*See also:* Maya; Olmecs; Teotihuacán.

## FURTHER READING

Blanton, Richard E., G. Feinman, S. Kowalewski, and L. Nicholas. 1999. *Ancient Oaxaca: The Monte Albán State.* New York: Cambridge University Press.

Coe, Michael, and Rex Koontz. 2013. *Mexico: From the Olmecs to the Aztecs*. 7th ed. New York: Thames & Hudson.
Miller, Arthur G. 1995. *The Painted Tombs of Oaxaca: Living with the Dead*. New York: Cambridge University Press.
Powell, Eric A. 2016. "Zapotec Power Rites." *Archaeology*, September/October 2016. https://www.archaeology.org/issues/227-1609/trenches/4741-trenches-mexico-zapotec-ritual
Zorich, Zach. 2013. "Deconstructing a Zapotec Figurine." *Archaeology*, February 28, 2013. https://www.archaeology.org/issues/81-1303/trenches?start=5

# Mughal Empire

The Mughal Empire was a Muslim empire that ruled across the subcontinent of South Asia, encompassing modern-day India, Pakistan, Afghanistan, and Bangladesh, from the sixteenth to the nineteenth century CE. At its peak, the empire commissioned impressive architectural projects, embraced policies of religious tolerance, and successfully administered a massive population across a vast territory. Most famously, the Taj Mahal was built by one of the Mughal emperors, Shah Jahan. After the death of its last great ruler, Aurangzeb, the empire set into a period of decline. It ultimately ended when the British government took direct control of India in 1857.

## INHABITANTS

Babur, the founder of the Mughal Empire, was descended from Mongols and Turks. He grew the empire from present-day Afghanistan in the west to present-day Bangladesh in the east and from modern-day Kashmir in the north to the Deccan Plateau in central India. Eventually, even parts of southern India were incorporated into the empire. In this way, the Mughal Empire was ethnically and culturally diverse, encompassing inhabitants of various descent from all around South Asia. This also meant that the Mughal Empire came to contain a population of multiple religions. While the dynasty itself was Muslim, its constituents were not only Muslim but also Hindu, Jain, and Sikh, as those religions were already prominent in India when the Mughals arrived. This also included the bhakti, a devotional movement of Hinduism, which was very popular at the time of the empire's initiation.

## HISTORICAL BACKGROUND

The Mughal Empire was founded by Babur in 1526. Babur came from a family of military leaders and rulers: he was a descendant of the Turko-Mongol military leader and ruler Timur Lang (Tamerlane) and the famous conqueror Genghis Khan. In 1504, Babur acquired possession of what is now eastern Afghanistan by capturing the city of Kabul, but the empire was not officially established until Babur defeated the sultan of Delhi in a battle at Panipat, a city about ninety kilometers north of Delhi. After conquering more territory in northwest India, the first Mughal emperor, Babur, died. He was succeeded by his son, Humayun, whose tenure as a

*Bangladesh*

A low-lying countryside at the convergence of some of Asia's largest river systems leaves Bangladesh vulnerable to a rising sea and other challenges brought on by climate change.

Comprising much of the ancient region of Bengal, Bangladesh sits on the nexus of the Meghna River snaking down from the northeast, the Brahmaputra River flowing down from the Himalayas, and the Padma River, the primary distributary of India's famed Ganges River. Bengal has been inhabited for tens of thousands of years. By the mid-first millennium CE, the region saw a rise in urban centers, similar to that across the rest of the northern Indian subcontinent. The region of Bengal was known from early on as a strong naval power, conquering regions around the Bay of Bengal and beyond. While local authority often prevailed over the region, Bengal was also intermittently ruled by the major empires that dominated India, including the Maurya, Gupta, Pala, and Mughal Empires. Hindu, Buddhist, Jain, and Muslim rulers led the region at different points. The British took control of region in the mid-eighteenth century. Following World War II, Bengal was divided in half, with West Bengal becoming a part of India and East Bengal becoming a part of the Dominion of Pakistan. After the Bangladesh genocide, East Bengal broke off from West Pakistan, forming the nation-state of Bangladesh in 1971.

Situated at the point where three major waterways issue into the sea, Bangladesh is at a particularly precarious position given the earth's changing climate. The country already faces consistent flooding. Monsoon season rages in the country from June to September, and Bangladesh may bear the brunt of any excess rainfall upriver within its rivers' vast watersheds. The nation's low-lying countryside contributes to the problem. Bangladesh is one of the most densely populated nations on earth and has already seen waves of climate refugees. These migrations and the overall hardship of the Bangladeshi people stand to intensify with the rising sea level.

---

Mughal ruler was more tumultuous than that of his father. In 1543, he was driven west and lost possession of the throne in India to Sher Shah, an Afghan ruler. Humayun recovered sovereignty only after an Indian civil war enabled him to reclaim it through battle in the year 1555. He died shortly thereafter, restoring Mughal sovereignty just in time for his son, Akbar, to inherit the throne at age thirteen.

Akbar became one of the greatest rulers of the empire. His accomplishments included building a new palace and establishing the capital at Fatehpur Sikri, in the present state of Uttar Pradesh; instituting administrative systems for the empire; and enacting policies of religious tolerance. Importantly, Akbar integrated Persians as well as Indian Muslims and Hindus into his administration and abolished the tax on non-Muslims. He ruled until his death in 1605, when his son Jahangir succeeded to the throne. It was during Jahangir's reign that the British East India Company began to set roots in India. In 1613, they established their first "factory" in the region, which was actually a secure warehouse to store goods, and the first British ambassador to India, Thomas Roe, visited Jahangir's court in 1615.

After his death in 1627, Jahangir was succeeded by Shah Jahan, who is most famous for commissioning the construction of the Taj Mahal. He began to undo the policy and culture of religious tolerance established by Akbar. In 1632, he ordered the destruction of all recently built Hindu temples. Shah Jahan had four sons, each of whom held governorships during his reign and fought for succession to the throne when he fell ill. Ultimately, Aurangzeb acquired the throne and held his father prisoner in the Red Fort at Agra, which had been the site of the empire's capital since 1585, until Shah Jahan's death in 1666. Aurangzeb, like Jahangir, worked to reverse Akbar's legacy of religious tolerance, likely due, at least in part, to pressures from religious scholars and growing opposition between Hindus and Sikhs. Aurangzeb also expanded the territory of the empire considerably during his reign, even as the presence of the European powers, especially the East India Company, continued to grow.

## CULTURE AND SOCIETY

At its peak, in the sixteenth and seventeenth centuries, the Mughal Empire was one of the most powerful and wealthiest in the world. It established effective public administration, set up a revenue collection system based on the measurement of land, and implemented a system of legal justice. It also carried out many civil works projects, including building roads, minting silver coins for currency, and constructing religious and secular architectural works.

Even though it was a Muslim empire, under Mughal rulers such as Akbar, religious tolerance was encouraged through policy. As a result, society under Mughal rule remained relatively diverse and multidimensional. However, certain rulers who were less keen on supporting religious diversity did suppress the flourishing of other religions, such as when Shah Jahan ordered the destruction of recently built Hindu temples during his reign.

Mughal architecture first became a prominent feature of the empire under Akbar. Under the rule of Jahangir, at the beginning of the seventeenth century, arts such as poetry and painting flourished. He was a significant patron of local culture and was able to do so because of the stability of the empire ensured by his father, Akbar, whom he succeeded. But Mughal art and architecture reached its peak under Shah Jahan, who commissioned the Taj Mahal for his wife.

## DEMISE

Aurangzeb's death in 1707 initiated the period of the Mughal Empire's decline. During this time, various groups, including the Afghans, Rajputs of northwest India, and Marathas of west India, made attempts to take the place of the decaying empire. The eighteenth century also saw the growth of British interest and presence in the subcontinent. On May 10, 1857, a number of *sepoys*, or Indian infantrymen, in the East India Company's army broke out in rebellion against the British in the town of Meerut, about forty kilometers away from Delhi. The revolt then spread to other units of sepoys across north and central India, and battle raged on in many areas well into the year 1858. Ultimately the British contained and quashed the rebellion. The British established formal governance over the Indian subcontinent, officially ending the Mughal Empire. The last Mughal emperor, Bahadur Shah, was deposed and exiled to Rangoon in Burma (now Myanmar).

## RECENT DISCOVERIES AND CURRENT STATUS

The influences and legacies of the Mughal Empire are without a doubt still present in South Asia today. One of the first major architectural projects the empire constructed in India was the fort at Agra in north India, which would eventually come to be neighbored by the famous Taj Mahal. The Agra Fort, which really appears as a walled city, was established as a UNESCO World Heritage Site in 1983. Humayan's Tomb is also an important architectural feature of the empire. It was commissioned by the emperor Humayan's first wife, Bega Begum, in 1558 and designed by Persian architects. It was the first garden-tomb on the Indian subcontinent and is located in Delhi. Humayan's Tomb was declared a UNESCO World Heritage Site in 1993.

Shah Jahan commissioned two of the most prominent remaining features of Mughal rule. The first is the Red Fort in Delhi, which served as one of the main residences for Mughal emperors. It is notable for its red sandstone ramparts, or defensive walls. On the day of India's independence from the British, India's first prime minister, Jawaharlal Nehru, raised the Indian national flag at the Lahori Gate at the Red Fort. Shah Jahan's other legacy comes in the form of the famous Taj Mahal. He commissioned this monument as a memorial for his wife, Mumtaz Mahal. Construction began in 1632 and was completed twenty years later in 1652. For the Taj Mahal, Shah Jahan used milky white marble as opposed to the traditional sandstone. Today, it houses the tombs of both Mumtaz Mahal and Shah Jahan. The Taj Mahal was designated a UNESCO World Heritage Site in 1983 and is also considered one of the Seven Wonders of the World.

Finally, the emperor Aurangzeb left a religious and architectural legacy in the form of the Badshahi Mosque in Lahore, the ancient capital of Punjab and present-day capital of Pakistan. The mosque was commissioned in 1671 and completed in 1673. It represents hallmark features of Mughal architecture, including a carved red sandstone exterior and marbly inlay. It was the largest mosque built during the Mughal era and is now an iconic tourist site in Pakistan.

*Rebecca Waxman*

*See also:* Mongol Empire; Pataliputra.

## FURTHER READING

Prasad, Ishwari. 1974. *The Mughal Empire*. Allahabad: Chugh Publications.
Tadgell, Christopher. 1990. *The History of Architecture in India*. London: Phaidon Press.

# Mycenae

Mycenae was a Greek superpower through the Bronze Age. During its height in the second half of the second millennium BCE, Mycenae was the premier power in Greece. The Homeric epics, the oldest texts in the Greek alphabet, though written centuries after the fall of Mycenae, depict the king of Mycenae, Agamemnon, as the most powerful king on the Greek side of the Trojan War.

The city stood in the northeast region of the Peloponnesus, the southernmost part of the Greek mainland, and was connected to the rest of Greece by the narrow isthmus of Corinth. The Peloponnesus is named after Pelops, Agamemnon's mythical grandfather. The city was perched on a ridge a little over ten miles from the Argolic Gulf, and the ruins lie between the cities of Argos, Corinth, and Nemea, which all rose to prominence in the eras after Mycenae's demise.

In many ways, the ruins are typical for a Mycenaean city. The Mycenaean civilization, which derived its name from Mycenae but was not a cohesive state in the modern sense, spread throughout much of mainland Greece and into the Aegean Sea. Mycenae and other Mycenaean sites were built around a palace with a megaron—or grand hall—and featured large fortified walls. The ruins of Mycenae are also famous for their large Lion Gate and artifact-rich shaft graves.

## INHABITANTS

The name *Mycenaeans* can denote either the inhabitants of Mycenae or the broader group who belonged to what we today call the Mycenaean civilization. This section describes the former group, but the residents of Mycenae shared much in common with the inhabitants of other settlements within the Mycenaean culture, especially the other palace-centered cities on the Greek mainland. Later Greeks traced the Mycenaeans' rulers back to major mythological dynasties. According to these later stories, Perseus, the son of Zeus, founded the city, and it was eventually taken over by Atreus, the son of Pelops and the father of Agamemnon.

The people spoke an early form of Greek and had a writing system, known today as Linear B; however, writing seems to have been confined to a small class of court officials and was used to keep track of administrative records. The Mycenaeans worshipped an early form of Greek polytheistic religion; how much their religion resembled that of later Greeks—which we know much more about—is a topic of debate. The Homeric epics, which acted as a basis for later Greek religion, claim to depict individuals of the Mycenaean age, centuries earlier, but there is no consensus in how accurately they do so.

## HISTORICAL BACKGROUND

Mycenae grew in wealth and influence through the Bronze Age, culminating in its pinnacle in the later second millennium BCE, when it was a leading power across the Aegean and beyond. Mycenae's existence predates the Bronze Age, with the site showing signs of settlement from as early as the fifth millennium BCE. The fortifiable acropolis in a fertile region strategically close to the Isthmus of Corinth and the Argolic Gulf rendered the site an ideal location for settlement, and Mycenae was inhabited continually from this Neolithic origin, experiencing increases in population and wealth through the Early Bronze Age.

Mycenae continued to blossom through the early second millennium BCE, and the shaft graves known today as Circle A and Circle B attest to the growing wealth and power of Mycenae in the seventeenth and sixteenth centuries BCE. Circle B is slightly older than Circle A; they are named after the order in which they were rediscovered. Circle A contained more wealth, exhibiting the ongoing rise in

The so-called Lion Gate adorns the city of Mycenae's main entrance. It was constructed in the mid-thirteenth century BCE, at the height of Mycenaean power. (Mino Surkala | Dreamstime.com)

Mycenae's status. Both sets of shaft graves were built outside of the fortified acropolis of Mycenae, although an expansion of the walls later enclosed Circle A within the walls. Upon finding five golden death masks in Circle A, Heinrich Schliemann, eager to tie his astounding new discovery to the Homeric epics, claimed, "I have gazed upon the face of Agamemnon." However, Agamemnon, if he was a based on a real historical figure, would not have lived until centuries after the burial, which was rediscovered by Schliemann.

By the middle of the second millennium BCE, Mycenae had grown into a major Aegean power. Although the culture shared by Mycenae and a number of other mainland cities and settlements is known today as the Mycenaean civilization, scholars do not believe Mycenae itself was the capital of a unified state. It was, however, a leading city in a culture on the rise. Until ca. 1450 BCE, the rival Minoan civilization, centered in Knossos and other cities on Crete, proved to be the dominant power in the Aegean, controlling trade networks and exporting culture. However, from ca. 1450 to 1370 BCE, the major Minoan sites appear to have been captured and occupied by Mycenaean forces from the mainland, marking the end of the Minoan era. The Mycenaeans were the dominant culture of the Aegean for the next two centuries.

As wider Mycenaean culture flourished, the city of Mycenae did as well. In the mid-fourteenth century BCE, the inhabitants rebuilt the fortifications that enclosed the acropolis. This final iteration of the wall, which survives in places today, was built from massive blocks and is known as cyclopean. This term was used by later observants and refers to the Cyclopes, a large, one-eyed race who were thought to have lived before humankind and were credited with fitting such large blocks into place. Other construction projects beautified the area within the walls, including the palace. The famous Lion Gate was put into place in the mid-thirteenth century BCE. During this era, the elite of Mycenae moved away from the shaft graves like those found in Circle A and Circle B and began utilizing Tholos tombs.

## CULTURE AND SOCIETY

The city of Mycenae shared its culture and society with a number of other second-millennium BCE Greek settlements, collectively known today as Mycenaean Greece. The major Mycenaean cities, like Mycenae, were on the Greek mainland and were centered around a palace, which itself was built around a megaron, or grand hall. The king, known as the *wanax* in Mycenaean Greek, held court from his megaron, which was the city's center of political and economic life. The script known today as Linear B was used to keep administrative records. Mycenaean art features pottery, frescoes, jewelry, and other media and shows a broad influence from Minoan culture.

The Homeric epics, the earliest and most influential works in the Greek alphabet, depict Mycenaean society and culture. In these epics, Agamemnon, the strongest leader on the Greek side of the Trojan War, ruled Mycenae, which is likewise depicted as the most powerful Greek city at the time. These epic poems come at the end of a centuries-long oral tradition; however, they were not written down until about four centuries after the events were purported to have taken place. There is a fierce scholarly debate as to whether these texts offer an accurate glimpse of the historical Mycenaeans. A common middle-of-the-road answer is that the texts primarily describe the era in which they were first written down (ca. 800 BCE), but certain details and aspects—carried down by the oral tradition—have survived from Mycenaean times.

## DEMISE

The city of Mycenae fell in the twelfth century BCE in conjunction with the so-called Late Bronze Age collapse. In Mycenae, there were signs of a slight decline before the final full-scale demise; however, it was right around this time that Mycenae led the famed invasion of Troy that has been memorialized in the Homeric epics. Therefore, plenty of influence and resources remained in the city at this late stage, and the city's fall can be fully attributed to the Late Bronze Age collapse. This phenomenon saw massive upheaval all across the eastern Mediterranean and into the Near East. Not only was Mycenae overturned but also all of the other Mycenaean palaces across the Greek mainland as well as other powerful cities across these regions.

Scholars debate what caused this widespread upheaval. Some point to migrations of peoples, the so-called Dorian invasion or the arrival of the Sea Peoples attested in contemporary Egyptian records. Others point to climate change or natural disasters such as earthquakes as the cause of both the widespread migrations of peoples and the violence across powerful urban centers. Other still look to the advent of ironworking and the accompanying weaponry. The site of Mycenae was intermittently resettled in the later Archaic, Classical, and Hellenistic eras but never wielded nearly the same influence as it did during the Bronze Age.

## RECENT DISCOVERIES AND CURRENT STATUS

Ever since the sensational finds of Kyriakos Pittakis and Heinrich Schliemann in the mid-nineteenth century CE, Mycenae has been one of the most important archaeological sites in the eastern Mediterranean, and excavations have been ongoing since. Mycenae is listed, together with the remains of Bronze Age Tiryns, about ten miles away, as a UNESCO World Heritage Site.

*Anthony Vivian*

*See also:* Knossos; Troy.

## FURTHER READING

Mylonas, George E. 2006. *Mycenae—A Guide to Its Ruins and History*. Athens: Ekdotike Athenon.
Schofield, Louise. 2007. *The Mycenaeans*. Los Angeles: J. Paul Getty Museum.
Shelmerdine, Cynthia W. 2008. *The Cambridge Companion to the Aegean Bronze Age*. Cambridge: Cambridge University Press.
Ventris, Michael, and John Chadwick. 2015. *Documents in Mycenaean Greek: Three Hundred Selected Tablets from Knossos, Pylos and Mycenae with Commentary and Vocabulary*. Cambridge: Cambridge University Press.

# N

## Nazca

Nazca culture emerged in southern coastal Peru around 200 BCE and flourished until around 500 CE. By 750 CE, the civilization had fallen into decline. While Nazca crafts, architecture, and social practices are relatively well known among researchers, the culture's great popular fame comes from the Nazca Lines. Carved into the sands of the Nazca desert, some 800 miles of these lines depict individual images of animals, trees, and flowers that are best seen from high overhead. Indeed, some images were discovered only through the use of satellite imaging techniques. The mystery of the lines is, Why were they created in the first place, and why were they made on the scale that they were so that one can see them best from Earth's atmosphere?

### INHABITANTS

The Nazca lived along the southern coast of what is now Peru. We know little about the people themselves, but we do know that they were agricultural and irrigated their farmland. We also know that they had contact with other Andean peoples, as elements of their pottery work became popular in the ceramic work of the Huari region after 500 CE. Also, the Nazca used wool in their textiles, yet llamas and alpacas could not have lived in the coastal regions. This is further evidence of trade with cultures that existed in the highlands. Finally, some Nazca mummies have been found displaying tropical bird feathers on their shrouds.

Some researchers believe that the Nazca represented less of a unified political culture and were instead separate chiefdoms that occasionally operated together. This conclusion comes from the fact that agricultural techniques and art production were similar across the communities, yet individual towns were laid out very differently.

Many Nazca tombs have survived; in fact, this is where the greatest number of Nazca artifacts have been found. Much information has been gathered from these tombs. For example, there does not seem to be a difference between male and female burials, indicating some level of equal status between genders. The deceased were placed in a seated position and were often surrounded by skulls; these skulls show evidence of elongation through wrapping, which mirrors other civilizations found in this area during this and surrounding time periods. It is also clear that tombs could be reopened and additional mummies added; some researchers suggest that this indicates the Nazca practiced some form of ancestor worship. Trophy heads, or heads strung together, were often also buried with the mummies;

such morbid designs also appeared in Nazca artwork. Finally, some sacrificial burials may have been performed and were particularly gruesome. Eyes were blocked, and mouths were filled with excrement and sewn shut. Tongues may have been removed and stored separately.

## HISTORICAL BACKGROUND

Many archaeologists hold that the Nazca civilization was an outgrowth of the earlier Paracas culture, which existed in the same area from roughly 800 BCE to 100 BCE. The discovery of pottery artifacts with dramatically different coloring and firing techniques led to the conclusion that the Nazca were separate from the Paracas, who had come earlier. The culture was then named for what was believed to be the center of its civilization: the Nazca drainage area from the Rio Grande.

While knowledge of the of the details of Nazca life is somewhat limited, two major cities are thought to have been part of Nazca society: Ventilla, the main urban capital, and Cahuachi, a possible pilgrimage location. Ventilla spanned almost 500 acres and included terraced housing as well as ceremonial mounds and walled courts. An extensive aqueduct system was present there. The area was also close to irrigated farmland, thus allowing for agricultural success.

Meanwhile, Cahuachi is located around thirty miles inland and along the bank of the Nazca River. This meant the area had year-round water access. No domestic architecture has been found here, thus supplying additional evidence of Cahuachi's status as a pilgrimage location. The area, just under 3,000 acres, is naturally hilly, and several adobe mounds exist that appear to take advantage of the natural hills. The largest, called the Great Temple, is sixty-five feet high, but all the mounds are connected by a walled plaza. Holes in the ground suggest that worshippers set up tents to protect themselves from the sun, while textile and pottery rubbish suggest religious feasts, possibly related to harvest festivals.

## CULTURE AND SOCIETY

Much of what we know about the Nazca comes from their pottery and textile artwork. Both were very advanced and included delicately embroidered mantles and clay panpipes and jars. Similar items had been found from the Paracas cultures, but the Nazca had advanced their technology. Specifically, they had learned the ceramic technique of slip casting, allowing them to make more delicate versions of the Paracas panpipes and delicate spouts and handles for their jars.

Their artwork was filled with carefully stylized human, animal, and plant figures; some of the same designs can be seen in the Nazca Lines. The Nazca also used gold to create masks that adorned their cloth-wrapped mummies. The Nazca Lines themselves are distinguished by their coloring; by scraping away the dark surface layer of the stone on the plain, the lighter earth underneath was exposed. This allowed the designs to be visible from above as well as on the ground. (Over time, however, many of the lines filled in, making them harder to discover from the surface but still visible as part of a pattern from above.)

To deal with the extremely low rain conditions of the area, the Nazca built sophisticated aqueduct systems, cisterns, and galleries; this ensured a reliable water supply during the dry season and minimized the threat of evaporation of collected water. Elaborate spiral ramps allowed people to descend into the water areas, which were lined with cobblestones from the river.

## DEMISE

Nazca civilization is believed to have been driven into decline by an El Niño weather event. Their agricultural practices had left the land vulnerable, and heavy rains caused severe, destructive flooding. According to the most recent research, the Nazca's mistreatment of the environment around them was a major factor in the society's destruction. According to British researchers, the Nazca heavily depended on a local tree called the huarango; this tree preserved nitrogen in the soil, helped maintain natural irrigation, and held down the soil during rainy seasons. Researchers examined the soil record in the area and found that the huarango was very common at the beginning of Nazca society. Then, in the same record, one could see evidence of huarango being rapidly replaced by maize (corn). Maize is a staple crop for civilizations in the area. However, clear-cutting of the huarango trees to create farmland and produce wood for building and for fuel made the soil vulnerable to the El Niño event, which would have caused flooding and mudslides in the area. At this point in the soil record, maize suddenly disappears, and new kinds of shrub plants appear. Nazca society had largely vanished or, in any case, become greatly diminished as people sought new resources and alternative ways of life.

## RECENT DISCOVERIES AND CURRENT STATUS

The Nazca Lines have been designated a UNESCO World Heritage Site. They have become one of the most famous tourist attractions in Peru. In both 1998 and 2000, severe mudslides threatened to destroy the lines. Master plans were created to preserve them over time, but the lines remain vulnerable owing to the operation of the Pan-American Highway, which runs through the area. In 2018, a tractor trailer left the roadway and caused severe damage to some lines.

In 2019, over a hundred new Nazca Lines were discovered by Japanese researchers who used satellite photographs and artificial intelligence (AI) technology to uncover the figures. The researchers also identified two types of images created by the lines; those over fifty meters and those under fifty meters. They believe that the larger images served ritual purposes, while the smaller ones may have served as waypoints to orient travelers.

The irony of the way in which Nazca culture disappeared was that the same El Niño that harmed these people at one time may have aided them. Prior to the final environmental destruction, researchers have noted, similar El Niño events likely helped fill the aqueducts that allowed the Nazca to survive in a dry climate.

*Michael Shally-Jensen*

*See also:* Machu Picchu; Tiwanaku.

## FURTHER READING

Bourton, Jody. 2009. "Logging 'Caused Nazca Collapse.'" BBC Earth News, November 2, 2009. http://news.bbc.co.uk/earth/hi/earth_news/newsid_8334000/8334257.stm

Daley, Jason. 2019. "Archaeologists Identify 143 New Nazca Lines." *Smithsonian Magazine*, November 21, 2019. https://www.smithsonianmag.com/smart-news/ai-helps-identify-1-143-new-nazca-lines-180973621/

Reinhard, Johan. 1985. *The Nazca Lines: A New Perspective on Their Origin and Meaning*. Nampa, ID: Pacific Press.

# O

## Old Goa

Old Goa is a town on the western coast of the Indian subcontinent in what is now the Indian state of Goa. It is situated on the banks of the Mandovi River to the north, with the Arabian Sea to the west, and a number of hills surround the area. Old Goa was historically a port town with consistent trade, but it reached its peak during the fifteenth and sixteenth centuries under Muslim and then Portuguese rule.

The city has had many names throughout its history. Prior to the arrival of the Portuguese to the region in the early sixteenth century, the village was known as Ella (sometimes spelled Ela). They renamed it Goa, but when it was replaced as the capital, it became referred to as Old Goa, or Velha Goa (*velha* meaning "old" in Portuguese).

Today, in Old Goa, one can mostly see evidence of its history as part of the Portuguese colonial empire. It is especially prominent for its beautiful Catholic architecture, including churches and cathedrals. However, remains of Hindu and Muslim edifices can still be found as well. Reflective of the various stages of its multifaceted history, the town is now home to a religiously, ethnically, and culturally diverse population.

### INHABITANTS

From the second century CE until 1312, Old Goa was ruled by various Indian kingdoms. This included the Kadamba dynasty, an ancient royal family of the present-day state of Karnataka in southern India; the Vijayanagara Empire, based in the Deccan Plateau of southern India; and the Shilaharas of modern-day

---

*Lemuria*

Lemuria was a continent theorized to have existed in the Indian Ocean. In 1864, recognizing that lemurs lived in India and Madagascar but not in the intervening lands, zoologist Philip Sclater proposed a continent, now lost, that existed at one time and connected India and Madagascar. It was far from just lemurs that were thought to have lived on Lemuria: the proposed continent received significant attention when fellow zoologist Ernst Haeckel suggested that the sunken continent was the birthplace of humankind. Haeckel had long been suggesting Asia as the birthplace of our species as opposed to Africa, which was consensus opinion of the scientific community then as now, and Lemuria gave him the opportunity to offer a more moderate iteration of his original proposal. Lemuria flourished in the minds of scientists for about half a century before a better understanding of plate tectonics made the need for a lost continent under the Indian Ocean superfluous.

Maharashtra. Old Goa, known then as Ella, was the main local port during the pre-Muslim and pre-Portuguese era. Languages spoken in these dynasties during these periods included Sanskrit, Marathi, and Kannada, among others. Waves of immigrants arrived in each respective era and blended with these original inhabitants to create the town's current mosaic population.

## HISTORICAL BACKGROUND

It is possible that the history of Old Goa as a port town could reach back all the way to the second century CE, during the ancient period of the Mauryan dynasty in India. Trade and contact in the general region of Goa can also be traced back to this time. We know for certain that Old Goa was active starting in the first few centuries CE.

Old Goa remained a part of the various Hindu kingdoms until 1472, when it was conquered by the Muslim Bahmani kingdom. Under the Bahmani sultanate, the port of Ella at Old Goa had a number of foreign trade links, including Cairo, in Egypt, and Venice, in Italy. The Bahmani sultanate dissolved shortly thereafter, so Old Goa was incorporated into one of its five successor states: the Bijapur sultanate. During this period, under the rule of Adil Shah, Old Goa became the capital city until the Portuguese conquest in 1510.

After conquering the area, the Portuguese maintained authority over Old Goa until 1961, totaling over four whole centuries, thus indelibly transforming the once Hindu town into a veritable site of hybrid imperial culture. During the early period of Portuguese rule, primarily in the sixteenth century, Old Goa became a bustling metropolitan site as the empire's capital. In 1730, the city was designated as the Portuguese capital for all Asian colonial occupations. Over the course of the sixteenth century, the Portuguese built many royal, public, and secular buildings and structures there. As various Christian groups arrived, more chapels, churches, cathedrals, and convents were constructed.

By 1543, the population of Old Goa amounted to roughly 200,000 people. It was a booming capital and port city.

## CULTURE AND SOCIETY

Traditionally, throughout the first millennium CE, the primary religions practiced in Old Goa were Hinduism and Jainism. However, the Bahmani and Bijapur sultanates were Muslim dynasties and therefore introduced Islam to the area. During this period, Old Goa was also a port where Muslim devotees making pilgrimage to Mecca passed through. Famously, when the Portuguese arrived, they brought Catholicism to their new colony. Therefore, by the sixteenth century, Old Goa was a multireligious hub of Hinduism, Jainism, Islam, and Christianity.

In addition to many famous sites of Portuguese religious and historical architecture, Old Goa once housed many important Hindu and Muslim edifices. Modern-day scholars have identified remains of the port wall at Ella. Old Goa was also the site of the Brahmapuri temple, a center of learning for Brahmins. Within this complex was the Gomanteshwar temple, which was founded by Kalamadevi, a queen of the Kadamba dynasty. Another important Hindu structure there was Madhava temple, which was a pilgrimage center for Hindus during the Vijayanagar period.

Prior to the region's conquest by the Portuguese Empire, Old Goa was an educational, religious, and cultural center. It was also a site of shipbuilding, since it was a port town, as well as goldsmithing. It had a long history of sea trade with other towns on the west coast of India, including trading horses, and possibly beyond via the Arabian Sea. These horses were in great demand in regions such as the Deccan Plateau. It also had a number of wells, which were buried due to plague.

Because it was a port town, Old Goa attracted local, regional, and even overseas traders and merchants, thus bringing in a relatively diverse population. This became an especially cosmopolitan crowd once commerce boomed and trade expanded during the sixteenth century. Old Goa was even called the "Rome of the Orient," attracting many European tourists.

## DEMISE

Old Goa did not experience a demise per se. Rather, it was transformed over time. The port city transferred between various hands of power prior to the arrival of the Portuguese, and then reached its peak of prosperity during Portuguese rule in the sixteenth century. In the seventeenth century, however, the city suffered a serious of severe challenges. As the malaria and cholera epidemics ravaged the area, Old Goa's prosperity began to dwindle. It was virtually abandoned, with its population dramatically decreasing to only 1,500 people by the year 1775. However, Portugal still maintained sovereignty, as the broader region of Goa remained the last European colony in India. Finally, it was incorporated into the Republic of India in 1961, fourteen years after the country's independence from British colonial rule.

## RECENT DISCOVERIES AND CURRENT STATUS

Today, Old Goa—specifically its churches and convents—has been named a UNESCO World Heritage Site. The site includes seven remaining monuments from the period of Portuguese colonization and missionary work: the Basilica of Born Jesus, the Sé Cathedral of Santa Catarina, the Chapel of St. Catherine, the Church and Convent of St. Francis of Assisi, the Church of Our Lady of Rosary, the Church of St. Augustine, and the Chapel of St. Cajetan.

One of the surviving features of the Portuguese period in Old Goa is the Basilica of Born Jesus (*Basílica do Bom Jesus*, in Portuguese). It was built in 1605, with marble flooring, inlaid precious stones, and elaborate gilded altars. Notably, the basilica holds the mortal remains of Saint Francis Xavier, a Jesuit who died on a sea voyage to China in 1552. The relic attracts devotees from around the world, especially for a once-per-decade viewing of the body. The Basilica of Born Jesus was India's first Minor Basilica and is regarded as one of the best examples of baroque architecture in the subcontinent. UNESCO designated the basilica a World Heritage Site in 1985.

Another remarkable relic of Portuguese rule still standing in Old Goa is the Sé Cathedral of Santa Catarina. Construction of the cathedral began in 1562 and was completed in 1619. The cathedral was built to commemorate the victory of the Portuguese Empire under Afonso de Albuquerque over the Muslim army, resulting in the capture of the city in 1510. Since this day of triumph fell on the day of the feast of Saint Catherine of Alexandria, the cathedral was dedicated in her honor. It was constructed in Portuguese-Gothic architectural style, with a Tuscan exterior, and houses in its tower the "Golden Bell."

Today, Old Goa is a popular tourist site for Indian and international travelers alike, owing to its status as a UNESCO World Heritage Site and its rich visual and architectural history of empires and centuries gone by.

*Rebecca Waxman*

*See also:* Ajanta Caves; Madurai; Vijayanagara.

**FURTHER READING**

D'Souza, Alvita M. 2007. *Reconstructing the Urban Maritime History of Goa: A Study of the Port-Capitals of Chandrapur, Gopakapattana, and Ella.* Goa University, June 17, 2022. http://irgu.unigoa.ac.in/drs/handle/unigoa/3906

Pearson, M. N. 1984. "Goa during the First Century of Portuguese Rule." *Itinerario* 8: 36–57.

Prasad, Om Prakash. 1987. "Two Ancient Port Towns of Karnataka—Goa and Bangalore." *Proceedings of the Indian History Congress* 39: 55–61.

## Olmecs

The Olmecs were a people of ancient Mexico whose culture arguably set the pattern for later pre-Colombian civilizations in Mesoamerica. Their homeland was the Gulf Coast lowlands of southern Veracruz and western Tabasco, north of the Yucatán Peninsula. Olmec culture emerged as early as 1200 BCE and flourished from about 800 BCE to 400 BCE. During this time, Olmec economic and political influence extended into the central Mexican highlands and reached southeast along the Pacific coast to what is today El Salvador.

The Olmecs are best known for the images of rulers and gods they carved into massive basalt monuments, for the great earthen mounds and paved courts they built at their religious centers, and for the fine art and craftwork they produced in jade, stone, and pottery.

**INHABITANTS**

The name *Olmec* comes from a later Aztec (Nahuatl) term for "people of the rubber country"; rubber trees existed in the region and were made use of. Little is known about the language spoken by the Olmec, although most scholars are inclined to think it was a Mixe-Zoquean language of a kind still spoken by a small number of speakers in the area.

Colossal heads have been found within the Olmec heartland, some up to nine feet high. They are sculpted of basalt and represent helmeted figures with broad-nosed, thick-lipped, and somewhat flattened features. At various times, some observers have sought to explain these characteristics by suggesting an "African connection," but there is no convincing evidence for such a link. The idea also runs counter to what is known about the peopling of the Americas. A similar argument, based on the facial features found in stylized Olmec masks and figurines, has been put forth for a Chinese Bronze Age connection—but, again, the evidence is questionable. It is nevertheless the case that Olmec figurative art was extraordinarily creative and can cause one to wonder what may lie behind it. Olmec deities included gods of rain, fire, spring, wisdom, and death. A number of Olmec motifs indicate that human sacrifice likely took place, probably including war captives but also perhaps children.

## HISTORICAL BACKGROUND

In the early formative period of Mesoamerican cultures, villages began to transition from small-scale farming societies to more complex, stratified ones based in towns and cities. The Olmec represented the first and among the most distinctive civilizations to arise in Mesoamerica. By 1200 BCE, Olmec culture was well developed at San Lorenzo, a civic-ceremonial center rather than a city proper. There were perhaps 1,000 people living in the vicinity, with elites occupying the "urban" area and overseeing religious rites and trade and commoners living in rural areas and growing the crops on which the residents depended. The Olmecs reworked the surface geography in San Lorenzo to create a level central space with a sacred mound rising from the center, probably to reflect mythological beliefs.

In about 900 BCE, Olmec power shifted to another center, La Venta. It is not known why exactly San Lorenzo was abandoned and La Venta given prominence. It could have been a result of ecological changes or a political disruption of some kind. In any case, both centers were home to impressive public works projects that included large clay pyramidal structures, ceremonial courtyards, and effective drainage systems. The clay mound at La Venta measures 110 feet in height and features two adjacent courtyards bounded by adobe platforms and dirt mounds. Other buildings, such as altars and tombs, were spread out over a large area and display elaborate stone carvings. Together with the settlements in the hinterland, La Venta likely served a population of over 10,000.

## CULTURE AND SOCIETY

As noted, the Olmec aesthetic was complex. Besides massive heads, it featured various chubby baby-like figures with elongated heads, almond-shaped eyes, slim noses, and downturned mouths. There are also sundry shamanic figures and "ecstatic" masks, at once realistic and abstract. One ubiquitous mythical figure, often cut in jade, resembles both a human and a jaguar. This Olmec "were-jaguar," with its cleft head and grim mouth (often fanged), has been interpreted as a water spirit, an intermediary between the human and the supernatural worlds. The themes of bloodletting and sacrifice are also evident in Olmec artistic renderings.

The Olmecs seem to have been the first to play a ritualized ball game that later became popular throughout Mesoamerica. A hard rubber ball was moved about a court by opposing teams whose players used their bodies, not their hands, to pass the ball through a small hoop at each end of the court. The losing team was apparently put to death. On the great Olmec portrait heads, the leatherlike helmets worn by the subjects may well represent protective gear used in ball games.

Olmec society was stratified and made up of rulers, priests, warriors, craftspeople, and commoners. Outside the heartland region, the Olmec traded exotic raw materials such as jade for both food staples and luxury goods. Other Olmec trade items included incised stone axes and pottery bowls, which have been found far outside La Venta. The basalt for the colossal heads was mined some sixty miles away, indicating a sophisticated logistics system and the use of mass labor. Mosaics fashioned from serpentine blocks were drawn from imported materials and presented at ritual sites as offerings to the gods.

## DEMISE

For nearly 400 years after 900 BCE, La Venta projected Olmec power and influence in the region. A few lesser centers also existed. The Olmecs never built cities but instead lived in small dwellings near the main civic-religious centers. By around 400 BCE, La Venta was abandoned for reasons unknown to us. Thereafter, another site, Tres Zapotes, to the northwest, became the final Olmec center, lasting, albeit with less influence, for another couple of centuries. The Olmec cultural legacy persisted into later times, however, and inspired many of the subsequent civilizations of Mesoamerica.

## RECENT DISCOVERIES AND CURRENT STATUS

For a long time, the source of Olmec jade remained unknown. In 2002, however, scientists discovered large deposits of jade in the mountains of Guatemala after landslides exposed them following a hurricane. Later that same year, and again in 2006, archaeologists presented evidence of what they believe to be the earliest form of writing in the New World, dating to about 650 BCE and 900 BCE, near the Olmec sites of San Andrés (near La Venta) and San Lorenzo, respectively. Several of the glyphs in these artifacts bear a rough similarity to later Maya pictographs, suggesting an early influence. No one has yet deciphered the Olmec glyphs, however.

Recent research has also brought to light that a number of pottery items and other artifacts previously thought to have originated with the Olmec as trade items were in fact copied by people outside the Olmec heartland who were influenced by their style. This suggests the impact of Olmec civilization on the wider region.

Today, both San Lorenzo and La Venta remain available for limited research and viewing, though each has been substantially degraded over the centuries. Both have associated museums for visitors, as does Tres Zapotes.

*Michael Shally-Jensen*

*See also:* Maya; Tenochtitlán; Teotihuacán; Tula.

## FURTHER READING

Coe, Michael D., and Rex Koontz. 2013. *Mexico: From the Olmecs to the Aztecs.* New York: Thames & Hudson.

Diehl, Richard A. 2005. *The Olmecs: America's First Civilization.* New York: Thames & Hudson.

Grove, David C. 2014. *Discovering the Olmecs: An Unconventional History.* Austin: University of Texas Press.

## Olympia

Olympia was a sanctuary in southwestern Greece that served as the host of the original Olympic Games. Not to be confused with Mount Olympus in northern Greece, where Zeus and the other Olympian gods were said to live, Olympia was a religious center near the city-state of Elis. The location is less than ten miles from Elis itself and just over ten miles to the west coast of the Peloponnesus, the large mountainous region of southern Greece connected to the rest of mainland Greece by the Isthmus of Corinth. The settlement sat near the Alpheus River, which flows east to west into the Ionian Sea, and on the Kladeus River, a tributary that flows south into the Alpheus.

At its height, Olympia included dozens of temples, treasuries, and athletic venues. The Temple of Hera was the oldest temple at Olympia, and although most of the temple has not survived, the torch of the Olympic flame is lit at its altar at the beginning of each iteration of the modern Olympic Games. The massive Temple of Zeus, which housed the famous and enormous chryselephantine statue of Zeus, served as the spiritual center of ancient Olympia since its construction in the fifth century BCE; however, it survives only as a foundation. Most of Olympia's other ancient structures have been similarly left in some state of disrepair after centuries of abandonment.

### INHABITANTS

The site of Olympia shows signs of inhabitation from the second millennium BCE. From an early stage and throughout its height in the first millennium BCE and beginning of the first millennium CE, Olympia was a religious hub for the worship of Zeus and other gods. Its status as a Panhellenic sanctuary opened the city to all free Greeks and others as a place of worship. Therefore, the population fluctuated depending on pilgrimages and festivals and peaked during the Olympic Games held in the summer once every four years.

Several columns of the massive fifth-century BCE Temple of Zeus at Olympia remain. The temple once housed a colossal chryselephantine statue of Zeus. (Bo Li | Dreamstime.com)

## HISTORICAL BACKGROUND

The site that came to be known as Olympia was first called Altis, a name derived from the local word for *grove*. Forests still covered much of the space through the early years of inhabitation. The site was already a religious sanctuary in this early stage. Among the early structures were a bouleuterion—or council house—and treasuries from several nearby city-states. Chief among the archaic ruins was a Temple of Zeus and Hera. When the later Temple of Zeus was built, this former structure became the Temple of Hera.

Greece was not unified at this time, but the site's status as a sanctuary allowed individuals from across the Greek-speaking world and beyond to come and worship. Greek city-states built and maintained treasuries within the sanctuary to house their citizens' often expensive offerings to the gods. These city-states ranged from Byzantium (modern-day Istanbul) to the northeast, Cyrene (in modern-day Libya) to the south, and multiple Sicilian city-states to the west. Despite the open nature of Olympia and other Panhellenic sanctuaries, a nearby city-state exerted authority over the administration of the various sites. In the case of Olympia, that city-state was Elis, located less than ten miles to the northwest.

The Olympic Games were first held in 776 BCE. This date was calculated in the fourth century BCE, but it soon became canonical, and Olympiads—four year blocks of time based on the Games—were soon used to date other events in Greek history, which did not previously have a unified calendar. Sporting events have a long history; there is evidence for ad hoc sporting events in Greece—as well as

Egypt and Mesopotamia—before this time. Records of Olympic victors show that for the first four decades or so, the Games remained a relatively local affair, with winners primarily coming from nearby Messenia and the rest of the western Peloponnesus. Afterward, winners began appearing from farther and farther afield.

From the inception of the Olympic Games, the inhabitants of Elis, or Eleans, served as the officials of the event. In the seventh century BCE, the inhabitants of Pisa, or Pisatans, wrested control of the sanctuary and, therefore, the Games away from the Eleans. Pheidon, the powerful tyrant of Argos in the eastern Peloponnesus, seems to have played a role in helping the Pisatans usurp this authority. They ran the Games for years before the Eleans took back control of the important and growing event. Our dates for the Pisatans' control of the Olympic Games are not completely certain, but 668 to 580 BCE is a standard estimate.

The fifth and fourth centuries BCE are often considered a high point in Olympia's existence. A large building program more than doubled the permanent structures in the sanctuary. These new buildings included treasuries, temples, bathhouses, the final version of the Olympic Stadium, and the Olympic Hippodrome. The Pelopion was a tomb and altar for the mythological figure Pelops, who lends his name to the larger region, the Peloponnesus. King Phillip II had the Phillippeion built to commemorate his pivotal victory at the Battle of Chaeronea in 338 BCE; it was the only structure in the sanctuary built for a living man. The Leonidaion was the largest structure at the site and was used to house athletes present for the Olympic Games. The new Temple of Zeus became the crown jewel of Olympia; inside sat the famous chryselephantine statue of Zeus, which was over forty feet tall and carved by the famous sculptor Phidias.

The sanctuary at Olympia and the Games hosted there continued to thrive under the Hellenistic successor kingdoms and eventually under the Romans. The site continued to be enhanced with additional structures. However, Roman leaders did not always treat the location or the event with the respect that had become standard. The Roman general Sulla moved the Games to Rome for an Olympiad in 80 BCE, but this move proved temporary. After changing the year in which the Games were to be held, the emperor Nero participated in the Olympics of 67 CE and was declared the winner in every competition he entered, no matter how poorly he performed. After the emperor's death, this iteration of the Games was considered null and void.

## CULTURE AND SOCIETY

The culture and society of Olympia revolved around the worship of Zeus and other gods as well as the Olympic Games, which were held every four years. The Olympics began in 776 BCE as a mostly local affair, with a single day and a single event: a foot race around the stadium. However, the Games quickly attracted competitors from farther away and expanded to include other events and extra days. In 684 BCE, almost a century after its initiation, the Games expanded from one day of events to three; two centuries later, it grew again to five days. There were chariot races and the pankration, among other events. The latter was a UFC-style fighting competition where anything was permitted except biting and eye gouging. Women could enter chariots into the chariot races but were otherwise barred from competing. The gathering at Olympia for the Games was also a cultural event, attracting poets and fine artists. Other Panhellenic games (i.e., the Pythian, Nemean, and Isthmian Games) sprouted up in the three off years when the Olympics were not being held; however, they were never as popular as the Olympic Games.

## DEMISE

The entire Roman Empire went through a period of upheaval in the third century CE. Olympia, then under Roman control, experienced a particularly tumultuous century. Earthquakes damaged many structures. In 267, the Goths invaded and looted the site, and the sanctuary was partially fortified as a result. The final Olympic Games of antiquity were held in 393 CE, after which Emperor Theodosius I banned them. Christians partially converted the site to a place for Christian worship, but it was always primarily known as a pagan site. As part of the Christian backlash against pagans, Emperor Theodosius II had the Temple of Zeus destroyed in 426 CE. The Olympic Games have cropped up in various forms at different places since the demise of Olympia, including most famously the modern Olympic Games which commenced in 1896.

## RECENT DISCOVERIES AND CURRENT STATUS

Olympia is a UNESCO World Heritage Site, and serious excavations have been underway there since the early nineteenth century. In March 2021, a bronze bull from the early first millennium BCE was found near the foundation of the Temple of Zeus. The flame for all of the modern Olympics Games is lit via a parabolic mirror at the altar of the Temple of Hera before being brought by torch to the location of the Games.

*Anthony Vivian*

*See also:* Delphi; Rome.

## FURTHER READING

Nielsen, Thomas Heine. 2007. *Olympia and the Classical Hellenic City-State Culture. Historisk-filosofiske Meddelelser 96.* Copenhagen: Royal Danish Academy of Sciences and Letters.

Raschke, Wendy J. 1988. *The Archaeology of the Olympics: The Olympics and Other Festivals in Antiquity.* Madison: Wisconsin University Press.

Sealey, Raphael. 1976. *A History of the Greek City States, 700–338 B.C.* Berkeley: University of California Press.

Valavanis, Panos. 2004. *Games and Sanctuaries in Ancient Greece: Olympia, Delphi, Isthmia, Nemea, Athens.* Los Angeles: J. Paul Getty Museum.

# P

## Paestum

The Latin name *Paestum* refers to the original Greek colony of Poseidonia, founded on Italy's west coast about eighty miles south of modern-day Naples. The Greeks chose this site for a colonial settlement around 600 BCE for its excellent harbor and land access. Built on the river Sele, the city occupies a fertile agricultural plain with access to the Lucanian hills, where the Greeks could collect wood and stone for construction. As an important port city, Paestum had sea access via a lagoon adjacent to the city.

After its early period as a Greek colony, the city was subsequently conquered by the Lucanians. It next became a Roman colony in the third century BCE, giving aid and resources to the Romans during the Punic Wars. The city saw varying degrees of Roman influence in the following centuries before being abandoned in the early medieval period. The site has a rich abundance of archaeological material, including several well-preserved Greek temples.

### INHABITANTS

From at least the eighth century BCE, Greek city-states sent out groups of citizens to establish colonies throughout the Mediterranean. Though initially a process to facilitate long-distance trade, Greek colonization resulted in the formation of cities in France, Spain, Italy, and around the Black Sea, eventually including upward of 500 known colonies. Each new colony maintained some sort of affinity with its mother city (*metropolis*) in Greece and functioned as a way to spread Greek culture around the Mediterranean.

Southern Italy and Sicily, especially, were the sites of numerous Greek colonies, together known as Magna Graecia ("Great Greece"). Poseidonia, named in honor of the Greek god Poseidon, was founded by colonists from Sybaris around 600 BCE. Over the course of the next century, it became a dominant commercial and political power in the region.

Initially built close to the coast, the colonists of Poseidonia soon moved their habitation inland. The city was built on a grid system with a central square (*agora*) and defensive walls. Among numerous other buildings, the Greeks constructed temples to Hera and Athena. The city was also the location of the sanctuary dedicated to Hera (the Foce del Sele, "mouth of the River Sele"), an important pilgrimage site for Greeks. The inhabitants of Poseidonia eventually expanded even farther inland to control the surrounding region, and the city became powerful enough to mint its own coinage.

## HISTORICAL BACKGROUND

Near the end of the fifth century BCE, Poseidonia was taken over by the Lucanians, an Indigenous Italic tribe. This change was not necessarily an overt conquest but rather a slow integration of Indigenous peoples and cultural elements into the city. The changing of the city's name to Paestum is probably a result of Lucanian influence. The city remained a thriving cultural center during this period, continuing to produce pottery and other art, including a series of tomb paintings discovered in a necropolis outside the city walls.

Paestum may have first drawn Rome's attention after the campaign of Alexander of Epirus. This uncle of Alexander the Great made war upon the Lucanians and Samnites of Italy in the 330s BCE. It is unclear whether he occupied Paestum in the course of the war. In any case, Alexander made peace with Rome but was soon murdered by Lucanians in his court. Shortly thereafter, Rome conducted its own war against the Samnites with the aid of the Lucanians in 326 BCE. By the end of the century, Rome was militarily active everywhere around the city of Paestum.

Paestum came under Roman control after the Pyrrhic War, fought between Rome and Pyrrhus of Epirus, in the third century BCE. The Romans formed their own colony at Paestum in 273 BCE, granting the city Latin rights. This designation meant that the city's inhabitants were given a special set of rights as a form of limited Roman citizenship. As an ally to Rome, Paestum supplied naval support during the Second Punic War (218–201 BCE) between Rome and Carthage. And the city remained loyal to Rome during the Carthaginian general Hannibal's invasion of Italy.

## CULTURE AND SOCIETY

During its period as a Greek colony, Paestum contained two sacred areas in which three Doric-style temples still stand. These well-preserved temples were built in the fifth and fourth centuries BCE and are characterized by their massive size and unique design. The Doric order denotes the simple circular capitals atop columns in each temple, as opposed to more intricate column designs. Each temple is also characterized by the entasis of its columns, indicating the apparent curvature of the columns as the diameter of each column decreases upward.

There are two temples dedicated to the goddess Hera located close together in the city. The first was built out of limestone around 550 BCE. For a time, this temple was called the Basilica because archaeologists believed it to be a Roman civic building. The long side has eighteen columns, while the short side has nine, an unusual design not found in many other Greek temples. This design was perhaps the result of the two doors used to enter the temple. The columns running down the middle of the inner chamber (cella) suggest a possible dedication of the temple to more than one god.

The second temple to Hera was built around 460 BCE. It has a six-by-fourteen column plan and is the best preserved of all the temples in Paestum. Built of limestone, this temple has an unusual appearance because its rather wide columns are arranged close to one another. Its inner chamber contains a double row of Doric columns, and at one time, the temple had a roof made of tiles and wood. The temple is possibly dedicated to Poseidon in addition to Hera, and there is evidence that several other deities were worshipped there.

The final temple is dedicated to Athena, though it was for a time believed to be dedicated to Ceres, the Roman goddess of agriculture. On the other side of the town center from the Hera temples, the Athena temple was built around 510–500 BCE. It incorporates a mix of Doric and Ionic column designs (the Ionic order is defined by columns with scroll or spiral capitals). This blended design suggests a sort of transitional architectural style for the period.

During the Roman period, the city's forum was oriented around these two sacred areas. The city's new identity as a Roman colony was reflected in a rebuilding program and the incorporation of various Roman building types. This new construction included a Temple of Peace in the second century BCE as well as a Roman amphitheater.

## DEMISE

Paestum began to lose its prominent status in the second century BCE. Though a second colony was founded there in 71 CE, economic decline and lack of cultural relevance were compounded by the eruption of Mt. Vesuvius in 79 CE. This catastrophic event buried the nearby city of Pompeii and seems to have slightly affected some of Paestum's own buildings. Despite these setbacks, there were occasional periods of revival and rebuilding in the first two centuries CE.

In this later period, Paestum was isolated due to its being bypassed by a newly constructed Roman highway and the abandonment of its harbor. The marshy area around the city had a bad reputation for being inhospitable. Still, there appears to have been a vibrant Christian community in the city. In the fifth century CE, the Athena/Ceres temple was converted into a Christian church dedicated to the Virgin Mary, and Paestum was chosen as the seat for a bishop. This activity at the church is evidenced by a cemetery near the building.

In the seventh century, the Lombards, a Germanic group, invaded the region and further destabilized Paestum. The city remained inhabited until its sack by Muslim invaders in 871 CE. As a result, the bishop of Paestum was forced to move his seat to Capaccio. The church in Paestum was still visited on occasion, and some bishops of Capaccio attempted to restore it.

## RECENT DISCOVERIES AND CURRENT STATUS

Paestum is recognized as a UNESCO World Heritage Site under the official name Cilento and Vallo di Diano National Park with the Archaeological Sites of Paestum and Velia. The three well-preserved Greek temples are the site's main draw for tourists.

*Chris Bingley*

*See also:* Pompeii; Rome.

## FURTHER READING

Boardman, John. 1999. *The Greeks Overseas: Their Early Colonies and Trade*. 4th ed. London: Thames & Hudson.

Cerchiai, Luca, Lorena Jannelli, and Fausto Longo. 2002. *The Greek Cities of Magna Graecia and Sicily*. Los Angeles: Getty Publications.

Graham, Alexander John. 1983. *Colony and Mother City in Ancient Greece*. 2nd ed. New York: Ares.

Gualtieri, Maurizio. 2013. "Greeks, Lucanians and Romans at Poseidonia/Paestum (South Italy)." In *A Companion to the Archaeology of the Roman Republic*, edited by Jane DeRose Evans, 369–386. Hoboken, NJ: Wiley-Blackwell.

# Pataliputra

Pataliputra, the capital of multiple ancient empires, sat on the southern bank of the Ganges River in northeastern India. The city meets the Ganges River as it flows southeast down from the Himalayas to present-day Bangladesh and the Bay of Bengal. The Gandaki River, flowing from the north, and the Son River, flowing from the south, both issue into the Ganges in the vicinity of Pataliputra, making the location a hub for river transportation. The city lies between New Delhi, approximately 600 miles to the northwest, and Calcutta, approximately 300 miles to the southeast. The region surrounding the city has a humid subtropical climate with an average relative humidity of 60 percent. The temperatures average over ninety degrees Fahrenheit from March through September, and monsoon season drops heavy amounts of rain from June to September.

The modern city of Patna, which boasts a population of over two million inhabitants, surrounds the ancient ruins of Pataliputra and remains a major cultural and economic hub in Bihar, India. Among the modern city's streets, excavations of the ancient ruins have been ongoing. Important archaeological sites can be found at Kumhrar, Agam Kuan, and Bulandi Bagh. It was at the latter site that the famous Pataliputra capital was found in the late nineteenth century.

## INHABITANTS

Pataliputra has been inhabited continuously since before the fifth century BCE, making it one of the oldest cities of continuous inhabitation on the globe. The primary language of the city has been Magadhi, which is native to Magadha, the region surrounding Pataliputra. Many other languages have been and continue to be spoken among the city's diverse population. Among these, Bengali from the east and Hindi from the west have been particularly prominent. Although the population today largely practices Hinduism, the city played an important role in the Buddhist and Jain belief systems and was traditionally home to followers of these faiths.

## HISTORICAL BACKGROUND

The settlement that later came to be known as Pataliputra first appeared in the historical record in the early fifth century BCE as Pataligram. Both Buddhist

> **Shambhala**
>
> Shambhala is a kingdom existing on a spiritual plain according to Indo-Tibetan Buddhism. The name of the city is derived from a real place, Sambhal, in north central India. The spiritual city first appeared in Hindu mythology. The *Vishnu Purana*, an ancient Sanskrit text, says that Shambhala will be the birthplace of the final form of Vishnu and thereby usher the world into a new era. In the Buddhist tradition, the kingdom features in the Kalachakra tradition, a group of Buddhist texts originally from the eleventh century CE and also written in Sanskrit. There are traditionally thirty-two kings of Shambhala. Suchandra, the first king, is responsible for the enlightenment of Shambhala. He is the first of seven Dharmarajas, the initial kings of the spiritual realm, who are followed by twenty-five Kalki kings. The Dalai Lamas claim to be manifestations of Pundarika, the second Kalki king. Some believe Shambala inspired the mythical Tibetan realm of Shangri-La.

and Jain texts describe the life of King Ajatashatru of Magadha. A ruler of the Haryanka dynasty, Ajatashatru is said to have gained the throne by arresting and executing his father, King Bimbisara. He continued his father's program of aggressive expansion. Ajatashatru moved the capital of Magadha from Rajagriha to Pataligram. The latter had previously been a smaller settlement, but Ajatashatru fortified it into a proper capital, which later dynasties and empires also used for their capital long after the last Haryankan king. The rapid expansion of Magadha continued under the Shishunaga and Nanda dynasties in the fifth and fourth centuries BCE, respectively. Pataliputra continued to serve as the capital and power base for the growing kingdom in this time period. The Nanda kings consolidated the gains of the Haryankans and Shishunagas and continued to grow the power of Magadha. It was the prospect of fighting the Kingdom of Magadha under Nanda leadership that forced the army of Alexander the Great to rebel and turn back to the west.

The Mauryan Empire overtook the region, including Pataliputra, and built upon Magadha's previous success. Chandragupta Maurya founded the empire toward the end of the fourth century BCE, and it quickly expanded across northern India. Megasthenes, the Greek ethnographer, visited Pataliputra during this time and described a magnificent capital city surrounded by large wooden walls with dozens of gates and hundreds of towers. The Mauryans continued to thrive under Chandragupta's successors, who extended the empire's sway southward down the Indian peninsula. Ashoka, Chandragupta's grandson, controlled almost the entire Indian subcontinent and played a large role in sparking the spread of Buddhism around Asia. He also began replacing the wooden structures of Pataliputra with stone ones.

After the reign of Ashoka, the Mauryan Empire began to shrink, and finally, in 185 BCE, the Shungas took Pataliputra. The Shungas ruled a regional empire for about a hundred years followed by the rules of the Kanvas, the Andhrabhrtyas, and various Bengali princes. The Gupta Empire was the next massive empire to be centered in Pataliputra. Sri Gupta founded the empire in the late third century CE. The empire reached its territorial apex in the fourth and fifth centuries, ruling over almost all of northern India. A cultural and literary zenith corresponded with the empire's political pinnacle. It was at this time that the

*Mahabharata* and *Ramayana*, the two major epic poems written in Sanskrit, crystalized into something of a final form. The Gupta Empire finally unraveled in the sixth century.

After the fall of the Gupta Empire, the center of power in northeastern India appeared to shift slightly westward. Pataliputra was still an important political, cultural, and economic center but no longer served as the capital to the large empires that ruled over northern India and beyond. The Kannauj Empire and the empire established by Harsha both had their capitals at Kannauj, which was also on the Ganges River, about 400 miles upriver (northwest) from Pataliputra. The Pala Empire controlled much of northern India from the eighth to the twelfth centuries, and Pataliputra served as one of several capitals for this empire, which was the final major Buddhist power to rule in India.

## CULTURE AND SOCIETY

The culture and society of Pataliputra has gone through much evolution through the city's millennia of continuous habitation. A diverse range of influences has shaped the city's culture and society. Patna, the modern name of the city, is derived from a Hindu goddess, and the city has spent much of its existence as a hub for the practice of Hinduism. However, other Indian religions view the city as important for their own reasons. Chandragupta Maurya, who founded the Mauryan Empire in the late fourth century BCE, became a Jain monk following his abdication; his descendant Samprati, another Mauryan emperor, also practiced Jainism. Other Mauryan emperors practiced Buddhism, which originated not far from Pataliputra. The second and third Buddhist councils were held in the city. Emperor Ashoka hosted the latter and is largely responsible for spreading Buddhism out from India by sending out Buddhist missions in all directions.

The era in which the Mauryans ruled Pataliputra also saw abundant and unprecedented contact and exchange with the Hellenistic West. The famous Pataliputra capital is a large sandstone Greek-style capital that weighs almost a ton. Other archaeological evidence of this contact abounds. The Gupta Empire is often considered the golden age of Indian history, and the two major Sanskrit poems, the *Mahabharata* and *Ramayana*, more or less came into their final form under the Guptas. More recently, the Sikhs have considered Patna City, a neighborhood of Patna, sacred because Guru Gobind Singh, the tenth Sikh Gurum, was born there in 1666.

## DEMISE

Pataliputra continued to thrive as a city after the fall of the Pala Empire in the twelfth century CE but no longer served as a regional capital. Political power shifted to other regions. In subsequent periods, Pataliputra and the surrounding region of Bihar were ruled by Bengali powers to the east and powers such as Delhi to the west in turn. Through the Sena Empire, the Delhi and Bengal sultanates, the Sur and Mughal Empires, and under the Nawabs of Bengal and British, the city persevered. Now known as Patna, it remains an important cultural and economic hub at an important crossroads of the Ganges River system.

### RECENT DISCOVERIES AND CURRENT STATUS

Remains from the eras of Pataliputra's past lie among the bustling modern iteration of the city, Patna. Excavations have been ongoing, including at the sites of Kumhrar, Agam Kuan, and Bulandi Bagh.

*Anthony Vivian*

*See also:* Mughal Empire; Vijayanagara.

### FURTHER READING

Ashvini Agrawal. 1989. *Rise and Fall of the Imperial Guptas*. New Delhi: Motilal Banarsidass.
Raychaudhuri, H. C., and B. N. Mukherjee. 1996. *Political History of Ancient India: From the Accession of Parikshit to the Extinction of the Gupta Dynasty*. Oxford: Oxford University Press.
Sastri, Kallidaikurichi Aiyah Nilakanta, ed. 1988. *Age of the Nandas and Mauryas*. 2nd ed. New Delhi: Motilal Banarsidass.
Singh, Upinder. 2016. *A History of Ancient and Early Medieval India: From the Stone Age to the 12th Century*. Noida: Pearson.

## Pecos Pueblo

In its heyday, Pecos Pueblo housed over 2,000 people and rose to five stories. The pueblo stood between Glorieta Creek and the Pecos River, just north of where the two converged. The location allowed the pueblo to control trade with the Plains

Although now in ruins, the Pecos Pueblo once housed thousands of inhabitants within its multistoried construction. Its solid, stone construction has largely survived the centuries. (National Park Service)

Indians to the north and the inhabitants of the Rio Grande Valley to the south. Among vast woodlands, the pueblo was perched on the southern face of the Santa Fe Mountains, the southernmost subrange of the Sangre de Cristo Mountains, which are, in turn, the southernmost subrange of the Rocky Mountains.

The solid stone construction of the pueblo has allowed much of it to survive the centuries, although it has not been inhabited full time since the 1830s. Still multi-storied in places, the pueblo survives among relics from other eras. In addition to the Spanish mission built near the pueblo, an early twentieth-century ranch and an American Civil War battlefield can also be found close by.

## INHABITANTS

The inhabitants of Pecos Pueblo were part of the group known collectively today as Puebloans. They cultivated maize, squash, and beans using irrigation systems developed from the nearby Glorieta Creek and Pecos River, and they operated within large trade networks that incorporated the cultures of the Rio Grande Valley to the south and the Plains Indians to the north. The Puebloans had a rich religious culture that explored the relationships between the human and natural worlds and featured kivas: large, circular, subterranean rooms used for worship and religious ceremonies. The inhabitants of Pecos Pueblo spoke a branch of the Kiowa-Tanoan family of languages called the Towa language; it is also known as the Jemez language, as it is still spoken today at Jemez Pueblo.

## HISTORICAL BACKGROUND

For millennia before Pecos Pueblo rose to five stories, Native Americans inhabited the region. At very early stages, more than ten millennia ago, big game hunters roamed the area tracking game such as mastodons. Big game hunting gave way to hunting and gathering, which, in turn, methodically gave way to a more settled lifestyle. From the eleventh century BCE to the eighth century CE, the regions around what would become Pecos Pueblo were inhabited by peoples now known as Basketmakers, thanks to their extensive construction and use of baskets. By the eighth century, the Basketmakers had settled into a more sedentary lifestyle. At some locations across what is today the Four Corners region of the American Southwest, they constructed large pit houses for themselves. Some of these also featured rooms above ground. Having long grown maize and squash, they began cultivating beans as well.

Around the ninth century, the people living near the convergence of Glorieta Creek and the Pecos River also began building pit houses, similar to those in other locations in the region. By the eleventh century, these pit houses were supplemented with aboveground buildings: small, multifamily pueblos. Over the twelfth and thirteenth centuries, the population increased across the Rio Grande Valley and Four Corners regions. A rise in pueblo construction dovetailed with the increase in population, both around the Pecos River valley and beyond. The site that would later become Pecos Pueblo was just one of a couple dozen pueblos dotting the Pecos River valley at this time, including nearby Forked Lightning Pueblo and Rowe Pueblo.

The following period saw the population of this sprawling region continue to rise, but instead of resulting in more pueblos as it did earlier, the increasing population now began to consolidate their settlements. Some pueblos were abandoned, while several across the region grew rapidly in size. An exemplary case of this phenomenon was the Pecos Pueblo, which ballooned in size to become the premier pueblo in the entire region. Around the fourteenth century, the inhabitants of an estimated 50–100 small villages coalesced to form the burgeoning hub that was Pecos Pueblo. The site succeeded over others largely because of the ideality of its location, which allowed it, among other things, to command trade networks to the north and south. At its height, the pueblo was home to around 2,000 people and rose as high as five stories.

The Pecos Pueblo thrived for centuries. Pecos was recognized as the region's premier pueblo both among the Puebloans themselves at Pecos and other major pueblos and among the Spanish when they arrived in the sixteenth and seventeenth centuries. At this time, Pecos Pueblo was known as Cicuye for its ability to support 500 warriors among its population. The Spanish established a Franciscan mission near the site of the pueblo in the early seventeenth century. This mission, similar to other missions set up near other major pueblos, attempted to convert the populations to Christianity and otherwise control the lives of the Puebloans. In 1680, the residents of Pecos Pueblo banded together with those of other pueblos and expelled the Spanish from the region. At Pecos, they built a kiva—a local religious structure—in front of the Spanish mission as a show of defiance. The rebellion was successful; however, the Spanish returned in 1692 and reestablished themselves in the region.

## CULTURE AND SOCIETY

The residents of Pecos Pueblo made up a portion of Puebloan culture and society that thrived in what is today the Four Corners region of the southwestern United States. They spoke Towa, a tonal language. Tribal rules forbid the transcription of the language, but it lives on in spoken form at Jemez Pueblo. Material culture from the region features pottery and textiles. Their religion helped stitch together the community of Pecos Pueblo and featured prominently in the Pueblo Revolt of the late seventeenth century. The faithful utilized kivas—round subterranean rooms—for worship and ceremonies, and religious festivals typically featured traditional dance. The society relied on the cultivation of maize, squash, and beans. At its height, Pecos Pueblo was the most influential site in the entire region, and it wielded great control over trade networks with the people of the Rio Grande Valley to the south as well as the Plains Indians to the north.

## DEMISE

The decline of the Pecos Pueblo was sparked by the arrival of the Spanish. Although the Puebloan people were able to expel the Spanish from the region in 1680, the imperialists returned a dozen years later and entrenched themselves. After this point, Pecos Pueblo did not resist as fiercely as other pueblos in the area.

Throughout the eighteenth century, diseases that originated in Europe decimated the community. By the 1830s, Pecos Pueblo was a shell of its former self, and the remaining population moved to Jemez Pueblo, about ninety miles to the west. The culture that flourished at Pecos Pueblo has lived on at Jemez, as has their Towa language. Although the Spanish undid the political consequences of the late seventeenth-century Pueblo Revolt, the event seems to have afforded the Puebloan people a slight measure of autonomy in their future relationship with the Spanish, which aided the survival of their culture and religion.

## RECENT DISCOVERIES AND CURRENT STATUS

The state of New Mexico purchased the 341 acres of land that included and surrounded Pecos Pueblo in 1935, making it a state monument. In 1965, the federal government took over control of the monument under the Lyndon B. Johnson administration. It has remained in federal hands since. In the 1990s, 1000s of more acres were added to the national park.

*Anthony Vivian*

*See also:* Ancestral Puebloans; Spanish Missions in North America.

## FURTHER READING

Decker, Carol Paradise. 2011. *Pecos Pueblo People through the Ages, Stories of Time and Place*. Santa Fe, NM: Sunstone Press.
Kantner, John. 2004. *Ancient Puebloan Southwest*. Cambridge: Cambridge University Press.
Knudten, Cori, and Maren Bzdek. 2020. *Crossroads of Change: The People and the Land of Pecos*. Norman: University of Oklahoma Press.
Whiteley, Peter M., ed. 2018. *Puebloan Societies: Homology and Heterogeneity in Time and Space*. Albuquerque: University of New Mexico Press.

# Pergamon

Pergamon thrived as a regional power in northwestern Anatolia for centuries. The city was built a little less than twenty miles from the Aegean coast, opposite the large island of Lesbos, and the town of Elaia served as Pergamon's port during the city's heyday. Pergamon occupied a strategic position overlooking a plain that the Caicus River had cut between the mountains. For the Hellenistic and Roman periods, the city was the major power in this region of Anatolia known as Mysia. At its peak, Pergamon was the most influential city in all of Anatolia.

The city center was divided into two halves, the upper and lower acropolises. The upper acropolis was the heart of the city and featured temples to Dionysus and Athena, a large theater, a large library, the main agora, and the Pergamon altar. The frieze of the Pergamon altar was looted by Germany and currently resides in Berlin. The lower acropolis housed a gymnasium as well as temples to Hera and Demeter. Outside of the city proper was the large Sanctuary of Asclepius, which served as a hub of ancient medical thinking and practice, and a Roman-era temple to the Egyptian gods Isis and Serapis.

## INHABITANTS

The inhabitants of Pergamon were Anatolian Greeks. They spoke Greek, but their culture was a distinctly Anatolian strain of Greek. The city was intermittently ruled by Eastern powers. They traced their city's history back to Telephos, the son of Heracles (anglicized: Hercules). In the city's heyday under the Attalid dynasty, the inhabitants prided themselves on their culture and viewed their city as a second Athens. They worshipped a pantheon of Greek gods, which persisted and grew through the city's Roman era. A major Roman-era temple was dedicated to two Egyptian gods, Isis and Serapis, importation of foreign gods being a common Roman practice.

## HISTORICAL BACKGROUND

Pergamon was founded well before its prime and had a regional presence through the Archaic and Classical periods of Greek history. The earliest current archaeological records date back to the eighth century BCE. The length and nature of inhabitation at the site before this is a matter of scholarly debate.

The city enters the written historical record in the very early fourth century BCE, at which point, it, like most of the other Greek-speaking cities on Anatolia, was under Achaemenid Persia's sphere of influence. Xenophon is the earliest extant author to mention the city, calling it "Pergamos" in his *Anabasis*, which describes events at the turn of the fourth century BCE. He states that it was at Pergamon that he released thousands of his own men returning from their failed venture into Persia to the Spartan Thibron, who was launching his own ultimately unsuccessful expedition into Persia. A few decades later, Orontes I used Pergamon as a base of operations.

After Alexander III of Macedon conquered the Persian Empire and then promptly died, Pergamon—along with the rest of western and northern Anatolia and Thrace—came under the rule of Lysimachus, one of several competing successor kings. Lysimachus appointed Philetaerus as the leader of Pergamon; however, Philetaerus betrayed Lysimachus in 282 BCE, joining his own and Pergamon's fate to Seleucus, a rival successor king. Philetaerus's line—known as the Attalid dynasty—would rule Pergamon for the next century and a half. Two generations after Philetaerus, Attalus I declared Pergamon autonomous for the first time in centuries and granted himself the title of king. Under his sucessor, Eumenes II, the Kingdom of Pergamon reached its farthest territorial capacity, incorporating much of western Anatolia.

Pergamon continued to flourish under the Attalid dynasty until 133 BCE. With no male heirs, King Attalus III granted the Kingdom of Pergamon to Rome in his will. During his life, he witnessed the expanding power of Rome, and he believed such a move would obviate a violent Roman takeover. Claiming to be a member of the royal family, Aristonicus challenged the move, but he was defeated by Roman forces in 129 BCE, which then completed Rome's annexation of Pergamon. The city thrived as a part of Rome's province of Asia for the next several decades.

Pergamon played a major role in the Mithridatic Wars before becoming an influential regional power under Roman rule. Upset at the Romans, Mithridates VI, king of Pontus, orchestrated the killing of all Roman and Italian citizens across Pergamon and other Anatolian cities on a specific date in the spring of 88 BCE. After more than two decades of war, the Romans defeated Mithridates VI, and the Romans punished Pergamon for its role in the war by removing its status as a free city and exacting a tribute. Albeit no longer autonomous, Pergamon continued to thrive under Roman rule. Writing in the first century CE, Pliny the Elder described Pergamon as the most influential city in the entire region. In the early second century, the city was extensively refurbished, first under the Roman emperor Trajan and then under his successor, Hadrian.

## CULTURE AND SOCIETY

Pergamon boasted a culture and society that were equal parts Greek and Anatolian. Agriculture sustained the society, but the city was also embedded into the Aegean and Anatolian worlds through extensive trade networks. A sophisticated water supply system ensured that the city was well hydrated. During its height under the Attalid dynasty and into its Roman period, the city served as an intellectual hub and exported culture throughout the region. They constructed a grand history for their own city, linking themselves to Heracles through his son Telephos and to the Trojan Cycle of epics through the area of Teuthrania.

As an intellectual hub, Pergamon was home to some of these eras' most influential thinkers, particularly—though not exclusively—philosophers and physicians. The city's philosophical reputation spanned centuries and included members of a variety of schools, including the Peripatetic and Neoplatonic schools. Sosipatra, the fourth-century CE Neoplatonic philosopher, moved to Pergamon following her husband's death and became a renowned mystic philosopher. Asclepius was the Greek god of healing, and Pergamon's Sanctuary of Asclepius became a leading ancient medical center and a hub for medical thinking and writing as well as medical practice. Galen, the influential physician and prolific medical writer, worked out of the city's Sanctuary of Asclepius.

## DEMISE

Pergamon began to decline in the third century CE, a tough century for most regions within the Roman Empire, and although it continued to experience ups and downs, its overall influence waned steadily from there. Pergamon suffered a major earthquake in 262 and later—like many other Roman cities—a Gothic invasion. The city changed hands many times through the centuries between the Byzantines, Arabs, Seljuks, Nicaeans, and eventually the Ottomans. While this was occurring, the city's population decreased and consolidated into a more defensive settlement entirely on the city's acropolis.

### RECENT DISCOVERIES AND CURRENT STATUS

Pergamon has been a UNESCO World Heritage Site since 2014. The city has been undergoing consistent excavation since the 1860s. The archaeological finds up until World War I were largely stolen and brought to Germany, including the famous frieze of the Pergamon Altar. Since then, they have gone to the local Bergama Museum. Excavations are ongoing and currently overseen by Felix Person of New York University's Institute for the Study of the Ancient World.

*Anthony Vivian*

*See also:* Ephesus; Troy.

### FURTHER READING

Evans, Richard. 2014. *A History of Pergamum: Beyond Hellenistic Kingship.* London: Bloomsbury Academic.
Green, Peter. 1993. *Alexander to Actium: The Historical Evolution of the Hellenistic Age.* Berkeley: University of California Press.
Mattern, Susan P. 2013. *The Prince of Medicine: Galen in the Roman Empire.* Oxford: Oxford University Press.
Picón, Carlos A., and Seán Hemingway. 2016. *Pergamon and the Hellenistic Kingdoms of the Ancient World.* New York: Metropolitan Museum of Art.

## Persepolis

Secluded in the southern Zagros Mountains, Persepolis rests on a raised terrace built in the broad Marv Dasht plain. Its English name comes from the Greek for "Persian city"; the Persians knew it as Parsa, which similarly means "city of the Persians." The remains of the former Achaemenid Persian capital are thirty-seven miles from the modern urban hub of Shiraz, but the location was likely chosen in large part thanks to its proximity to a different city: Pasargadae, the Achaemenid capital before Persepolis, is a winding fifty-mile road from Persepolis. The spot's isolated and easily fortified nature provided another reason for the choice of location.

Darius I, also known as Darius the Great, founded the city to be his new capital in the late sixth century BCE. Several palaces and smaller structures fill the terrace, built by him and his successors. To make room, the terrace was partly cut into the mountain, and the buildings were primarily made of limestone and mud brick. Today, although the vast palace complexes are mostly gone, their foundations remain, with many columns still reaching up. Many of the city's artifacts, especially the Persepolis bull and many bas-reliefs, have been looted from the site and are displayed across Europe and North America.

### INHABITANTS

As a planned city that served as a residence to the Achaemenid kings, Persepolis's original inhabitants were the construction workers of Darius I, who founded the city, followed by his court and staff. The original workforce included many physical laborers brought in from different parts of the Achaemenid Empire. It also contained top architects and craftsman from other Persian urban centers. The design of Persepolis is thought to have been largely modeled on Darius's palace at Susa, the king's parallel construction in the West. They did not live in the grand halls they were building, but temporary housing was set up on site during the construction. The city was built to be a perpetual testament to the kings' power, and scant evidence of these original inhabitants survives. Eventually, Darius's court and staff moved in. However, Persepolis's remote location made it difficult to reach during Iran's wet winter season. Persepolis served as a treasury for Persian royalty and could act as a safe haven if necessary, but under normal circumstances, it was not meant to be more than a seasonal residence for the Achaemenid kings.

## HISTORICAL BACKGROUND

Darius I founded Persepolis around 515 BCE as a seasonal residence and a standing monument to his power. He ended up ruling for three and a half decades, adding territory to his empire's eastern, northern, and western borders. However, in the beginning of his reign, his hold on power was tenuous, and many see this fragile environment as part of his decision to build the city of Persepolis. When King Cambyses II was earlier campaigning in Egypt, his brother Bardiya (known as Smerdis in Greek sources) seized the throne back in Persia. On his way back to reclaim the throne, Cambyses died, leaving Bardiya as sole ruler. Darius and six other aristocratic coconspirators overthrew Bardiya, and Darius became king. The new king claimed the real Bardiya had died long before and that the recently deceased ruler was an impostor. However, many powerful forces within the empire were unhappy with Darius's ascension, and he was forced to spend the initial part of his reign putting down revolt after revolt. This circumstance likely encouraged Darius to found a new capital that was remote, easy to defend, and removed from the squabbles of the previous capital.

Darius began construction on Persepolis in the first decade of his reign, in 515 or perhaps a few years before. He constructed a grand staircase known as the Persepolitan stairway up to a large elevated terrace. Upon this platform, he oversaw the completion of three main structures: the Apadana, the Palace of Darius, and the Council Hall. The Apadana was Darius's receiving hall, the walls below which featured bas-reliefs of the twenty-three nations of the Achaemenid Empire paying tribute to Darius. He began various other building projects in his newly formed city, which were then completed by his son.

When Darius died, his son Xerxes ascended the throne and took over the construction at Persepolis. Although he had to put down revolts in Egypt and Babylon, he did not face the same fierce challenges to his succession that his father did. At Persepolis, he completed some of the buildings started by his father, such as the Royal Treasury. He also began new projects at the royal city, including two of the location's grandest structures: the Gate of All Nations and the Throne Hall, also known as the Hall of 100 Columns. He also built a harem that included twenty-two apartments, replete with an enclosed garden.

Just as Darius and Xerxes ruled the Achaemenid Empire at its territorial peak, they are credited with being the main builders responsible for Persepolis.

Nevertheless, later rulers continued to add to the Persian capital. Of particular note, Artaxerxes I, son of Xerxes, completed his father's Throne Hall, and Artaxerxes III reinvigorated construction at Persepolis in the fourth century, adding a palace of his own.

## CULTURE AND SOCIETY

Because Persepolis served as a seasonal headquarters for the Persian kings, its culture and society are that of the Achaemenid royal court. In addition to the spacious receiving halls and king's quarters, there was lodging for military personnel as well as the royal harem. A vast and diverse array of artifacts speak to the royal culture that was found in this capital city. The city itself was built as a testament to the various kings' power, so many of the bas-reliefs and other artwork decorating the city illustrate this power. Some of the bas-reliefs depict celebrations of Nowruz, the Persian New Year, pushing some to argue that the city's primary function was the royal celebration of this holiday. Administrative texts show the broad organization that kept the court running smoothly. The Achaemenids were *the* superpower of the wider Near East in this time period. The Apadana palace coin hoard, named after the palace complex it was found in, showcases the wealth of the Achaemenids, as do the colossal remains themselves.

## DEMISE

Alexander III of Macedon, also known as Alexander the Great, invaded and conquered the wealthy and expansive Achaemenid Empire in the 330s BCE. When his army beat Darius III's at Gaugamela, in the final decisive pitched battle of the conquest, Alexander took his army farther east. After taking Babylon and Susa, the Macedonian army set its sights on Persepolis. Darius had all but abandoned these urban centers as he fled north to Ecbatana and then toward Bactria. Nevertheless, Ariobarzanes, a Persian satrap also known as Ariobarzanes the Brave, made a heroic last stand at the so-called Persian Pass en route to Persepolis. After holding the pass for about a month with a small Persian force, Alexander's army flanked him and took Persepolis. He allowed his army to loot the Persian capital for days and stationed them there for five months.

A fire broke out during this time, and accounts differ about whether it was intentional and, if so, who lit it and why. One anecdote popular among later Greek historians was that Thais, a hetaera from Athens, incited the arson as revenge for the Persians burning the old Temple of Athena back in 480. Persian historians indicate this looting and fire as responsible for the loss of myriad early Persian texts and works of art. The looting has continued into the modern era; Western powers have taken artifacts from the ruins and displayed them in museums far from Iran.

## RECENT DISCOVERIES AND CURRENT STATUS

Persepolis has been a UNESCO World Heritage Site since 1979. In the 1930s, the Persepolis Fortification Archive and Persepolis Treasury Archive, two important sets of Achaemenid administration texts inscribed on tablets, were found at Persepolis. More recently, fragments of a Greek-style plaque depicting Herakles and Apollo were discovered.

*Anthony Vivian*

*See also:* Ctesiphon; Susa.

## FURTHER READING

Curtis, J., and N. Tallis, eds. 2005. *Forgotten Empire: The World of Ancient Persia.* Berkeley: University of California Press.

Llewellyn-Jones, Lloyd. 2013. *King and Court in Ancient Persia 559 to 331 BCE.* Edinburgh: Edinburgh University Press.

Soheil, Mehr Azar. 2018. *The Concept of Monument in Achaemenid Empire.* London: Routledge.

Wilber, Donald Newton. 1989. *Persepolis: The Archaeology of Parsa, Seat of the Persian Kings.* London: Darwin Press.

# Petra

A striking city carved into sandstone cliffs in present-day Jordan, Petra wielded control over important trade routes up through the first century CE. The name means "rock" in Greek, but the city was known as Raqmu to its Nabatean inhabitants. On the northern Arabian Peninsula, about 100 miles south of Jerusalem as well as the Mediterranean port of Gaza and 60 miles north of the Red Sea, Petra sat on a global crossroads. The city's strength rested on its defensibility and secure water supply. The region's rugged geography enhanced its defensibility, and the Nabatean inhabitants took great strides to construct aqueducts, wells, and dams to ensure the population's water supply in the arid region.

Despite centuries of erosion and abandonment, many of Petra's buildings remain in good condition. The most famous building, Al-Khazneh, or the Treasury, was recently voted one of the New Seven Wonders of the World. Despite its name, it seems to have been a mausoleum for the first-century CE king Aretas IV. Additionally, many elaborate tombs and religious buildings comprise the cityscape. Although the Great Temple and the Temple of the Winged Lions are in ruins, Ad Deir, or the Monastery, and the freestanding Qasr al-Bint have survived largely intact. A large amphitheater cut into the sandstone has also survived.

## INHABITANTS

The Neolithic site Beidha, just a few miles from Petra, stands as proof that the area was inhabited at least as far back as ca. 7000 BCE. Before founding the city of Petra around the fourth century BCE, the Nabateans started out as one of several Bedouin tribes ranging the Arabian Peninsula in search of water and pasture. Although Petra was founded earlier, most of the major building projects seem to have been undertaken in the second and first centuries BCE as well as the first century CE. In addition to their Arabic roots, the Nabateans also had connections

Al-Khazneh, which translates to "the Treasury," was carved directly into the sandstone cliff. The dating of this magnificent structure is disputed, but many suggest a date in the first century CE. (Angela Ostafichuk | Dreamstime.com)

to regional Aramaic culture. This duality is reflected in their language. Their primary language was a dialect of Arabic, yet they also spoke Aramaic to communicate with neighbors. The Nabatean alphabet was derived from the Aramaic alphabet and later, in turn, developed into the Arabic alphabet.

## HISTORICAL BACKGROUND

Originally Bedouin nomads, the Nabateans are believed to have settled in Petra by the fourth century BCE. The area allowed them to control the important trade routes that crisscrossed the region and beyond, including the lucrative incense trade route. This allowed them to quickly surpass their fellow Bedouin tribes in wealth and reputation. The exact chronology of when the Nabateans built Petra is not known. While it seems likely that Petra existed in the fourth century BCE in some capacity, it also appears that the impressive building projects for which the city has become famous were built in later centuries. Although much of Nabatean history remains unclear and scholars still debate the dates of Petra's construction, we do have rich information on the Arabian kingdom. Nabatean inscriptions play a central role in our understanding of their history and culture. This story is then supplemented by outside sources, particularly the Old Testament, Diodorus, Strabo, and Josephus.

An episode dated to 312/311 BCE showcased the already established reputation of the Nabateans and seems to have indicated the existence of Petra. The episode comes from Diodorus's writings three centuries later but relying on earlier, now lost, sources. According to Diodorus, Antigonus I, one of the successors of Alexander the Great and the leader of the Seleucids, conquered the Levant and caught wind of the Nabateans' wealth. He sent two armies to raid their territory, both unsuccessful. The first army of 4,000 infantry and 600 cavalry succeeded with a surprise attack on "the Rock" before the Nabateans returned the favor with a surprise counterattack that left almost the entire invading force dead. The second army failed to gain entrance to "the Rock." Many have identified this location as an early iteration of what would become Petra.

Diodorus also mentions the Nabateans engaging less successfully with another successor kingdom, the Ptolemies, who ruled Egypt, across the Red Sea. After harassing Ptolemaic merchant ships on the Red Sea, the Ptolemies punished the Nabateans accordingly. Aretas I is the first Nabatean king for whom we have solid evidence. A Nabatean inscription bears his name and has been dated to the mid-second century BCE (though some contend the inscription may refer to one of his successors of the same name), and he is mentioned in the Old Testament book 2 Maccabees. Here he is described as an ally to the Maccabees of Judaea in their war against the Seleucids. However, his own successor, Aretas II, and the Hasmonean descendants of the Maccabees fell into conflict with one another.

The first half of the first century BCE saw the Nabateans at the peak of their influence. Obodas I inherited the war against the Hasmoneans from his predecessor, which he concluded by winning a decisive victory. He also repelled an invasion from the Seleucids, killing their king, Antiochus VII Dionysus, in the process. For his victories, he was deified by the Nabataeans, and a temple was built to worship him at Avdat, where an inscription refers to him as a god. After the brief rule of Rabbel I, Aretas III took the throne. He ruled a powerful state that was secure in its defenses at Petra but also exerted its influence outward and controlled many of the trade routes through Arabia and beyond.

Although the Nabatean Kingdom and its capital of Petra were at their pinnacle in the middle of the first century BCE, they found themselves in the path of Rome's rapid expansion. As Pompey was conquering much of Rome's eastern frontier, he sent the Roman general Scaurus to Petra. Petra's strong defenses allowed the Nabateans to hold out, but they were still forced to pay a tribute to Rome. Later, Herod the Great, who ruled Judea as a client king for Rome, forced the Nabateans to become his vassals. The Nabatean Kingdom experienced a brief resurgence under Aretas IV in the early first century CE. During his reign, Augustus Caesar recognized the independence of the Nabateans, and the kingdom centered in Petra was once again autonomous and prosperous. After seeing its fortunes shrink in the second half of the first century CE, the Nabatean Kingdom was officially annexed by Rome in 106 CE.

## CULTURE AND SOCIETY

Although no Nabatean literature has survived, a number of inscriptions provide us with the Nabatean language as well as glimpses at Nabatean culture and society. Many inscriptions prove religious in nature, and the knowledge we can glean from these is supplemented by architecture, coinage, and other material remains. The Nabateans had a polytheistic religion that shared a pantheon with other pre-Islamic Arabic religions. Dushara, a god of Mount Shara, south of Petra, eventually became of particular importance to the Nabateans, appearing on their coinage even after the kingdom had been annexed by Rome.

The Nabateans were renowned for their engineering and architecture. Their buildings carved into the sandstone at Petra intrigued and impressed outsiders in antiquity, as they do today. The Nabateans likewise gained prestige for their ability to secure a water supply for their desert city. They engaged in agriculture, again putting their engineering ability to use to extract the most from their desert climate; however, they primarily relied on their control of the western Arabian trade routes. This control gained them wealth and rendered them a regional power.

## DEMISE

Petra and the remainder of the Nabatean Kingdom lost their autonomy once and for all when the kingdom was annexed by Rome in 106 CE. Nevertheless, the city continued to prosper for some time. The trade routes still passed through Petra, as did the wealth that traveled on them, even though the city did not wield the same monopolistic control over these routes as it once did. Eventually, as other regional urban centers, such as Palmyra, grew under Roman rule and maritime trade increased, the influence of Petra shrank. A major earthquake caused serious damage to the city in 363 CE. The city carried on as a shell of its former self before being abandoned and largely forgotten about by the outside world until its rediscovery in 1812.

## RECENT DISCOVERIES AND CURRENT STATUS

In 2016, satellites and drones helped archaeologists rediscover a colossal ancient structure half a mile south of Petra. It is the second-largest known structure in Petra and has been tentatively dated to the second century BCE. Scholars are still trying to determine its function, as it was slightly removed from the main part of the city. Petra has been a UNESCO World Heritage Site since 1985, and in 2007, Al-Khazneh, the most recognizable building in Petra, also known as the Treasury, was voted one of the New Seven Wonders of World.

*Anthony Vivian*

See also: Baalbek; Phoenicians; Ur.

## FURTHER READING

Healey, John F. 2001. *The Religion of the Nabataeans: A Conspectus.* Leiden, Netherlands: Brill.
McKenzie, Judith. 1990. *The Architecture of Petra.* Oxford: Oxford University Press.
Negev, Avraham. 1986. *Nabatean Archaeology Today.* New York: New York University Press.
Taylor, Jane. 2012. *Petra and the Lost Kingdom of the Nabataeans.* London: I. B. Tauris.

# Phoenicians

The Phoenicians were an ancient people whose homeland was on the eastern seaboard of the Mediterranean but who also founded cities in North Africa, Sardinia, and Spain. They were especially known for their maritime trade, naval power, and alphabet, which influenced Greek writing and other languages. The chief Phoenician cities from the second and first millennia BCE were Tyre, Sidon, Byblos, and Arwad (Arvad), all located on the coastal plain of present-day Lebanon, southern Syria, and northern Israel. From their home base, the Phoenicians established colonies farther afield in the Mediterranean region. The most powerful of these settlements was Carthage (located in modern Tunisia), which between the seventh and third centuries BCE was the center of a great empire and the source of a whole Carthaginian civilization. (The present entry looks at pre-Carthaginian Phoenicia; for information on Carthage and its history, see Carthage.)

## INHABITANTS

There are a number of mysteries surrounding the Phoenicians, and one of them concerns their name. We do not know what they called themselves. The name "Phoenicians" was given to them by the Greeks in the first millennium BCE. The Bible does not use "Phoenicians." Homer used it but more often mentions "Sidonians" in place of "Phoenicians." The Phoenicians seem to have called their own home territory in the Levant by its original Semitic name, Canaan. And, indeed, the inhabitants of the old Phoenician cities were of Canaanite (West Semitic) descent; evidence of Aegean and Cypriot intermixing, however, suggests a broader Levantine identity. The Phoenician language was a direct descendant of Canaanite, as were various aspects of Phoenician culture.

The Phoenician kings of Tyre, Sidon, and Byblos are known from about ninety Phoenician inscriptions found in Lebanon and Cyprus, but these sources do not supply much information on political and cultural matters. Some information on religion has been gathered from inscriptions and from a brief summary in Greek by Philo of Byblos (64–161 CE) of a work by one Sanchuniaton, a Phoenician scholar of about the seventh century BCE. In addition, coins from Tyre, Sidon, Byblos, Arwad, and Cyprus offer indirect cultural and historical information. Surviving partial texts from Egypt and Malta indicate that Phoenician records were kept on papyrus. Besides these, archaeological evidence together with later Roman sources remain the key sources of information about the Phoenicians and their world.

## HISTORICAL BACKGROUND

Phoenicia emerged as a trading and manufacturing center quite early in the history of the Near East. Merchants exported cedars from its inland mountain region to Old Kingdom Egypt (ca. 2600–ca. 2100 BCE). By the second millennium BCE, the Phoenician cities of Byblos, Sidon, Tyre, and Arwad—along with the Amorite/Syrian city of Ugarit—had achieved prominence as seaports, trading in textiles, dyes, glass, cedar, wine, weapons, metalwork, and ivory carving.

Phoenicia as a whole, however, was never politically powerful. Its cities were often forced to make tribute payments to their larger neighbors. They were Egyptian vassals through much of the Bronze Age (to ca. 1200 BCE), when Byblos was the most significant city among them. During the Iron Age (ca. 1200–535 BCE), Tyre and Sidon came to exceed Byblos in political and economic importance. With the waning of Egyptian domination, Phoenicians enjoyed a period of independence between 1200 and 860 BCE. It was during this period that King Hiram of Tyre provided materials and personnel to King Solomon of Israel in connection with the building of the temple in Jerusalem and that Jezebel, the daughter of King Ethbaal of Sidon, became the wife of King Ahab of Samaria (northern Israel).

By the first half of the first millennium BCE, Phoenicians were actively exploring the Mediterranean as far as Gibraltar, on the eastern edge, and even to Cádiz (Iberia), on the Atlantic. They established a colony there (ca. 700) and on the Tunisian coast at Carthage (ca. 800). Phoenician traders may even have reached the British Isles. They would work for foreign powers as well. Phoenician warships were a valued asset to the Persian Empire. Under the patronage of the Egyptian pharaoh Necho II (609–593 BCE), Phoenician ships were said to have circumnavigated the African continent, a feat not accomplished again until the sixteenth century by the Portuguese. Phoenician enterprise turned the Mediterranean into one of the greatest maritime trading environments in history. Also during this period, Phoenician culture—a complex blend of Levantine, Egyptian, Greek, Anatolian, and Mesopotamian influences—reached its peak. The famous Phoenician alphabet was laid out in the second millennium BCE, and by 800 BCE, it had been adapted by the Greeks, who subsequently transmitted alphabetic writing to Rome and parts of Western Europe.

After 860 BCE, the Phoenician city-states fell under Assyrian tutelage. When they failed to pay tributes, campaigns against them were launched by Sargon II (r. 721–705 BCE), by Sennacherib (r. 705–681 BCE), and by Esarhaddon (r. 680–669 BCE). Sidon was largely destroyed, but Tyre survived, albeit in a diminished condition. These punitive campaigns and the burden of tribute prompted the Phoenicians to establish new colonies in Cyprus and the western Mediterranean. When the Assyrian Empire finally gave way to Babylonia in the late seventh century BCE, Phoenicia became a territory of Babylon. Then, with the taking of Babylon by the Persian Cyrus the Great in 535 BCE, Phoenicia was absorbed into the vast Persian Empire. Phoenician cities provided ships and sailors for the Greco-Persian Wars against the Greeks. By then, however, the political and economic significance of the Phoenicians had shifted from their homeland in the Levant to their colonies, especially Carthage in North Africa.

## CULTURE AND SOCIETY

The economy of Phoenicia was based on agriculture and maritime trade. Fishing was also important. The government of Phoenician cities throughout the pre-Carthaginian era and after (from ca. 3000 to ca. 500 BCE) was based on hereditary monarchy. In these monarchies, a close connection existed between royal privilege and priestly power. For example, one king of Tyre was himself a high priest, and at Sidon, the king functioned as priest of the temple dedicated to the goddess Ashtart. Below the royal-priestly ruling class stood the wealthy merchants, and below them were the small manufacturers, farmers, fishers, tradespeople, and ordinary workers.

The Phoenicians were also widely known for their arts and crafts. One of the chief commodities of Phoenician trade was a purple dye obtained from murex seashells. In addition, Phoenician purple cloth produced using this dye was highly valued. Renowned, too, were Phoenician ivory carving and metalwork. From ivories and terra-cotta figurines, we know something about Phoenicians' physical appearance and dress. Far less is known about the Phoenicians' armor and weapons. One custom for which they were known is the burying of the dead in rock-cut chamber tombs, inside of which were placed various amulets and trinkets for good luck in the afterworld.

The Phoenician pantheon of gods varied somewhat from city to city. At Byblos, the main deities were Baal Shamim (Lord of Heaven) and Baalat (the Lady of Byblos). Other deities included Baal Hammon (perhaps, Lord of Braziers) and the goddess Tanit, both of whom also became important in western Phoenicia. At Tyre, the local *baal* (lord) was known as Melqart Baal (Lord of the City), whom the Greeks equated with Heracles and who also had a famous temple in Cádiz, near the Pillars of Heracles (Hercules). At Sidon, the main deities were Baal Shamim (the Lord of Heaven), Ashtart (a goddess of love and war), and Eshmun (a healing god). Phoenician temple ritual centered on sacrifice. Types of sacrifices included an atonement offering, a peace offering, a whole burnt offering, and a meal offering. Sacred sex appears also to have been practiced, a rite possibly performed for fertility purposes. Biblical and Roman references to child sacrifice find little material support in the archaeological data.

Phoenician script employed a twenty-two letter alphabet that was nearly identical to that used later in biblical Hebrew. The Phoenician alphabet itself may have been a descendant of a writing system used by the peoples of Canaan during the Middle Bronze Age (ca. 1700–ca. 1500 BCE), but the Phoenicians did pass their own alphabet to the Greeks during the early first millennium BCE.

## DEMISE

Persian, and then Macedonian, dominance over the Levantine cities of Phoenicia took their toll. One Persian ruler, Artaxerxes III (r. 359–338 BCE), crushed a revolt in Phoenicia led by Tennes, the ruler of Sidon. Artaxerxes punished the residents by executing Tennes, destroying parts of the city, and deporting part of the population to Babylonia.

Then, during Alexander the Great's conquest of Persian lands that began in 334 BCE, he decided he would take the Mediterranean coastline down to the border of Egypt. At first, the Phoenicians (and others) of Tyre welcomed Alexander, but they refused him the honor of performing a sacrifice at the Temple of Melqart. Consequently, Alexander put the city under siege, which lasted for seven months. In the end, the city was conquered, and the center of Phoenician power shifted to Carthage, in the West.

## RECENT DISCOVERIES AND CURRENT STATUS

In 1923, the French archaeologist Pierre Montet discovered inscriptions made in the Phoenician alphabet on the sarcophagus of a king of Byblos; subsequently, Montet uncovered eight other royal tombs in the city. Later excavations by others in the cities of Sidon and Tyre revealed valuable collections of artifacts, including large quantities of painted pottery. Evidence for Phoenician civilization also comes from sites in Cyprus, the Aegean, Malta, and elsewhere, as well as from its neighbors: reliefs found in the Assyrian city of Nineveh depict Phoenician warships in detail, including the great eyes painted on their prows.

Tyre and Byblos were named UNESCO World Heritage Sites in 1984, partly in an effort to limit damage done by ongoing armed conflicts and haphazard urban development. Tyre, in particular, suffered from both problems in addition to facing the effects of coastal erosion, which has only increased in recent years. For its part, Sidon, which experienced destruction more than once in ancient times, is of interest to visitors today, mostly for its medieval Christian castle, built by the Crusaders in 1228 CE.

*Michael Shally-Jensen*

See also: Assyrians; Babylon; Carthage; Persepolis.

## FURTHER READING

Culican, William. 1971. *The First Merchant Adventurers: The Ancient Levant in History and Commerce*. New York: McGraw-Hill.
Elayi, Josette. 2018. *The History of Phoenicia*. Translated by Andrew Plummer. Atlanta: Lockwood Press.
Moscati, Sabatino, curator. 1999. *The Phoenicians*. New York: Rizzoli.
Quinn, Josephine Crawley. 2018. *In Search of the Phoenicians*. Princeton, NJ: Princeton University Press.

## Pompeii

Arguably one of the most famous archaeological sites in the world, Pompeii was preserved in ash by the eruption of Mount Vesuvius in 79 CE. The ancient city is located in what is now the *comune* (municipality) of Pompei, between Naples (ancient Neapolis) and Sorrento (ancient Surrentum), in the Campania region of Italy. Ancient Pompeii was a Mediterranean harbor town with a strategic position on the Sarno River on the fertile plains of Campania, indicating it enjoyed considerable economic success and stability.

The excavated city provides detailed insight into everyday life in a Roman town. The ash and pumice from Mount Vesuvius preserved grand public buildings, lavish private homes, graffiti-laden taverns and businesses, and a variety of religious buildings. In addition to these structures, pottery, metals, and organic materials such as food remains, wood, plants, and human and animal bodies were preserved. As these organic materials decomposed, they left a void in the surrounding ash, allowing archaeologists to create plaster casts of what had once been there—a new scientific technique. It is these plaster casts along with the high quality of structural and artistic preservation that make Pompeii such a unique and renowned place.

## INHABITANTS

The original inhabitants of the area around Pompeii were a native Italian, Oscan-speaking group that settled in the fertile Campanian plains as early as the tenth century BCE. Many of these early settlements became trading posts because of Campania's central location within Italy and its connections to both the sea and inland river routes. At the beginning of the eighth century BCE, Greeks from Euboea set up trading posts in the region, and by the end of the sixth century, they controlled most of the Bay of Naples. The Etruscans, a people native to northern Italy, were also active in the Campania region during these two centuries and set up towns along with the Greeks.

The circuit walls of Pompeii, two temples, and the original grid plan were laid out at the end of the sixth century BCE. It is unclear whether the population of the city was Greek, Etruscan, or a mix of both with native peoples, but by the fifth century BCE, the city was under Samnite control, a native Italian, Oscan-speaking tribe. The Samnites held Pompeii until the early third century BCE, when Rome conquered the Bay of Naples. This blended town was an allied city of Rome until 80 BCE, when it was resettled by Roman military veterans as a Roman *colonia* (colony). Throughout its long history, Pompeii has had a varied and diverse population composed of native and conquering peoples and their enslaved peoples.

## HISTORICAL BACKGROUND

There are two histories of Pompeii: one of the city itself and one after its demise. Pompeii's central and well-connected location allowed the town to thrive from the beginning. Greeks, Etruscans, and Samnites flocked to the Campanian plains before Rome's interest in the south of Italy. Pompeii, however, is widely known as a Roman town because of its status at the time of Vesuvius's eruption. In 79 CE, Pompeii was a prosperous Roman trading town with people and goods from across the empire. The city became an ally with Rome in the third century BCE after the Samnite Wars but was not settled as a full Roman colony until 80 BCE at the end of the Social War. At this time, the citizens of Pompeii received Roman citizenship, and Latin became the official language. This change in status brought with it Roman architecture, governing, institutions, and culture.

At the beginning of the Imperial period, under the reign of Augustus (27 BCE–14 CE), Pompeii saw increased wealth and prosperity as well as physical changes. New public buildings were constructed for Roman needs, and homes in the southeast corner of the city were demolished for an amphitheater. A covered theater was also built, and administrative buildings were added to the forum. Water flowed more freely within the city with the addition of an aqueduct, and trade and commerce flourished.

In 59 CE, there was a riot in the amphitheater that is depicted in a fresco found in the town and corroborated by the ancient historian Tacitus. Just three years later, in 62 CE, Pompeii was struck by a massive earthquake that damaged large portions of the city. There is archaeological evidence that the city was not yet rebuilt when the eruption buried it in 79 CE. The date that Mount Vesuvius erupted is currently a point of contention between archaeologists and ancient historians. The traditional date is August 24, although recent analysis of graffiti, plant remains, and other organic materials at the site push the date later, to October 17. Regardless of the date, a violent volcanic eruption both destroyed and preserved the city in 79 CE.

The history of Pompeii did not end with the eruption of Vesuvius. Small groups returned to the site of the eruption in an attempt to recover their belongings or loot the wealthier parts of the city, but soon after, the location was forgotten. It would not be found again until Domenico Fontana, an Italian architect, uncovered some ancient Roman walls covered in frescoes and graffiti in 1592. He did not make his discovery public, so the city remained buried. In the seventeenth century, a few small inscriptions were found, but it was not until the eighteenth century that excavations truly began. In 1748, Spanish military engineer Rocque Joaquin de Alcubierre excavated parts of Pompeii looking for treasures for the king of Naples. The city, however, was not identified as Pompeii until 1763 with the discovery of an inscription. From the end of the eighteenth century through the beginning of the nineteenth, large sections of the town were uncovered, including the famous House of the Faun and the House of the Tragic Poet.

In 1863, Giuseppe Fiorelli took charge of the excavations and introduced scientific notation and techniques. He developed the plaster cast method that captured the forms of the victims in Pompeii by filling the spaces left in the ash where their bodies had decomposed with plaster. He also divided the city into the system of nine regions, blocks, and homes that we still use. Excavation and conservation campaigns continued throughout the nineteenth and twentieth centuries.

## CULTURE AND SOCIETY

The remains of Pompeii reveal a bustling a market and trading town specializing in *garum* (a fish-based sauce). Unlike other archaeological sites, not only were the grand temples and villas preserved but also the workshops, graves of lower-class citizens, and take-out restaurants frequented by all walks of life. The majority of the preserved buildings are from the Roman period, but the blueprint of previous "versions" of the town can be seen. As the city grew, the walls were expanded with blocks on a grid pattern that were of mixed domestic, commercial, and industrial buildings.

Pompeii had several entertainment zones that included two theaters, one open-air and one covered, and a large amphitheater built 150 years before the Colosseum in Rome. The city also had at least five public bathhouses, all beautifully and intricately decorated. Communal bathing was a hallmark of Roman culture for all classes of citizens. Men would spend their afternoons at the baths, enjoying the different pools and steam rooms, meeting friends, and conducting business. Water was supplied to the baths, and the rest of the city, by an aqueduct, although most residents also collected rainwater.

The religious, political, and commercial center of any Roman city was its forum. The center of Pompeii was in the southwest corner of the city. In the second century BCE, it was transformed from its humbler state to its current monumental form. The Temple of Jupiter (later the Capitolium), the market, and the law court (Basilica) were constructed, and the forum was paved with stone. Temples to Apollo and Venus stood outside the forum; smaller temples throughout Pompeii honored Jupiter, Asclepius, and Minerva, and there was a small but lavish temple to the Egyptian goddess Isis. She was very popular in Pompeii, as evidenced by the wealth of the temple, and demonstrated the diverse population of the city.

Pompeii is known for its various villas and townhouses with rich wall paintings and furnishings that depicted Greco-Roman myths, the natural environment, and daily life. These images and those found at the humbler taverns, or "fast-food" establishments, and brothels as well as the graffiti found throughout city paint a vivid picture of daily life in a Roman town.

## DEMISE

Our most complete account of Pompeii's demise comes from two letters from Pliny the Younger to the historian Tacitus. According to his account, just after midday, fragments of ash and pumice came raining down, destroying many homes, and it quickly covered the city in more than nine feet of volcanic debris. Heated toxic gas and pyroclastic material filled the city by the next morning, and ash continued to fall, burying the city further along with its inhabitants and goods. When the catastrophic event was over, Pompeii was covered in nineteen to twenty-three feet of pumice and ash.

## RECENT DISCOVERIES AND CURRENT STATUS

Today, the Archaeological Park of Pompeii is one of the most visited tourist sites in the world. There have been no large-scale excavations since the 1960s; instead, archaeologists have been focused on reconstruction, preservation, and documentation of the exposed ruins. In 2012, the Great Pompeii Project began treating unexcavated areas behind street fronts to preserve exposed walls. In 2019, small-scale excavations resumed in Regio V. In November 2020, the remains of two men were found, and the next month, a *thermopolium*, or tavern, was discovered. Terra-cotta containers were found intact as well as samples of food remains. The tavern was painted with brightly colored, detailed frescoes.

*Katie Tardio*

See also: Paestum; Rome.

## FURTHER READING

Beard, M. 2008. *The Fires of Vesuvius: Pompeii Lost and Found.* Cambridge, MA: Belknap Press of Harvard University Press.
Berry, J. 2007. *The Complete Pompeii.* London: Thames & Hudson.
Buttersworth, A., and R. Laurence. 2006. *Pompeii: The Living City.* London: Phoenix.
Dobbins, J., and P. Foss. 2007. *World of Pompeii.* New York: Routledge.

# R

## Roanoke Colony

Roanoke Island, in present-day North Carolina, was the site of the first attempt at English settlement in North America. The colony was founded in 1585 at the behest of Sir Walter Raleigh, under a charter obtained from Queen Elizabeth I. Located on the Outer Banks, the island colony was occupied by settlers only briefly (ten months) before all returned to England. A second group arrived in 1587; yet by 1590, there was no sign of them. While some clues regarding their fate have been uncovered, it is not known for certain what became of them.

### INHABITANTS

The original inhabitants of the land, of course, were an Algonquin Native American people known variously as the Roanoac (Roanoke) or Secotan. In fact, the chief of the Roanoke, Wanchese, traveled to England with an English expeditionary force and another chief, Manteo, of the Croatan tribe, in 1584. The two Indigenous groups would continue to play a role in Roanoke colony's evolution, just as the Powhatan people played a significant role in the unfolding of the later Jamestown colony on the James (Powhatan) River in Virginia.

The initial group of English settlers on Roanoke Island consisted of 108 colonists, all men. They were part of a larger contingent carried by a fleet of vessels, but most of the rest of the group ended up being diverted to other activities. The settlers included the scientist and ethnographer Thomas Harriot and the metallurgist Joachim Gans. John White served as a mapmaker and artist. Arriving in the summer of 1585, the colonists built a small fort and lived in relative isolation—albeit with some contact with the Native peoples. Soon, though, they experienced sickness and starvation. The following year, they returned to England.

The second expedition arrived in 1587. Among the 117 colonists were 17 women and 9 children. Many were probably members of the English middle class seeking their fortunes in the New World. One of the women, Eleanor Dare, the daughter of then governor John White and the wife of colonist Ananias Dare, gave birth to a girl. The child was christened Virginia Dare and was the first child of English parents born in the New World. Ultimately, this second population of settlers vanished from the scene, leaving behind only the lingering mystery of what had become of the Roanoke colony.

### HISTORICAL BACKGROUND

In the mid-1500s, England claimed the lands between present-day Maine and North Carolina. The English called the area Virginia in honor of Queen Elizabeth

I, who was known as the "Virgin Queen." Britain was then in competition with Spain, which had begun settling the southern half of the New World, and France, which had begun exploring the northern half. (Portugal was also active in the hemisphere.)

Walter Raleigh, trusted adviser to Queen Elizabeth, sent two navigators, Philip Amadas and Arthur Barlowe, to the New World in 1584. They came upon and explored Roanoke Island, which is situated inside the far edge of the Outer Banks, in Albemarle Sound. Deciding that it was suitable for a colony, they returned to England, carrying with them Wanchese of the Roanoke and Manteo of the Croatan; they also brought a few New World products with them, such as tobacco and potatoes. (Both eventually became extremely popular.)

Raleigh then commissioned his cousin Sir Richard Grenville to sail seven vessels, with 108 men aboard, to the region. They departed in late April 1585. Once across the Atlantic, the fleet first navigated through the Caribbean, making stops, before arriving at Roanoke Island in August. The settlers erected a fort on the northern end of the island. When Grenville returned to England for supplies, a new governor, Ralph Lane, was named. The colonists explored the area and developed a tentative relationship with the Native peoples, who helped them obtain food.

As in the case of the Spanish in their colonies, however, the Roanoke settlers were primarily interested in discovering gold and other riches; they did not devote sufficient attention to sustaining the colony over the long run. Consequently, food became scarce, frictions developed (both internally and with the Native peoples), and the

"The Lost Colony" was drawn around the turn of the twentieth century. The piece depicts the discovery of the famous "Croatoan" inscription after the demise of the Roanoke colony. (The Miriam and Ira D. Wallach Division of Art, Prints and Photographs: Picture Collection, The New York Public Library. "The Lost Colony" New York Public Library Digital Collections)

settlers put their hope in the arrival of supply ships from the homeland. When ships did finally arrive, they were those of Sir Francis Drake's fleet; the privateering sea dog Drake had to be persuaded to carry the colonists home to England. Three men were left behind—and never seen again. Shortly afterward, Grenville returned to Roanoke with supplies. Finding the site abandoned, he left fifteen men on the island with a two-year supply of provisions; he instructed them to maintain the colony while he returned to England. Subsequently, some of these men were killed in hostilities with Native tribes from the mainland; the others were never heard from again.

In 1587, Raleigh sent out a new expedition, this time with ninety-one men, seventeen women, and nine children. John White was named governor. The group was supposed to found a city called Raleigh on the Chesapeake Bay, but navigation concerns on the part of the ship's master resulted in the party's being left on Roanoke Island. Such a beginning must have seemed inauspicious in light of what was known of the previous settlement and the absence of any survivors from it. Nevertheless, this new group got to work in the name of the queen.

White returned to England in 1588 to set up shipments of additional supplies for the colony. On his arrival, however, he encountered difficulties because Elizabeth was then making preparations to battle the Spanish Armada. No large ships could be spared; two smaller vessels were allotted, but they were subsequently ransacked by French pirates. The Anglo-Spanish War delayed White's return to Roanoke by two years.

## CULTURE AND SOCIETY

There is little information on the daily lives of the settlers. Through a combination of historical, archaeological, and other methods—including Native American oral traditions recorded in the decades after the demise of Roanoke—researchers have put together a picture of what likely took place during the time it operated as a colony. It appears that an overriding concern among the settlers was exploration for riches, in part to gain an advantage over Spain. Besides precious metals, the colonists sometimes looked for passages to the Far East, at a time when no one really knew whether the Pacific Ocean might lie beyond the Chesapeake. The English followed a number of fantastic leads provided them by Native guides, all the while failing to cultivate good relations with the Native peoples (although they fared better in some cases than in others).

American historians tended to ignore the place of Roanoke in the development of the continent until 1834, when George Bancroft's popular *History of the United States* was published. Bancroft related a story of noble enterprise (under Raleigh, Grenville, etc.), unfortunate betrayal (by the pilot of the 1587 Chesapeake venture), threats by hostile Native tribes, undaunted courage among the colonists, and terrible tragedy in the colony's loss. He brought attention to Virginia Dare in particular as the first English child born in what would become the United States. Although Bancroft's story was incomplete and exaggerated, it served its purpose of bolstering the national myth regarding the white/British heritage of the Americans and the superiority of that heritage over others.

## DEMISE

In 1590, when John White returned to Roanoke after being away for two years, the colony was gone. All that he found was the word "Croatoan" carved on a barkless patch of a tree. White concluded that the colonists must have gone to the south with the Croatan; he was unable, however, to perform a search due to weather conditions and matériel problems. The colony's fate remained a mystery. It would be seventeen years before a successful English settlement was established, at Jamestown, Virginia. Indeed, John Smith, the lead English figure in that colony's founding, heard stories from Native contacts about a strange place to the south called "Ocanahoan," where men wore European clothing; others mentioned the name "Roonocock." Smith dispatched two search parties, but neither one discovered any evidence of the lost colony or learned the whereabouts of its inhabitants. Ironically, Jamestown itself would eventually be abandoned (1699) when the colonial capital was moved to Williamsburg (then Middle Plantation).

## RECENT DISCOVERIES AND CURRENT STATUS

Various ideas have been put forth over the centuries concerning the fate of the colonists. These include the notions that (1) they were integrated into one or more of the local tribes; (2) they attempted to sail home but sank or otherwise failed; and (3) they were attacked by (a) the Powhatan or (b) the Spanish. Despite this long history of speculation, no major advance in the study of Roanoke occurred until 1998, when scientists determined through tree ring analysis that both Roanoke and Jamestown had been founded at times of extreme and sustained drought. Under such conditions, the colonists' food supply from crops would have been drastically diminished and their ability to obtain fresh water severely impacted. It is likely, too, that their strained relations with the surrounding Native peoples suffered more so because of the drought.

In 2016, researchers working in Bertie County, North Carolina, at the far western end of Albemarle Sound, some sixty-five miles from Roanoke Island, discovered artifacts that they believe could have belonged to the Roanoke settlers. It is difficult to say for sure, but the site under excavation does correspond to a "fort" symbol drawn on a map by John White. It is possible that the settlers relocated there.

Today, Fort Raleigh, on the northern end of the island, is a National Historic Site. The site of Governor Lane's 1585 fort was located during an archaeological dig in 1947–1948 and was reconstructed in 1950. The accompanying museum contains exhibits related to the colony and the cultural heritage of the Native Americans as well as material concerning the island's later significance during the Civil War and Reconstruction. A dramatization of the settlement's history, *The Lost Colony*, is performed in the summer months under the sponsorship of the Roanoke Island Historical Association. (Similar "living history" programs are part of Historic Jamestown.)

*Michael Shally-Jensen*

*See also:* Shaker Villages.

## FURTHER READING

Horn, James P. P. 2010. *A Kingdom Strange: The Brief and Tragic History of the Lost Colony of Roanoke*. New York: Basic Books.
Kupperman, Karen Ordahl. 2007. *Roanoke: The Abandoned Colony*. 2nd ed. Lanham, MD: Rowman & Littlefield.
Lawler, Andrew. 2018. *The Secret Token: Myth, Obsession, and the Search for the Lost Colony of Roanoke*. New York: Doubleday.
Oberg, Michael Leroy. 2008. *The Head in Edward Nugent's Hand: Roanoke's Forgotten Indians*. Philadelphia: University of Pennsylvania Press.

# Rome

Rome occupied a strategic location that allowed its people to dominate the surrounding landscape and eventually most of the Mediterranean. Located fifteen miles from Italy's west coast, Rome lay along the Tiber River. Providing access to the coast downriver and central Italy upriver, the Tiber gave Rome easy access to trade and a naturally defensible location inland. The city is traditionally held to have been built upon seven hills just east of the river, a layout that provided additional defense. As a river port and road hub, Rome was able to take advantage of the surrounding populations and natural resources, including timber, stone building materials, and metals.

After an early period of kingly rule, Rome formed a republic that expanded its dominion over all of Italy and much of the Mediterranean through a series of military conquests. In the first century BCE, Rome's first emperor, Augustus, solidified his power, a seminal event that led to the rule of a series of royal dynasties. The empire began to fragment in the fourth century before being permanently divided in 395 CE. The sacking of the city by the Goths in 410 has been conventionally understood as the end of ancient Rome, but the city flourished during the medieval period and still exists today as a vibrant metropolis.

## INHABITANTS

According to Roman mythology, the city was founded by its first king, Romulus, in 753 BCE. Romulus and his brother Remus were descendants of the Trojan hero Aeneas and twin sons of the god Mars. But after a dispute in which Romulus killed his brother, he founded a settlement on the Palatine Hill. Romulus offered asylum to exiled and fugitive men in Rome, later violently subjugating the Sabine people.

Some of this mythology corresponds to what can be documented about early Rome. Italy has been occupied at least from the Neolithic period, and a series of migrations in the Late Bronze Age resulted in a diverse group of Italian peoples from which the Romans emerged. Archaeological evidence shows the presence of several small villages on the site of Rome that were occupied from at least 1200 to 1000 BCE. These villages had rounded huts with thatched roofs, and the inhabitants subsisted on herding and farming.

During the ninth and eighth centuries BCE, settlements in Rome expanded from the Palatine to the Capitoline and Forum. And the seventh century witnessed

### Venice

Venice has been flooding for centuries and is slowly sinking into the sea.

Unlike most major Italian cities, Venice was not founded until after the fall of the Western Roman Empire, although the Veniti people, the city's namesake, lived in the region for centuries before Rome was even founded. Coming from the north, the Lombards conquered Oderzo in the mid-seventh century CE, and Venice, more isolated on islands in the lagoon, became the new center of power for the locals trying to avoid the reach of the Lombards. Paolo Lucio Anafesto was elected as the first doge in 697, which is the traditional date for the founding of the Republic of Venice. The republic thrived for over a millennium, building an overseas empire that included islands and shorelines on both sides of the Adriatic Sea, swaths of southern Greece, and Cyprus.

The Venetian metropole became a cultural hub and exported its culture across the Mediterranean, Europe, and beyond. The Venetians were known for their glasswork and Renaissance paintings. For a stretch in the mid-second millennium, Venice was a world leader in printing. Venetian architecture is varied and influential, particularly Venetian Gothic and rococo styles.

Venice has always been an aquatic city, famous for the canals woven through its ancient blocks. In the mid-second millennium, the Venetians diverted the rivers that discharged into the Venetian Lagoon to prevent the lagoon's natural silting and thereby help prevent attacks from the mainland. The city has been flooding seasonally for centuries. Flood tides fill much of the city surface, starting in the autumn, through the winter, and into the early spring, giving the city a distinct marine smell. These floods only stand to get longer and deeper as the city faces two troubling trends: the slow but steady sinking of the urban area and the rising sea.

much monument building, transforming the city from a group of huts to a true urban center. There is some archaeological evidence for kingly rule in the sixth century BCE; these royal rulers were advised by a senior council (the Senate) and a popular assembly.

## HISTORICAL BACKGROUND

From at least the eighth century BCE, the Romans had begun to expand outside the original site of their city. And indeed, Roman mytho-history chronicles the interactions of Italian peoples and their often violent incorporation into the Roman cultural fold. From roughly 500 to 300 BCE, the Romans had several major battles with outsider groups, including the Sabines, Latins, and Etruscans. Occupying a large portion of Italy's west coast and sharing much in common with the early Romans, the Etruscans had thriving urban centers, a trade network in natural resources, and a rich culture that produced art and architecture before being subsumed by the Romans.

The regal period in Rome ended in 509 BCE with the ousting of King Tarquinius Superbus ("Tarquin the Proud") and the establishment of the Roman Republic. The constitution established by the Romans, though not an actual written document, divided power between several popular assemblies and the elite political body the Senate. In this system, a Roman political career followed a set order of political offices (*cursus honorum*). The highest political offices were consuls, praetors, and censors. Two consuls were elected annually to preside over assembly and Senate meetings, propose laws, and oversee military command. Praetors were law officers of the Roman court system. And censors supervised the Roman census and were responsible for public works.

The Punic Wars (264–146 BCE) were a series of conflicts fought between Rome and its archenemy Carthage, located in North Africa. Rome solidified its dominance in the Mediterranean through these wars and other conflicts. After incorporating Italy, it expanded its control into Spain, Africa, and Greece.

The end of the republic was a century-long process in which a series of Roman leaders solidified increasingly more political and military power for themselves. Marius was elected consul an unprecedented seven times, enacting a series of military reforms that created an army loyal to him. His successor, Sulla, was appointed dictator, a special temporary office that the Romans had created for moments of crisis. As dictator, Sulla enacted a series of constitutional reforms and had his political enemies purged from the city. Finally, Julius Caesar, fresh from a successful military campaign in Gaul, had created an army loyal to him alone. He marched on Rome and was proclaimed dictator for life, among other honors. Caesar was ultimately assassinated by a conspiracy of senators in 44 BCE.

Caesar's nephew Octavian used the power vacuum created by his uncle's assassination to solidify his own hold on power in Rome. As Caesar's adopted son, he inherited a large amount of wealth and began calling himself *divi filius* ("son of a god"), since Caesar had been deified after his death. After a civil war in which Caesar's assassins were defeated, Octavian fought another war against Caesar's formal general Mark Antony and Queen Cleopatra VII of Egypt.

After the defeat of Antony and Cleopatra at the Battle of Actium in 31 BCE, Octavian's power in Rome was total. He was christened Augustus by the Senate in 27 BCE and ruled as sole emperor until his death in 14 CE.

## CULTURE AND SOCIETY

The Romans had a patriarchal and militaristic society that thrived on patriotism, the dispensation of authority, and the respect for ancient precedent. Roman life was dominated by the upper classes, and social relationships were based around a patron and his clients. Successful aristocratic patrons had careers in the military, the law, or politics. Their clients were a largely educated class in Rome who supported themselves through more meager employment and the benefaction of their patrons.

Family life was oriented around the *paterfamilias*, the male head of the household. According to tradition, this patriarch had the power of life and death over all members of the family. Roman women were therefore ideally chaste and modest, and this was reflected in Roman legislation against adultery that largely punished women. Despite this clear double standard, many women did hold professional jobs outside the household. Rome also had a large population of slaves who served as the state labor force, in businesses, and in private households. Slave manumission was a common practice, and these freedmen often went on to illustrious careers, though many often became the clients of their former masters.

Roman religion was polytheistic and focused on rituals, including prayer, animal sacrifice, and interpreting omens. Romans served as priests of the various gods and celebrated a multitude of religious festivals and holidays, which took up 159 days of the year. Entertainment in Rome included the performances of drama and comedy in the theater, chariot racing in the Circus Maximus, gladiatorial battles, and other spectacles.

## DEMISE

Much scholarly ink has been spilled on the "decline and fall" of Rome. The city did indeed transform and change in the later period of antiquity, but its complete destruction is an exaggeration.

Following the death of Augustus in 14 CE, his descendants ruled as the Julio-Claudian dynasty until 68 CE. A series of dynasties followed until the Crisis of the Third Century, in which thirty-four different emperors and usurpers ruled during a twenty-six-year period. The advent of the Emperor Constantine brought radical change to the empire. In addition to being the first Christian Roman emperor, Constantine moved the capital of the empire to the newly renamed city of Constantinople in 330.

Rome was hardly neglected as a result. The city was still where the Senate met, and Constantine spent lavishly on buildings in Rome. Though few emperors during the subsequent period visited the city, they directed funds to improve public buildings to appease the city's substantial population.

In 410, the Goths occupied and plundered Rome for three days. Pagans in the city claimed that this was a result of Rome's adoption of Christianity, to which the bishop Saint Augustine responded with his opus *The City of God* (*De civitate Dei*). The symbolic importance of this event therefore outweighed any lasting impact on the city, which slowly recovered over the next decade.

## RECENT DISCOVERIES AND CURRENT STATUS

Rome was made the capital of a unified Italy in 1870, and today it is a bustling metropolis, UNESCO World Heritage Site, and tourist destination.

*Chris Bingley*

*See also:* Carthage; Paestum; Pompeii; Syracuse.

## FURTHER READING

Beard, Mary, and Michael Crawford. 2002. *Rome in the Late Republic.* London: Duckworth.
Cornell, Tim. 1995. *The Beginnings of Rome: Italy and Rome from the Bronze Age to the Punic Wars (c. 1000–264 BCE).* London: Routledge.
Stambaugh, John E. 1988. *The Ancient Roman City.* Baltimore: Johns Hopkins University Press.
Treggiari, Susan. 2002. *Roman Social History.* London: Routledge.

# S

## Scythians

The Scythians were one of the ancient steppe peoples, nomads who dominated the steppeland north of the Black Sea in Eurasia during the seventh to fourth century BCE. They represented a powerful force during the Classical and early Hellenistic ages of Greece and defended their territory against the Persians and others as well. Scythians were among the first masters of the horse, and they engaged in scorched-earth tactics in wars. Yet, they are also known for their exquisite depictions of animals—often in violent scenes—in fine gold and silver works. Scythian culture was described by the Greek historian Herodotus in the fifth century BCE; it is also known through modern archaeological investigations.

### INHABITANTS

The Scythians lived on the south Russian steppe between the Carpathian Mountains to the west and the Don River to the east. They were one of a number of similar nomadic nations inhabiting a region where borders were variable and ill defined. The population of ancient Scythia, as their homeland was called, was not entirely homogeneous; they likely had mingled with other peoples, such as the Turks, Mongols, and Huns. According to Herodotus, the country was ruled by a principal tribe, the Royal Scyths, who were of Iranian stock and called themselves "Skolotoi." More generally, the name *Scythia* was used by Greek writers to refer to any northern barbarian from the Eurasian steppe, extending from the Carpathians to Manchuria in the Far East. It was, however, the warrior pastoralists of the so-called North Pontic region who were the true Scyths, and they formed a singular political entity that lasted until the fourth century BCE. They were an Indo-European people who spoke a language akin to Old Persian.

### HISTORICAL BACKGROUND

Until the end of the eighth century BCE, virtually nothing is known about the Scythians, though they probably had settled in the north central section of the Eurasian steppes sometime in the second millennium BCE. During the Zhou dynasty of China, the Emperor Xuan (r. 827–782 BCE) drove the Xiongnu tribal confederation from his borders, thus starting a chain reaction of wars and migrations as each population was pressured to shift westward. At the end of the eighth century, the Scythians were attacked by a tribal confederation from the East known as the Massagetae, causing the Scythians to, in turn, cross the Volga River and attack the Cimmerians, driving them into central Europe and the Caucasus.

> **Kitezh**
>
> Legend has it that the city of Kitezh sits at the bottom of Lake Svetloyar, which is located just over 300 miles west of Moscow. The tale of the mythical city began circulating in the eighteenth century, but it purports to recount events in the early thirteenth century. According to the story, when the Mongols invaded the Grand Duchy of Vladimir, they came upon Yuri II, the grand duke of Vladimir, at Kitezh. Rather than retreat or move to defend themselves, Yuri II and the citizens of Kitezh prayed before the approaching army. Lake Svetloyar swallowed the city whole before it could be reached by the attacking Mongols. Some say that the city is still visible at the bottom of the lake, but only to the pious. The story of Kitezh puts a romantic spin on Yuri II's life, who in reality was killed by the Mongols in the Battle of the Sit River.

The Scythians remained in central Asia. At first, they fought against the Assyrians, but they later allied with them against the Mannai, Medes, Babylonians, and others. They reached the height of their power in the last third of the seventh century, when they could roam and make war in nearly any direction. They raided Syria and Palestine and even went as far south as the border of Egypt. Ultimately, the Medes pushed the Scythians out of the Near East, by which time they were splintered into several communities.

## CULTURE AND SOCIETY

As the dominant force in the steppes, the Scythians were a nomadic tribal people organized around a powerful chief. Chiefs possessed a large number of gold weapons and ornaments, and this treasure was always placed in their tomb after death. The Scythians were expert equestrians and likely the first such horse riders in southern Russia. Some experts believe that women fought alongside men. (The evidence here, based on a few burial sites, is scanty but nonetheless suggestive.) At the same time, like most nomads, the Scythians kept cattle and moved seasonally in search of grass for grazing. There was even some division of labor based on tribe, with warrior tribes roaming more widely for political gain and farming tribes operating between the Dnieper and Don Rivers to supply foodstuffs and produce goods for trade. Scythian exports of wheat, fish, timber, and slaves were important to Greek cities on the Black Sea, especially Athens and its confederacy.

While the Scythians erected no permanent temples, they did worship several gods and conduct rituals in their honor. Chief among these deities seems to have been Tabiti, a goddess of fire and probably also the mother goddess. Other gods included Papoeus, Tabiti's powerful male counterpart, and gods of earth, sun, moon, and war. Human captives were sacrificed to these deities to maintain earthly harmony and win favor.

Scythian art centered on animal representations and more abstract design and was used to adorn saddles, blankets, rugs, clothing, swords, and vases. The finest works are in metal and beautifully realized. Naturalistic, stylized, and imaginary creatures often appear together in a single design: a beast of prey attacking a herd

> **Thule**
>
> Thule was the land of the far north, as conceptualized by writers of the ancient Mediterranean. Thule first appears in geographical accounts as early as the fourth century BCE. It became a staple of Greek and Roman geography, appearing in numerous works, including those of Strabo and Pliny the Elder. Although always representing a land in the far north, Thule was described differently by different authors. For example, Pytheas, the oldest extant author to discuss Thule places it on a northern point of the European continent. The Roman historian Tacitus, on the other hand, claims that Romans circumventing Britain saw Thule to their north, which would render it an island north of the Scottish mainland. The Nazis appropriated the idea of a mythical northern land as the supposed birthplace of the Aryan race.

animal is a typical theme. In the best examples of this art, there is a notable vitality and drama.

## DEMISE

When the Babylonians and Medes marched upon the Assyrian capital of Nineveh in 615–614 BCE, the Scythians were persuaded by the Assyrians to help repel the attack. Only two years later, however, the Scythians turned against Assyria and aided its enemies in sacking Nineveh. Before long, the Medes, in turn, sought to undo their Scythian allies, killing some and driving most of the rest back through the Caucasus into Scythia. A number of small Scythian communities remained on the southern shores of the Black Sea and in parts of Armenia, ultimately blending with the populaces there.

In their homeland, the Scythians, in about 512 BCE, defended themselves against a large-scale attack by the Persian king Darius I during the latter's expedition to Greece. Although already in decline, they performed a similar feat against one of Alexander the Great's generals in 325. In the fourth and third centuries BCE, however, the Scythians were finally driven from their lands by the Sarmatians, a related Iranian people from the East. By the end of the third century BCE, the south Russian steppe was known as Sarmatia, and the Scythians no longer existed as a distinct nation, although tribes of them remained in the Balkans and in the Asian section of the steppes.

## RECENT DISCOVERIES AND CURRENT STATUS

By far, the most notable recent discovery related to Scythian culture was the mummified remains of a tattooed women buried in a frozen tomb in the high Altai region of Siberia, near the borders of Mongolia, China, and Kazakhstan. Discovered in the Pazyryk valley in 1993, the woman had undoubtedly been an important figure in her time, as she was buried with six horses and wore, within her decorated coffin, a fine silk blouse and thigh-high leather riding boots along with some elaborately designed jewelry. Her frozen grave preserved her remains relatively well and gave rise to the name "Ice Maiden." (She may have only been twenty-five years old at death.) The only question was whether she was Scythian. Although details of the burial site generally match those found closer to the Scythian homeland and correspond to much of what Herodotus had to say about Scythian burial practices, the location in the Far East and various other aspects of the site have led most scholars to conclude that, at best, she was a representative of what are known as the "wider Scythian cultures," of which little is known other than that they shared some aspects of material culture and may have been related linguistically. The particular culture to which the Ice Maiden belonged is termed Pazyryk culture. Since her discovery, a few other less spectacular finds have turned up on the Eurasian steppes.

*Michael Shally-Jensen*

*See also:* Mongol Empire; Van.

### FURTHER READING

Braund, David, ed. 2005. *Scythians and the Greeks: Cultural Interactions in Scythia, Athens, and the Early Roman Empire.* Exeter, UK: Exeter University Press.
Cunliffe, Barry. 2020. *The Scythians: Nomad Warriors of the Steppe.* New York: Oxford University Press.
Simpson, St. John, and Svetlana Pankova. 2017. *Scythians: Warriors of Ancient Siberia.* London: Thames & Hudson.

## Shaker Villages

The Shakers, or the United Society of Believers, were a celibate religious sect in the United States that established some twenty neatly maintained villages in the late 1700s and early 1800s. They also came to be known for their finely crafted furniture and other objects of material culture.

Based in Christian worship, the sect acquired its nickname from its members' practice of whirling, trembling, or shaking during religious services. Participants believed that they could rid themselves of sin or wicked habits by engaging in such ecstatic religious exercises. Sex was also out of the question in the Shaker worldview.

In their time, the Shakers met with some outside opposition but were also admired for their well-managed farms, strong work ethic, and ingenuity in producing cleverly designed, functional objects and marketable goods. Several Shaker villages, operated today as museums, stand as testaments to Shaker society.

### INHABITANTS

Shakerism reached the height of its prominence between 1840 and 1860. During this period, its membership grew to about 6,000. Approximately twenty Shaker societies were established, notably in Mount Lebanon, New York; Harvard and Hancock, Massachusetts; East Canterbury, New Hampshire; Enfield, Connecticut; and Sabbathday Lake, Maine. Other successful communities were created in Ohio, Kentucky, and Indiana.

Shakerism mainly appealed to rural farming folk who for one reason or another were disillusioned with the main Protestant denominations and willing to live celibately and communally—that is, with all property held in common—in the interest of attaining "perfection" in God's eyes. The promise for believers was that, in doing so, they would help bring about the Second Coming of Christ. The sect was known by several different names: the United Society of Believers in Christ's Second Appearing, the Millennial Church, and the Children of Truth, or Alethians (from the Greek word for truth).

Shaker "communism" stressed that property and profit were to be held in common for the good of all. The sect also held that all humanity—men and women, Blacks and whites, Indians and whites, pioneers and planters, scions and paupers, adults and children—deserved to be treated equally. Accordingly, women in Shaker society took their places as equals with men in both the spiritual and temporal operation of the community. On the other hand, nonwhite membership remained negligible throughout the sect's history.

## HISTORICAL DEVELOPMENT

American Shakerism has its roots in a group of Quakers from Manchester, England, and in particular the efforts of one Ann Lee. Lee had been a member of the Church of England (Anglicans) when she became attracted to a religious sect of "Shaking Quakers," led by James and Jane Wardley, in 1758. The group practiced an ecstatic form of worship in which they claimed possession by the Holy Spirit, spoke in tongues, and healed the sick. They also believed that the Second

The Shaker village of Hancock, Massachusetts, was founded in the late eighteenth century and remained active until 1960. This site is known for its Round Stone Barn, built in 1826. (Lee Snider | Dreamstime.com)

Coming of Christ would be in the form of a woman and that the public confession of sins was necessary for salvation and membership in the group.

Lee spent a decade and a half with the Wardleys, railing against conventional religion and its contradictions. She sometimes disrupted Anglican worship services by dancing, speaking in tongues, and expressing iconoclastic views. Following one such incident in 1770, she was jailed. While there, she had a series of visions. In one, she said that she saw the union of Adam and Eve, not as a divinely ordained act of procreation but, rather, as a form of lustful self-indulgence; she concluded, therefore, that sexual activity among God's earthly children must be avoided. In another revelation, Lee said that she received a command to go to America, which she did in 1774.

Already in England, Lee had been granted the honorific title "Mother" because of her leadership ability among the Shaking Quakers. In the New World, she extended her reputation by encouraging a small band of followers accompanying her to clear land and build a settlement at Niskeyuna (now Watervliet), New York, not far from Albany. From there, she led a two-year evangelical mission through eastern New York and New England, trusting that her religious message would catch on. Although Lee died in 1784 without having attracted a large body of converts, Shakerism grew under her successors, Joseph Meacham and Lucy Wright. The two established the first stable Shaker community at New Lebanon, New York, in 1787. From there, the movement expanded in New England and advanced westward into Kentucky, Ohio, and Indiana. Opposition to it also mounted.

## CULTURE AND SOCIETY

The Shakers believed that "Mother Ann" was the source of God's latest and most profound revelation to humankind; her successors carried on her legacy. Besides celibacy, open confession of sins, communal sharing of possessions, and equality of the sexes, the Shakers practiced pacifism and consecrated labor, or the application of work in the service of God and community. They rejected the Calvinist doctrine of predestination and emphasized free will and the perfection of the individual through faith and work. In their well-planned, self-sufficient communities, separated from the outside world, the Shakers engaged in a variety of unconventional yet emotionally moving forms of worship, including ring dances, trances, ecstatic shouting, prophetic revelations, healings, and speaking in tongues—all regarded as proof of the Holy Spirit's presence. Believers would sit quietly in meditation until overcome by a spiritual power, causing them to tremble or shake violently.

The Shakers did not actually forbid marriage, but they considered it less defensible than celibacy and separation by gender. During daily work and worship services, men and women in most communities did come together, converse, dance, and enjoy each other's company.

Shaker villages or communities consisted of two or more "families" of thirty to sixty persons each, made up of men, women, and adopted children. Each family lived in its own large house with separate entrances, stairways, and sleeping quarters to keep the sexes apart. Spiritual oversight of the family or community was entrusted to four elders, two men and two women, who received their instructions from the ministry. Business affairs, including farming, manufacturing, and the marketing of goods, were the responsibility of the deacons or trustees, also usually two men and two women. While the deacons were accountable to the elders, the latter were answerable only to the ministry, which had ultimate supervision over the entire community. The ministry consisted of two elders and eldresses chosen from among the various family elders.

As unique as their social and religious practices were, the Shakers were equally well known for their industriousness, their avoidance of extremes in dress and decoration, their hospitality, and their creative practicality. The attractive simplicity of Shaker furniture has won a large audience of admirers and collectors. The ingenuity of the Shakers was also expressed through some of their inventions, including the circular saw (originally pedal powered), the washing machine (water or steam powered), the metal pen point, the clothespin, and the flat-edged broom. The famous "Shaker chair" actually had a number of different styles and functions, one notable version of which allowed the sitter to tilt back against a wall for comfort. The Shakers were also the first to sell packaged seeds in the United States.

## DEMISE

Naturally, the Shaker practice of celibacy posed a challenge for the long-term prospects of the sect. Without marriages and the creation of offspring, the sect could only grow through recruitment, which never really occurred at the level needed. Young people on the outside tended to be interested in intimacy—and marriage—with other young people; therefore, Shakerism tended to be a religious community of the old, particularly as villages aged and their "families" with them.

Like other utopian communities, secular and religious alike, the Shakers relied on a variety of "bonding mechanisms" to hold people together within the group and keep them committed to the collective ideal. These mechanisms included charismatic, and somewhat authoritarian, leadership; a "special" outlook grounded in an ascetic lifestyle; and restricted contact with the outside world. Such mechanisms can, and in this case did, also work *against* the longevity of the group. Outside critics at the time felt that Shaker practices violated the American notion of individual freedom; some also considered that they disrupted families, oppressed women (equality was never total), and "brainwashed" disciples. In short, Shakerism was charged with being a cult—and not without justification.

By the 1870s, Shaker membership had dwindled to less than 2,500; within twenty years, it was under 1,000; and by the start of the twentieth century, it was down to 500 or less. Shakerism's rather mysterious religious principles and rituals, and its simple, small-scale approach to agriculture and material culture, began to look less and less promising in the context of a burgeoning, industrial-capitalist society. In this respect, it mirrored the Anabaptist denominations (Amish, Mennonites, Hutterites) but was hindered by the absence of procreation. By the 1970s, the sect was virtually extinct.

## RECENT DISCOVERIES AND CURRENT STATUS

Only one Shaker village, Sabbathday Lake, Maine, remains active today; it has two or three members. Places where Shaker buildings and artifacts have been preserved and may be experienced by visitors include Pleasant Hill and South Union, Kentucky; Canterbury and Enfield, New Hampshire; Mount Lebanon and Watervliet, New York; Shaker Heights, Ohio; and Hancock Village (Pittsfield), Massachusetts.

At Hancock Village, for example, visitors can see how the Shakers lived in their heyday. Crops are grown as they were by the original inhabitants, and animals are kept in the great three-story Round Stone Barn. At the Meetinghouse, costumed guides demonstrate how the Shakers worshipped by performing the trembling dance that gave the sect its name. At the Brick Dwelling, visitors see the separate dormitory rooms for men and women. Other exhibits display the simple but finely crafted Shaker furniture and Shaker inventions. There are also demonstrations of basketmaking, weaving, and other crafts. Shaker drawings and script were unique in their own right, and in the accompanying store, one may purchase books illustrating these.

In the final analysis, human geography—and history—worked against the Shakers and their worldview. Some recent archaeological excavations have revealed that Shaker villagers occasionally succumbed to worldly pleasures, such as whiskey, perfume, tobacco, and cosmetics. Even in a closed community, it seems life had a way of intervening.

*Michael Shally-Jensen*

*See also:* Roanoke Colony.

## FURTHER READING

Garrett, Clarke. 1998. *Origins of the Shakers: From the Old World to the New World*. Baltimore: Johns Hopkins University Press.
Kirk, John T. 1997. *The Shaker World: Art, Life, Belief*. New York: Harry N. Abrams.
Morse, Flo. 2016. *The Story of the Shakers*. New York: Countryman/W. W. Norton.
Stein, Stephen J. 1992. *The Shaker Experience in America: A History of the United Society of Believers*. New Haven, CT: Yale University Press.
Swank, Scott. 1999. *Shaker Life, Art, and Architecture: Hands to Work, Hearts to God*. New York: Abbeville Press.

# Spanish Missions in North America

Created as part of Spain's colonial empire in the period from the sixteenth through the early nineteenth century, Spanish missions in the American (U.S.) South and Southwest reveal much about the confluence of nations and peoples in these regions. The Spanish North American frontier, as the entire historic development is called, consisted of three main geographic divisions. The most extensively settled area was the western "borderlands," including colonial Mexico's northern provinces from Texas (Tejas) to California (Las Californias). The eastern area centered on St. Augustine (San Augustín), Florida, and extended northward along the coast (to the Carolinas) and westward into the panhandle. There was also, for a period between 1763 and 1803, an effort to settle the expanse of the Louisiana Territory (Luisiana), then under the Viceroyalty of New Spain after France's concession. However, this last effort did not amount to much in the larger scheme of things. In each region, a combination of forts, Catholic missions, and towns arose. From this grand colonization effort, a rich legacy of Hispanic culture was born and spread through conquest, conversion, and historical circumstance.

## INHABITANTS

There was considerable variation in the composition of the Spanish frontier settlements over time and place. In seeking to introduce Catholicism along with European methods of agriculture, the missions primarily targeted sedentary Amerindian peoples that were easier to control militarily and more adaptable to agriculture and herding. A few attempts were made to convert nomadic or semi-nomadic Indigenous groups possessing strong warrior traditions, such as the Apaches and Comanches, but these efforts came to naught.

At the missions, which featured churches and other buildings, priests gave the Indians religious instruction and supervised their labor. Some missions proved more successful than others in producing converts and achieving economic stability. They developed sizable (albeit forcibly formed) "congregations," worked farmlands, and maintained herds of sheep or cattle. In many cases, a town arose adjacent to a mission and was occupied by a mix of Spanish, Hispano (of Spanish descent), Indigenous, mestizo, and, later, Anglo residents, over time producing a rich Hispanic culture that continued to flourish into succeeding centuries. An adjacent fort, or presidio, housed soldiers and served to defend the settlement against foreign incursions or warring tribes; it also maintained the peace internally by enforcing colonial law.

## HISTORICAL DEVELOPMENT

Spanish expeditions in search of slaves and wealth landed on Florida's shores in the early sixteenth century. In 1539, Hernando de Soto led 600 men into Florida, and over the next four years, he and his military successor, Luis de Moscoso, led their conquistadors through the peninsula and up into the Carolinas and interior areas of southeastern North America. Indian resistance in Florida was largely quelled, though large parts of the interior remained unconquered.

The first permanent Spanish settlement in *La Florida*, St. Augustine (1565), actually arose as a defense against French Huguenots who were seeking to establish a colony in the region. The Spanish governor there was charged with driving out the French Protestants and securing Spanish control. After 1573, Franciscan priests built a string of Spanish missions along the Atlantic and Gulf coasts.

In the American Southwest, it was Francisco Vázquez de Coronado who led a Spanish expedition into the Pueblo country of Arizona and New Mexico in 1540, in search of the mythical Seven Cities of Gold (Cibola). Disappointed, Coronado ranged as far as Kansas before giving up. His grand failure put an end to European exploration in the region for decades. The first missions in New Mexico were established by friars accompanying Juan de Oñate's expedition for silver in 1598. Oñate, the son of a silver baron in Mexico, brought 500 colonists along with 10 Franciscan missionaries into the upper Rio Grande Valley. At the Tewa town of Yúngé, which Oñate renamed San Gabriel, the conquistador established his first capital. Abuses of the Native population, however, prompted one pueblo, Acoma, to revolt (1599); the Spaniards consequently killed or enslaved hundreds of its inhabitants. By 1608, other such incidents, along with charges of incompetence, led to the viceroy's removal of Oñate. That same year, the secular settlement of Santa Fe was begun.

Over the next century, Franciscan priests founded more than forty additional missions along the Rio Grande and surrounding areas. The mission at Santa Clara, New Mexico, was founded by Father Alonso de Benavides in 1627. By 1680, missions had been established among most of the Pueblo Indian peoples and the Navajo.

In Texas, Spanish missions were founded in response to France's settlement of Louisiana. The first such mission was founded in 1690, near what is now Weches, Texas, but it failed due to Indian hostility. More successful enterprises were established in east Texas in the early 1700s. San Antonio became the home of several missions, including, from 1744, San Antonio de Valero, which later became the Alamo. Toward the end of the eighteenth century, the Franciscan missions in Texas began to decline because the population of potential converts had decreased. Nevertheless, civilian communities centered on livestock and farming developed around the presidios of San Antonio and La Bahía (near Goliad, Texas) and in the secular settlement of Nacogdoches.

Between 1687 and 1711, the Jesuit missionary and explorer Father Eusebio Kino established many missions and *visitas* (country chapels) in northern Mexico, Baja California, and southern Arizona. One of the most prominent of these was Mission San Xavier del Bac, south of modern-day Tucson. In California, meanwhile, Father Junípero Serra accompanied the expedition of José de Gálvez in 1769 and founded the Mission San Diego de Alcalá, the first of twenty-one Franciscan missions in California. San Diego was followed in 1770 by Monterey, which became the provincial capital of Upper California seven years later. San Francisco (1776) and Santa Barbara (1782) became equally prominent presidio and mission sites. The last California mission was San Francisco Solano (1823), located in the Sonoma Valley.

## CULTURE AND SOCIETY

Spain's goal in the new land, once the prospect of gold and silver had diminished, was not to eliminate the Indians but to turn them into Christian subjects in support of the Crown. Native lands could be put to use generating income (including taxes), and Native souls could be saved for the glory of God. The missions were paternalistic institutions that provided for their Indigenous charges while depriving them of their independence and dignity. In the early decades, Spanish elites thought that they might create separate "republics" for Indians and non-Indians, but through the forces of intermarriage and acculturation, Indians, to a degree, were absorbed into the Hispanic population. Hispanics, Indians, and mestizos, in turn, were drawn into the mission's sphere and to surrounding secular towns. Indian women in particular became socially and economically integrated into Hispanic society in towns like Los Angeles. Indeed, in some locations, it was the market economy and the world of work that brought together Indian and Hispanic cultures and societies, more so than the religious work of the missions. It was primarily in secular contexts that the Spanish language spread, not in Latin-centric instructional and liturgical contexts. Throughout the colonial period, Spanish enjoyed prestige as the language of the elites as well as the regional lingua franca.

Before the mid-1800s, the North American Southwest along with California were held by New Spain, that is, Mexico. Separated by distance and terrain, and reliant on different economies, each region—Texas, New Mexico, and California—developed its own distinct cultural features. These different communities tended to be referred to by different names: Tejano (in Texas), Hispano (in New Mexico), and Californio (in California). Anglo-Americans also began to migrate to these areas in later decades; the growing presence of Anglos in the Southwest resulted in permanent change for the Mexicans/Hispanics and Indians living there. After the 1840s, the United States took control of the region and transformed it into its own new frontier, although long-standing local and regional cultures continued to thrive.

The design of the missions reflected Gothic, Moorish, and Romanesque architectural styles—influences brought to the New World by the Spanish. Paintings on interior walls sometimes depicted southwestern landscape elements or the artistic traditions of the Indians—both of which later carried over into "Southwestern style." A hybrid style was also evident in food and dress. Place names often reflected either Spanish or Native American terms, with some places carrying two names (or even three, after the Anglos arrived). The English language was also affected by the Spanish-Mexican vocabulary used on the frontier, with words like *rodeo* and *corral* entering the lexicon.

The growth of the Spanish Empire also exposed the Native Americans to the Europeans' diseases, against which they had little immunity. An epidemic in New Mexico in 1640, for example, killed 3,000 Indians. Critics then and now charged that the mission system destroyed much of the Indians' Native culture and turned them into an exploited and degraded labor force. This was particularly the case in some of the California missions, where strict work protocols had to be followed and harsh penalties were meted out when breaches occurred. There were sporadic rebellions by the Indians over time, the most significant being a Pueblo rebellion led by a San Juan (Pueblo) Indian named Popé in 1680. In that conflict, some 400 Spaniards were killed and most of the rest were driven from Santa Fe and northern New Mexico, although they later returned. By 1834, the Mexican government had secularized most remaining missions, using them instead for nonreligious purposes, such as government outposts or trading centers.

## DEMISE

Throughout the colonial era, the Spanish Crown was advised by resident governors about the status of its frontier provinces in North America. Even in Mexico, where its power remained strong, the Crown faced significant challenges in maintaining a far-flung empire. The perpetual pressure on the colonial treasury required constant management, and the mission-presidio system could advance only so far through the conversion of souls and the use of Indian labor. In the 1720s, and again in the 1760s, regional inspections of the system were conducted. By then, Florida had already suffered a series of raids by the English, and at the end of the Seven Years' War, in 1763, Spain transferred St. Augustine and other mission sites to Great Britain in exchange for Havana, which the British had captured during the war. Much of the Spanish population in Florida chose to relocate to Cuba as a result. After the American Revolutionary War, the Seminole Indians gained ground on the peninsula.

In 1776, a new governmental structure was instituted in Mexico and the borderlands of Texas, New Mexico, Arizona, and California. Some economic expansion took place by making use of tribal alliances to quell the warring Apache, but by the early 1800s, Texas was starting to be occupied by Anglos seeking to establish a presence there. The Adams-Onís Treaty of 1819 formally ceded Florida to the United States and moved the boundary of Spanish Texas south to the Sabine River, throwing open the doors to Anglo immigration.

New Mexico, having experienced reconquest in the 1690s (following Popé's rebellion), saw the reestablishment of churches at many pueblos, but without direct control by the friars over the Indians. Economic ties between the Pueblos and the growing Spanish population expanded. Hispanic settlement centered on Santa Fe, which served as both the provincial capital and a fort. Peace was secured with the Comanche and Apache in the late 1700s, and New Mexico rose to prominence as a silver mining, sheepherding, and trading region. Meanwhile, in Arizona, revolts by the Pima and Yuma in 1751 and 1781, respectively, caused Spain to draw back somewhat and concentrate its forces in Tucson, which did not develop into a major center of Hispanic culture until sometime later in its history.

In California, Spain had always had only a tenuous "empire" and had no knowledge of areas lying beyond the coastal missions. In the long run, the idea of making loyal and self-sustaining colonists out of the Indians did not succeed. Even by the late 1700s, Indian deaths exceeded births within the mission system. Agricultural production was sustained only under a regime of forced labor. The work to secularize the system began after Mexico won its independence from Spain in 1821 and was completed by the mid-1830s. The land was transferred to *mayordomos*, or property overseers. Within a few decades, most of the adobe arches, red-tiled roofs, and cultivated lands of the old missions had fallen into disrepair.

## RECENT DISCOVERIES AND CURRENT STATUS

Today, old walls of stone and adobe remain the most prominent reminders of Spain's once expansive imperial presence in what is today the United States. These structures mark preserved or reconstructed presidios, churches, mission buildings, elite homes, and, occasionally, simpler facilities for teaching and housing Indians. Many of them now serve as museums or public parks and draw millions of tourists annually. Some of them, however, such as Salinas Pueblo Mission (New Mexico), are less frequently visited than others.

On the Atlantic coast of northern Florida, about forty miles south of Jacksonville, the grand Castillo de San Marcos of St. Augustine, the oldest masonry fort in the United States, stands situated in the oldest continuously inhabited European-founded settlement on the continent. Far to the west, in south central Texas, stand the remains of the old stone Misíon San Antonio de Valera, which was abandoned after 1793 and turned into a fort known as the Alamo. It became the site of the famous Battle of the Alamo, fought over the issue of Texas independence from Mexico, in 1836. Farther west, in Santa Fe, New Mexico, stands an elongated one-story adobe building called the Palace of the Governors, which is the oldest continuously occupied building in the United States. Farther to the west, near Tucson, Arizona, is the impressive Mission San Xavier de Bac, the original of which was destroyed during an Apache attack but which was erected anew in the 1780s and 1790s. Finally, in present-day Orange County, California, the remains of the palatial Mission San Juan Capistrano can be found, one of a number of such historic remnants of Spain's former claims in Alta California.

Although these buildings may now represent "history," the descendants of Spain's missionaries, conquistadors, and explorers settled throughout the Crown's North American colonial territory, building communities from Florida (and the Caribbean) to the Pacific. In between, the Spaniards introduced lasting bodies of language and culture along with such Western economic mainstays as horses, sheep, and cattle. Mexico's, and later the United States', inheritance of this legacy has changed it significantly but not overwritten or erased it. (Mexico was not named New Spain for nothing!)

Most of the recent archaeological findings relating to Spanish missions in North America serve to round out our understanding of this rich history rather than to supply major missing elements or profoundly alter our understanding.

*Michael Shally-Jensen*

*See also:* Ancestral Puebloans; Machu Picchu; Pecos Pueblo; Tenochtitlán.

## FURTHER READING

de la Teja, Jesús F., and Ross Frank, eds. 2005. *Choice, Persuasion, and Coercion: Social Control on Spain's North American Frontiers.* Albuquerque: University of New Mexico Press.

Douglass, John G., and William M. Graves, eds. 2017. *New Mexico and the Pimería Alta: The Colonial Period in the American Southwest.* Boulder: University Press of Colorado.

Fontana, Bernard L. 1994. *Entrada: The Legacy of Spain and Mexico in the United States.* Albuquerque: University of New Mexico Press.

Lake, Alison. 2006. *Colonial Rosary: The Spanish and Indian Missions of California.* Athens: Swallow Press/Ohio University Press.

Milanich, Jerald T. 1999. *Laboring in the Fields of the Lord: Spanish Missions and Southeastern Indians*. Washington, DC: Smithsonian Institution Press.

Officer, James E. 1987. *Hispanic Arizona, 1536–1856*. Tucson: University of Arizona Press.

Weber, David J. 1992. *The Spanish Frontier in North America*. New Haven, CT: Yale University Press.

## Stonehenge

Stonehenge is a colossal monument in Wiltshire, England, built during the Neolithic and Bronze Ages. Construction began as early as the fourth millennium BCE, with the bulk of the building occurring in the third millennium BCE. Scholars still debate the site's functions, but it was closely associated with both burial and events on the solar calendar. During the Neolithic and Bronze Ages, Stonehenge was located in the most densely populated portion of what is today the United Kingdom. It stands in the middle of southern England, less than ten miles north of Salisbury and about eighty miles west of central London.

The site is partially preserved and features a series of concentric circles. The outer ring is a ditch, which was dug as the first phase of construction. Walking past the ditch toward the main stone monument in the center, an observer would then cross two concentric circles of holes, the so-called Y and Z holes. The circles of the inner stone monument remain partially standing: the outer circle features giant thirteen-foot, twenty-five-ton vertical standing stones topped with large horizontal lintel stones. These horizontal stones were meant to connect to make a complete ring. Inside this circle, there is a ring of smaller bluestones. Within the next level, there is a horseshoe of trilithons: groups of two standing stones topped with one horizontal lintel stone. These stones range up to twenty-four feet and fifty tons, and three of these trilithons remain standing. Within this level, there is a horseshoe of smaller bluestones. What has come to be known as the altar stone lies in the middle; some scholars believe this stone stood vertically in Stonehenge's heyday. Multiple features within these concentric circles are oriented toward sunset on the winter solstice or, conversely, to sunrise on the summer solstice.

---

### Avalon

Avalon was an island within the mythological world of King Arthur and eventually became one of the most important locations in the myth, perhaps second only to Arthur's court at Camelot. The oldest surviving mention of the island comes in Geoffrey of Monmouth's twelfth-century CE *History of the Kings of Britain*. In this and subsequent works, Avalon is depicted as an island strongly associated with magic. Arthur's magical sword, Excalibur, was forged in Avalon, and Arthur himself traveled to the island in an attempt to recover after receiving mortal wounds in the Battle of Camlann. Morgan, the witch and fairy, is said to rule the island as queen. Some identify the mythical city of Avalon with Glastonbury Tor, which was formerly an island. Some Arthurian stories have Glastonbury Tor as Arthur's final resting place, which dovetails with Avalon's prominent role at the end of Arthur's life.

## INHABITANTS

While Stonehenge is a rich archaeological site, there is still much we do not know about those who built and used it. The site appears to have fulfilled a religious function, including acting as ceremonial burial site. DNA evidence suggests that a wave of farmers originating in the eastern Mediterranean reached Great Britain at around the turn of the fourth millennium BCE. These people may have brought with them a tradition of constructing monuments from large standing stones. Later, the so-called Bell Beaker people settled the region in the mid-third millennium BCE. While locals were forefront in the construction and use of the site, some of the human remains attest to the fact that people came from far distances to visit or be buried at the site.

## HISTORICAL BACKGROUND

The earliest construction at the site of Stonehenge dates to the late fourth millennium BCE; however, archaeological records from the surrounding region attest to the fact that the area had been inhabited for millennia before that. Some suggest that postholes dating to approximately 8000 BCE may show signs of Mesolithic rituals. Other construction occurred in the area in the fourth millennium BCE, just centuries before the first phase of Stonehenge. A large nearby cursus—a long cylindrical trench known as the Stonehenge Cursus—has been dated to approximately 3500 BCE.

The first iteration of the monument was a large circular ditch about 360 feet in diameter and dated to roughly 3100 BCE. Bones from large mammals—deer and oxen—were interred in the ditch. Gaps in the ditch were left in the south and northeast so that individuals could enter the inner circle without having to traverse the ditch. This earliest iteration of the monument also included fifty-six holes in a ring just inside the main trench. Men, women, and children were interred in these holes as well as in the main ditch. Bones from dozens of individuals have been analyzed, and it is estimated that perhaps 150 individuals were originally interred.

---

*Camelot*

Camelot is the castle and court of King Arthur, the legendary British ruler. Many of the stories about Arthur come from English, Welsh, and French sources, but the earliest tales of Arthur make no mention of Camelot. Chrétien de Troyes's twelfth-century French poem *Lancelot, the Knight of the Cart* is the oldest extant work to make mention of Camelot. Later, beginning with the Lancelot-Grail cycle of the next century, the location became the canonical home and power base for King Arthur. According to legend, the castle sits surrounded by fertile plains and woodlands along a river, downstream from Astolat, another legendary castle within the Arthurian mythological world. The fabled castle of Camelot has fixated modern culture. Despite the consensus that the city is fictional, people have proposed sites across England and Wales as the historical Camelot. In American culture, Camelot denotes John F. Kennedy's White House, a name first coined by his widow, Jacqueline Kennedy.

The builders appear to have stood something up in the pits; the consensus is that the pits held timber posts, although some have suggested bluestones.

The next iteration of the monument featured the construction of the massive stone structures that have become synonymous with Stonehenge. Beginning a few centuries after the trench was dug, in the middle of the third millennium BCE, this phase of the site was the first to see stone structures (provided that the theory about earlier bluestones is not true). This stage of construction featured two main types of stones: large sarsens (ranging from twenty-five to fifty tons each) and relatively smaller bluestones. The sarsens appear to have been taken from almost twenty miles to the north and the bluestones from even farther. The builders transported at least some of the bluestones from Preseli Hills, about 200 miles northwest in what is today Wales.

The builders used these sarsens and bluestones to form four concentric circles within the ditch dug several centuries earlier. Large sarsens lined the outer circle. Horizontal lintel stones were placed on top of the vertical stones and—assuming that the monument reached completion—connected to form a complete ring. Just inside this level was a circle of bluestones. Further inside, the builders constructed a horseshoe of sarsen trilithons. These were the largest stones brought into the complex, weighing up to fifty tons. Like the outer ring of sarsens, these too were accompanied by an arrangement of bluestones placed just within, although there is evidence that all the bluestones were rearranged into their final positions post-construction. Other stone structures were erected in this period, including the station stones and the so-called slaughter stone, all outside of the central stone structure but inside the outer ditch.

## CULTURE AND SOCIETY

Stonehenge experienced its centuries-long heyday well before written records were kept in Great Britain, but the site itself tells us of the culture and society of those who built and used it. The site was a monument used for burials from an early stage. The location appears to have hosted ritualistic burials and events on the solar calendar, particularly the winter and summer solstices. It was not, however, constructed for long-term inhabitation. The Salisbury Plain, which houses Stonehenge, was in the thick of the most densely populated region of the United Kingdom through Stonehenge's peak, that is, late fourth, third, and early second millennia BCE. Some animal remains that were found at Stonehenge originated from as far away as the Scottish Highlands, hundreds of miles to the north, suggesting Stonehenge held a broad renown. Some scholars have suggested that for periods in the mid-third millennium BCE, thousands of individuals gathered at the monument on the winter and summer solstices.

## DEMISE

The height of Stonehenge's construction and usage was the middle of the third millennium BCE, from which the site saw a gentle centuries-long decline. Major construction, including the placement of the sarsen megaliths, appears to have

Sarsens are the largest stones at Stonehenge. The prominent sarsen trilithons of the inner horseshoe comprise the most well-known portion of site. (Justin Black | Dreamstime.com)

ceased around 2400 BCE. For the next several centuries through the turn of the second millennium BCE, minor construction continued; the bluestones appear to have been rearranged multiple times in this timeframe. Finally, around 1600 BCE, two concentric circles of holes, known today as the Y and Z holes, were dug between the outer ditch and the central stone monument. This was the final known phase of construction at the monument.

Although construction ceased and its functions morphed with time, Stonehenge continued to be visited and appreciated in later centuries. Round Barrows, Bronze Age earthen burial mounds, dotted the area surrounding Stonehenge, confirming the location's close association with burial. In the middle of the second millennium, locals carved numerous ax-heads and daggers into four of the large sarsens at Stonehenge. Around 700 BCE, a little over a mile from the monument, a hill fort was constructed, known today as Vespasian's Camp, after its previous misidentification as a Roman fort. After the Romans arrived to the island in 43 BCE, they, too, appreciated and frequented the monument.

## RECENT DISCOVERIES AND CURRENT STATUS

Stonehenge is a UNESCO World Heritage Site. Excavations have been occurring since the seventeenth century as archaeologists seek to extract more information from this important glimpse at prehistoric life in Britain. The twenty-first century has witnessed important finds in the area surrounding the monument. In 2011, pits within the nearby Stonehenge Cursus were found that connect this structure to the main Stonehenge monument. Additional Neolithic structures and mounds were found in 2014 near the village of Durrington, about two and a half miles from Stonehenge. Finally, in early 2021, preparation for the construction of a proposed tunnel unearthed a number of Neolithic and Bronze Age artifacts.

*Anthony Vivian*

*See also:* La Tène Celtic Culture.

## FURTHER READING

Burl, A. 1999. *Great Stone Circles*. New Haven, CT: Yale University Press.
Chippindale, Christopher. 2012. *Stonehenge Complete*. 4th ed. London: Thames & Hudson.
Cunliffe, Barry, and Colin Renfrew, eds. 1997. *Science and Stonehenge*. Proceedings of the British Academy 92. Oxford: Oxford University Press.
North, John. 1997. *Stonehenge: Ritual Origins and Astronomy*. New York: HarperCollins.

# Susa

Referred to in some early sources as Shushan, Susa was a city in ancient Elam, a country in what is now southwest Iran. Some of the earliest written documents from Mesopotamia describe the peoples of Susa and Elam as enemies or conquered subjects. By the thirteenth century BCE, Susa was frequently interfering in Babylonian and Assyrian affairs and embarking on conquests in parts of Mesopotamia and Iran.

Besides being the principal city of the relatively short-lived Elamite Empire (ca. 1250–1100 BCE) and of the longer-lived but comparatively less significant Neo-Elamite civilization (1100–612 BCE), Susa also had a storied history as the administrative capital of the Achaemenid Persians under Darius I (r. 521–486 BCE) and as part of the later Parthian Empire (247 BCE–224 CE).

Among the notable archaeological finds at Susa have been the "victory stele" of Naram-Sin, king of Akkad (r. 2261–2224 BCE), and the famous Code of Hammurabi of Babylon (r. 1792–1750 BCE); both objects had been taken as war booty during raids in Mesopotamia. In addition, the biblical book of Esther, which relates the story of a Hebrew woman in Persia during the time of Xerxes I (r. 486–465 BCE), Darius's father and predecessor, is set in Susa.

## INHABITANTS

The Elamites seem to have called their country Haltamti, possibly meaning "the Lord's land." Elam/Haltamti was composed of fertile lowlands along the Persian Gulf interior highlands on the Iranian plateau to the east. It was from the highlands of Elam that neighboring Sumer and Akkad, to the west, obtained wood, metals, semiprecious stones, and horses. Elamite civilization borrowed considerably from Sumer. Most of the Elamites' written records were in the Elamite language, which has only been partially deciphered and has no known relationship with any other tongue.

## HISTORICAL DEVELOPMENT

The third millennium BCE was marked by mutual raiding between the Elamites and the Sumerians, with the Elamites often coming out ahead. Based on the records of Sargon of Akkad, conqueror of both the Sumerians and the Elamites in the twenty-fourth century BCE, we know that an Elamite federation operated under distinct yet equal tribal rulers. Prior to their contact with the Akkadians, the Elamites had been using a form of pictographic writing; under Akkadian influence, however, they adopted a system of cuneiform signs.

In addition to being overcome by the kings of Akkad, Susa was brought under the Third Dynasty of Ur (ca. 2100–2000 BCE). The last ruler of Ur, however, was captured by Elamite sovereigns who briefly reestablished their independence. In the second millennium BCE, Elam and Mesopotamia were invaded by northern peoples such as the Hurrians and Kassites. For about 300 years thereafter (i.e., from 1600 BCE), the history of Susa and Elam become obscure.

After about 1300 BCE, Elamite monarchs made incursions into Babylonian and Assyrian territory as well as in various directions in Iran. This middle period of Elam's history (ca. 1300–1130) was the era of King Untashgal (ca. 1265–1245) and his successors. It was notable for its spectacular architecture and sculpture, as primarily evidenced at the site of Chogha Zanbil, about nineteen miles southeast of Susa. (The remains of a great ziggurat are there.)

After Nebuchadnezzar I of Babylon defeated the Elamites around 1130 BCE, Susa's history again goes dark. The city came into prominence once more after 750 BCE, when it became a powerful enemy of Assyria. It was finally sacked by the latter's King Ashurbanipal in 636 BCE, followed by a takeover by the Medes (of northern Iran) in 617 BCE. Thenceforth, it became a province in the Persian empires and their successors.

## CULTURE AND SOCIETY

Susa enjoyed access to the Persian Gulf and also to a major east–west trade route; therefore, it became militarily and economically important, with much commerce and industry anchoring it.

Although it had a long and significant early history, the city probably reached its height in the thirteenth century BCE, when a string of aggressive Elamite rulers challenged Assyria for control of lower Mesopotamia. This period was also one of significant building activity by the Elamites, evidenced above all by the great ziggurats at Susa and Chogha Zanbil. (The former was destroyed by Ashurbanipal.)

The arts of the Elamites reached a high level. There are impressive examples of painted pottery, stone relief work, and metal and stone sculpture, among other forms. From finds at Susa, we learn that the Elamites drew on Achaemenid Persia for dress designs and a few social customs. The Achaemenid kings, in turn, drew on Elamite expertise to populate parts of the Persian bureaucracy, as attested by Elamite clay tablets found at the Persian ceremonial center of Persepolis.

Besides speaking a unique language not related to any other, ancient or modern, the Elamites were unusual for having a matriarchal social structure. That is, although their rulers were male, succession to the throne was through the female line; a new king was called the "son of his sister."

Nevertheless, the female deities that originally dominated Elamite religion's pantheon were ultimately overshadowed by male gods, with Inshushinak, Susa's protector god, being the most prominent.

## DEMISE

In the sixth century BCE, Elam became a satrapy of the Persian Empire. Under Persian rule, Susa was rebuilt by Darius I (r. 521–486 BCE) and his heirs, and it served as one of the three major Persian capitals (Persepolis and Ecbatana being the other two). At the time of Darius's father, Xerxes, it served as the setting for the biblical story of Esther, where it is called "Shushan the palace."

Susa was captured by Alexander the Great in 331 BCE, and it became a center of Greek influence under his immediate successors. Alexander held a mass wedding of Macedonian men to Persian women at Susa in 324 in anticipation of establishing a unified nation, but he died (at age thirty-two) the following year. Susa remained a cultural center under the Parthians (of northeastern Iran) after 140 BCE; there is a relatively large Parthian cemetery at the site. Under the Sassanian ruler Shapur II (r. 309–379 CE), Susa was ravaged because it was believed to be a Christian center. Thereafter, it fell into insignificance—except, of course, to those who maintain an interest in ancient history.

## RECENT DISCOVERIES AND CURRENT STATUS

Susa was first encountered by Western researchers in 1850. Since the late nineteenth century, it has been under almost continuous excavation by French archaeologists. The main objects of interest at the site are four large mounds representing the citadel, the Palace of Darius I, and two sections of the ancient city.

Susa was declared a UNESCO World Heritage Site in 2015.

*Michael Shally-Jensen*

*See also:* Ctesiphon; Persepolis; Ur.

## FURTHER READING

Álvarez-Mon, Javier, Gian Peitro Basello, and Yasmina Wicks, eds. 2018. *The Elamite World*. New York: Routledge.
Frye, Richard N. 1993. *The Heritage of Persia*. Costa Mesa, CA: Mazda Publishers.
Harper, Prudence O., Joan Aruz, and Francoise Tallon, eds. 1992. *The Royal City of Susa: Ancient Near Eastern Treasures from the Louvre*. New York: Metropolitan Museum of Art.

## Syracuse

Syracuse was a bustling economic and cultural hub near the southeastern tip of Sicily that grew into a major central Mediterranean power. In the eighth century

BCE, Greek colonists from Corinth first established the city on the small island of Ortygia, just off the coast of Sicily proper. Over time, the city grew to incorporate large swarths of Sicily beyond Ortygia and sent off colonies of its own. The city blossomed in the fifth and fourth centuries when powerful tyrants made the city the strongest in the region and nurtured a vibrant cultural scene. Ultimately becoming the most powerful city on Sicily, Syracuse found itself caught directly between the two growing Mediterranean superpowers of Rome and Carthage during the first two Punic Wars.

The present-day city of Syracuse encompasses a rich assortment of ruins from Syracuse's many different eras. Perhaps the most distinctly Syracusan is the Temple of Apollo first built on Ortygia in the sixth century BCE, the oldest surviving Doric temple on Sicily. It was subsequently converted into a cathedral under Byzantine rule and a mosque under Islamic rule. Other ancient structures include a Greek theater and Roman amphitheater. The Fountain of Arethusa is a natural fountain on the island of Ortygia, where the ancients claimed the nymph Arethusa surfaced from the underground after attempting to flee the river god Alpheus from Arcadia, back in Greece.

## INHABITANTS

Sicily, including the region surrounding Syracuse, had been continuously inhabited for millennia before the first Phoenician and Greek colonists arrived. These earlier inhabitants were divided into three peoples: the Sicanians, the Elymians, and the Sicels. The Sicanians are thought to be the island's first settlers, and the Sicels primarily resided on the eastern parts of the island. According to Thucydides, Archias, a colonist from Corinth drove local Sicels off the small island of Ortygia and founded Syracuse in 734 BCE. This was just a year after the first Greek colonists under Thucles from Chalcis founded Naxos, just up the coast. These two colonies were the first of dozens that the Greeks founded on Sicily, particularly on the eastern coast. The Syracusans themselves sent out five additional colonies on Sicily over the next century and a half. The Greek colonization of the eastern parts of the island coincided with the Phoenician colonization of the western parts, which began several decades before, around 800 BCE.

## HISTORICAL BACKGROUND

One of the earliest Greek colonies on Sicily, Syracuse soon ballooned into a regional superpower. Archias led a contingent of Corinthian colonists and established the city in 734 BCE. Driving off some local Sicels, they first settled on the small island of Ortygia, before the city overflowed onto the main part of Sicily. It grew so fast that it sent out five colonies of its own into nearby parts of southeastern Sicily. The ideality of the location, especially its two natural harbors, contributed to the growing success of the city.

The fifth century BCE saw Syracuse become the most powerful city on Sicily. In the early decades of the century, tyrants originally centered in the nearby Greek colony of Gela attempted to expand their power and consolidate all of southeastern Sicily. Hippocrates of Gela first went about expanding his power base, and Gela became the premier city in the region. Although he did besiege Syracuse, he was not able to conquer the city. His successor, Gelon, continued these ambitious plots and was able to accomplish what Hippocrates could not, conquering Syracuse. He did so by reinstating the Gamoroi, the erstwhile Syracusan aristocratic class who had recently fallen out of power. After becoming tyrant of Syracuse, Gelon quickly helped Syracuse surpass Gela and become the regional powerhouse, in part by forcing major populations from other cities that he controlled to move there. Allied with Theron, the tyrant of Acragas, Gelon beat a Carthaginian force at the Battle of Himera in 480 to become the major power on the island.

Already the primary force on Sicily, Syracuse continued to grow in influence for the remainder of the fifth century BCE. Hiero I, the tyrant of Syracuse after Gelon, ushered in a cultural high point for the city, bringing in some of the most talented poets from Greece. He also led Syracuse and allied Greek cities to victory against the Etruscans at the Battle of Cumae in 474, thereby halting the Etruscans advancing influence in southern Italy. Thrasybulos established a democracy in Syracuse in 467, and the city continued to prosper as a democracy. From 415 to 413, under the democratic leadership of Hermocrates, the city warded off two Athenian fleets aiming to conquer the city. The Syracusans then sent forces east to aid Athens's enemies. A contingent of Syracusans likewise joined Cyrus the Younger's unsuccessful bid for the Persian throne.

Syracuse continued to flourish as a regional power before getting squeezed between the two Mediterranean superpowers of Rome and Carthage. Dionysius I overthrew the democracy and became tyrant in 405 BCE, ending about six decades of democratic rule. He continued the fight against Carthage and exerted Syracuse's influence in the wider Mediterranean, gaining a foothold on the Italian peninsula and meddling in affairs in Greece. After Dionysius I's death, the city was beset by internal strife as opposing claims to the throne vied for control. After a brief occupation by Pyrrhus of Epirus, Hiero II rose to power in 270 and ended this factional strife with his fifty-five-year rule. In the First Punic War, he fought on the side of the Carthaginians and then the Romans in turn. It was not until the Second Punic War that Rome besieged and conquered Syracuse, three years after Hiero II's death.

## CULTURE AND SOCIETY

Syracuse boasted a cultural hub that was often fostered by its tyrants. Ruling in the early fifth century BCE, Hiero I made Syracuse into the cultural hotspot of the western Greek world. His court featured a who's who of his generation's leading poets. Aeschylus, Simonides, Pindar, Bacchylides, and Epicharmus all traveled there to perform. The natural philosopher Xenophanes also spent time there. Dionysius I rejuvenated Syracuse's cultural scene in the early fourth century, stocking his court with the leading intellectuals of his day. Philistus, the native Syracusan historian, was a patron of the tyrant. Following his predecessor Hiero's lead, Dionysius also brought in leading thinkers from abroad. He brought in the philosopher Plato and the poet Philoxenus but treated them both poorly. The polymath Archimedes was related to and closely linked with Hiero II, who played a crucial role in Archimedes's "Eureka" moment: the tyrant tasked the mathematician with determining whether a votive crown was pure gold, and he did so by using water displacement to calculate its density, reportedly shouting, "Eureka!" (Greek for "I have discovered!") while running down the street naked after having his epiphany in the bath. The city's culture flourished at other points in its history, including later eras, after the city lost its autonomy. Under the Emirate of Sicily, the 200-year Muslim rule of the island, the city experienced a cultural renaissance and blossomed with Arab poets, including the influential Ibn Hamdis.

## DEMISE

Although Hiero II first sided with the Carthaginians against the Romans, he swapped allegiances partway through the First Punic War and remained loyal to the Romans for the last four decades of his long reign. His death came just a year after the decisive Carthaginian victory over the Romans at the Battle of Cannae in the Second Punic War. His successor, Hieronymus, swapped Syracuse's allegiances back to the Carthaginians but was assassinated after only thirteen months in power. Like the Athenians, Carthaginians, and others before them, the Romans besieged the city of Syracuse. Unlike their predecessors, the Romans were successful. After a three-year siege, the Romans took the city in 212 BCE, ending Syracuse's autonomy and status as a central Mediterranean power.

The city remained an economic hub with a large population under the Romans and beyond. It served as the capital of Sicily under Roman rule, and the Syracusans were eventually granted Roman citizenship along with the rest of the Sicilians. In the seventh century CE, the Byzantine emperor Constans II moved to Syracuse and proposed a permanent change of the empire's capital from Constantinople to Syracuse; he was assassinated before being able to carry out his plan. Though no longer independent, the city persevered as an influential regional player through the cycle of different rulers that it, like the rest of Sicily, has experienced up to the present.

## RECENT DISCOVERIES AND CURRENT STATUS

Syracuse and the Rocky Necropolis of Pantalica are together a UNESCO World Heritage Site.

*Anthony Vivian*

*See also:* Athens; Carthage; Granada; Rome.

## FURTHER READING

Champion, Jeff. 2010. *Tyrants of Syracuse*. Vol. 1, *480–367 BC*. Barnsley, UK: Pen and Sword Military.

Champion, Jeff. 2012. *Tyrants of Syracuse*. Vol. 2, *367–211 BC*. Barnsley, UK: Pen and Sword Military.

Dummett, Jeremy. 2010. *Syracuse, City of Legends: A Glory of Sicily*. London: I. B. Tauris.

Strassler, Robert B. 1998. *The Landmark Thucydides: A Comprehensive Guide to the Peloponnesian War*. New York: Touchstone.

# T

## Taxila

Known as Takshashila to its inhabitants, Taxila was founded right around the turn of the first millennium BCE and hosted one of the world's earliest and most famous universities. The city stood by a tributary to and just east of the Indus River, a major thoroughfare that flows southeast down from the Himalayas to the Arabian Sea. Taxila likewise occupied an important liminal space between East and West on the Silk Road, which connected the Indian subcontinent and China to the Near East and the West. It was located on the outskirts of the region known as Gandhara in ancient times; today, the remains sit very near where the Punjab and Khyber Pakhtunkhwa provinces meet Islamabad Capital Territory in present-day Pakistan, less than twenty miles northwest of Islamabad, the capital of Pakistan.

As different empires from the East and West ruled this important city, Taxila saw four major waves of construction, leaving us with four distinct ruined settlements. The site known as Hathial is the oldest, showing signs of inhabitation as early as 1000 BCE through about 400 BCE. Bhir, immediately to Hathial's west, was active from around the sixth to the first century BCE. Sirkap, the third site, lies just to the north and thrived for the final two centuries of the first millennium. Finally, Sirsukh makes up the most recent site, having been established in the first century CE. This final site sits slightly removed from the others, farther to the north. Among other ruins, a number of Buddhist monasteries, stupas, and other structures bear witness to Taxila's erstwhile reputation as an important center of Buddhist culture.

### INHABITANTS

The surrounding region was inhabited for millennia before Taxila itself was established at the turn of the first millennium BCE. After the city's founding, during the early centuries of the first millennium BCE, Gandhari, a Prakrit language, was prevalent in the region, as was the historical Vedic religion and Brahmanism. The region would continue to be a hotbed of different religions through Taxila's existence. The onset of Achaemenid Persian rule from the west in the sixth century BCE ended local control of Taxila. It also infused the city with a wider diversity and a place on the world stage. The city retained this cosmopolitan nature under the rule of later empires.

### HISTORICAL BACKGROUND

Located just to the east of the Indus River, Taxila lay in the heart of the Indus valley, home to one of the world's oldest civilizations. The Indus valley civilization flourished from the mid-fourth millennium BCE to the mid-second millennium BCE throughout the wider region. The site of Saraikala, which was very close to the future location of Taxila, was inhabited in the Neolithic, Bronze, and Iron Ages. Hathial shows signs of inhabitation from around 1000 BCE, making it the oldest known iteration of the city of Taxila itself. Among other artifacts, red burnished ware has been found at the site. There are indications of trade and commerce between this early iteration of Taxila and surrounding locations, particularly the city of Pushkalavati, about seventy-five miles to the northwest. Bhir, just to Hathial's west, was the next site of Taxila to be founded, around the sixth century BCE.

In the late sixth century, Darius I, the Achaemenid king, conquered large swaths of land to his empire's east, including Taxila. In 515 BCE, Darius led his massive multinational army eastward into Bactria and other regions in and around present-day Afghanistan. They stationed for the winter in Gandhara, close to Taxila, before moving south to conquer the Indus valley the next year. As the capital of the vast Persian Empire's easternmost province, Taxila rose in prominence. The university of Taxila—an early influential center for higher education—thrived during this era. The Persian conquest was the first in a long succession of foreign rulers from the West and East: starting from the sixth century BCE, at least eight different foreign powers would control Taxila for the remainder of its prominence.

In 326 BCE, Alexander III of Macedon, like Darius before him, traveled through Taxila in his conquest of the Indus valley. At Taxila, he sacrificed to the gods and celebrated gymnastic and equestrian competitions. However, three years later, he was dead, and his newly forged empire fractured. Six years after that, forces under Chandragupta Maurya—the founder of the Maurya Empire—conquered Taxila and the surrounding regions from the east. Chanakya, the adviser to Chandragupta Maurya and an influential intellectual, is thought to have taught at the university of ancient Taxila. Under Ashoka, Chandragupta Maurya's grandson and successor, Taxila became a hub for Buddhist thinking and teaching.

The Maurya Empire began to fade after the reign of Ashoka, and in the second century BCE, Taxila was once again taken over by a power from the West, this time by what came to be known as the Indo-Greek Kingdom. It was under this kingdom that Sirkap, a separate settlement at Taxila, was founded. For the remainder of the first millennium BCE, Taxila was ruled by the Indo-Greek Kingdom, the Indo-Parthian Kingdom, and the Indo-Scythians intermittently. The university of ancient Taxila and the city's deep connection with Buddhism continued to flourish in this era. In the first century CE, Kujula Kadphises, the founder of the Kushan Empire, conquered Taxila. Sirsukh, Taxila's final major settlement, was founded by Kushan leaders to the north of the city's existing boroughs. The city remained under Kushan control for about three centuries until the arrival of the Gupta Empire in the mid-fourth century. Taxila thrived under the Guptas for about a century before a long period of decline set in.

## CULTURE AND SOCIETY

Taxila lay on the crossroads between East and West. This fact, coupled with the city's location on a tributary to the important Indus River, made the city an important trading hub from an early stage. Later in its existence, as it served as an eastern post for powers to the west and a western post to powers on the Indian subcontinent in turn, the city gained a diverse and international flavor.

The culture and society of Taxila largely revolved around its university. It differed from a university in our strict modern sense of the word; teachers created and controlled their own programs without institutional gatekeeping or oversight. It was a premier institution of higher education in its day, attracting teachers and scholars from across India, China, the Near East, and beyond. A who's who of intellectuals traveled to the city to form and teach their own programs.

Taxila's renown as a mecca of higher learning predates its association with Buddhism, but since its Mauryan era in the late fourth and third centuries BCE, the city became closely linked with the religion and grew into an influential center of Buddhist teaching and learning. According to one tradition, the *Mahabharata*, a major Sanskrit epic that began as an oral epic, was first recited in Taxila. The Gandharan Buddhist texts, the oldest surviving Buddhist texts from the early centuries of the first millennium CE, were found not too far from Taxila.

## DEMISE

The migration southward of nomadic peoples originally from the steppes to Gandhara and the other regions around Taxila eventually spelled the end for the city. A series of raids from distinct nomadic peoples beginning in the mid-fifth century started the process in earnest. The Kidarites first pillaged Taxila, but the Guptas were able to chase them away and retain control of the city. However, the Hephthalites and Alchons followed in subsequent decades. These invasions wreaked particular destruction on the many Buddhist structures throughout the region. This process was exacerbated by Mihirakula, an Alchon ruler, who held control of the city in the early sixth century. He oversaw the systematic destruction of stupas, temples, monasteries, and other Buddhist sites. By the time Xuanzang, a Buddhist monk from China, visited the city in 630, he described a city already largely in ruin.

## RECENT DISCOVERIES AND CURRENT STATUS

Taxila is a UNESCO World Heritage Site. Among the ruins are the four major settlements of Taxila (Hathial, Bhir, Sirkap, and Sirsukh), the prehistoric site of Saraikara, and a number of Buddhist structures. The Global Heritage Fund included Taxila with eleven other sites in its 2010 report on Global Heritage in peril. Steps have been taken since then to shore up the preservation of the site.

*Anthony Vivian*

*See also:* Ai-Khanoum; Harappa and Mohenjo-Daro; Pataliputra.

## FURTHER READING

Dwivedi, Sunita. 2020. *Buddha in Gandhara*. New Delhi: Rupa Publications.

Marshall, John. 2013. *Taxila: An Illustrated Account of Archaeological Excavations 1913–1934*. 3 vols. Cambridge: Cambridge University Press.
Salomon, Richard. 2018. *The Buddhist Literature of Ancient Gandhara: An Introduction with Selected Translations*. Somerville, MA: Wisdom Publications.
Stoneman, Richard. 2021. *The Greek Experience of India: From Alexander to the Indo-Greeks*. Princeton, NJ: Princeton University Press.

# Tenochtitlán

Tenochtitlán (pronounced tay-nōch′-tee-tlan′) was the capital of the Aztec Empire of ancient Mexico. The city was located on an island in the western part of what was then Lake Texcoco. Modern Mexico City now occupies most of the former lake basin, including the island that had been the site of the ancient city of Tenochtitlán.

The city was founded in 1325 CE (or 1345, per some authorities) and eventually grew to support a large population. A second group of Aztecs, or Mexica, settled on the nearby island of Tlatelolco in 1358. Both settlements began as small villages of thatch huts, but with the continued growth of Aztec culture, they developed into city-states (*altepetl*) that eventually merged into a single metropolis. The Aztecs reigned over much of central Mexico until the Spanish conquest in the sixteenth century.

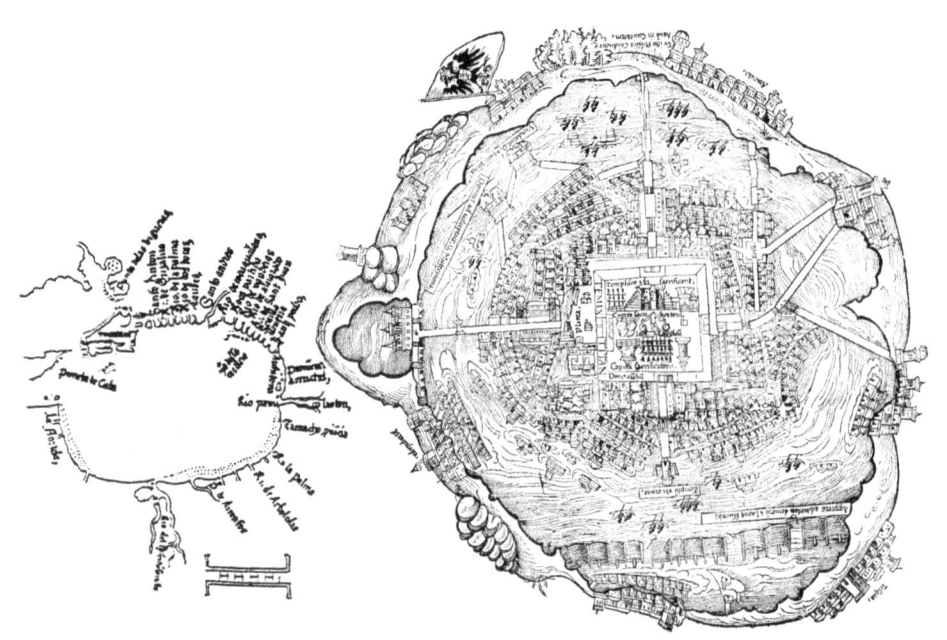

This engraved map of Tenochtitlán appeared in the first edition of Hernán Cortés's letters. It shows the Aztec capital as seen by its Spanish conquerors in the early sixteenth century. (Map of Tenochtitlan and the Gulf of Mexico, from "Praeclara Ferdinadi Cortesii de Nova maris Oceani Hyspania Narratio" by Hernando Cortes (1485–1547) 1524)

Tenochtitlán was joined to the mainland by three human-built causeways and surrounded by artificial islands—reclaimed marshland—where produce was cultivated. Because the lake water was salty, an aqueduct supplied fresh water to the city from nearby Chapultepec. A dike sealed off part of the city from the lake as a flood control measure. Tenochtitlán was laid out on a grid plan and covered more than 4.6 square miles. Together with a number of palaces (for priest rulers), there was a central plaza, the Tecpan, containing two temple pyramids where human sacrifice was practiced. (A rack of skulls displayed their remains.) Also in the city was a ballcourt for playing the famed ritual sporting game of Mesoamerica, a market center, a variety of stone calendars and sculptures, and other buildings for official functions. The palaces of Montezuma II (now situated beneath the National Palace of Mexico) and other rulers were located outside the precinct walls.

## INHABITANTS

The term *Aztec* is generally used to refer to a range of ethnically and culturally related peoples in central Mexico—people who shared a common language (Nahuatl), origin myths, and basic social and political attitudes. More specifically, *Aztec* designates members of one of the most prominent of those groups, the Mexica of Tenochtitlán and surrounding areas. (*Mexica* is sometimes used in place of *Aztec*.)

In the Valley of Mexico, between the fourteenth and early sixteenth centuries, a person's identity and loyalty were linked to his or her home city-state, or *altepetl*. These city-states were ruled by dynasties of kings and princes of greater or lesser importance. Each city-state controlled a particular population within a specific geographic area, and each one distinguished itself by honoring its own collection of local deities and myths and by stressing the value of its own history and religious rites. Therefore, the differences between these entities were more matters of emphasis than of philosophy. Still, the shifting alliances among the various city-states produced a situation akin to perpetual warfare over the centuries. The Mexica called their own city Tenochtitlán, or "Place of the Rock-Cactus Fruit." By the time the Spaniards arrived in 1519, Tenochtitlán had a population of over 200,000, making it the largest city in the New World.

The language spoken by the Aztecs throughout central Mexico was Nahuatl (meaning "good speech"). The same language is spoken today by more than a million people in Mexico and Central America. Belonging to the Uto-Aztecan language family, it is distantly related to such languages as Paiute, Comanche, and Hopi, which are spoken in the present-day western United States.

## HISTORICAL BACKGROUND

Before settling at Lake Texcoco, the Mexica and other Aztec peoples—the Xochimilca, Tepaneca, and Acolhua, among others—had resided in northern Mexico and lived as seminomadic hunters and gatherers. According to myths and histories, the Mexica left their homeland in the early twelfth century and, over the course of several decades, traveled southward to establish centers in central

Mexico (including the site of Xochimilco). They discovered a valley already populated with small competing city-states of Indigenous peoples.

The Mexica spent the next seventy-five years as minor players struggling to ally themselves with different rulers of city-states. After a series of political maneuverings, they found themselves essentially banished to the marshy lowlands of Lake Texcoco, where they settled on an island. The Aztec patron god, Huitzilopochtli ("Hummingbird of the South"), indicated to them that they would realize their destiny upon witnessing an eagle on a cactus. Thus it was that they encountered their defining vision at Texcoco, the eagle/cactus emblem, symbolizing their power. Immediately, they constructed (in 1325) a small temple in honor of Huitzilopochtli.

In 1337, a separate group of Mexica moved to a connected northern island to establish the city of Tlatelolco. The two adjacent cities remained in a state of mutual toleration until 1473, when the inhabitants of Tenochtitlán forced a merger, as it were, under the threat of the ax. By then, they had already made alliances with two neighboring city-states. For the next several decades, this so-called Triple Alliance would expand its control throughout central and southern Mexico, forming the Aztec Empire.

## CULTURE AND SOCIETY

The Aztecs produced a large number of codices, or manuscripts, based on glyphs (pictographs) and other elements. They created maps, historical narratives, records of tribute, and various calendrical and religious works. Most of these manuscripts were destroyed during or after the Spanish conquest, but a number of copies, or works drawing on the originals, were constructed by Native scribes in the colonial period. Additional knowledge about the Aztecs comes from archaeological investigations, including those at the Great Temple (Templo Mayor) in downtown Mexico City and at sites elsewhere in central Mexico.

The Aztecs were accomplished in a variety arts and sciences. They erected massive precision-engineered pyramids of impressive height and beauty. Practiced astronomers, they mapped the skies and were able to predict eclipses and the movement of nearby planets. They developed a calendrical system of great accuracy and accrued substantial bodies of agricultural and medical knowledge. They expressed themselves artistically in fine works of stone, metal, shell, and feathers. They also practiced human sacrifice for religious purposes, hoping thereby to appease their angry gods.

Each Aztec city-state was headed by a dynastic ruler; under certain circumstances, however, leadership was shared among priests and secular rulers. Politics and religion were deeply interconnected in Aztec society. Priests sanctioned Aztec rulers, and Aztec rulers participated in religious ceremonies. During key moments, virtually the entire populace was expected to participate in religious rituals. The Aztecs were polytheistic; that is, they believed in a pantheon of gods and goddesses. The most important areas of worship were creation, the sun (especially in times of warfare), and rain or fertility. Every major deity had its own temple, its cult of priests and priestesses, and its unique religious rituals.

Central to the Aztecs was the belief that the universe had been created and destroyed four times; the Aztecs of central Mexico lived in the fifth world, or fifth sun. This sun was created by the gods at Teotihuacán, a great (non-Aztec) city built centuries earlier northeast of Lake Texcoco. By Aztec times, it was in ruins, yet impressive all the same. Aztec myth held that one of the primordial gods had sacrificed himself to become the sun. Therefore, it was incumbent on the Mexica people to repeat the process (symbolically) by presenting blood sacrifices to the sun god and other great deities.

Aztec society was divided between nobles and commoners, with some intermediate groups, such as expert artists and craftspeople, filling out the whole. Nobles functioned as political advisers, judges, priests, governors, tax collectors, and scribes. They reinforced their social status through the conspicuous display of luxury goods along with enjoying other privileges, such as temple schools for their children and the right, for men, to have several wives. Commoners, on the other hand, were monogamous, and young men trained as soldiers in addition to carrying out duties in farming, fishing, transportation, and manufacturing. Women, whether of noble or common lineage, learned to weave cloth by hand (using cotton or maguey fibers), and commoner women prepared food and assisted nobles domestically. They also tended fields, especially when the men were out warring.

Throughout the Valley of Mexico and beyond, agriculture was a central preoccupation. Several varieties of maize (corn), beans, chili peppers, and squash were cultivated. The maguey (agave) plant was used to concoct a fermented beverage as well as to supply fibers for cloth and needles for sewing. To the south, cotton and cacao (chocolate) were grown. Gold, obsidian, jadeite, and turquoise were mined for use in the manufacture of luxury goods and trade items. The Aztecs and their neighbors, in turn, obtained large quantities of exotic goods through regional trade.

In addition, with every military conquest, the Aztecs and their allies demanded regular payments of tribute goods from conquered city-states. Such political payments supported the elite lifestyle of the nobles. The tributes also helped to sustain the city-states' populations in times of famine, supplied military needs, and provided high officials with trade goods for ongoing trading activities. Warfare thus served two major purposes: it allowed for the exaction of tribute from conquered enemies, and it furnished the state with foreign captives to use in sacrificial ceremonies.

## DEMISE

With the arrival of the Spanish conquistador Hernán Cortés in late 1519, Tenochtitlán faced a new challenge. Cortés was initially greeted by Montezuma II, and the two entered into discussions; but the encounter soon turned antagonistic. Over the next year, Tenochtitlán was besieged several times by the Spaniards, and Montezuma was made a hostage (later being killed). A smallpox epidemic, brought by the Europeans, hit the Aztec capital in 1520; tens of thousands of Mexica died. The invaders took down most of the city's buildings and eventually started erecting colonial Mexico City on Tenochtitlán's corpse. Because the destruction was thorough and a new city arose in its place, ancient Tenochtitlán is barely visible today. The site of the Templo Mayor (Great Temple), however, was (re)discovered in 1978, and excavations there have revealed a great deal of valuable information. Similarly, other sites and sources continue to reveal long-lost secrets about Aztec history and culture.

## RECENT DISCOVERIES AND CURRENT STATUS

Today, archaeological digs continue to take place in the heart of Mexico City in an effort to learn more about the urban center's colonial past and its ancient predecessor, Tenochtitlán. Alongside existing buildings, in basements, in subways, under roadways, and among modern sewer lines, researchers have been busy uncovering new details about Aztec life. In 2011, a large cache of ceremonial goods was located under a plaza. Elsewhere, stone carvings revealing details of human sacrifice were discovered. Numerous trade goods, such as jade-and-turquoise masks, obsidian mirrors, shellwork, and adornments featuring jaguar teeth have been found. The ruins of an elite school were identified beneath the rubble of a modern building that collapsed in a 1985 earthquake. It has become clear that the Templo Mayor was the major religious site and also that large-scale sacrifices took place just before or at the onset of the Spaniard's arrival—perhaps to win the pleasure of the gods in the face of an incoming threat.

*Michael Shally-Jensen*

See also: Teotihuacán; Tula.

## FURTHER READING

Atwood, Roger. 2014. "Under Mexico City" and several related articles. *Archaeology*, July/August 2014. https://www.archaeology.org/index.php/search-page?q=tenochtitlan&search=Go

Berdan, Frances F. 2014. *Aztec Archaeology and Ethnohistory*. New York: Cambridge University Press.

Carrasco, David. 2012. *The Aztecs: A Very Short Introduction*. New York: Oxford University Press.

Coe, Michael D., and Rex Koontz. 2013. *Mexico: From the Olmecs to the Aztecs*. 7th ed. London: Thames & Hudson.

Mundy, Barbara E. 2015. *The Death of Aztec Tenochtitlan, the Life of Mexico City*. Austin: University of Texas Press.

Rojas, José Luis de. 2012. *Tenochtitlan: Capital of the Aztec Empire*. Gainesville: University Press of Florida.

Schwartz, Stuart B., and Tatiana Seijas, eds. 2018. *Victors and Vanquished: Spanish and Nahua Views of the Fall of the Mexica Empire*. 2nd ed. Boston: Bedford/St. Martin's.

# Teotihuacán

Located about thirty miles northeast of modern Mexico City, near the former Lake Texcoco in the Valley of Mexico, Teotihuacán (pronounced tay-oh-tee-wah-khan') was the first great city of the pre-Columbian civilizations of Mesoamerica. It arose as a small farming settlement around 200 BCE and by 100 CE had started to develop as a major religious, political, and commercial center. At its peak (ca. 500 CE), it supported some 150,000 people and served as the capital of a powerful state or empire.

Teotihuacán was known for its great assemblage of monumental architecture, which was laid out in an impressive urban grid pattern encompassing eight square miles. Near the southern end of the main north–south road, called the Avenue of the Dead, stood the Pyramid of the Sun, 250 feet high and 650 feet square at its base (and mostly intact today). It had terraced sides and stairs leading to the summit. At the opposite end of the avenue stood the Pyramid of the Moon, about half the size of the sun pyramid. In another section, there was a large sunken courtyard, the Ciudadela, which was surrounded by temples. The city had canals that brought drinking water to the inhabitants along with a sewer system. A striking design element repeated in one of the city's temple buildings is the sculpted head of the Feathered Serpent, generally identified with the Aztec god Quetzalcoatl. The name *Teotihuacán*, in fact, is an Aztec word meaning "city of the gods." However, the site was virtually vacated by the time the Aztecs encountered it.

## INHABITANTS

What is known about the people of Teotihuacán is that they were something of a multiethnic population that nevertheless differed culturally from their Olmec predecessors and their Maya neighbors to the south. Clearly, their society was stratified and included farmers, craftspeople, merchants, bureaucrats, and, at the top, priest rulers. Hieroglyphics found on murals and pottery suggest that the people were literate, yet no written documents have been found to back up that prospect.

Besides temples and palaces, the city contained apartment buildings for residents. Craft workers—stonemasons, potters, sculptors, and painters—occupied a distinct neighborhood featuring workshops and related facilities. More luxurious homes for the ruling class sported decorative murals depicting human rituals and revered (or feared) animals such as jaguars and coyotes. Some masks or busts that survive show elaborate headdresses, painted faces, and extravagant jewelry, but such luxury items were likely limited to priests and gods. There is evidence that immigrants from surrounding areas took up residence in the city and maintained their ethnic identities over generations rather than assimilating entirely to Teotihuacán culture.

## HISTORICAL BACKGROUND

Permanent agricultural villages were present in Mesoamerica since about 2500 BCE, long before the rise of Teotihuacán. Olmec civilization, centered on the coastal forests of the Gulf of Mexico region north of the Yucatán Peninsula, flourished between about 1200 BCE and 600 BCE. The inhabitants of Teotihuacán were certainly influenced by the Olmecs, as were the Maya, the Zapotecs, and others. Both grew maize and potatoes and used surplus labor for the construction of temples and other public works (mammoth stone heads, in the case of the

Olmecs). Both had religious and, so it seems, warrior classes to uphold the culture and defend the state. With the passing of Olmec society, however, new centers of civilization developed in Mexico, one of which was Teotihuacán. Scholars consider that Teotihuacán's population got an early boost when, in about 50 CE, a major eruption of the Popocatépetl volcano brought refugees streaming in from the countryside.

Partly overlapping in time with Teotihuacán, the Maya, whose territory was Yucatán and Guatemala, flourished at different times and places within that region between 350 BCE and 1200 CE. Some Maya art and artifacts from the Early Classical period (250–550 CE) indicate intrusions by Teotihuacán into various lowland Maya cities, such as Tikal and Copán. It is thought that one reason this occurred was that the obsidian resources were considered good in the south—obsidian tool production being a central preoccupation of the Teotihuacanos. Another site of clear Teotihuacán influence was the lowland city of El Tajín, which flourished between 500 and 1200 CE.

## CULTURE AND SOCIETY

Teotihuacán operated as a ceremonial center for civic-religious functions and as a merchant city. The chief deity of the inhabitants was a god, Tlaloc, who granted water and plant cultivation to humans in exchange for human sacrifice and territorial expansion. The building of the pyramids and temples was likely ordered by a priestly elite and organized by a military force that recruited labor and kept workers in line; it is possible, too, as recent research in Egypt has shown, that workers viewed their efforts as bringing spiritual benefits to themselves and their families. Both the people of Teotihuacán and the Aztecs cremated their dead and worshipped some of the same deities, including Tlaloc and the Feathered Serpent (Quetzalcoatl), or god of the wind. Sacrifices, both animal and human, took place in front of crowds of spectators from atop the pyramids and elsewhere.

The city's commercial status derived from its manufacture of obsidian knives, scrapers, and points as well as its export of raw obsidian, obtained from nearby mines. In addition, shell, mica, and textile materials were both imported and exported. Other noted manufactures included plaster-coated, decorated cylindrical vases and small clay figurines representing household gods and other entities. Fine masks of greenstone and other materials, some with inlaid eyes of obsidian or shell, were highly valued and illustrate the Teotihuacán art style. It seems that the city's leaders built no forts, supply depots, or external roads to maintain control of any far-flung areas; yet, Teotihuacán's presence was surely dominant in the region for centuries.

## DEMISE

After 600 CE, Teotihuacán's power began to decline, probably because of internal stresses but also because of issues concerning agricultural production. By 650, it had lost its dominance, and shortly thereafter, it was looted and burned, perhaps by raiders from the city-state of Cholula to the southeast. Its temples now empty, it continued to house a remnant population in crude structures erected out of the remains of former palaces. Cholula seems to have inherited Teotihuacán's religious prestige, while the Toltecs took up its imperial aspirations. The city's pyramids became places of pilgrimage for the later Aztecs.

## RECENT DISCOVERIES AND CURRENT STATUS

Apart from continuing to fill out the picture of daily life and the cultural development of the city over time, researchers at the site have in recent years discovered evidence—in the form of material artifacts along with results from human bone analysis—that suggests a link between certain Maya populations and the ruling elite of Teotihuacán. It may turn out that such a finding cannot be applied across the board, or it may be that we will never know for sure. A lack of preserved human remains, despite the identification of over 130 burials sites, makes a firm determination difficult.

An ancient tunnel beneath the Temple of the Feathered Serpent was also recently found, echoing a similar tunnel beneath the Pyramid of the Sun (once thought to be a natural cave). Archaeological work there has proceeded slowly, with numerous new objects and fragments being documented. The meaning of these underground complexes is not clear, though they may have served as courses for pilgrims or places for the ritual induction of religious adepts.

Scholars have also recently proposed that the name of the city may originally have been Teohuacan, or "city of the sun." Spanish colonists may have altered the name in the course of describing it to their sponsors at home.

Teotihuacán was designated a UNESCO World Heritage Site in 1987. As one of the biggest tourist attractions in Mexico, its standing is fairly secure at present. Nevertheless, pressure has been building lately to develop parts of the surrounding area, something that could potentially affect the ancient city.

*Michael Shally-Jensen*

*See also:* Maya; Monte Albán; Olmecs; Tenochtitlán; Tula.

## FURTHER READING

*Archaeology*. 2018. "Teotihuacan May Have Been Renamed by the Spanish." January 24, 2018. https://www.archaeology.org/news/6298-180124-mexico-teotihuacan-aztecs
Coe, Michael D., and Rex Koontz. 2013. *Mexico: From the Olmecs to the Aztecs*. New York: Thames & Hudson.
Pasztory, Esther. 1997. *Teotihuacán: An Experiment in Living*. Norman: University of Oklahoma Press.
Schuster, Angela M. H. 1999. "New Tomb at Teotihuacan." *Archaeology*, updated March 2, 1999. https://archive.archaeology.org/online/features/mexico/
Storey, Rebecca. 1992. *Life and Death in the Ancient City of Teotihuacán*. Tuscaloosa: University of Alabama Press.

# Thebes

For half a millennium, the city of Thebes was one of the most important locations in ancient Egypt. From roughly 1550 BCE to 1069 BCE (with a brief interruption during the rule of Akhenaten, 1353–1336 BCE), it was Egypt's capital and main cultural center. Thebes had been a minor trading post as far back as 2316 BCE, but as the priests of Amun, who worshipped this particular Egyptian god, gained power within the city, Thebes grew in stature and became a place from which the pharaohs ruled in splendor for centuries. Thanks to these rulers' building efforts, during the New Kingdom period (1550–1069 BCE), Thebes came to feature two great religious and cultural sites of lasting renown: the temples at Karnak and Luxor. The city was located on the Nile, about 500 miles south of the delta; Karnak was situated in the northern section of Thebes, and Luxor lay to the south.

## INHABITANTS

The Greek historian Herodotus referred to Egypt as "the gift of the Nile," a phrase that captures the complete dependence of the Egyptians on the river. Flowing from south to north for thousands of miles through an arid desert, the Nile annually overflowed and deposited fertile silt that made farming possible. In fact, the Egyptians called their country Kemet, meaning "black land." Besides food crops, the Nile gave the people a means of transportation and commerce. It also produced a sense of commonality among settlements that encouraged the creation of a single state (albeit one that was occasionally split asunder). With vast expanses of desert lying to the east and the west, the Nile cataracts (sharp changes in level, usually with waterfalls) situated along the river's southern stretch, and the Mediterranean Sea located at its northern boundary, Egypt enjoyed natural defenses against outside invasion as well as an enduring source of water and spiritual and artistic inspiration.

Ahmose I, founder of the Eighteenth Dynasty, expelled the foreign invaders known as the Hyksos about 1570 BCE, thus marking the start of the New Kingdom. For the next 500 years, Egypt oversaw an empire extending from the Euphrates River in the east to the fourth cataract of the Nile River (in present-day Sudan). The temples and other buildings of the Eighteenth Dynasty (1549–1292 BCE) are recognized as the apogee of Egyptian architecture, while the many gold artifacts in Tutankhamun's preserved tomb remind us of the staggering wealth that Egyptian royalty possessed at the time. Ramesses II (r. 1279–1213 BCE), the pharaoh mentioned in the Hebrew Bible, was especially notable for his many monuments, including the impressive temples at Karnak and Luxor.

## HISTORICAL BACKGROUND

After Ahmose drove out the Hyksos and established Thebes as his capital, the city became known as the source of Egypt's liberation from foreign oppression. Also during the New Kingdom period, the god Amun, or Amun-Ra, became the most powerful deity in the Egyptian pantheon. Originally the god of Thebes and of fertility, Amun saw his status elevated during this time. He was considered the creator of the universe and was said to have created Thebes as the centerpiece of that creation.

During this same period, Thebes became the largest city in the world. Contemporaneous writers stated that most of the cities were built on the model of Thebes.

Yet, less is known about the city itself than the two temple complexes of Karnak and Luxor and the priestly cult that sustained them. At one point, around 1230 BCE, the pharaoh Ramesses II moved his capital to Per-Ramesses, on the delta; but the priests of Amun retained Thebes as their capital, essentially dividing the power of the Egyptian rulers and starting the decline of the New Kingdom's glory.

For most of its life, then, Thebes was a mainstay of Egyptian culture and history. The Valley of the Kings and the adjacent Valley of the Queens are found in the nearby Theban Hills, part of the larger Theban Necropolis on the west bank of the Nile, opposite the ancient city. Among the many rock-cut monuments, there are the mortuary temples of the pharaohs Seti I, Amenhotep III, Hatshepsut, Tutankhamun, and Ramesses III. Thebes itself featured an awe-inspiring Avenue of Sphinxes leading to the Temple of Karnak.

## CULTURE AND SOCIETY

While the great mortuary complexes and temples of pharaohs such as Seti I and Hatshepsut are justifiably renowned for their design and construction, Karnak—the modern name for the Temple of Amun—is notable for a different reason. The ancient Egyptians had several names for the area, calling it the Throne of the Two Lands, the Finest of Seats, and the Sacred Spot. The Egyptians believed that when the world was created, a mound first emerged from the waters of chaos; it was on this mound that Amun had stood to create Thebes and then the rest of the world. Therefore, this was the most sacred spot in all of the world and the best place to build a Great Temple to the creator god. The temple also honors other important gods, including Osiris, Isis, Ptah, Mut, and Montu. Various Egyptian rulers who wanted to be remembered also contributed to the temple's expansion over time. Indeed, this is one of Karnak's most unique features: unlike other building projects that were created to honor a specific ruler, at Karnak, each pharaoh added his or her own flourishes and augmentations. The complex is one the largest religious sites in the world, with scholars estimating that three buildings the size of Notre Dame Cathedral could fit inside the main temple alone. In total, the ruins comprise over 200 acres.

The construction of Karnak had certainly begun by the Middle Kingdom period (around 2040 BCE) and continued through the end of the last, the Ptolemaic dynasty, when Thebes was conquered around 30 BCE. It is possible that some kings of the Old Kingdom (beginning around 2613 BCE) first erected structures on the site. Within the festival hall of Tuthmose III (r. 1479–1425) is a list of Old Kingdom rulers, and some scholars believe that Tuthmose may have removed monuments from the time of the Old Kingdom to make room for his own.

Unlike the mortuary complexes in the Valley of the Kings and the Valley of the Queens, Karnak was in regular use as a Temple of Amun. Thebes held dozens of festivals and celebrations focused on the temple, which led to an increasingly powerful priesthood.

Luxor, meanwhile, seems to have served a different purpose. Lying on the east bank of the Nile, it apparently was not dedicated to any particular god or pharaoh. Instead, scholars believe that Luxor's glory revolved around the renewal of kingship in general. The pharaohs of the New Kingdom may have been crowned there. A pathway leads directly from Karnak to Luxor, and it is believed that Luxor may have played a key role in the Festival of Opet, an annual celebration of Thebes, Amun-Ra, the pharaoh, and Egyptian civilization. Stations were created for the gods at different places along the pathway, and it is thought that statues of Amun were carried from Karnak to Luxor as part of the celebrations.

## DEMISE

Eventually, the priests of Amun grew powerful enough to challenge the authority of the pharaoh. During the Third Intermediate Period (1069–525 BCE), the Theban priests came to claim not only Thebes but all of Upper Egypt. It was then, too, that the city began to decline. By the seventh century BCE, the Nubian pharaoh Tantamani had made Thebes his capital, briefly reigning over both Egypt and the Kingdom of Kush. In 667 BCE, however, the Assyrian king Ashurbanipal invaded Egypt, and in the following year, he sacked Thebes and drove out Tantamani (who returned to Nubia/Kush).

Another sack occurred at the hand of the Persians in 525 BCE. Karnak was, to a degree, repaired and renovated, but its glory days were over. By the time of the Roman takeover in the first century BCE, Thebes was little more than a few empty streets, and Karnak and Luxor were half-forgotten monuments to an ancient religion. Under the Christian emperor Constantine II (r. 337–340 CE), all pagan temples were ordered closed. Nevertheless, there is evidence that Coptic Christians held church services in the buildings for some time.

## RECENT DISCOVERIES AND CURRENT STATUS

While little remains today of Thebes itself, the Karnak and Luxor temples are among the most visited spots on the planet in the global tourism industry. In fact, Luxor is now the name of the modern city that encompasses what used to be Thebes and its two religious centers. As recently as 2019, there were plans to turn the ruins of the area into the world's greatest "open-air museum," creating more hotels and entertainment venues linked not just to Karnak and Luxor but to the nearby Theban Necropolis. The plan is controversial, however, and has been met with resistance.

In 2019, archaeologists announced that an expansive tomb had been discovered within Luxor. It belonged to a royal master of seals named Shedsu-Djehuty and appears to date back to the Eighteenth Dynasty. The tomb is more than 540 square yards in area and has eighteen entrance gates.

In 2020, meanwhile, researchers used medical scans, 3D printing, and an electronic voice box to recreate the voice of a mummified priest named Nesyamun, who lived during the eleventh century BCE. It is thought that Nesyamun was a priest at Karnak or Luxor. The same research team expects that, in the near future, they may be able to reconstruct the singing of the priests of Amun.

*Michael Shally-Jensen*

*See also:* Abu Simbel; Assyrians; Deir-el-Bahri/Djeser-Djeseru; Memphis and Saqqara.

## FURTHER READING

*Egypt Independent.* 2020. "Researchers Listen to the Voice of Karnak Temple Priest 3,000 Years after His Death." January 24, 2020. https://egyptindependent.com/researchers-listen-to-voice-of-karnak-temple-priest-3000-years-after-his-death/

Hawass, Zahi A. 2006. *The Royal Tombs of Egypt: The Art of Thebes Revealed.* New York: Thames & Hudson.

Lewis, Aiden. 2019. "Expansive New Kingdom Tomb Unveiled in Egypt's Luxor." Reuters, April 18, 2019. https://www.reuters.com/article/us-egypt-archaeology/expansive-new-kingdom-tomb-unveiled-in-egypts-luxor-idUSKCN1RU2E7

Snape, Steven R. 2014. *The Complete Cities of Ancient Egypt.* New York: Thames & Hudson.

Strudwick, N., and H. Strudwick. 1999. *Thebes in Egypt: A Guide to the Tombs and Temples of Ancient Luxor.* Ithaca, NY: Cornell University Press.

# Timbuktu

Located in Mali, on the southern edge of the Sahara Desert, just north of the great bend of the Niger River, Timbuktu was once an important center of commerce and Islamic culture. It played a central part in two great empires of the African Middle Ages: the Mali Empire and the Songhai Empire.

Among Timbuktu's notable buildings are the Sankoré, Djingareyber, and Sidi Yahia mosques, all of which are pounded-clay or clay and rubble stone structures dating from the Songhai era. Known in the past as a great center of Islamic theological and legal scholarship, today, Timbuktu is home to the Ahmed Baba Institute, which collects and preserves centuries-old books and manuscripts.

## INHABITANTS

Timbuktu has long been at the crossroads of migrating and competing peoples and cultures but has generally been made up of an array of Songhai, Tuareg, Bambara, and other groups over its history. The empire of Mali controlled a large area of West Africa in the fourteenth century. Under its most famous ruler, Mansa Musa (r. 1312–1337), it became the most powerful state in Africa at the time, extending from the upper Senegal River in the west to the bend of the Niger River in the east and from the upper Volta River in the south to the Sahara in the north. Its rulers, or *mansas*, were devout Muslims who made pilgrimages to Mecca, bringing home honor and glory and accruing great wealth in the course of managing the empire.

The Songhai state ruled an even larger area of West Africa from 1464 to 1591. Timbuktu and Djenné, along with its capital of Gao, served the empire's numerous merchants and soldiers and helped to maintain a profitable trade network, which by then extended southward to the tropical forests and northward across the Sahara. Songhai, too, was overseen by noted rulers, including its founder, Sunni Ali (r. ca. 1464–1492), and the powerful Askia Muhammad Touré (r. 1493–1528). They continued the strong Islamic tradition of Timbuktu and the other cities while also reigning over a large number of non-Muslims in the empire's population.

## HISTORICAL BACKGROUND

Timbuktu was a working market town by the twelfth century, its location well suited to serving the fishing and farming communities of the middle Niger area as well as the caravans traveling across the Sahara. In the fourteenth century, Mansa Musa, the emperor of Mali, enlarged Timbuktu's mosques, encouraged the creation of an Islamic school, and enhanced the city's status as a center of Muslim culture. Both the empire and its leader benefited from a change in European currency, whereby copper and silver coins were replaced with gold. Much of the gold that made this possible was extracted from mines controlled by Mali. The noted Berber traveler and writer Ibn Battuta, who visited Mali in 1352–1353, remarked on the splendor of the golden objects in Malian courts, yet objected, at the same time, to the pandering to the king by his courtiers. Mansa Musa himself, who had brought a 100-camel entourage to Mecca during his hajj (pilgrimage) there, is sometimes considered to have been the richest man of all time, possessing such vast gold reserves that he could cause precious metal prices in the hemisphere to rise or fall depending on the transactions he chose to make.

The Songhai people were accomplished traders and soldiers during the early medieval period, but they came to be controlled, first, by the Kingdom of Ghana and then by the Kingdom of Mali. In 1464, however, the Malian cities of Timbuktu and Djenné were captured by the Songhai leader Sunni Ali and his forces. The Songhai state grew into an empire as Ali expanded his authority. He established laws, created a centralized system of rule, and promoted the development of trade. Under Ali, the Songhai exported not only gold, salt (valued as a preservative), and agricultural products but also slaves.

Following Ali's death in 1492, one of his generals, Muhammad Touré, a Soninke, took over the throne. Muhammad established the Askia dynasty in 1493 and reigned as Askia Muhammad. Under his rule, the Songhai Empire reached its greatest extent. He made Islam its official religion, promoted Islamic scholarship, and engaged in holy wars (jihads). He also established an efficient bureaucracy and maintained a standing army. Yet, while those living in Songhai's major cities adopted Islamic culture, those in the countryside continued to follow traditional African religions.

It was also during the reign of Askia Muhammad that Timbuktu again became one of the major cultural centers on the continent. The University of Timbuktu (or University of Sankoré), which was really a collection of mosques and a scholarly community that endured over time, drew thousands of Islamic scholars from across the Muslim world.

## CULTURE AND SOCIETY

Timbuktu was an important administrative city in central Mali as well as a historic trading center, lying at the junction of trade routes on the southern edge of the Sahara and north of the Niger River. The city consisted of merchants, administrators, Islamic educators, soldiers, farmers, fishers, laborers, servants, slaves, and others. In addition, shifting encampments of nomads often ringed the city. By the 1500s, there were around 100,000 residents.

A publication from 1525, *History and Description of Africa*, by a Moroccan traveler called Leo Africanus, brought Timbuktu to the attention of the West. The writer reported on the dazzling wealth the city possessed in gold coin and ingots and noted the magnificence of its army as well as the great learning of its many judges, scholars, and priests. Timbuktu seemed almost fable-like in Leo Africanus's account, and European travelers began to seek the city out. It was so difficult to reach, however, and so few made it and came back, that the very word *Timbuktu* came to mean something impossibly distant, at the far corners of the earth. By the mid-1800s, when Europeans finally arrived in force and were able to return to tell the tale, Timbuktu was well past its prime.

The "mud" architecture of both Timbuktu and Djenné is striking. Major structures employ wooden frames that are then packed with fine clay. Some buildings, such as the Great Mosque at Djenné, feature large conical towers and elaborate parapets. Despite occasionally needing minor maintenance, these mud-and-wood fabrications have stood the test of time and serve as symbols of the sophistication and splendor of the culture that erected them.

## DEMISE

The Songhai ruler Askia Muhammad was overthrown by his son Askia Musa in 1528, and thereafter the empire began to decline. Trade routes shifted farther to the south, a civil war erupted, and droughts and disease swept the region. After Songhai was attacked and defeated by Morocco in 1591, Timbuktu began to fade. Little protection was provided against subsequent Fulani and Tuareg incursions. The French established an outpost at Timbuktu in the 1890s, but the city never regained its past glory. It became part of Mali in 1960.

## RECENT DISCOVERIES AND CURRENT STATUS

During the late twentieth century, efforts were begun to revive Timbuktu's cultural legacy. The city was designated a UNESCO World Heritage Site in 1988. Two years later, it was classified as an endangered site because of encroaching desert sands. It was removed from the endangered list in 2005, following the implementation of conservation programs.

Concerns for the safety of the site's cultural heritage returned when a coalition of Tuareg separatist rebels and Islamist fighters (Ansar Dine) seized control of the city in early April 2012. The Ansar Dine leaders soon imposed strict Islamic law and destroyed many of the city's shrines to Islamic saints and other structures it considered idolatrous. They also burned numerous historic documents. In late January 2013, however, the Islamists were expelled by a military force made up of elements from France and Chad as well as the Malian army. A number of the destroyed shrines were later rebuilt by local stonemasons under UNESCO supervision. International efforts had also been put in place to protect the city's literary heritage by moving books and manuscripts to safe harbors outside the area of Islamist control.

*Michael Shally-Jensen*

*See also:* Ife.

## FURTHER READING

Hammer, Joshua. 2016. *The Bad-Ass Librarians of Timbuktu: And Their Race to Save the World's Most Precious Manuscripts*. New York: Simon and Schuster.

Kane, Ousmane Oumar. 2016. *Beyond Timbuktu: An Intellectual History of Muslim West Africa*. Cambridge, MA: Harvard University Press.

Kryza, Frank T. 2006. *The Race for Timbuktu: In Search of Africa's City of Gold*. New York: Ecco.

# Tiwanaku

The city of Tiwanaku (also spelled Tiahuanaco) was the seat of an Amerindian empire in the central Andes region of South America from roughly 200 to 1000 CE. The empire spanned a vast amount of territory and was influential in the world of Andean civilizations of the time. At its peak, the Tiwanaku Empire extended through parts of present-day Peru, Bolivia, and Chile. The city itself was located near Lake Titicaca, one of the area's major topographical features and considered by the inhabitants to be the center of the world and the origin of the universe. As a mytho-religious center, a center for art production, and a political epicenter, the city was crucial to the shaping of Andean culture during the period of its existence. It was, nevertheless, abandoned by about 1100 CE, probably because of severe drought but likely also because of internal conflict. At an altitude of over 12,000 feet, Tiwanaku had the distinction of being the ancient world's highest city.

## INHABITANTS

The inhabitants of Tiwanaku did not have a written language, so even the name of the place has been passed down through the Incas and the Spanish; in fact, Tiwanaku may not have been its original name. The city was inhabited by an Indigenous population as early as 200 CE, but it reached its peak somewhere after 500 CE. As many as 20,000–30,000 people may have lived there. (Some estimates range as high as 50,000 or 70,000.)

Tiwanaku is a somewhat peculiar urban site in that it has many residential buildings but few storehouses or administrative buildings. Instead, the city seems to have been focused on its religious significance and its residential community. On the flat, swampy lands beside Lake Titicaca, farmers built drainage ditches and raised crops of potatoes and quinoa. To keep the potatoes edible after the harvest, the people freeze-dried them, laying them out on ridges in the fields to freeze at night and then dry under the daytime sun.

There were different types of residential buildings in the city. Some were created in compounds, constructed from adobe, and built on cobblestones. Others

The Gateway of the Sun, a part of the Kalasasaya Temple, is the most recognizable remain from Tiwanaku. It was made from a single block of stone and features highly debated religious iconography. (Dmitriyrnd | Dreamstime.com)

had finer construction, using high adobe walls around courtyards while the buildings themselves were made of carefully cut stone. This pattern clearly indicates the existence of a class system similar to those of other Andean civilizations.

## HISTORICAL BACKGROUND

The area around Lake Titicaca was settled as early as the second millennium BCE. People made use of the llama, alpaca, and vicuña for wool clothing, transportation, and, when necessary, food. The lake provided fish and reeds, which were used to fashion boats, roofs, and mats. Potatoes, quinoa, and oca (a tuber) were cultivated in the fields, and metals, including gold, copper, and tin, were extracted from the nearby mountains. The cold altiplano conditions, however, did preclude the growth of trees and may have dampened population growth generally, whereas warmer, more fertile areas to the south did not face these same restrictions.

One reason why Tiwanaku may have been so successful and influential in the region was its location. Besides the fishing and farming resources provided by Lake Titicaca—not to mention the symbolic import of the lake—the city also benefited from being accessible from different directions and from the year-round rainfall it enjoyed. Residents devised a method to ensure sufficient water for their crops and to keep those crops warm enough to ward off the frost caused by the cold desert air. At its peak, the city covered more than 3.5 square miles.

## CULTURE AND SOCIETY

Like other Andean civilizations, Tiwanaku was based on a clearly defined division of labor. This structure factored into its eventual efforts at military conquest and political control of a large number of people and vast areas. It is known that ancient Peru, for example, underwent several periods of regional growth and militaristic expansion. The Tiwanaku Empire was thus based on a social organization and technological means that were common to the various peoples of the ancient central Andes, such as the later Inca.

In the mythology of the region, Lake Titicaca was considered the center of the world. According to that mythology, the two islands situated on the lake were the sun and the moon. The first race of people were stone giants, who were later replaced by humans.

Tiwanaku, therefore, had great religious significance. Many major stone buildings and monuments there now make up the ancient city's ruins. Interpreting their nature and meaning, however, can be difficult, as many of them were at some point moved from their original positions. It is thought that various monuments were originally placed so as to line up with either the rising sun or the midday sun, but this is not certain.

Two types of stone walls were constructed at Tiwanaku, those that used irregular blocks and those that used carefully cut and fitted straight-edged blocks. Many of these blocks show grooves where ropes were placed to move them into position more easily. Sophisticated tools and technology were used to create these building blocks, including bronze and lead clamps and sockets to improve the fit and durability of the walls.

Among the major temples in Tiwanaku are the Akapana Temple, the Semi-Subterranean Temple, and the Kalasasaya Temple. The last is the most famous, as it contains the Gateway of the Sun in its northwest corner. Carved from a single massive block of stone, the gateway has relief carvings of creatures that are either angels or demons with bird heads. In the center of these figures is a deity who is associated with a Chavín sacred figure and may have been a predecessor of the Inca creator god Viracocha. The elaborately carved figure is crying, possibly to signify rain, and has a face similar to a mask. Nineteen rays extend from his head, and he holds a staff in each hand. The significance of the gateway itself, on which these figures appear, continues to be debated. When it was found by Europeans, it was broken and lying on its side; it may have been moved from its original location.

Several massive stone figures appear in the city. Many researchers believe that these statues may have been the first attempt to represent the stone giants who are part of Andean mythology.

Like other cultures of the time, the residents of Tiwanaku were skilled with both textile work and ceramics. The designs they employed appear in other ancient cultures in the area, indicating that those cultures either absorbed the designs from Tiwanaku or that Tiwanaku incorporated them from the outside—or perhaps, simply, there was a two-way communication. Pottery from Tiwanaku has a distinctive orange base color, and tall vessels that have been partly buried in the ground are common. Some vessels were modeled after human heads but with distinctive features, implying that they were intended to represent a specific person rather than a generic figure.

Weaving from Tiwanaku has several distinctive and innovative features, including difficult-to-achieve diagonal patterns and floral decorations. In some cases, such work has been linked to trading networks and to llama caravans that moved across the Tiwanaku Empire's different areas.

## DEMISE

The reason that Tiwanaku fell into decline is hotly debated. There was a massive drought around 1000 CE, and some researchers think that the drought led to agricultural collapse and widespread hunger, which would have reduced the power Tiwanaku had over the surrounding civilizations. Others believe that the drought occurred shortly after the city fell; the evidence here is the violent shattering of pottery and buildings, as the city presumably experienced some kind of sudden uprising or attack. In any case, researchers are sure that the production of Tiwanaku ceramics suddenly stopped around 1000 CE and that the city's urban core was empty within a few decades.

After the city's demise, aspects of Tiwanaku culture were represented in some civilizations that came after. The Inca, for one, borrowed heavily from its architecture, sculpture, and road design, going so far as to import stone masons from the Lake Titicaca region when they began constructing their most important cities. Meanwhile, civilizations to the south borrowed some words (it is thought) and certain art patterns from Tiwanaku.

## RECENT DISCOVERIES AND CURRENT STATUS

Tiwanaku is a UNESCO World Heritage Site, a fact that became particularly important in 2009 when Bolivia was attempting to reconstruct what is called the Akapana pyramid in the city. Adobe was being applied to damaged areas, but researchers had not conclusively demonstrated that the material or the method was appropriate.

In 2013, marine researchers were examining the floor of Lake Titicaca when they uncovered an ancient ceremonial site. They found a variety of artifacts, including figurines made from lapis lazuli and ceramics, a ceremonial medallion, and incense burners. These artifacts were all considered to have played a part in both the material world and the religious worldview of the Tiwanaku people. The prevailing view is that such objects were consecrated to the gods and thrown into the center of the lake as a tribute.

*Michael Shally-Jensen*

*See also:* Machu Picchu; Nazca.

## FURTHER READING

Blakemore, E. 2019. "Hints of Mysterious Religion Discovered in World's Highest Lake." *National Geographic Magazine*, April 1, 2019. https://www.nationalgeographic.com/culture/2019/04/evidence-ancient-religion-discovered-lake-titicaca/#close

Janusek, John Wayne. 2008. *Ancient Tiwanaku*. New York: Cambridge University Press.
Kolata, Alan L. 1993. *The Tiwanaku*. Cambridge, MA: Blackwell.
Protzen, Jean-Pierre, and Stella Nair. 2017. *Stones of Tiahuanaco: A Study of Architecture and Construction*. Los Angeles: Cotsen Institute of Archaeology Press.

# Troy

Troy's location on the northwest coast of Asia Minor, modern Turkey, was forgotten in antiquity. It was located on what is now called the Hisarlik archaeological mound that was also the site of the later Hellenistic and Roman town of Ilium (or Ilion). Troy held a strategic position on the Dardanelles, a narrow channel that connects the Aegean Sea to the Black Sea, northwest of Mount Ida. This was an important trade route in the ancient world, enabling the people of Troy to flourish during the Bronze Age (ca. 3000–1200 BCE). Until the nineteenth century, Troy was considered a mythical location related to Homer's *Iliad* and *Odyssey*.

## INHABITANTS

The question of who inhabited Troy has been a topic of scholarly dispute since the 1980s, when excavations at the Hisarlik mound resumed. The Trojans, or the Dardanoi, are a real people with a mythical past. Their ethnicity and the nature of their language remain a mystery, but their material culture ties them to other Anatolians groups, like the Luwians. In the ancient world, they were considered a non-Greek people and fought against the Greeks in the Trojan War of Homer's *Iliad* and *Odyssey*. With the fall of Trojan Troy in the tenth century BCE, its original inhabitants abandoned the region. In the seventh century, the town was reoccupied by Greek settlers, who were later sacked in the first century BCE by the Romans. Through its history, Troy was an agricultural and trading center with a diverse population from the Mediterranean, Near East, and Anatolia.

## HISTORICAL BACKGROUND

The history of this legendary city is twofold. There is the history of the city itself and the archaeological history of the site. The approximate location of Troy has been a topic of intrigue for centuries for its role in the Trojan War of Homer's *Iliad* and references to it in the works of the ancient Greek authors Herodotus and Strabo. In 1822, Charles Maclaren was the first to suggest the Hisarlik hill as the site of Homeric Troy, but no excavations took place because Greek scholars still considered the town to be mythological. In the 1860s, the Calvert family purchased the mound and began digging test pits around the site, discovering the Roman settlement. They joined forces with Heinrich Schliemann, a wealthy German businessman and archaeologist, and in the 1870s, large-scale excavations began at the newly identified city of Troy. Between 1870 and 1890, Schliemann conducted seven major and two minor archaeological campaigns. After Schliemann's death in 1890, the excavations were continued (1893–1894) by his colleague Wilhelm Dörpfeld and later (1932–1938) by Carl Blegen of the University of Cincinnati.

Hisarlik mound was 105 feet (32 m) above the plain when excavations began, and it contained many clearly distinguishable layers filled with archaeological material. Schliemann and Dörpfeld identified a sequence of nine main layers, which we use to talk about the different periods of habitation at Troy. In each of these nine periods, a town was built, occupied, and ultimately destroyed. Each settlement was destroyed by fire, earthquake, or both. After each disaster, the inhabitants simply leveled out the debris and rebuilt the city. The nine periods of ancient Troy are labeled I to IX. The bottom and oldest layer in Troy I. Troy I to V correspond roughly to the Early Bronze Age (ca. 3000–1900 BCE). Schliemann mistakenly identified Troy II as Homer's Troy because of its large fortification walls, city plan, and large cache of gold, silver, bronze, copper, and ceramic artifacts, which he named "Priam's treasure" after the fabled king of the *Iliad*.

Troy VI and VII belong to the Middle and Late Bronze Age (ca. 1900–1100 BCE). The city was enlarged in these periods, and a large limestone wall that was fifteen-feet (4.5 m) thick at the base rose to a height of more than seventeen feet (5 m). Dörpfeld identified this period as Homer's Troy because of this large fortification; however, Troy VI was destroyed by a violent earthquake a little after 1300 BCE, not by an attack. Also, the presence of archaeological material from the Mycenaean culture indicates that this level was too early for the Trojan War. Troy VIIa was immediately built after the earthquake. Buildings completely filled the citadel, and every house was equipped with storage jars of food, as if special measures were taken to withstand a siege. This evidence, combined with the fact that this level was destroyed by a large fire and held many human remains, led Blegen to classify Troy VIIa as the Troy destroyed by Greeks in the *Iliad*. Troy VIIa is still considered the most likely level for this legendary war.

## CULTURE AND SOCIETY

For the ancient Greeks, the Trojan War was a real historical event that took place during the Mycenaean period, at the end of the second millennium BCE, outside the gates of Troy. Many Greek heroes, such as Achilles, Ajax, and Odysseus, fought in this mythical war, and their stories are what make Troy such a mysterious and awe-inspiring place. During the earliest periods of Troy (I–V), the city was a fortified stronghold that served as the capital of the region. The king, his family, officials, advisers, and slaves all lived within the walls, with most of the population living on the farmable land nearby. This large populace would come into the fortified city and take refuge in times of danger.

Troy VI and VII had a large population of at least 5,000 people and trade contacts in Anatolia (modern Turkey) and the Greek Aegean. Troy VI was a trading center for both Near Eastern and Mediterranean goods, with evidence of both Anatolian and Mycenaean Greek pottery. During these periods, there was a thriving wool industry, and new settlers had come to the city, bringing with them domesticated horses. The city had large decorative pillars that flanked the south gate and tightly packed houses constructed within the walls of the citadel that were connected by cobbled streets. This is a significant change from the earlier periods with the majority of the population living outside of the walls, indicating that the area was no longer safe. With the destruction of Troy VII, the city was abandoned until the seventh century, when it became a Greek and then Roman (first century BCE) town.

## DEMISE

After the fiery destruction of Troy VIIa, the city entered a period of decline. Troy VIIb has evidence of a smaller number of inhabitants, but by 1100 BCE, they had vanished. For the next four centuries, until 700 BCE, the site was abandoned. In the seventh century BCE, Greek settlers reoccupied Troy, and it was given the Hellenized name of Ilion (Troy VIII). The Romans sacked Ilion in 85 BCE and then partially restored it and settled Roman colonists there (Troy XI). The Roman town, now called Ilium, was given a new theater by Emperor Augustus, and he also restored the Temple of Athena. Ilium remained a sizable Roman town until the founding of Constantinople in 324 CE. Little is known of the town after that, but the Romans did connect this city with Trojan Aeneas, a mythical founder of Rome, demonstrating their collective memory and mythological connection of the area with Homer's Troy.

## RECENT DISCOVERIES AND CURRENT STATUS

After a lapse of about fifty years in the twentieth century, excavations at Troy resumed. The current campaign began in 1988 under the direction of the German archaeologist Manfred Korfmann and the American archaeologist Brian Rose from the University of Cincinnati. It is using modern scientific techniques to review the findings of previous excavations and explore new areas of the site. In 1996, the Turkish government created the Historical National Park at Troy to protect the site as well as open it up to visitors. In 1998, it became a UNESCO World Heritage Site, and in 2018, the Troy Museum opened in the village of Tevfikiye, just a half mile away from the archaeological site.

*Katie Tardio*

*See also:* Ephesus; Knossos; Mycenae.

## FURTHER READING

Cline, E. 2010. *The Oxford Handbook of the Bronze Age Aegean (ca. 3000–1000 BC).* Oxford: Oxford University Press.

Latacz, J. 2004. *Troy and Homer: Towards a Solution of an Old Mystery.* Oxford: Oxford University Press.

Rose, C. 2013. *The Archaeology of Greek and Roman Troy.* Cambridge: Cambridge University Press.

Sweeney, N. 2018. *Troy: Myth, City, Icon.* New York: Bloomsbury Academic.

## Tula

Tula (pronounced too'-la) was the capital city of the Toltec Empire, which dominated much of southern Mexico and the surrounding area from the tenth through the twelfth century CE. It is located about forty miles northwest of present-day Mexico City, farther north than earlier Mesoamerican capitals. The city arose after the decline of both Teotihuacán, just to the south of Tula, and Maya civilization, centered on the Yucatán Peninsula. Tula became the center of a major Toltec trading network that reached from the American Southwest to Costa Rica.

Tula encompassed an area of about four square miles and housed a population of some 30,000–50,000 at its height (950–1150 CE). The city featured pyramids, a temple with sculpted columns, great halls or palaces, a large open plaza, ballcourts, and statues known as *chacmools* that depict reclining men holding sacrificial knives and bowls on their stomachs—which are said to be for receiving the beating hearts of sacrificed persons. The colossal columns (called atlanteans, for "Atlas-like") that have come to symbolize Toltec civilization depict costumed warriors ready for battle. Most Tula building structures displayed carved or stuccoed friezes.

### INHABITANTS

The Toltecs represented a group of blended Indigenous elements in Mesoamerica, comprised mainly of Nahua, Otomí, and Nonoalca ethnicities. The Nahua, related to the later Aztecs, had invaded the center of Mexico from the northwest around the beginning of the tenth century CE. They are referred to in the Spanish chronicles as "Chichimec Toltecs." The Nonoalca, for their part, likely brought the traditions of Teotihuacán civilization and developed other cultural elements as well. The Otomí, too, had ties to Teotihuacán and to the wider Valley of Mexico. The Toltecs and their empire were of such stature that many of the region's later peoples, including the Aztecs, claimed descent from them. It was the Aztecs who related what they knew of Toltec culture and history to the Spanish conquistadors.

### HISTORICAL BACKGROUND

The Toltecs moved into the area they occupied in the Valley of Mexico after the collapse, in the late seventh century CE, of the great city of Teotihuacán. They took over and further developed trade routes that stretched throughout much of Mesoamerica. Immigrants from surrounding areas flocked to the Toltec homeland. By the ninth century, the city of Tula was well established and served as the center of a growing empire.

For a century or more, the Toltecs seem to have shared close contacts with the Maya center of Chichén Itzá. According to both central Mexican and Maya annals, the Toltec king Topiltzin (r. ca. 980–999) renamed himself Quetzalcoatl (the principal deity) and fled Tula for Chichén Itzá. (He may have been running after an unsuccessful attempt to reform religious practices such as sacrifice.) While the

Toltecs eventually came to occupy Chichén Itzá, there is no evidence that they conquered the Maya. Rather, they most likely were in communication with the Maya beforehand and shared cultural elements with the Maya that appear at both Tula and Chichén Itzá. Thus, forms of art and architecture such as sculpted columns—atlanteans, serpent columns, and others—and the reclining *chacmool* figures could first have been displayed at Chichén Itzá and then adopted at Tula. Similarly, some styles at Chichén Itzá suggest secondary adaptations by later Toltec inhabitants.

## CULTURE AND SOCIETY

The precise outlines of the Toltec Empire have not been determined, yet Toltec influence in the region surely reached far and wide. As some scholars have argued, the expansion of the empire may have been carried out by independent Toltec warlords rather than by an all-powerful king ruling from the center. Thus, the Toltec "Empire" was less a unified entity than a network of aligned districts (as was the case with Maya civilization).

The most important deity in Toltec civilization was Quetzalcoatl (also called Kulkucán). The Toltecs demanded tribute from their neighbors and took human sacrifices to appease their gods. They displayed the skulls of their victims on wooden racks and created artworks that featured war, death, and sacrifice. Among the works at the Toltec capital of Tula are sculptured panels showing jaguars and coyotes and others depicting eagles eating human hearts. The Aztecs admired the Toltecs and pointed proudly to their architectural achievements, religious heritage, and warrior tradition.

Toltec subsistence centered on maize cultivation and the growing of beans, squash, and other crops. Irrigation was practiced on a small scale. The hunting of game supplemented the diet. Trade was extensive, with pottery, stone implements, textiles, animal skins, feathers, and other goods reaching settlements lying well beyond the Toltec heartland.

## DEMISE

Toltec power waned in the mid-twelfth century, as droughts disrupted agriculture and Tula experienced factional strife and conflicts with neighboring states, particularly Cholula. It came under heavy pressure from displaced peoples of the northwest seeking refuge. About 1150, Tula was ravaged and set aflame. Some Toltecs fled to the Valley of Mexico, where their traditions lived on in the Aztec era.

As for King Topiltzin, even before Tula's demise, he had been forced into exile and went to the Gulf Coast (Chichén Itzá), where he died at the end of the tenth century. Legend has it that before his departure from Tula, he promised to return in the year 1519. Thus, when the Aztecs encountered the Spanish conquistador Hernán Cortés in 1519, they debated whether he was Topiltzin returned from the dead. By then, Topiltzin had been deified and was identified in myths with the planet Venus, or the morning and evening star.

## RECENT DISCOVERIES AND CURRENT STATUS

At Tula, archaeologists have worked since 1940 to excavate and restore the great temples and adjacent buildings. The colossal atlantean figures, or Toltec warriors, have been restored and returned to their places in Pyramid B, where they once supported a roof. The so-called Burned Palace, contiguous with Pyramid B, has been determined to be the center of Toltec administration. Sections of housing near the Tula River have been identified as well.

In 2007, researchers uncovered the remains of twenty-four children near Tula, aged five to fifteen years, whose throats had been cut. It is believed that they were sacrificial victims to Quetzalcoatl or Tlaloc, the rain god.

*Michael Shally-Jensen*

*See also:* Maya; Tenochtitlán; Teotihuacán.

## FURTHER READING

Davies, Nigel. 1977. *The Toltecs, until the Fall of Tula.* Norman: University of Oklahoma Press.

Diehl, Richard A. 1983. *Tula: The Toltec Capital of Ancient Mexico.* New York: Thames & Hudson.

Miller, Mary Ellen. 2012. *The Art of Mesoamerica: From Olmec to Aztec.* 5th ed. New York: Thames & Hudson.

# U

## Ur

Ur was one of the oldest and most important cities in ancient Mesopotamia during the time of the Sumerians and Babylonians (ca. 3500–1750 BCE). It is also known, from its mention in the Bible, as Ur of the Chaldees (Ur Kasdim) and is said to have been the birthplace of the prophet Abraham.

The city was situated on the Euphrates River, in the southern part of Sumer, close to the Persian Gulf; at the time, the gulf ranged farther inland than it does now. Today, the city's remains lie in southern Iraq, about 220 miles southeast of Baghdad. Two of Ur's contemporaneous neighboring city-states were Eridu and Uruk, the latter known for its development of writing (cuneiform) and the great Sumerian poem *The Epic of Gilgamesh.*

The major monument at Ur (as with other ancient Sumerian cities) was the ziggurat, a word meaning "summit" or "pinnacle." Dating from a somewhat later period in the city's history (ca. 2100 BCE), the Ur ziggurat consists of a large platform measuring 190-by-130 feet with great staircases ascending it that open onto an upper terrace, which originally featured a temple to the moon god.

Besides such cultural achievements, the Sumerians are known for the systems of canals, dikes, and reservoirs they constructed; the measuring and surveying instruments they developed; the arithmetic and astronomical systems they employed; their work in areas such as metallurgy, pigmentation, cosmetics, and perfumes; and the medical knowledge they applied in the preparation of various herbal and mineral treatments. (For a full discussion of Sumerian "firsts," see Kramer 1988.)

---

### *Iram of the Pillars*

Iram is a city—or perhaps a people—mentioned in the Qur'an. Another common name for the city is Ubar, and T. E. Lawrence coined the name the Atlantis of the Sands for the city. The passage within the Qu'ran asks the reader to consider the fate of Iram, which is said to have had lofty pillars. Those who have taken Iram to be a historical city have long searched the southern Arabian Peninsula and beyond in search of the city. Some have associated it with contemporary megacities such as Alexandria or Damascus. Others have sought out cities lost to the desert. For instance, in the 1990s, a team of archaeologists suggested that Shisr, an archaeological site in present-day Oman, is home to the remains of Iram. Although these claims often garner much attention when they are made, they have thus far failed to sway a consensus of scholars.

## INHABITANTS

Ur was a trading center strategically located near the Tigris and Euphrates Rivers at a time when large-scale human settlements were first beginning to form. With the Sumerian invention of cuneiform, around 3200 BCE, commercial activity and forms of government control, such as taxation, expanded. The Sumerians used cuneiform to record information about food production, trade, and royal history and to compose literary epics, myths, and hymns.

The Sumerians believed that humans had been fashioned of clay—the most abundant material in the region—and existed to supply the gods with food and shelter. Prayers, offerings, and sacrifices were presented at the temple, which was managed by a body of priests. The gods of Sumer resembled humans in appearance and behavior, and a rich mythology concerning their activities was created.

The city itself was said to belong to the god having responsibility for it on the day the world was created. Most of the actual land was initially held by the residents of Ur—the crop farmers, cattle breeders, fishermen, merchants, scribes, and artisans making up the bulk of the populace. Over time, as the danger of attack by surrounding peoples increased, a strong form of kingship came into being, supplemented by the priesthood. The ruler of Ur defended the city from its rivals, sought to enlarge its territory and influence, maintained the irrigation system essential to the survival of its citizens, built roads and monuments to the gods, and administered law and justice.

The language spoken by the Sumerians was a non-Semitic one that had no sister languages (i.e., it was a language isolate). The neighboring Akkadians, Amorites, and, later, Babylonians, on the other hand, all spoke Semitic languages (a group that includes Arabic, Hebrew, and Aramaic).

The Ziggurat of Ur is the most significant ruin from Ur and one of the more recognizable sites from ancient Mesopotamia. Built in the late third millennium BCE, the massive structure was associated with worship of the moon god, Nanna. (Rasool Ali | Dreamstime.com)

## HISTORICAL BACKGROUND

Although there is evidence for the occupation of the site of Ur as early as the fifth millennium BCE, the city began to flourish in the first half of the third millennium BCE, when it established authority over all of Sumer. For the next several centuries, control of Sumer changed hands among the various city-states and, in the later third millennium, passed to the Semitic "hero-kings" of Akkad, including the great empire builder Sargon (r. 2334–2279 BCE).

By the end of the millennium, Ur had reestablished itself as the predominant power. It was at this time, during what is called the Third Dynasty, that the great ziggurat was completed and Ur reached its height: its empire encompassed not only Sumer and Akkad but adjacent lands, such as Elam (in what is now southern Iran) and the northern region of Mesopotamia. During the reigns of Ur-Nammu (2047–2030 BCE) and Shulgi of Ur (2029–1982 BCE), an urban community of over 50,000 residents emerged, augmented by numerous slaves (captured foreigners). High-ranking officials lived in great luxury. A famous decorated panel from around 2500 BCE known as the Standard of Ur depicts a procession of goods being brought to ruling elites by lines of enslaved bearers. Important persons were buried in special tombs, along with treasures of gold, silver, and semiprecious stones; the deceased were often accompanied by retinues of servants and animals as well as collections of utilitarian items needed in the afterlife.

## CULTURE AND SOCIETY

Sumer in its heyday consisted of nearly a dozen city-states. Each was a walled city surrounded by several villages and hamlets. The main feature of Ur and other Sumerian cities was the temple, situated on a high terrace atop a massive staired structure known as a ziggurat. In the temple, there stood a statue of the god—the moon god Nanna, in the case of Ur—along with an offering table and an assortment of rooms used by the priests. The temple and associated ziggurat were built primarily of sun-dried brick, with many walls and columns featuring geometric patterns and sometimes paintings. The temple compound housed the residences and workplaces of scribes and artisans; unskilled workers and laborers lived outside the city walls. Temples employed women, including enslaved women, to do the spinning and weaving.

Ur's economy was based on agriculture. Given the region's dry climate, it was necessary to establish irrigation systems to bring water from the Euphrates River that bordered Ur on the east. Barley and wheat, along with textiles, were traded for stone, metals, and other commodities that were scarce in the area. Cows, sheep, goats, and other animals were raised for food, animal by-products, and trade. The ruling elite oversaw most foreign trade, but sometimes licenses were granted to private citizens for the same purpose. At first, women could buy and sell property, but in later centuries, the independence of women declined in favor of a patriarchal system.

Ur's society was hierarchical, consisting of nobles—that is, the royal family, priests, and other high officials—at the top, followed by property-owning clients or vassals in the middle, and then the commoners and slaves. In some cases, commoners could own or farm land, though they usually did so as part of a larger family group. Slaves could sometimes earn profits and buy their freedom, but toiling away in a life of servitude was their usual fate.

The Sumerians worshipped a pantheon of gods. While the moon god, Nanna, was central to Ur, other leading deities included An (heaven), Ki (earth), Enlil (lord of the air), and Enki (lord of the deep). In addition, there were many lower-ranking deities in charge of the numerous natural and cultural phenomena that made up the world. A body of universal laws, which the gods themselves were supposed to adhere to, kept the universe operating harmoniously.

Music was part of this worldview, as song accompanied by instrumental music was used in both ritual contexts and during feasts and celebrations. Well-designed harps and lyres have been recovered from some of the royal tombs, and hymns recorded in cuneiform have also been retrieved.

Sumerian mathematics was based on the number sixty. One finds traces of this same numerical system today in, for example, timekeeping (60 minutes in an hour, 60 seconds in a minute) and geometry (360, or $60 \times 6$, degrees in a circle).

Troves of Sumerian clay tablets have been recovered, many of which are commercial, legal, or administrative in nature. However, as many as 5,000 of these are literary works such as myths, epics, hymns, lamentations, proverbs, fables, and dialogues. A number of Sumerian myths feature the culture hero Enki, who bestowed civilization on humankind and saved the Sumerians from the great flood. At the same time, Enki succumbed to the temptation of eating the forbidden fruits of Dilmun—the paradise of the gods—and nearly died as a result. Another popular figure was Inanna, the talented yet cruel goddess, who entered the Netherworld in defiance of divine law, returning to the normal world only after her husband, Dumuzid, agreed to take her place.

## DEMISE

Shulgi of Ur was one of the more notable rulers in the ancient world, combining patronage of the arts and letters with great skill as a soldier and statesman. During his reign, Ur served as the capital city of the Sumerian state and prospered economically and culturally. After his death, however, hordes of nomadic Amorites from the west flooded the city, leaving it weakened. About 2000 BCE, the Elamites, Sumer's long-standing enemy on its eastern flank, sacked Ur and left much of Sumer ravaged.

Over the next two centuries, a constant power struggle took place involving several Sumerian city-states, which by then had become predominantly Semitic in language and culture. Then, about 1760 BCE, the great king Hammurabi of the Amorites succeeded in unifying the region, establishing Babylon in the north as the capital. With this transfer of power, a new historical era was opened, namely, that of Babylonia and its rivalry with Assyria to the north.

Despite its changing fortunes, Ur remained an important center of moon devotion in Babylonia. Over the succeeding centuries, figures such as Nebuchadnezzar

II and Cyrus the Great of Persia (both from the sixth century BCE) gained esteem by restoring and augmenting the great temples of Ur.

Sometime after around 550 BCE, during the Achaemenid/Persian period, another great disaster struck Ur. The Euphrates River appears to have changed its course, leaving Ur stranded some ten miles to the west of the river's banks. Researchers believe that the damage done to the city's transportation and irrigation systems would have proved fatal, causing Ur to fall to ruins.

## RECENT DISCOVERIES AND CURRENT STATUS

Ur was "discovered" by Western investigators in 1852, but it was only through excavations conducted under the British archaeologist Leonard Wooley in the 1920s and early 1930s that information about the city's history came to light and our knowledge of early Mesopotamian culture was broadened. Many objects from the Royal Tombs of Ur were transferred to the British Museum (London) and the Iraq Museum along with the University of Pennsylvania Museum of Archaeology and Anthropology, whose researchers contributed to the Wooley excavations. The famous ziggurat of Ur was damaged during the 1991 Persian Gulf War but remained undamaged during the 2003 allied military campaign in the Iraq War.

In 2009, the University of Pennsylvania and Iraqi officials reached an agreement to resume archaeological research at the site. In that same year, the Global Heritage Fund began developing a plan for the conservation of the city's remains, augmented in 2013 by a joint Italian-Iraqi effort.

*Michael Shally-Jensen*

*See also:* Assyrians; Babylon; Hittites.

## FURTHER READING

Crawford, Harriet E. W. 2015. *Ur: The City of the Moon God.* London: Bloomsbury Academic.
Fagan, Brian M. 2007. *Return to Babylon: Travelers, Archaeologists, and Monuments in Mesopotamia.* Rev. ed. Boulder: University of Colorado Press.
Kramer, Samuel Noah. 1988. *History Begins at Sumer: Thirty-Nine Firsts in Recorded History.* 3rd ed. Philadelphia: University of Pennsylvania Press.
Zettler, Richard L., and Lee Horne, eds. 1998. *Treasures from the Royal Tombs of Ur.* Philadelphia: University of Pennsylvania Museum of Archaeology and Anthropology.

# V

## Van

Van, known during its heyday as Tushpa, thrived as the capital of the Kingdom of Urartu from the ninth to the seventh century BCE and went on to serve as a regional stronghold for a succession of powers up through the modern period. The ancient, heavily fortified citadel, in present-day southeastern Turkey, is called Van Citadel or Van Castle today. It stands between the modern city of Van, a few miles to the east, and Lake Van, the large body of water less than a mile to the west. The ancient citadel stands over a fertile plan in the mountainous highlands, not far from the source of the Tigris River.

The citadel was built and fortified on top of a natural mound. The hill looms several hundred feet over the plain and stretches horizontally from near the shore of Lake Van eastward for almost a mile. The builders constructed the citadel into the long ridge and south-facing slope of the natural rise. The original Urartian capital and later iterations of the city included the fertile plain to the south, which the citadel overlooks. Many inscriptions have survived from Tushpa's peak, including those marking tombs. A large cuneiform inscription commissioned by Xerxes I in the first half of the fifth century BCE in Old Persian, Babylonian, and Elamite stands about seventy feet above ground. Carved into the cliff face, the inscription praises Ahura Mazda and glorifies Xerxes himself. Remains from two large palatial complexes and walls as high as thirty feet dominate the site.

### INHABITANTS

The immediate region has been inhabited for at least seven millennia: an excavation just south of Van Citadel shows signs of human inhabitation at 5000 BCE. The citadel itself was first built in the ninth century BCE as the capital of the emerging Kingdom of Urartu. Its inhabitants spoke Urartian and worshipped a polytheistic pantheon of gods. They wrote their language in a cuneiform script, and their epic literature resembled that from other locations in the Near East and the Mediterranean. Their economy and society was based on agriculture. After Urartu fell, Armenia rose and dominated the area. The modern rediscovery of Urartu was taken as a source of pride for Armenians, and many understand the Urartians as forerunners of the Armenian people.

### HISTORICAL BACKGROUND

The Kingdom of Urartu, with Van as its capital, became a major player in the ninth century BCE in the region that is today southeastern Turkey, northwestern

Iran, and Armenia. The area was known at the time as Nairi, which also denoted the inhabitants of the area, a loosely connected group of different local peoples. The Urartian people were originally just one of the many groups that made up the Nairi. The name *Uruartri* is first attested back in a thirteenth-century Assyrian inscription, and the Urartians lived in the shadow of the colossal Middle and Neo-Assyrian Empires for their entire existence.

In the ninth century BCE, the Urartians consolidated the Nairi peoples under their rule. This process is largely credited to King Aramu, the oldest recorded king of Urartu, who ruled in the mid-ninth century. He controlled the land around Lake Van from his capital of Arzashkun on the Neo-Assyrian Empire's northern border. Shalmaneser III, the emperor of Assyria, invaded the nascent kingdom and captured Arzashkun. Sarduri I reestablished Urartu's prescience in the region, moving the capital to Van, or Tushpa, as it was known then. Much of the city's construction began at this stage; the oldest archaeological records for the site point to this period.

With Van as its highly fortified capital, Urartu took advantage of an uncharacteristically quiet Neo-Assyrian Empire and expanded its reach under successive kings. This occurred over the reminder of the ninth century BCE and the first half of the eighth century BCE. Ishpuini, Sarduri I's successor, extended the kingdom to the southwest, conquering the important religious center of Musasir. The kingdom's expansion continued under his successor, Menua, who also revamped domestic infrastructure and centralized the administration. Next came Argishti I, who likewise broadened Urartu's borders, especially to the northwest, where he founded a citadel at Erebuni, which has evolved into Yerevan, the present-day capital of Armenia. Finally, the kingdom reached its territorial peak under Argishti I's successor, Sarduri II. At this time, Urartu ruled a wide stretch of land from its capital of Tushpa, ranging from Lake Urmia and Lake Sevan in the east to almost as far as the Mediterranean in the west.

While Urartu controlled a large swarth of the Near East under Sarduri II, it proved to be overextended and faced a steep decline through the latter half of the eighth century BCE. Tiglath-Pileser III, the newly crowned emperor of Assyria, defeated Sarduri II, the Urartians, and their allies in a watershed battle in 743 BCE. Rusa I, Sarduri II's successor, was beleaguered by continued attacks from the Assyrians in the south and raids from the Cimmerians to the north. Shortly after ascending the throne of the Neo-Assyrian Empire, Sargon II, like Tiglath-pileser III three decades earlier, set his sights northward toward Urartu. In 714 BCE, Sargon II's Assyrian army defeated the Urartian army of Rusa I. However, given a confluence of factors, the Assyrian army did not advance on Tushpa. Rusa I survived the defeat but committed suicide shortly thereafter.

The Kingdom of Urartu experienced a brief resurgence in the first half of the seventh century BCE. King Argishti II chased the Assyrian army out of Urartu and led the kingdom through three decades of relative prosperity. His son Rusa II succeeded him and oversaw four additional decades of a flourishing Urartu, with Tushpa likewise flourishing. After Rusa II's death in 639 BCE, Urartu fell into a period of decline. Assyria never fully conquered Urartu, but the latter eventually became dependent on the former. After the Median Empire grew rapidly and overtook the Neo-Assyrian Empire, the Medes took over Urartu shortly thereafter. The city of Van, formerly Tushpa, continued to thrive under a succession of colossal empires, and Armenia grew out of former Urartu.

## CULTURE AND SOCIETY

Urartian culture and society blossomed at Van—then known as Tushpa—among other cities of the region. The Urartian language, which is a part of neither the Semitic nor the Indo-European family of languages, was supplemented in the latter parts of Urartu's existence with a Proto-Armenian language. Urartian survives in a cuneiform script, from which we can read about Urartu's polytheistic religion. While distinct in many ways, Urartian mythology shows links to the mythologies of other cultures in the Near East and Mediterranean. The Urartian art that has survived includes pottery, cylinder seals, and frescoes but is perhaps best known for its bronze ware and figurines. Urartian society was largely agricultural. The state constructed impressive irrigation systems for the areas in need of them. The elite at Van ruled from the citadel and oversaw the fertile valley to the south as well as a varying swath of the surrounding region.

## DEMISE

After Van was captured by the Medes and the Kingdom of Urartu was dissolved in the beginning of the sixth century BCE, the city continued to serve as a regional stronghold for centuries, though no longer as the capital of an autonomous kingdom. Beginning in the sixth century BCE, the region was ruled by a line of Near Eastern superpowers: the Medes, Achaemenid Persia, and the Seleucid Empire. Meanwhile, Armenians, particularly the Orontid dynasty, wielded increasing local power. This power crystallized into the Kingdom of Armenia in the fourth century BCE, and although Van never served as capital for this kingdom, it was an important political and economic hub for the Armenians. The Sassanids, Byzantines, Seljuks, Ottomans, and later iterations of Armenia all ruled over the region at various points. Timur I's forces destroyed the citadel in the later fourteenth century, but the region later returned to prosperity. The area has witnessed much violence since the turn of the twentieth century, particularly the Armenian genocide, which raged around Van and in neighboring territories in the 1910s.

## RECENT DISCOVERIES AND CURRENT STATUS

The Van Citadel is on UNESCO's Tentative List of World Heritage Sites in Turkey. The citadel now lies abandoned between the modern city of Van and Lake Van. The site features impressive remains ranging back to the Urartian period. Two palatial complexes dominate the site, with foundations carved into the landscape supplemented by structures and buildings made from mud bricks. Several stone-cut tombs have survived, including ones from the Urartian era.

*Anthony Vivian*

*See also:* Ctesiphon; Scythians.

## FURTHER READING

Hovannisian, Richard G. 2004. *The Armenian People from Ancient to Modern Times.* New York: Palgrave Macmillan.
Payaslian, Simon. 2008. *The History of Armenia.* New York: Palgrave Macmillan.
Piotrovsky, Boris B. 1969. *The Ancient Civilization of Urartu.* Translated by James Hogarth. Spokane, WA: Cowles Book Co.
Sagona, Antonio, and Paul Zimansky. 2009. *Ancient Turkey.* London: Routledge.

## Vijayanagara

Vijayanagara, Sanskrit for "City of Victory," the erstwhile capital of the empire of the same name, stands on the south shore of the Tungabhadra River. The site is about 150 miles from where the river, flowing east, connects to the Krishna River, which eventually issues into the Bay of Bengal. Vijayanagara sits in the central inland region of the southern portion of the Indian peninsula, in the present-day state of Karnataka, not far from its border with the state of Andhra Pradesh. The Arabian Sea looms less than 200 miles to the west, and the southern tip of the Indian peninsula stands about 600 miles to the south.

Major remains dot the landscape of present-day Vijayanagara. The most impressive area is Hampi, right on the bank of Tungabhadra River. This site served as the religious epicenter of Vijayanagara and features impressive Hindu temples and structures as well as Jain and Muslim buildings. Among the sprawling site, Virupaksha temple, the oldest and most popular temple at Vijayanagara, is preeminent. A royal and political center also sat in the middle of a wider urban area north of the town of Kamalapura and south of the religious center at Hampi.

### INHABITANTS

The inhabitants of Vijayanagara were of various southern Indian ethnicities, especially Kannada and Telugu. The two major spoken languages were likewise Kannada and Telugu, both Dravidian languages. Hinduism was the main religion of the city as well as the wider empire. Many Hindu inhabitants viewed their empire as a Hindu stronghold during a time of increasing Muslim expansion from the north. Nevertheless, religious tolerance was generally practiced within the empire itself, and the city of Vijayanagara included a not insignificant number of Jain and Muslim inhabitants.

### HISTORICAL BACKGROUND

Before serving as the capital to an empire that controlled the entire southern Indian peninsula, Vijayanagara was a pilgrimage site with temples to Shiva and other Hindu gods. It primarily functioned as this religious site before transforming into the power base for what would become the Vijayanagara Empire. Two sons of Sangama founded

> ### Kumari Kandam
> 
> According to certain Tamil writers, Kumari Kandam was a continent stretching south from India that has since sank into the Indian Ocean. Ancient Tamil and Sanskrit texts have long depicted a lost continent off the Indian subcontinent. As the Tamil Renaissance flourished in the latter half of the nineteenth century, Western scientists were positing a lost continent of Lemuria to account for the existence of lemurs on India and Madagascar but not the lands between. Tamil writers connected the tales from ancient texts to the recent theory of Lemuria and illustrated an ancient Tamil motherland that hosted two Sangams, or literary academies, each lasting for thousands of years. From the 1930s, they have used the name Kumari Kandam, a phrase from *Kanda Puranam*, a fifteenth-century Tamil text, to denote the continent. The existence of this continent would render the Dravidian family of cultures—and Tamil specifically—the world's oldest culture and humankind's common ancestor.

the empire: in 1336, Harihara ruled first, and his brother Bukka succeeded him a couple of decades later. Bukka first used the city of Vijayanagara—then primarily a religious site known as Hampi—as his capital. There is a disagreement among historians over the origins of this family. Some contend that the brothers were Kannadigas from the Hoysala Empire in southwestern India; others argue that the family was Telugu from the Kakatiya Kingdom in southeastern India. The brothers rapidly expanded their sphere of control from the Tungabhadra River valley to the entire southern portion of the Indian peninsula in the fourteenth century.

The empire's early fourteenth-century success was consolidated and expanded upon in the fifteenth and sixteenth centuries, as the city of Vijayanagara became one of the largest metropolises on the globe. The empire's success was in the face of constant attacks from the sultanates to the north, particularly the Bahmani sultanate. Deva Raya II set Vijayanagara's sights overseas, gaining influence in Sri Lanka and Burma. All the while, the city of Vijayanagara was growing at a remarkable pace. The once relatively small pilgrimage site of Hampi had expanded to include additional temples, and the city sprawled to the south, becoming one of the primary urban centers in all of southern India. The end of the fifteenth century saw the end of the Sangama dynasty. The Saluva dynasty only ruled for several years before being overthrown, in turn, by the Tuluva dynasty.

Vijayanagara continued to thrive under the Tuluva dynasty. Much of this success resulted from the deft leadership of Krishnadevaraya. When he ascended the throne in the early sixteenth century, his rule was fragile and threatened from many angles. After multiple recent coups, the kingship was not wholly safe from ambitious nobles within the kingdom. Moreover, the Portuguese and other European powers were becoming increasingly interested in colonizing and controlling India. Nevertheless, Krishnadevaraya strengthened his empire to meet these challenges as well as the ongoing threats from the sultanates in the north. He included Muslim calvary and archers in his newly fortified army. The city and the empire continued to prosper until the devastating Battle of Talikota in 1565. After the battle, the city was destroyed, and the empire continued under the Aravidu dynasty, who moved the capital to Penukonda.

## CULTURE AND SOCIETY

Vijayanagara was a pilgrimage site for faithful Hindus long before it became the capital of the Vijayanagara Empire and a bustling megacity. It retained its status as a center for Hindu culture and society through its existence. Sanskrit, the classical Indo-Aryan language and sacred language of Hinduism, experienced a revival under the Vijayanagara Empire. Many of the new works were important commentaries on classic texts such as the Vedas, but new works were composed as well. Literature in other local languages, including Kannada, Telugu, and Tamil, likewise flourished.

Vijayanagara has become famous for its architecture. Hampi, the original pilgrimage site on the bank of the Tungabhadra River, features a rich variety of impressive sites. There are many elaborate temples and other structures to be found at Hampi; the site is dominated by four large temple complexes—Virupaksha, Krishna, Vitthala, and Achyutaraya—displaying a range of influences and architectural styles. Vijayanagara society was predicated on a caste system. Although the Hindu empire was consistently at war with Muslim sultanates from the north, tolerance of non-Hindus was largely the policy within the empire's borders and within the city of Vijayanagara.

## DEMISE

The city of Vijayanagara was thriving as a regional powerhouse through the middle of the sixteenth century, then it underwent a sudden reversal. On January 23, 1565, the army of Rama Raya, the king of Vijayanagara, faced off against the army of a coalition of four sultanates to Vijayanagara's north in the Battle of Talikota. The battle proved catastrophic for the Vijayanagara Empire. Rama Raya was himself captured and executed, and the remainder of the Vijayanagara army fled, leaving the capital city open to enemy soldiers. They, in turn, plundered and razed the city, abruptly ending its status as one of the globe's largest metropolises and a major political hub. The Vijayanagara Empire survived in a diminished form for decades, but Tirumala Deva Raya, Rama Raya's successor, moved the capital from Vijayanagara to Penukonda. The city never recovered; the inhabitants largely left the urban area. Physical evidence of the 1565 destruction of the city remains in the city's ruins to this day.

## RECENT DISCOVERIES AND CURRENT STATUS

The structures that remain from Vijayanagara's heyday and before are widespread, diverse, and numerous. The majority of these appear in and around the site of Hampi, which is a UNESCO World Heritage Site. Hampi was on UNESCO's Endangered World Heritage List from 1999 to 2006 but has since been removed. Excavations are ongoing, and the temple complexes at Hampi are a popular tourist destination.

*Anthony Vivian*

See also: Anuradhapura; Madurai.

## FURTHER READING

Fritz, John M., and George Michell, eds. 2006. *New Light on Hampi: Recent Research at Vijayanagara.* Mumbai: Marg Foundation.
Jackson, William J. 2017. *Vijayanagara Voices: Exploring South Indian History and Hindu Literature.* London: Routledge.
Reddy, Srinivas. 2001. *Raya: Krishnadevaraya of Vijayanagara.* New Delhi: Juggernaut.
Sastry, K. A. Nilakanta. 2006. *Further Sources of Vijayanagara History.* Hong Kong: Hesperides Press.

## Vinland

Vinland, or *Vínland* in Old Norse, refers to a part of North America encountered in about 1000 CE by the Viking explorer Leif Erikson. The most detailed accounts of Vinland (or "Wine Land") and the various Vinland voyages appear in the *Saga of the Greenlanders*, first written sometime in the thirteenth century, and in the *Saga of Erik the Red*, which is thought to have been composed before 1265 CE. There is also an early mention of Vinland in Adam von Bremen's historical treatise of about 1075, which discusses Norse paganism and other aspects of the Viking Age.

The land in which Vinland lay was likely first sighted by a European around 986, when the Norse-Icelandic merchant Bjarni Herjólfsson was blown off course while traveling to Greenland. Subsequently, Leif Erikson (son of Erik the Red) led an expedition that identified Helluland ("Flat-Rock Land"; probably Baffin Island) and Markland ("Forest Land"; probably Labrador) along with Vinland, where his group remained for a year. It was Erikson who named the place, in recognition of the wild grapes the group found there. His brother Thorvald went to Vinland around 1004 and stayed for three years; he became the first European to contact the Indigenous people there, whom he referred to as *skrælingjar* ("savages" or "barbarians"). Another Icelandic explorer, Thorfinn Karlsefni, led an expedition to Vinland in 1010, inviting a few women aboard as well as a crew of men. Leif Erikson's sister Freydis also landed in Vinland, around 1013, in competition with two brothers, Helgi and Finnbogi. (She had them both killed.) Vinland was probably

---

### Brasil

The island of Brasil, or Hy-Brasil, is a mist-covered island west of Ireland, according to Irish folklore. Not related to the nation-state of Brazil, the name is thought to be connected to the Bresail, an ancient Irish clan. According to lore, the island is close enough to be visible from Ireland's west coast but was entirely cloaked in mist for all except one day every seven years. When approached by ship, according to some stories, the island would vanish. While not everyone believed in the supernatural aspects of the folklore, the island was long thought to be a real place, appearing on maps from the fourteenth to the nineteenth century. Explorations in search of Brasil began in the fifteenth century and carried on for centuries in vain. Some have connected Porcupine Bank, a shallow shoal 120 miles west of Ireland, with the mythical island.

abandoned by 1025, although trips to the region were still sometimes undertaken to obtain timber for the Norse settlements in Greenland.

The exact location of Vinland was long something of a mystery, with locales from Cape Cod to Newfoundland being suggested as possibilities. Then, in 1960, the Norwegian explorer Helge Ingstad discovered what looked to be a Viking settlement at L'Anse aux Meadows, on the northernmost tip of the Great Northern Peninsula, Newfoundland. Excavations began the following year, led by his wife, archaeologist Anne Stine Ingstad. Her team uncovered the remains of eight sod buildings clustered in the manner of an early medieval Icelandic or Norse Greenland homestead. Further, in 1965 Yale University revealed the so-called Vinland map, a world map apparently made in about 1440 and including the outlines of Vinland and Greenland. A new chapter in the Vinland saga had been opened.

## INHABITANTS

In the ninth and tenth centuries, Europe saw a major expansion of Scandinavian peoples. Viking warriors and merchants from Norway, Denmark, and Sweden plied the coasts and inland waterways of Europe and explored the islands of the North Atlantic. These Norsemen reached Iceland in the mid-ninth century and soon populated it, making it their home. By about 980, they had gone on to discover Greenland and established colonies on its southwestern coast. (They eventually encountered there the resident Inuit people, but there was no extended contact between the two.) The Greenland colonies became home to 3,000 or so Norse settlers, whose descendants continued to live there for several centuries afterward.

Given their maritime expertise, it was only a matter of time before the Norse settlers began exploring farther west. The coast of Labrador was about a five day's sail from Greenland (although it often took much longer), and the Norse Greenlanders needed timber for construction. By around 1000, the first serious attempts to explore and colonize the coastal areas of northeastern North America had begun. The tales that these venturers told were later written down, in Old Norse

---

### *Vineta*

Vineta was a mythical, Viking-era city supposed to have been located on the southern shore of the Baltic Sea. Appearing in a wide range of descriptions written between the tenth and twelfth centuries CE, it held a reputation as a wealthy and hedonistic city. Ibrahim ibn Jaqub's tenth-century, Arabic account is the oldest extant mention of the city. In the following century, Adam of Bremen depicted the city as an island on the Oder River and home to Slavs, Greeks, and others. Multiple twelfth-century works discussed the mythical city. For instance, the *Knytlinga Saga* narrates how the city was besieged by two different Danish kings. In these initial accounts and in the centuries since, Vineta has been linked with various historical cities. Some argue that Vineta was a real place that has since sunken into the Baltic Sea, perhaps off the island of Usedom or near the island of Ruden, north of the German coast. Others have identified it with Wolin, a city in present-day Poland.

and Old Icelandic, in the form of great literary sagas that became an integral part of Scandinavian—especially Icelandic—culture and history.

## HISTORICAL BACKGROUND

Determining the location of Vinland proved a puzzle for modern researchers. Given the name of the place and the fact that the sagas mention grapes and wine, most experts concluded that Vinland must be situated somewhere below the northern limit of wild grapes. New England, New York, and other areas were proposed. The Norwegian explorer Fridtjof Nansen considered that the presence of grapes and wine was legendary—as is much else in the sagas. The philologist Sven Søderberg suggested that *vin* in Vinland referred not to wine but to "pasture," since it operates that way in some Old Norse/Germanic place names. Others countered, however, that use of *vin* in that sense ceased well before the Vinland voyages were launched.

Drawing on all of the available information, the Ingstads concluded that Vinland probably was in northern Newfoundland, as earlier suggested by Canadian businessman W. A. Munn and Finnish geographer Väinö Tanner. In 1960, a search of the coasts was made, and at the northern tip of Newfoundland, in an area called L'Anse aux Meadows ("Bay with Grasslands"), some partially exposed habitation areas were discovered. During subsequent archaeological excavations, eight house forms were uncovered, and artifacts similar to those from other Norse sites were found. Comparative analysis and carbon-14 dating confirmed that the sites were both pre-Columbian and Norse, dating from about 1000 CE. It was not known at the time whether this might be one site among a number of others in "Vinland," or whether L'Anse aux Meadows even fell within "Vinland," but the site remains the only confirmed Norse or Viking settlement in North America and is widely accepted as a residence of the Vinland voyagers.

In 1965, Yale University published the heretofore unknown Vinland map, a world map showing Vinland to the west of Greenland; the map was said to have been made in Switzerland around 1440—before Columbus's voyage to the New World. In 1974, however, parts of the map were shown to be a forgery through the use of chemical analysis of the ink. Subsequent tests produced conflicting results, however. Today, the Vinland map is generally not accepted as authentic by scholars.

## CULTURE AND SOCIETY

The buildings at L'Anse aux Meadows were constructed of wooden frames and sod walls. The largest structure measures about ninety feet by fifty feet and features a "great hall" and other spaces. Its slightly convex walls show signs inside of the presence of sleeping platforms. There was a long, somewhat narrow hearth at the center of the house. Several smaller rooms opened off the main hall in a pattern similar to eleventh-century homesteads in Iceland. They likely served as storage rooms and possibly a lavatory. Several of the houses had stone ember pits identical with those found in Norse houses in Greenland.

Occupancy at L'Anse aux Meadows appears to have been short-lived, ten to twenty-five years, which corresponds roughly to the length of time recounted in the sagas. Among the artifacts found in the buildings are several iron nails and rivets, a primitive stone lamp similar to lamps found in Iceland and Greenland, a small whetstone of a type used in Scandinavia, a bone needle of Viking-era style, and a soapstone spindle whorl of the Late Classic Norse period. The whorl suggests that women were among the occupants of the houses. A bronze ring-headed pin and a single glass bead indicate the presence of adornments common at the time.

The area in which L'Anse aux Meadows is situated abounds in bog iron, which appears to have been smelted and utilized for a variety of implements. While the smelting pits have not all been located, large quantities of bog iron slag were found in one building that was apparently used as the smithy. Radiocarbon dating of charcoal associated with the slag indicated that it was approximately 1,000 years old. Some evidence of carpentry, including a boat rib, has also been found.

Excavations at the site have revealed no large middens, or refuse heaps, such as one might find at a long-inhabited human settlement. There is little evidence of any repair or rebuilding of the houses taking place, and no burial grounds have been located. The area does not appear to have been farmed. All this adds up to a picture of L'Anse aux Meadows as a site used as a winter base for crews engaged in exploration and commercial activities in the region. They lived largely on fish (salmon), uncultivated wheat (sandwort), and berries. This picture is more or less consistent with the saga accounts.

## DEMISE

The Icelandic sagas suggest that Vinland was abandoned because of conflict with the Indigenous inhabitants. These would likely have been the ancestors of the Beothuk or Montagnais. Although there is no archaeological evidence in support of warfare, two of the houses were deliberately burned, probably by the Norse themselves at the time of their departure. The fact that so few artifacts have been found suggests short-term occupancy and planned removal by the residents of their possessions. Besides hostilities with the Native peoples, a driving factor behind the abandonment of the settlement may have been the sheer distance involved in traveling between Greenland and Newfoundland, along with the small size of the "colony"—which numbered no more than 100 people (and probably less).

## RECENT DISCOVERIES AND CURRENT STATUS

The Canadian government named L'Anse aux Meadows a National Historic Site in 1968. Today, managed by Parks Canada, the site welcomes tourists and sponsors educational programs. One reconstructed building set apart from the remains of the original ones recreates life inside a Norse sod longhouse.

Not much of significance has been uncovered at the site since the initial excavations in the 1960s and a second round in the 1970s. One potentially interesting development was the identification, through satellite imagery, of a possible second Norse settlement at Point Rosee, at the southwestern end of Newfoundland. Excavations conducted in 2015 and 2016, however, turned up no signs of human habitation there.

*Michael Shally-Jensen*

*See also:* Iroquois Confederacy; Roanoke Colony.

**FURTHER READING**

Kunz, Keneva, trans. 2008. *The Vinland Sagas.* New York: Penguin Books.
Seaver, Kirsten A. 2004. *Maps, Myths, and Men: The Story of the Vinland Map.* Stanford, CA: Stanford University Press.
Seaver, Kirsten A. 2010. *The Last Vikings: The Epic Story of the Great Norse Voyages.* London: I. B. Tauris.
Wahlgren, Erik. 1986. *The Vikings and America.* London: Thames and Hudson.

# X

## Xianyang

Xianyang's ideal location led to it being the capital of the Qin state long before it became the capital of a unified China. It lies in a mountainous region on the north bank of the Wei River and near the larger Yellow River. Surrounded by mountains, the city lies in a fertile valley. The fertility of the soil and the spot's defensibility led to the ideality of the location. Today, Xianyang serves as a prefecture-level city in China's Shaanxi province. It neighbors and shares the same urban sprawl as Xi'an, a large city that is the capital of the same province. Emperor Qin Shi Huang's vast necropolis, replete with his terra-cotta army, sits just outside of town, a little over forty miles from Xianyang.

### INHABITANTS

The region around Xianyang has been occupied by humans for a very long time. About thirty miles from the ancient capital, Lantian man, a skeleton calculated to be 1,630,000 years old, was found. He is the oldest example of the *Homo erectus* subspecies on Asia and the second oldest in the world. Other Neolithic sites have been discovered in the area that measure thousands of years old. Fenghao, a twin city near Xianyang, composed of the two settlements of Feng and Hao, served as the capital to the Western Zhou dynasty from the eleventh to the eighth century BCE. In 350 BCE, Shang Yang, a statesman under Duke Xiao of Qin, designed the city of Xianyang, and Duke Xiao made the new city his capital and filled it with his subjects.

### HISTORICAL BACKGROUND

Xianyang was founded in the year 350 BCE to serve as the new capital for the state of Qin. Shang Yang rose up from a humble background to be a top adviser to Duke Xiao, the leader of the state of Qin. A practitioner of Chinese Legalism, he helped Duke Xiao reform the state, and many credit his administrative reforms as responsible for Qin's later success. Among other reforms, he convinced the duke to move his capital away from the powerful and potentially meddlesome aristocracy of Yueyang. They moved the capital to Xianyang, which at the time was newly built under the supervision of Shang Yang himself.

With Xianyang as its capital, the state of Qin grew in influence over the next century. This was amid what has come to be known as China's Warring States period, when seven major states, including Qin, constantly vied for supremacy. Shang Yang moved Qin closer to a meritocracy, granting successful soldiers land

and higher ranks within the military while stripping these distinctions from nobles whom he deemed unworthy. In the same vein, he abolished the practice of primogeniture. Some aspects of his reforms were draconian, but as a whole, they strengthened the military and economy of Qin. King Huiwen, Duke Xiao's successor, smarting from an old punishment, had Shang Yang killed, but the new king retained the statesman's reforms. The Legalist philosophy first instituted by Shang Yang was fine-tuned by Han Fei in the third century BCE.

Zheng, the man who would come to be known as Qin Shi Huang, became the ruler of Qin at the age of thirteen. Surviving a coup attempt and multiple attempted assassinations, he led a rapid string of conquests. Between the years 230 and 221 BCE, he led his army to conquer all six rival states In quick succession, he toppled the Han, Zhou, and Wei states between 230 and 225 BCE. Chu proved the most formidable of the other states, defeating an invading force of 200,000 Qin soldiers. Qin eventually conquered Chu with an invading force three times the size of the first. In 221 BCE, a year after finishing off what remained of Yan, Zheng defeated Qi, the final state to hold out against his conquests. After two and a half centuries of the Warring States period, Zheng had forcefully unified China and took the name Qin Shi Huang, which translates to "First Emperor of Qin." Although some dispute the etymology, most believe that the modern name *China* is derived from *Qin*.

Over the next decade, Qin Shi Huang sought to consolidate power and solidify the unification of China from his capital of Xianyang. He made the Qin seal script the official script of the entire empire, eliminating the variety of regional

Emperor Qin Shi Huang's massive terra-cotta army features over 8,000 individual soldiers along with hundreds of horses and chariots. The army stood buried for millennia until its excavation began in 1974. (Hbcs0084 | Dreamstime.com)

scripts that operated up until this time. He standardized the weights, measures, and currency as well as the length of cart axles. He brought China's previous form of feudalism to an end and divided his new empire into thirty-six administrative commanderies.

Meanwhile, a number of public works projects were conducted. He tore down walls that used to divide autonomous states within his empire and built walls to his northern frontier, antecedents to the Great Wall of China. He likewise built up Xianyang and the surrounding area with new palaces and infrastructure. He confiscated all the weapons from the empire not held by Qin individuals, melted them down, and used the metal to construct twelve large statues in Xianyang. Perhaps the most famous building project of Qin Shi Huang was his grand mausoleum and its terra-cotta army. In his later years, after a third unsuccessful assassination attempt, Qin Shi Huang became obsessed with his own mortality. This led him to build a colossal tomb for himself, which included thousands of terra-cotta warriors to protect him in the afterlife. His obsession with death also led him to seek out the Elixir of Life, which he believed would allow him to live forever. He is believed to have died from mercury poisoning from one or more of these elixirs. His dynasty—and Xianyang's status as capital—only survived him by a few years.

## CULTURE AND SOCIETY

Qin culture and society was largely influenced by the earlier Zhou dynasty, and although the Qin dynasty was short-lived, it had a lasting influence on later Chinese culture and society. The vast majority of individuals living the Qin state were nonaristocratic farmers. However, Xianyang was where the state's aristocracy would congregate. Shang Yang and Han Fei's Legalist approach to government helped organize the Qin administration and strengthen its military, allowing it to thrive in the third century BCE. The Qin's preferred philosophy of Legalism lessened the influence of other philosophies, such as Confucianism and Taoism. The focus on Legalism would carry on past the fall of the Qin dynasty and into the subsequent Han dynasty. When Qin Shi Huang unified China, he systematized Chinese culture and society to a degree not yet witnessed. Standardizing Chinese writing under the Qin script unified Chinese literature and culture for centuries to come. The most famous Qin art was buried in the ground for centuries. Qin Shi Huang's terra-cotta army contains 8,000 soldiers and hundreds of horses, all with unique handcrafted features.

## DEMISE

The death of Qin Shi Huang precipitated the rapid fall of the Qin dynasty and, with it, the city of Xianyang. Qin Shi Huang died while touring the eastern parts of his empire. Two months' travel from Xianyang, a band of his top advisers decided to conceal his death until they got back to the capital to obviate a potential uprising. In this time, they conspired to kill Fusu, Qin Shi Huang's eldest son and the heir apparent, and install his other son, Huhai, on the throne, who took the name Qin Er Shi.

China's second emperor proved immediately unpopular. He increased his father's already lavish spending on the military and public works, raising taxes to pay for it. He executed prominent members of the nobility and generals. Revolts arose, and Qin Er Shi showed himself unable to combat them. The newly formed empire descended into unrest. After losing the decisive Battle of Julu, Qin Er Shi was surrounded by his own men and forced to commit suicide. His successor, Ziying, inherited not an empire but the state of Qin.

In the power vacuum that resulted from Qin Er Shi's failure, the two most influential rebel leaders, Liu Bang of Han and Xiang Yu of Chu, vied for power. Liu Bang defeated his rival at the Battle of Gaixia and ushered in the Han dynasty rule of China. Although the Qin dynasty was short-lived, it set the stage for the stability of the Han dynasty. Liu Bang immediately had his adviser Xiao He plan a new capital, Chang'an. The new Han capital was also in the Wei River valley, to the immediate south of Xianyang.

## RECENT DISCOVERIES AND CURRENT STATUS

Excavations of Qin-era sites around Xianyang began in earnest around the 1950s. Finds have included palaces, tombs, roads, and other ancient structures. In 1974, archaeologists began excavating Qin Shi Huang's mausoleum and found the massive terra-cotta army. Digs have proven fruitful given the incredible magnitude of the remains. In 2012, a gigantic Imperial Palace was discovered at the site, measuring almost two million square feet. The Mausoleum of Qin Shi Huang has been a UNESCO World Heritage Site since 1987.

*Anthony Vivian*

See also: Chang'an.

## FURTHER READING

Clements, Jonathan. 2015. *The First Emperor of China*. London: Albert Bridge Books.
Cotterell, Arthur. 2007. *The Imperial Capitals of China: An Inside View of the Celestial Empire*. London: Pimlico.
Lewis, Mark Edward. 2007. *The Early Chinese Empires: Qin and Han*. London: Belknap Press.
Qian, Sima. 2009. *The First Emperor: Selections from the Historical Records*. Translated by Raymond Dawson. Oxford: Oxford University Press.

# General Bibliography

Ambler, C., N. Achebe, and W. H. Worger, eds. 2018. *A Companion to African History.* Hoboken, NJ: Wiley.

Avari, B. 2016. *India: The Ancient Past: A History of the Indian Subcontinent from C. 7000 BCE to CE 1200.* London: Taylor & Francis.

Chakrabarti, D. K., ed. 2006. *The Oxford Companion to Indian Archaeology: The Archaeological Foundations of Ancient India, Stone Age to AD 13th Century.* Oxford: Oxford University Press.

Chavalis, M. W. 2006. *The Ancient Near East: Historical Sources in Translation.* Malden, MA: Blackwell.

Collins, R. O. 2010. *The A to Z of Pre-Colonial Africa.* Lanham, MD: Scarecrow Press.

Cook, C. A., and J. S. Major. 2016. *Ancient China: A History.* London: Taylor & Francis.

Cowgill, G. L., and N. Yoffee, eds. 1991. *The Collapse of Ancient States and Civilizations.* Tucson, AZ: University of Arizona Press.

Crawford, M. H., and B. C. Campbell. 2012. *Causes and Consequences of Human Migration: An Evolutionary Perspective.* Cambridge: Cambridge University Press.

Diamond, J. 2013. *Collapse: How Societies Choose to Fail or Survive.* London: Penguin Books Limited.

Ellenblum, R. 2012. *The Collapse of the Eastern Mediterranean: Climate Change and the Decline of the East, 950–1072.* Cambridge: Cambridge University Press.

Erskine, A., ed. 2012. *A Companion to Ancient History.* London: Wiley.

Ford, T. H., and T. Bristow, eds. 2016. *A Cultural History of Climate Change.* London: Taylor & Francis.

Hoxie, F. E., ed. 2016. *The Oxford Handbook of American Indian History.* Oxford: Oxford University Press.

Kukla, G., H. N. Dalfes, and H. Weiss, eds. 2013. *Third Millennium BC Climate Change and Old World Collapse.* Berlin: Springer Berlin Heidelberg.

Lane, P., and P. Mitchell, eds. 2013. *The Oxford Handbook of African Archaeology.* Oxford: Oxford University Press.

Lewis, G. J. 2021. *Human Migration: A Geographical Perspective.* London: Taylor & Francis.

McLeman, R. A. 2014. *Climate and Human Migration: Past Experiences, Future Challenges.* Cambridge: Cambridge University Press.

Middleton, G. D. 2017. *Understanding Collapse: Ancient History and Modern Myths.* Cambridge: Cambridge University Press.

Moya, J. C., ed. 2011. *The Oxford Handbook of Latin American History.* Oxford: Oxford University Press.

Newitz, A. 2021. *Four Lost Cities: A Secret History of the Urban Age.* New York: W. W. Norton.

Owen, N. G., ed. 2014. *Routledge Handbook of Southeast Asian History.* London: Taylor & Francis.

Rufer, M., A. Nash, O. Kaltmeier, J. Raab, S. Rinke, and M. Foley, eds. 2021. *The Routledge Handbook to the History and Society of the Americas.* London: Taylor & Francis.

Schug, G. R., and S. R. Walimbe, eds. 2016. *A Companion to South Asia in the Past.* London: Wiley.

Schwartz, G. M., and J. J. Nichols, eds. 2010. *After Collapse: The Regeneration of Complex Societies.* Tucson: University of Arizona Press.

Shaw, I. 2003. *The Oxford History of Ancient Egypt.* New York: Oxford University Press.

Snell, D. C. 2005. *A Companion to the Ancient Near East.* Malden, MA: Blackwell.

Tainter, J. 1988. *The Collapse of Complex Societies.* Cambridge: Cambridge University Press.

de Tocqueville, A. 2016. *Atlas of Lost Cities: A Travel Guide to Abandoned and Forsaken Destinations.* Philadelphia: Running Press.

Weiss, H., ed. 2017. *Megadrought and Collapse: From Early Agriculture to Angkor.* Oxford: Oxford University Press.

Williams, A. R., ed. 2021. *Lost Cities, Ancient Tombs: 100 Discoveries That Changed the World.* Washington, DC: National Geographic.

Yoffee, N., and P. A. McAnany, eds. 2009. *Questioning Collapse: Human Resilience, Ecological Vulnerability, and the Aftermath of Empire.* Cambridge: Cambridge University Press.

# About the Authors and Contributors

## AUTHORS

**Michael Shally-Jensen** is an independent author and editor specializing in works on history, culture, and society. Among his previous books is ABC-CLIO's *Alternative Healing in American History: An Encyclopedia from Acupuncture to Yoga* (2019). He received his doctorate in cultural anthropology from Princeton University.

**Anthony Vivian** is a writer, historian, and adjunct professor. His historical writing focuses on ancient Greek historiography and Attic comedy, among other topics. He earned his PhD in history from UCLA in 2020.

## CONTRIBUTORS

**Chris Bingley** is a history writer and editor. His writing has focused on topics from the premodern world with a special focus on the ancient Roman and Late Antique Mediterranean. Chris received his PhD in history from UCLA in 2019.

**Katie Tardio** is a PhD candidate in classics at the University of North Carolina at Chapel Hill. She specializes in Roman archaeology of the provinces, specifically zooarchaeological analysis of foodways, trade, and ritual, as well as city landscapes, women in the ancient world, and day-to-day life within the Roman Empire.

**Rebecca Waxman** is a PhD student in history at the University of California, Los Angeles. She works on the histories of gender and sexuality in colonial and postcolonial South Asia, focusing in particular on sexual violence. She received her bachelor of arts in history from Wesleyan University in 2016.

# Index

Page numbers in **boldface** indicate main entries in the Encyclopedia.

Abu Simbel, **1–5**, 180
Abydos, **5–8**
Agriculture, 51, 79, 94, 110, 118, 143, 163, 165, 219, 247, 259, 280–281, 284, 293, 300
  decline, 96–97, 117, 175, 186, 205, 284, 295, 300
  development, 27, 70, 138, 141, 177, 184, 186, 224, 260
  economy, 5, 63, 171, 257
  farmers, 16, 23, 27–28, 54, 71, 101, 115, 123–124, 127–128, 136, 148, 172–174, 177, 181, 189, 191, 224–225, 238, 255, 259, 265, 283, 290, 292, 304, 323
  irrigation, 3, 16, 27, 29, 31, 33, 39, 59, 62–63, 77–78, 85, 130, 177–178, 184–185, 193, 203–205, 224, 300, 304–305, 307, 311,
  land, 43, 70, 77, 87–88, 115, 167, 171, 203–205, 217, 259, 262, 286, 306
  production, 27, 31, 39, 59, 262, 279, 290
  society, 3, 22, 25, 29, 39, 43, 79, 85, 115, 130, 184, 203, 211, 228, 235, 237, 252, 257, 281, 283, 290, 296, 305, 309, 311
Ai-Khanoum, **8–11**
Ajanta Caves, **11–14**
Aksum, **14–18**, 124
Alexander III of Macedon
  in Africa, 18–22, 95
  in Asia, 8–9, 34, 54, 59, 92, 112, 221, 227, 231, 234, 238, 253, 270, 276
  in Greece, 48, 88, 218
Alexandria, 15, **18–22**, 34, 118, 210, 303
Amarna, **22–26**
Amphitheaters, 8, 10, 21, 219, 232, 240–241, 271
Ancestral Puebloans, **26–30**

Angkor, **30–34**, 50
Animal husbandry, 39, 43, 85, 127–128, 130, 177
  bees, 19
  camels, 59, 290
  cattle, 59, 124, 252, 259, 263, 304–305
  chickens, 110, 130, 163
  dogs, 163, 179
  donkeys, 59
  elephants, 76
  goats, 59, 305
  horses, 19, 132, 158, 189, 209, 251–253, 263, 268, 276, 297–298, 322–323
  pigs, 163
  sheep, 59, 259, 262–263, 305
  water buffalos, 130
  *See also* Hunting
Antioch, **34–37**
Anuradhapura, **37–40**
Aqueducts, 35–36, 49, 75, 89, 112, 204–205, 232, 240–241, 279
Ashoka, 12, 37–38, 95, 221–222, 276
Assyrians, 7, 34, **40–45**, 57–58, 131–132, 181, 252–253, 310
Athens, **45–49**, 88, 96, 104, 111, 152, 227, 231, 252, 272
Atlantis, 43
Avalon, 264
Ayutthaya, **49–52**
Axes, 152, 158, 212

Baalbek, **53–56**
Babylon, 41–45, **56–60**, 73, 91, 131, 133, 230–231, 237–238, 252–253, 268, 303–307, 309
Bagan/Pagan, **60–64**
Bangladesh, 195

Barley, 59, 305
Baths, 75, 113, 129, 241, 273
Beans, 28, 69, 142, 172, 224–225, 281, 300
Bible. *See* Christianity, literature; Judaism, literature
Boats. *See* Seafaring, ships
Borobudur, **64–68**
Brahmanism, 38–29, 129, 275
Brasil, island of, 315
Bronze
  making, 33, 120, 128–129, 136
  statuary, 17, 51, 137, 182, 216, 297, 311, 318
  tools, 117, 158, 294
Buddha, 12–13, 37, 39, 51, 61, 65–68. *See also* Buddhism; Buddhists
Buddhism, 12–14, 32–33, 37–39, 51, 62–64, 66, 82, 154–155, 189, 190, 221–222, 275–277
  architecture, 12, 37, 39, 67, 156, 275, 277
  culture, 37, 62
  literature, 67, 189, 220–221, 277
  missionaries, 38, 95, 222
  monks, 12, 39, 154, 222, 277
  painting, 14, 39
  relics, 39, 189
  sculptures, 39, 67
  stupas, 37, 39, 49, 51, 60–61, 63, 65, 67, 81, 153, 169, 275, 277
  temples, 32, 49, 64, 64–68, 153
  *See also* Ashoka; Buddha; Buddhists
Buddhists, 12–14, 32, 50–51, 63, 65, 68 195, 220. *See also* Ashoka; Buddha; Buddhism
Buyan, 158

Cahokia, **69–73**
Camelot, 265
Canals, 32, 59, 62, 118, 154, 177, 248, 283, 303
Cannibalism, 29, 143
Carthage, **73–77**, 94, 218, 236–238, 249, 271–272
Cattle, 59, 124, 252, 259, 263, 304–305. *See also* Animal husbandry
Ceramics. *See* Pottery
Chan Chan, **77–80**
Chang'an, **81–84**, 154, 324
Chavín de Huántar, **84–87**
Christianity, 8, 55, 75, 89, 105, 121, 182, 208, 216, 250, 270
  architecture, 122, 239

Catholicism, 51, 144, 207–208, 259
churches, 17, 55, 89–90, 113, 121–122, 207–209, 219, 260–263
culture, 89, 96
doctrine, 35–36, 76, 113, 254–256
early church, 35–36, 73, 75, 88–89, 94–96, 111–113
leaders, 8, 17, 121, 288
literature, 35–36, 53, 54, 96, 113
missionaries, 110, 141, 258–262
rule, 8, 15–17, 87–89, 105, 119, 193, 250
*See also* Christians; Jesus Christ
Christians, 15, 34, 55–56, 74, 92, 96, 113, 120, 122, 208–209, 216, 219, 225, 288. *See also* Christianity; Jesus Christ
Churches. *See* Christianity, churches
Civil war, 18, 44, 70, 109–110, 195, 224, 246, 249, 291
Clergy. *See specific religions*
Climate change, 72, 80, 130, 200
  flooding, 30, 37, 64, 70, 130, 135, 139, 166, 184, 195, 248, 279
  droughts, 39, 184
  fires, 139, 184
  forests, 107, 109–110, 166, 175, 205
  investigative boxes, 30, 37, 64, 70, 135, 139, 166, 184, 195, 248
  rain, 17, 80, 110, 139, 186, 195, 205
Constantinople, 35, 76, **87–90**, 250, 274, 298
Copper, 28, 124, 128
  art, 71–72, 79, 135, 137, 297
  coins, 290
  mining, 124, 293
  tools, 117
Corn. *See* Maize
Cotton, 28, 39, 128, 148, 175, 181, 281
Ctesiphon, **90–94**
Cyrene, **94–97**, 214

Dams, 1, 4, 27, 232
Death. *See* Graves
Deir el-Bahri/Djeser-Djeseru, **99–102**
Delphi, 89, 94, **102–105**, 111
Deserts, 7, 20, 27, 115, 118, 138, 180, 185, 232, 235, 286, 289, 294, 303
  climate, 185, 235
  coast, 86
  inhabitants, 138, 180, 184
  sands, 4, 203, 291
Diamonds, 166
Dikes, 31, 159, 279, 303

# Index

Diseases, 72, 141, 145, 166–167, 175, 196, 226, 243, 255, 261, 291
Domesticated animals. *See* Animal husbandry
Drainage, 128–130, 211, 282–283, 292
  natural, 184, 204
Droughts, 29, 33, 134, 179, 186, 205, 246, 291–292, 295, 300
  risk of, 139, 184
  *See also* Climate Change; Rain

Earthquakes, 21, 35–36, 54, 63, 67, 87, 97, 112, 151, 165, 185, 193, 200, 216, 228, 235, 241, 282, 297
Easter Island, **107–111**, 162–163
Ephesus, **111–113**

Famine, 29, 179, 243, 281
Farming. *See* Agriculture
Fires, 20, 28, 35–36, 53, 76, 143, 175, 211, 231, 252, 297
  risk of, 139, 184
Fish and fishing, 34, 59, 110, 141, 143, 148, 163, 184, 238, 241, 252, 281, 290, 293, 318
  fishermen, 19, 238, 290, 304
  mythological, 46
Flooding, 37, 64, 70, 87, 112, 195, 205
  mythological, 159, 306
  risk of, 30, 37, 64, 70, 135, 139, 166, 184, 195, 248, 279
  seasonal, 127–128, 130, 248
  *See also* Climate change; Rain
Forests, 109–110, 135–136, 142, 153, 165, 166, 189, 214, 224, 265, 283, 289, 315
  climate change, 107, 109–110, 166, 175, 205
  rain, 30, 33, 64, 67, 84, 85–86, 107, 138, 173, 175–176
Frescoes, 39, 149–153, 193, 200, 240–242, 311. *See also* Painting

Games, 19, 70–71, 189
  ball, 174, 191–192, 212, 279, 299
  Olympic, 103, 213–216
  Pythian, 103–105
  war, 189
Garden of Eden, 57
Genocide, 141, 195, 311
Giza, **115–119**, 177–179
Gold, 260
  art and artifacts, 23, 25, 32, 44, 79, 85, 129, 147–148, 159, 182, 184, 193, 199, 204, 209, 210, 213–215, 252, 273, 286, 290, 297, 305
  currency and economy, 16, 75, 80, 124, 147–148, 290–291
  discovery, 166, 244, 251
  mining, 10, 124, 281, 290, 293
  mythological, 77, 259
Gomorrah, 53
Grain, 59, 75, 88, 123, 151, 252, 305, 318
Granada, **119–122**
Graves, 16–17, 18, 20, 25, 44, 69–71, 78, 115–118, 159, 173, 177–179, 180, 182, 185–186, 193, 198–200, 241, 252–254, 265, 267, 285, 305, 318
  burial, 6–7, 25, 28, 101, 158–160, 179, 184, 199, 203–204, 264, 266–267
  burial rites, 71, 100, 135, 159, 177, 238, 254
  cemeteries and necropolises, 5–6, 25, 81, 102, 116, 130, 158, 160, 177, 179, 182–183, 218–219, 270, 273, 287–288, 321
  *See also* Mummies; Tombs
Great Zimbabwe, **122–125**, 147
Guayaquil, 184

Harappa and Mohenjo-Daro, **127–130**
Hinduism, 32–33, 51, 66, 169–171, 194, 208
  architecture, 170–171, 207–208
  culture, 171, 208, 222, 314
  gods, 32, 222, 312
  leaders, 169, 195
  literature, 32, 221, 314
  rule, 64–66, 171, 208, 312–314
  Shiva, 32–33, 172, 312
  temples, 30–32, 168, 170–172, 196, 208–209, 312, 314
  Vishnu, 31–32, 169, 172, 221
  *See also* Brahmanism; Hindus
Hindus, 169, 171, 194–196, 209, 220, 312–314. *See also* Hinduism
Hittites, 1–2, 24, 41, 56, 60, **131–134**
Hollow Earth, 103
Horses, 19, 132, 158, 189, 209, 251–253, 263, 268, 276, 297–298, 322–323. *See also* Animal husbandry
Hunting, 11, 14, 24, 34, 43, 141, 143, 183–184, 189, 224, 300
  hunters, 124, 141, 224, 279
Husbandry. *See* Animal husbandry

## Index

Ife, **135–138**
Indigenous Australian cultures, **138–142**
Iram of the Pillars, 303
Iron, 17, 28, 124, 181, 318
   iron ore, 181
   smithing, 136, 158, 201
   tools, 157, 318
   weapons, 144, 157–158, 201
Iroquois Confederacy, **142–146**
Irrigation. *See* Agriculture, irrigation
Islam, 51, 93, 121, 148–149, 208, 210, 290–291, 313
   architecture, 120, 207–208, 312
   culture, 37, 120–121, 189, 208, 289–290
   leaders, 37, 120–121, 147, 189, 194–195, 208, 289–291, 314
   literature, 53, 189, 289
   mosques, 90, 93, 120, 122, 148, 197, 271, 291
   rule, 30, 44, 64, 119, 148, 169, 171, 194–196, 207–208, 271, 274, 292
   spread of, 15, 37, 67, 76, 119–120, 147, 208, 219, 290, 312
   *See also* Muhammad; Muslims
Ivory, 43–44, 75, 136, 213–215, 236, 238
   trade, 16, 75, 147–148, 236

Jade, 174, 192–193, 211–212, 281–282
Jails. *See* Prisons
Jainism, 194, 195, 208, 220–222, 312
Jakarta, 54
Jesus Christ, 36, 112, 209, 255–256. *See also* Christianity; Christians
Jews, 18–19, 34–35, 58, 92, 96, 120, 122. *See also* Judaism; Solomon
Judaism, 58–60, 96, 103, 234, 304
   leaders, 15, 56, 237
   literature, 15, 42, 53, 57, 58–59, 124, 131, 133, 233–234, 236, 238, 268, 270, 286, 303
   synagoges, 19, 121
   *See also* Jews; Solomon
Jungles. *See* Forests, rain
Jupiter. *See* Zeus

Khan, Genghis, 186–190, 194
Kilwa, 125, **147–149**
Kitezh, 252
Knives, 166, 284, 299
Knossos, **149–153**, 199
Kumari Kandam, 313
Kyoto, **153–156**

La Tène Celtic culture, **157–160**
Lagos, 135
Lapita people, **161–164**
Laws, 41, 57, 159, 178, 189, 290, 304, 321
   colonial, 259
   court, 242
   divine, 306
   Islamic, 291
   Legalism, 82, 321–323
   legal system, 132, 196
   legislators, 46–47, 104, 249
   legislature, 75–76, 248–250
   Roman, 89, 248–250
   texts, 43, 82, 189, 249, 289, 321–323
   *See also* Prisons
Libraries, 18–21, 40, 43, 112, 226

Machu Picchu, **163–168**
Madurai, **168–172**
Maize, 27–29, 69–71, 136, 142–143, 172, 175, 205, 224–225, 281, 283, 300
Maldives, 37
Manila, 30
Marble, 60, 121, 197, 209
Marduk, 42, 58–59
Masks, 25, 137, 199–200, 204, 211, 282–284
Maya, 107, **172–176**, 191–192, 212, 283–285, 299–300
Medicine, 24, 76, 94, 115, 238, 288
   study of, 227–228, 280, 303
Memphis and Saqqara, **177–180**
Meroë, 15–16, **180–183**
Metallurgy, 128, 181, 243, 303, 318. *See also* Bronze; Iron
Metalwork. *See specific metals*
Mining, 10, 124, 212, 281, 284, 293
   gold, 10, 124, 281, 290, 293
   silver, 262
Moche culture, 78, **183–186**
Mohenjo-Daro. *See* Harappa and Mohenjo-Daro
Mongol Empire, **186–190**
Monte Albán, 174, **190–194**
Mosques. *See* Islam, mosques
Mughal Empire, **194–197**, 222
Muhammad, 16, 93. *See also* Islam; Muslims
Mummies, 4, 6, 25, 179, 101–102, 185–186, 203–204, 253, 288. *See also* Graves; Tombs
Music, 18, 70, 83, 103, 135, 159, 166, 306

# Index

Muslims, 15–16, 34, 56, 93, 119, 122, 136, 147–148, 194–195, 208, 210, 289–291, 312. *See also* Islam; Muhammad
Mycenae, 134, 152, **197–201**, 297

Nazca, **203–206**
New Orleans, 70

Obsidian, 109, 174, 281–282, 284
Oil
  olive, 10, 75, 151
  sesame, 59
Old Goa, **207–210**
Olmecs, **210–213**, 283–284
Olympia, 105, **213–216**

Paestum, **217–220**
Pagodas. *See* Buddhism, stupas
Painting, 13, 83, 103, 152, 174, 196, 218
  architecture, 48, 174, 178, 305
  cave, 12–14, 140–141
  frescoes and murals, 12–14, 39, 138–141, 149–153, 172, 184, 193, 200, 240–242, 261, 305, 311
  masks, 283
  paint, 28, 72, 185
  painters, 283
  paintings, 36, 248
  pottery, 27–28, 48, 72, 129, 185, 239, 269
  ships, 239
  statues, 193
Papyrus, 21, 118, 178, 236
Pataliputra, **220–223**
Pecos Pueblo, **223–226**
Pergamon, 112, **226–229**
Persepolis, **229–232**, 269–270
Petra, **232–235**
Phoenicians, 73–77, 120, **236–239**
Piracy, 75, 245
Pompeii, 219, **239–242**
Polytheism
  African, 181–182
  Asian, 38, 127, 129, 252, 276
  Egyptian, 2–3, 5, 21, 23–24, 99, 179, 287–288
  European, 160
  Mediterranean, 46, 150, 198, 213–215, 226–227, 238, 250
  Mesoamerican, 172, 174–175, 210–212, 280–282, 283–284, 300

  Near Eastern, 43, 54–55, 59, 132, 235, 270, 304, 306, 309, 311
  North American, 29, 71
  South American, 79, 183, 295
  temples, 1–4, 5–7, 8, 13, 18–25, 43, 45, 48, 53–56, 58–59, 69–70, 84–87, 99–101, 102, 104, 111–113, 118, 131, 133, 160, 165–167, 172–174, 178–179, 182, 184, 186, 191–192, 204, 213–219, 226–227, 231, 232, 234, 237–238, 240–242, 271, 277, 279–288, 293–294, 298, 299, 301, 303–307
  *See also* Hinduism; Shinto
Potatoes, 244, 283, 292–293
  sweet, 108, 110
Pottery
  African, 7, 16–17, 136–137
  Asian, 83, 129
  European, 158
  Mediterranean, 48, 75, 152, 218, 239, 297
  Mesoamerican, 174–175, 210–212, 283, 300
  Near Eastern, 133, 269, 311
  North American, 27–28, 71, 143, 225
  Pacific, 161–163
  potters, 283
  potter's wheel, 28, 158
  sherds, 7, 136, 162–163
  South American, 79, 85, 183–186, 203–204, 294–295
Precipitation. *See* Rain
Prester John, 8
Priests. *See specific religions*
Prisons, 139, 256
  prisoners, 174–175, 183, 196, 256
  *See also* Laws
Pyramids
  African, 180–183
  Asian, 30, 32
  Egyptian, 1, 115–118, 177–180
  Mesoamerican, 172–176, 191–192, 211, 279–280, 283–285
  Near Eastern, 58
  North American, 70
  Pacific, 67
  South American, 183–184, 295, 299, 301

Rain, 177, 185
  climate change, 17, 80, 110, 139, 186, 195, 205

## Index

Rain (*cont.*)
   religion, 124, 185, 193, 211, 280, 294, 301
   seasonal, 12, 107, 185, 205, 220, 293
   *See also* Climate change; Droughts; Flooding
Rainwater, 241
Religion. *See specific religions*
Rice, 32, 39, 62–63, 148, 171
Rio de Janeiro, 166
Roads, 19, 22, 33, 27, 49, 129, 136, 165, 205, 219, 220, 229, 242, 273, 282–284, 288, 298, 324
   Bourbon Street, 70
   construction, 41, 113, 196, 304
   design, 295
   hub, 247
   raised, 31
   Royal Road, 34
   Silk Road, 34, 81, 83, 92, 171, 275
Roanoke colony, **243–247**
Rome, 15–17, 18, 21, 34–35, 40, 54, 73–75, 88, 92, 112, 115, 209, 215, 218, 227–229, 234–235, 237, 240–241, **247–250**, 271–272, 298
Rubber, 174, 210, 212

Sacrifice
   animal, 80, 175, 193, 238, 250, 276, 284, 304
   human, 71, 76–77, 79–80, 159, 167, 174–175, 183, 185, 192–193, 204, 211–212, 238, 252, 279–282, 284, 299–301
Salt, 83, 53, 290
Saltwater, 135, 279
Sculptures. *See* Statues
Scythians, 19, **251–254**, 276
Seafaring, 184
   boat burial, 7
   capabilities, 108, 161–163
   expedition, 139, 243–245, 315
   navigation, 161–163, 237, 244–245, 318
   navy, 19–20, 47–48, 74–75, 149, 245, 272
   outriggers, 108, 161
   seafarers, 8, 73, 108, 139, 148, 237, 244, 315, 318
   ships, 7, 20, 75, 94, 108, 118, 147–149, 158, 161, 184, 234, 237, 245, 293, 315
Sesame, 39, 59, 128
Seven Pagodas, 169

Sewers. *See* Drainage
Shaker villages, **254–258**
Shambhala, 221
Sheep, 59, 259, 262–263, 305. *See also* Animal husbandry; Wool
Shields, 144, 159
Shinto, 153–156
Ships. *See* Seafaring, ships
Shiva, 32–33, 172, 312
Sikhs, 194–196, 222
Silk, 75, 253
Silk Road, 34, 81, 83, 92, 171, 275
Silver, 260
   art and artifacts, 79, 148, 193, 251, 297, 305
   currency and economy, 41, 75, 196, 290
   mining, 262
Slavery, 16, 101, 115, 133, 136–137, 175, 187, 260
   slaves, 1, 5, 16, 20, 23, 43, 75, 133, 136, 148–149, 181, 240, 249, 252, 259, 290, 297, 305–306
   trade, 16, 70, 75, 110, 133, 135, 136, 147, 149, 290
Snow, 29, 138, 253–254
Socrates, 47, 96
Sodom, 53
Solomon, 15, 56, 237
Spanish Missions in North America, **258–264**
Spears, 71, 159
Squash, 28, 59, 69, 142, 224–225, 281, 300
Statues
   African, 2–4, 96, 99, 182, 288
   Eurasian, 14, 32–33, 36, 39, 42, 48–49, 51, 58, 83, 89, 112–113, 133, 137, 152, 213–215, 269, 305, 323
   Mesoamerican, 174–175, 279, 283, 300
   North American, 70–71
   Pacific, 65–67, 107–110
   South American, 80, 294–295, 299
Stonehenge, 157, **264–268**
Sugar, 39, 59
Susa, 58, 230–231, **268–270**
Swords, 16, 122, 157–159, 189, 252
   mythological, 264
Sydney, 139
Syracuse, **270–274**

Taro, 110, 163
Tartessos, 120
Tattoos, 163, 186, 253

# Index

Taxila, **275–278**
Temples. *See specific religions*
Tenochtitlán, **278–282**
Theatres, 35, 75, 102, 111–113, 226, 240–241, 250, 271
  amphitheaters, 8, 10, 21, 219, 232, 240–241, 271
  culture 166
Thebes, 1, 23–24, 100, 179, 181, **285–289**
Thule, 253
Timber. *See* Wood
Timbuktu, **289–292**
Tin, 120, 128, 293
Tiwanaku, **292–296**
Tombs
  African, 16, 181–182, 238–239
  Egyptian, 4–7, 18, 22, 25, 101–102, 116–117, 177, 179–180, 182, 286, 288
  Eurasian, 81, 122, 197, 200, 215, 218, 232, 238–239, 252, 253, 305–307, 309, 311, 323, 324
  Mesoamerican, 173–174, 191–193, 211
  Pacific, 66
  South American, 80, 186, 203
  *See also* Graves; Mummies
Troy, 200, **296–298**
Tula, **299–301**
Turquoise, 28, 281, 282

Ur, 41, 59, 269, **303–307**

Van, **309–312**
Venice, 248
Vijayanagara, 207, **312–315**
Vineta, 316
Vinland, **315–319**
Vishnu, 31–32, 169, 172, 221

Wheat, 59, 75, 88, 123, 151, 252, 305, 318
Wine, 75, 151, 159, 236, 315, 317
Wood, 72, 117, 135, 239, 269, 300
  art and artifacts, 109–110, 112, 136, 141, 179
  climate change, 107, 109–110, 166, 175, 205
  construction, 69, 72, 83, 117–118, 136, 143, 145, 217, 219, 221, 291, 317
  economy, 71
  fire, 20, 28, 35–36, 53, 76, 139, 143, 175, 184, 211, 231, 252, 297
  forests, 107, 109–110, 135–136, 138, 142, 153, 165, 166, 173, 175, 189, 214, 224, 265, 283, 289, 315
  timber, 181, 205, 217, 224, 265
  tools, 143, 177
  weapons, 144
Wool, 59, 184, 203, 293, 297. *See also* Animal husbandry; Sheep

Xianyang, 81, **321–324**

Ys, 159

Z, Lost City of, 84
Zeus, 20, 55, 198, 213–216, 242
  temples, 45, 53–55, 242
Ziggurat, 58–60, 260, 304–307

Lightning Source UK Ltd.
Milton Keynes UK
UKHW030249061222
413451UK00010B/182